KING

The Study of Urban Geography

Third Edition

To Mari

The Study of Urban Geography

Third Edition

Harold Carter
Gregynog Professor of Human Geography,
University College of Wales, Aberystwyth

Edward Arnold

Copyright © Harold Carter 1972, 1976, 1981

First published 1972 by
Edward Arnold (Publishers) Ltd
41 Bedford Square, London WC1B 3DQ
Reprinted 1973
First published as a paperback 1974
Reprinted 1974
Second Edition first published 1976
Reprinted (with corrections) 1977
Reprinted 1979
Third Edition first published 1981

British Library Cataloguing in Publication Data
Carter, Harold
  The study of urban geography. — 3rd ed.
  1. Cities and towns
  I. Title
  910'.09'1732   GF12S

ISBN 0-7131-6235-X Pbk

Filmset in Compugraphic 10 on 11 pt Baskerville by Colset
Private Limited, Singapore and printed in Great Britain by
Richard Clay (The Chaucer Press), Limited, Bungay, Suffolk.

Contents

Preface

This book is intended to provide an outline of urban geography for those undergraduates at universities or students in further education who wish to specialize in urban geography to an extent greater than is usually provided by general courses on human geography. Changes in the concepts of geographers, and in academic work generally, make it clear that such a work cannot be concerned with discrete blocks of subject matter, for the general problem under review is urbanism and the approach geographical. But this opens up a vast field of enquiry and within that field any finite study of this nature must be selective and present a personal view of what an undergraduate can and should be expected to consider. This view is my own and I am solely responsible for it. What I hope this volume does is provide a continuation from the elementary and general texts in human geography and a lead towards the more specialized studies which the graduate student would wish to follow. Perhaps it is worth adding that in the title the emphasis should be on *study* and not on the definite article!

This view of the study of urban geography has been built up by experience in teaching at Aberystwyth and by contact with fellow urban geographers in Britain and America. It is impossible to acknowledge all those who have in some way helped but I would particularly wish to mention Professors Robert McNee and Howard Stafford (Jr.) of the Department of Geography of the University of Cincinnati. Much of the material was discussed with them and with the graduate students of that Department in 1967–68. I would also like to put on record my appreciation of a Fellowship from the US National Science Foundation which enabled me to visit the United States and work for a year at Cincinnati. It was during that year that much of the basis of this book was established. I would also like to acknowledge the friendly and helpful comments of two other members of that Department, Dr K. B. Ryan and Dr Peter Halvorson, now of the Department of Geography at the University of Connecticut (Storrs).

I am also greatly indebted to my own graduate students who, from time to time, have critically examined much of the material and I would especially like to thank Dr W. K. D. Davies now at the University of Calgary and Dr C. R. Lewis of the Department at Aberystwyth. Finally Dr Ronald Jones of Queen Mary College read the manuscript and made many valuable suggestions both as to content and presentation.

The maps for the book were drawn by Mr Morlais Hughes, Mr M. Gelly Jones and Mr E. James, and I am grateful for their cartographic expertise. I would also like to acknowledge the ready help of Mrs Mair Jenkins in preparing the final version.

Lastly I would like to acknowledge the assistance of my wife both in a general and a particular sense. Not only has she accompanied me on many 'field excursions', and not always to the most attractive parts of towns and cities, but she also read and typed the original manuscript. It is appropriate that the volume be dedicated to her.

Preface to the second edition

In this second edition an attempt has been made to extend two themes which were introduced but not developed in the first edition. These are the behavioural approach, both in relation to central place concepts and the choice of residential location, and the citizen's image of perception of city space. Necessarily much is omitted or dealt with summarily, for the constraints of time, length and costs have all to be considered. Even so the conclusion has been completely rewritten in an attempt to relate the book to some broader issues. In addition a number of minor changes have been made and the references and recommended reading lists have been brought up to date.

I have had the advantage of discussing much of this material with Professor K. Corey of the Department of Community Planning at the University of Cincinnati and Professor W. K. D. Davies of the Department of Geography at Calgary, and I am grateful for their advice. My particular thanks are due to my colleague Dr C. R. Lewis, who shares with me the teaching of urban geography at Aberystwyth. He has helped both through constant discussion and by reading the additional matter. As usual, however, the final responsibility rests with the author.

Preface to the third edition

The choice in the preparation of this edition lay between either a substantial revision and updating but preserving much of the original, or a complete rewriting of the whole book. The first of these alternatives was chosen since it seemed sensible to build on a successfully established foundation. There have been considerable modifications. Two chapters of the second edition have been deleted, although some of their content has been retained and included in other chapters. Three new chapters have been added, on the housing market, on spatial inequalities in the city, and on the city in the developing world.

Both in the Introduction and in the last chapter some comment is made on the proposition that the urban geography here presented is outmoded since it deals with some observed characteristics of urbanism whilst not establishing in the first instance a view of the controlling socio-political and economic system from which those characteristics are ultimately derived. In short, the view that the starting point should be the general operation of the advanced capitalist system is not adopted and the 'facts' of urbanism somewhat arbitrarily constitute the point of departure. The basis, therefore, is an attempt to present in some logical form and order the work that has been published by urban geographers; it is a responsive rather than an innovative basis. The justification is that for the beginning student such an approach is the most appropriate, it starts from the known environment rather than a 'first cause'.

All social science can be regarded as value orientated. The values on which this book is based are, it is hoped, made clear. Certainly no assumption of the presentation of an 'absolute' set of 'facts' is made.

Once again I must acknowledge the great help I have had by discussing much of the specific material, as well as general principles, with my colleagues in the Department of Geography of the University College of Wales at Aberystwyth. I must again especially note the advice of Dr C. R. Lewis. I am also greatly indebted to Miss Linda James who has been responsible for typing not only the new chapters but also the many minor insertions and changes which have been made for this edition.

Harold Carter
Aberystwyth, Spring 1980

Acknowledgements

The author and publisher wish to thank the following for permission to reprint or modify copyright material:

Academic Press for a figure from 'The development of the industrial town 1730–1900' by H. Carter in *Historical geography of England and Wales* edited by R. A. Dodgshon and R. A. Butlin, 1976 (figure 9–10); The Acton Society Trust for a figure from 'A study of certain changes in land values, London 1950–64' by Bryan Anstey in *Land values* edited by Peter Hall, Sweet & Maxwell Ltd, 1965 (figure 9–1)[1]; Aldine Inc., Chicago, for two figures from 'How citizens view two great cities' by D. Francescato and W. Mebane in *Image and environment* edited by R. M. Downs and D. Stea, 1973 (figures 14–1A and B); the Association of American Geographers for a figure from 'A restatement of the transition zone concept' by R. E. Preston and D. W. Griffin, *Annals* **56,** 1966 (figure 9–15), a figure from 'Procedures in townscape analysis' by R. J. Solomon, *Annals* **56,** 1966 (figure 10–2); Almqvist & Wiksell Forlag, Stockholm, and George Allen & Unwin Ltd for a figure from *The industrial structure of American cities* by G. Alexandersson, 1956 (figure 3–1); Barrie & Jenkins Ltd for a figure from *Georgian London* by Sir John Summerson, 1945 (figure 7–2); E. J. Brill, Leiden, for two figures from 'Land use in the urban core' by W. Hartenstein and G. Staack in *Urban core and inner city* edited by W. F. Heinemeijer, M. Van Hulten and Hans D. de Vries Reilingh, 1967 (figures 9–5 & 9–13); Cambridge University Press for a figure from *Urban analysis: a study of city structure* by B. T. Robson, 1969 (figure 8–2); the author and David & Charles for a figure from *Urban geography* by D. T. Herbert, 1972 (figure 10–14); the author for a figure from *The hierarchy of commercial centres: a case study in South Wales* volume 2 by W. K. D. Davies, University of Wales Ph.D. thesis, 1964 (figure 6–2); Gustav Fischer Verlag, Stuttgart, for three figures from *The economics of location* by A. Lösch, 1939 (translation by W. H. Woglom, 1954, Yale University Press) (figures 4–7, 4–8 & 4–9); the editor and the American Geographical Society for a figure from 'The negro ghetto; problems and alternatives' by R. L. Morrill, *Geographical Review* **55,** 1965 (figure 10–8); the author for a figure from *Locational analysis in human geography* by Peter Haggett, Edward Arnold, 1977 (figure 4–5); Leonard Hill Ltd for a figure from *British shopping centres* by W. Burns, 1959 (figure 6–3); the editor and the Institute of Australian Geographers

---

[1] Figure numbers in brackets refer to those in this book.

for a figure from 'The distribution of an intra-metropolitan central place hierarchy' by R. J. Johnston, *Australian Geographical Studies* **6**, 1966 (figure 6−8); the editor and the American Geographical Society for a figure from 'Five cities of the Gangetic Plain' by O. H. K. Spate and E. Ahmad, *Geographical Review* Vol. 41 1950 (figure 16−2); George Allen and Unwin for a figure from *Housing policy and the housing system* by A. Murie, P. Niner and C. Watson, 1976 (figure 11−4). H.M.S.O., Department of the Environment for a figure from *Housing policy. A consultative document* Cmd 6851, 1977 (figure 11−1); Home Office, Community Development Project (C.D.P.) Information and Intelligence Unit for a figure from *Projects against houses. An alternative guide to housing finance* 1976 (figure 11−3); the editor and the Institute of British Geographers for a figure from 'Alnwick: a study in town plan analysis' by M. R. G. Conzen, *Transactions* **27**, 1960 (figure 7−3), for a figure from 'The urban regions of St Albans' by H. S. Thurston, 1953 (figure 10−1a), for two figures from 'Distribution of schizophrenics in Nottingham' by J. Giggs, *Transactions* **59**, 1973 (figures 15−1 & 15−2), one figure from 'The study of delinquency areas: a social geographical approach' by P. E. Lloyd and C. M. Mason *Transactions* New Series **3(1)**, 1978 (figure 15−5), one figure from 'The study of delinquency areas: a social geographical approach' by D. T. Herbert, *Transactions* New Series **1(4)**, 1976 (figure 15−4), and for a figure from 'Rural periodic day markets in part of Yorubaland' by B. W. Hodder, *Transactions* **29**, 1961 (figure 16−1); the author for two figures from 'Central place theory and the hierarchy and location of shopping centres in a city: Edinburgh' by R. Jones, IBG Study Group in Urban Geography, 1967 (figures 6−9 & 6−10); the author for a figure from 'Comments on "historical" factors influencing residential choice' by J. A. Silk, IBG Study Group in Urban Geography, 1972 (figure 10−15); the author for two figures from 'The development of by-law housing in Kingston-upon-Hull' by C. A. Forster, IBG Urban Study Group Salford Conference, 1968 (figures 10−3 & 10−4); the editors for a figure from 'The urban process under capitalism: a framework for analysis by D. Harvey, *International Journal of Urban and Regional Research* **2(1)**, 1978 (figure 15−7); Liverpool University Press for a figure from *The social and geography of Merseyside in the nineteenth century* by R. Lawton and C. G. Poole, 1976 (figure 10−12); the author and Longman Group Limited for three figures from 'The central place patterns of mid-Wales and the middle Welsh borderland' by C. R. Lewis in *Urban essays: studies in the geography of Wales* edited by H. Carter and W. K. D. Davies (figures 5−2, 5−5a & 5−5b); the author, Longman Southern Africa (Pty) Limited and the Human Sciences Research Council, Pretoria, for four figures from *Land use in central Cape Town: a study in urban geography* by D. H. Davies, 1965 (figures 9−4, 9−6, 9−7 & 9−8); Longman Group Limited for a figure from *People and housing in Third World cities* by D. J. Dwyer, 1975 (figure 16−5); Los Angeles Department of City Planning for three figures from *The visual environment of Los Angeles*, 1971 (figures 14.1A & B, 14.2 A, B & C, 14.3); the MIT Press for a figure from *The spatial dynamics of U.S. urban-industrial growth 1800−1914: interpretative and* *theoretical essays* by A. R. Pred, 1966 (figure 3−2); Macmillan for a figure from *Housing economics* by S. Charles, 1977 (figure 11−2); Methuen Ltd (ABP) for a figure from the essay by H. Carter in *Wales: a study in physical, historical and regional geography* edited by E. G. Bowen, 1957 (figure 7−1), and for a figure from 'Models of industrial locations' by F. E. I. Hamilton in *Models in geography* edited by R. J. Chorley and P. Haggett, 1967 (figure 13−4); George Philip & Son Limited and the University of London Institute of Education for a table from *The geography of Greater London* by A. E. Smailes, 1964 (figure 10−1B); Prentice-Hall Inc. for a figure from *Geography of market centres and retail distribution* by B. J. L. Berry, 1962 (figure 6−5), and for a figure from *Land resource economics: the political economy of rural and urban land resource use* by Raleigh Barlowe, © 1958 Prentice-Hall Inc. (figure 10−11); Presses Universitaires de France for a figure from *Étude sur le développement des villes entre Loire et Rhin au moyen-âge* by F. L. Ganshof, 1943 (figure 7−8), and for a figure from *La croissance de la banlieu parisienne* by J. Bastié, ¯964 (figure 12−1); Princeton University Press for two figures from *A history of city planning in the United States* by J. W. Reps, © 1965 Princeton University Press (figures 7−6 & 7−7), and for a figure from *Cairo: 1001 years of the city victorious* by J. Abu-Laghod, 1971 (figure 16−3); the Department of Geography, Queen Mary College, University of London for a figure from 'Crime rates as territorial social indicators' by D. M. Smith, *Occasional papers* **N11,** 1974 (figure 15−3); Routledge & Kegan Paul and the Humanities Press Inc. for a figure from *The west European city* by R. E. Dickinson, 1951 (figure 13−1); the author for two figures from *The middle order towns of Wales* by Gwyn Rowley, University of Wales Ph.D. Thesis, 1967 (figures 6−4A & 6−4B); the editor and the author for a figure from 'An approach to the study of a town as a central place' by D. Herbert, *Sociological Review* **9,** 1961 (figure 9−2); the Regents of the University of California Press for two figures from *The social areas of Los Angeles* by Eshref Shevky and Marilyn Williams, 1949 (figures 10−5 & 10−6); the author for two figures from 'City size distributions and economic development' by B. J. L. Berry, *Economic Development and Cultural Change* **9,** 1961 (figure 4−10); the University of Chicago Department of Geography and the author for a figure from *Private redevelopment of the central city* by L. S. Bourne, *Research Paper* **112,** 1967 (figure 10−10); the editor for a figure from 'Principles of areal functional organization in regional human geography' by A. K. Philbrick, *Economic Geography,* **33,** 1957 (figure 6−1A, B & C), for two figures from 'Cultural differences in consumer travel' by R. A. Murdie, *Economic Geography* **41,** 1965 (figures 6−12 & 6−13), for a figure from 'Delimiting the CBD' by R. E. Murphy and J. E. Vance Jr., *Economic Geography* **30,** 1954 (figure 9−3), for three figures from 'The industrial revolution and the emergence of Boston's CBD' by D. Ward, *Economic Geography* **42,** 1966 (figure 9−9A, B & C), and for a figure from 'The zone in transition: a study of urban land use patterns' by R. E. Preston, *Economic Geography* **42,** 1966 (figure 9−16); the editor for a figure from 'The spatial organization of residential areas in Accra, Ghana, with particular reference to aspects of modernization' by R. R. Brand, *Economic Geography* **48,** 1972 (figure 16−4); the editor for a figure from 'The squatters of Lima: who they are and what they want' by F. M. Andrews and G. W. Phillips, *Journal of Developing Areas* **4,** 1970 (figure 16−6); Columbia University Press for a figure from *The core of the city* by J. Rannels, 1966 (figure 9−14); The University of Hull Publications Committee for a figure from 'The segregation of immigrant communities in the city of Birmingham, 1961' by P. N. Jones, *University of Hull Occasional Papers in Geography* **7,** 1967 (figure 10−9); the University of Kansas Press for a figure from *Distribution of land values in Topeka* by D. Knos, 1962 (figure 8−8); the University of Illinois Press for a figure from *Urban land-use planning* by F. S. Chapin, 1965 (figure 8−9); Eastern Michigan University for a figure from *Community interaction and racial integration in the Detroit area: an ecological analysis* by R. V. Smith, S. F. Flory, R. L. Bashshur and G. W. Shannon, 1967 (figure 10−13); Northwestern University Department of Geography for three figures from 'The internal structure of retail nucleations' by B. J. Garner, *Northwestern University Studies in Geography* **12,** 1966 (figures 6−6, 6−7 & 6−11); the editor for a figure from 'The location of high status residential areas' by R. J. Johnston, *Geographische Annales* **48,** 1966 (figure 10−7); the University of Pennsylvania Press for two figures from 'An approach to metropolitan spatial structure' by D. L. Foley in *Explorations into urban structure* edited by M. Webber, 1964 (figure 1−2); the University of Pennsylvania Regional Science Association for a figure from 'A graph theory interpretation of nodal regions' by J. D. Nystuen and M. F. Dacey, *Papers of the Regional Science Association* **7,** 1961 (figure 5−1B); the editor for a figure from 'The location of urban land uses' by L. K. Loewenstein, *Land Economics* **39,** 1963 (figure 13−3); the University of Washington Press for a figure from 'The spatial organization of business land uses' by B. J. L. Berry in *Studies in highway development and geographic change* edited by W. L. Garrison *et al.*, 1959 (figure 8−6 which is the basis of figure 8−7); the author for a figure from *Two cities of Latin America* by A. H. Whiteford, Anchor Books (figure 8−3); and the University of Wales Press for a figure from *Roman frontier* by Nash Williams, 1954 (figure 7−9).

The publisher and author also acknowledge the use of non-copyright material from *The structure and growth of residential neighbourhoods in American cities* by H. Hoyt, U.S. Government Printing Office, 1939 (figure 8−5).

1

Introduction: The Study of Urban Geography

If it be regarded as a distinct systematic or topical study within the general field of geography, urban geography is a comparatively young branch of the subject. It was certainly not taught as a specialism in the same way as geomorphology or climatology, or indeed political geography, in university departments prior to the Second World War. This is easily understandable. Urban geography cannot claim to be a systematic study in the sense that it is concerned with those processes which, in the context of a culture, operate to create spatial patterns. These processes are economic, social and political and their study rightly generates the systematic themes within human geography. Urban geography, in contrast, considers all these processes in relation to one phenomenon, the city. It has tended, therefore, to concentrate on consequence, rather than process, though this tendency may perhaps be changing. Towns have always been of interest to the geographer and from the earliest times regional geographies have dealt with them. Thus Strabo in his *Geography* was well aware of the importance of location, 'the natural advantages [of a place] should always be mentioned, since they are permanent. Advantages which are adventitious are liable to change . . . those which continue, come to be regarded by posterity, not as works of art but as the natural advantages of a place; these, therefore, it is evident we must notice.'[1]

But in spite of the endeavour to place emphasis on advantages of location, the geographical study of towns became essentially descriptive. Strabo himself wrote of Lyons, 'Lugdunum, situated on a hill, at the conference of the Saône and the Rhône, belongs to the Romans. It is the most populous city after Narbonne. It carries on a great commerce, and the Roman prefects here coin both gold and silver money.'[2] This is followed by a description of the temple dedicated to Caesar Augustus. This sort of 'digest' account long stood as the standard way of dealing with towns although occasionally location was seen as a controlling factor. In the great atlas of town plans *Civitates orbis terrarum* published in the late sixteenth century, the wealth of Lyons is clearly related to its position, 'Its wealth comes from the afore-mentioned rivers, for because they pass many towns and flow into the sea, and because the city stands in the centre of Europe and is counted the heart of France, such rivers are a good means of conveying all things out of

---

[1] H. C. Hamilton and W. Falconer, Editors (1912): *The geography of Strabo*, 1, 182 (London).
[2] H. C. Hamilton and W. Falconer (1912), 287.

and into all the chief countries of Europe.'[3] But in general such relationships were rarely stressed. A typical example is William Frederick Martyn's *The geographical magazine, or new system of geography* published in 1793.[4] He comments that 'It is impossible in a work of this nature to expatiate on everything beautiful or curious in the various cities and towns which present themselves in different countries; nor can we do justice to the numerous architectural beauties with which England abounds.'[5] After dealing with London, Martyn continues, 'Bristol, reckoned the second city of England for its extent and population, is more remarkable for its commerce and opulence than for any curious or beautiful structures it contains: and indeed all the other towns and cities of England have little more to recommend them to our notice than their commerce and the conveniency of their situations.'[6] The whole geography of towns was in this way briefly dismissed, although the growing influence of industrialism meant that the detailed recording of the nature of trade and commerce became more important.

Even so there was little formal method. John Pinkerton in his *Modern geography, a description of the empires, kingdoms, states and colonies . . . in all parts of the world*[7] published in 1807 wrote, 'In giving a brief account of the chief cities and towns in England, a few of the most important shall be arranged according to dignity, opulence and population; and the others shall be stated without preference, in a kind of progress from the south-west to the north.'[8] In this progress the author becomes uneasy and excuses his omissions, 'In a chorography of England, Leicester and Shrewsbury might deserve description, but its geography can only embrace the most important topics.'[9] From this it appears that geography took on the aspect of a descriptive gazetteer, although it was only concerned with the principal parts: 'It's something like learning Geography . . . Principal Rivers . . . Principal Mountains . . . Principal Towns—Why what are those creatures making honey down there?' Thus Alice built up her geography of Looking Glass Land, although with an astute aside on the economic base, and it is not surprising that this approach resulted in a demand for an association, rather than a narration, of facts. This reaction was clearly apparent in the first issue in 1901 of the periodical now called *Geography* which contained a paper on 'The position of towns.'[10] 'The magnificence of a town's buildings,' wrote the author, 'the greatness of its population and commerce are stated as though they were causes of the town's importance, instead of being the most convincing proofs of peculiar advantages of position.'[11] And he

[3] R. Oehme (1965): *Old European cities*, 73 (London).

[4] W. F. Martyn (1793): *The geographical magazine: or new system of geography*. 2 volumes (London).

[5] W. F. Martyn (1793), **2**, 404.

[6] W. F. Martyn (1793), **2**, 405.

[7] J. Pinkerton (1807): *Modern geography; a description of the empires, kingdoms, states and colonies: with the oceans, seas and islands: in all parts of the world* (London).

[8] J. Pinkerton (1807), 77.

[9] J. Pinkerton (1807), 89.

[10] B. B. Dickinson (1901–2): The position of towns. *Geogl. Teach.* **1**, 97.

[11] B. B. Dickinson (1901–2), 97.

concluded, 'Let us once and for all give up the rote learning of towns, products and points of interest as separate facts in favour of a general but comprehensive grasp of distribution, and the logical consequences of physical position.'[12]

The replacement of description by interpretation of location laid the foundations for urban geography to develop as a special study. The first decade of the present century saw the appearance of two major works. Karl Hassert's *Die Städte geographisch betrachtet*, published at Leipzig in 1907,[13] was the first volume to present an outline of urban geography. Raoul Blanchard's *Grenoble, étude de géographie urbaine* published in 1911[14] was the first classical study of a single city. To a large extent, developments in urban geography mirrored those in geography as a whole. At this period the subject was finding a basis in working out the consequences of the physical environment, for in spite of the nebulous concept of 'man, the master of the possibilities' of the physical world, the great regional monographs were firmly based on lithology and relief. The association between the 'separate facts' lay in the causal effect of physical geography. It was inevitable that at the time the unifying basis of town study should be found in those factors of location which controlled urban development. Blanchard wrote in the foreword of his book, 'The basic concept of this study is to explain the origin and development of the town as a function of the physical conditions of its situation;'[15] and in the last lines he concluded, 'From its origin right down to its present extension, Grenoble is the town at the junction of types of terrain, at the confluence of rivers. In spite of human changes nature always asserts its rights, even on an organism as complex as a town.'[16]

There followed a whole series of studies,[17] which can conveniently be called the 'site and situation' variety, in which the main end was to demonstrate that the character of towns was to be derived from their physical locations.[18] The key word in such studies was 'nodality' — hence the vast range of diagrams attempting to demonstrate the nodal situation of settlements. In this sort of context there was little room for the further development of a true urban geography and little incentive to gather a multitude of single studies under the heading of the geography of towns.

The first general review of urban geography was made by Aurousseau in 1924.[19] He comments that city geography embraces such a large section of human geography that it is hardly a specialization at all. Thus at the outset, and in consequence of the problems involved in identifying urban

---

[12] B. B. Dickinson (1901–2), 108.

[13] K. Hassert (1907): *Die Städte geographisch betrachtet* (Leipzig).

[14] R. Blanchard (1911): *Grenoble: étude de géographie urbaine* (Paris).

[15] R. Blanchard (1911), 5.

[16] R. Blanchard (1911), 159.

[17] For example, J. Levainville (1913): *Rouen, étude d'une agglomération urbaine* (Paris).

[18] It is interesting to note that the only map, apart from one on general location, in H. J. Fleure (1924): Cities of the Po basin: an introductory study. *Geogl. Rev.* **14**, 345, is a map of January and July temperatures!

[19] M. Aurousseau (1924): Recent contributions to urban geography: a review. *Geogrl. Rev* **14**, 444.

geography as a systematic study, he is unsure about the nature of urban geography. An introductory section on method outlines Blanchard's approach and leads into the following statement: 'It is an astonishing fact that the greatest interest has centred upon the individual town. Geography is so deeply concerned with the distribution of things that an interest in town distribution seems to be an obvious consideration. Little attention has been given to it.'[20] Aurousseau then proceeds to note Fleure's contributions to the regional study of towns[21] and discusses the beginnings of functional study together with the early work on town status. Examples of town studies from different parts of the world are then given, and in conclusion 'the lack of extended studies in the United States' is recorded! The work makes extremely interesting reading for it stands at a point when rapid changes were taking place, the methods of the past and the problems of the future are uneasily associated in a review of a nascent specialism.

The changes noted above were largely a result of the reaction against the restricted aim of many town studies and this reaction was derived from two sources. The first was a direct rejection of the stereotyped 'site and situation' formula as it was slowly realized that such a limited consideration could not be abstracted from what was a complex, functioning economic and social system. Crowe, writing on methodology in 1938,[22] seized on the treatment of towns as indicative of the inability of geographers to penetrate beyond the superficial. He criticized the tendency 'to crystallize . . . upon the distribution of inanimate objects and the morphology of static patterns'. He pointed out that the application of the 'site and situation' formula was meaningless 'where site had nothing but historical interest and situation was viewed in terms of routes and not currents of movement.'[23] But already in 1933 Walther Christaller's great work on the central places of south-western Germany[24] had been published and, although its impact was not to be felt until the post-war years, the revolution Crowe had demanded was under way.

The second source of reaction came from the nature of town growth itself. The vast extension of urban areas under the stimulus of new modes of transport brought severe problems of interpretation. A site-situation approach was also meaningless when the large urban agglomerations had to be considered. In 1915 Patrick Geddes had been forced to devise a term for these new growths and the word 'conurbation'[25] came into circulation. The simple growth plan, the main element of the morphological approach was increasingly shown to be inadequate. In the 1920s the Chicago school of human ecologists was already considering the variety of economic and social forces

---

[20] M. Aurousseau (1924), 445.

[21] See note 18 and H. J. Fleure (1920): Some types of cities in temperate Europe *Geogrl. Rev.* **10,** 357.

[22] P. R. Crowe (1938): On progress in geography. *Scott, geogr. Mag.* 54.

[23] P. R. Crowe (1938), 18.

[24] W. Christaller (1933): *Die zentralen Orte in Süddeutschland* (Jena); translation by C. W. Baskin (1966): *Central places in Southern Germany* (Englewood Cliffs, N.J.).

[25] P. Geddes (1949): *Cities in evolution*, 14−15 (London).

which resulted in the segregation of urban land-uses.[26] The attention of geographers was thus directed towards the complexity of the townscape and away from the apparent simplicity of growth and general plan.

By the end of the Second World War, therefore, the situation had been reached where a rapid growth of urban geography was inevitable. Preliminary foundations had been laid and many of the basic ideas had been propounded, although in isolation. In many ways the subsequent expansion in urban geography was mainly concerned with the exploitation of ideas already in existence in the 1930s.

From a purely practical point of view there was an urgent need, certainly in most European cities, to deal with the terrible conditions brought about by uncontrolled nineteenth-century development. Wartime bombing resulted in the need for reconstruction. Redevelopment, reconstruction; both demanded planning. In one of the earliest post-war studies R. E. Dickinson wrote,[27] 'This book is not about planning. It is concerned with certain aspects of the inherent spatial or geographical structure of society upon which planning must be based, and it insists that knowledge of the anatomy of society must precede the treatment of its defects.'[28] The employment of many geographers in town planning and the interaction between academic urban geography and the practical and applied spheres of planning provided an active stimulus to development. Commercial concerns began to realize the need for rigorous analysis before developments were started and the study of store location and market survey[29] also impinged on methods of investigation in urban geography.

Finally, there were changes within academic geography itself which made the development of systematic studies more acceptable. The old convention of 'the relation between man and his (physical?) environment' with its impossible intellectual position, was slowly replaced by a new cliché, 'the areal differentiation of the earth's surface'. The 'physical basis' was accordingly deprived of its basic role; and, of the infinite variety of operative factors, no single one was given an *a priori* importance. In economic geography this change slowly released a flood of pent-up energy seeking the universal rather than the multiplication of detail. This flood finally burst through on the urban sector where 'model building' was first propounded in human geography. At the same time, urban areas had become such important parts of the landscape in western countries that the simplest geographical description had to come to terms with them: the need for systematic study was evident. The eastern states of America had to be interpreted in terms of 'Megalopolis',[30] the foundations of the contemporary

[26] For an outline see: G. Sjoberg (1965): Theory and research in urban sociology; chapter 5 in P. M. Hauser and L. F. Schnore (1965): *The study of urbanization*, 157 (New York).

[27] R. E. Dickinson (1947): *City region and regionalism* (London).

[28] R. E. Dickinson (1947), xiii.

[29] For example: W. Applebaum (1961): Teaching marketing geography by the case method. *Econ. Geogr.* **37**, 48. P. H. Thorpe, editor (N.D.): *Great Britain; a 'geographia' marketing and media survey* (London).

[30] J. Gottmann (1961): *Megalopolis, the urbanized northeastern seaboard of the United States* (New York).

geography of the Netherlands lie in Randstad, Holland,[31] not the sub-boreal peat.

All these conditions formed a great stimulus to the geography of towns and in the last two decades an enormous mass of literature has accumulated. But urban geography was never at the outset conceived as a well defined, systematic study; Topsy-like it just 'growed', although to such an extent that there is no need to present any argument for its recognition. But it had been developed by a large number of specialist workers engaged on particular aspects and at this stage, therefore, it became necessary to show that it formed a coherent field of study based on geographical principles of investigation. This need dominated much of methodological writing on urban geography during the 1950s. Mayer, in a series of papers,[32] outlined the main points on which geographers had concentrated and demonstrated these as forming related parts of a coherent systematic study. The general content of urban geography as propounded at that time can be summarized as follows.

At the outset the major concern was conceived to be a geographical one: 'Geography,' wrote Hartshorne, 'is concerned to provide accurate, orderly and rational description and interpretation of the variable character of the earth's surface.'[33] Since it was hoped, probably in vain, to be rarely inaccurate, seldom disorderly and never irrational, it was possible to omit the adjectives and argue that the geographer was concerned with the analysis of the variable character of the earth's surface. On that surface, the populations and the buildings agglomerated together to make up towns constituted the special interest of the urban geographer; they were to be abstracted from the totality for separate, topical study. Since the bulk of the population of the western world lived in towns and the problems of the urban environment were paramount at the time, the importance of the study in academic geography and its relevance to applied geography[34] needed no further stress.

The argument continued: the town as a unit feature of the earth's surface has, like all other features, two associated aspects. The first is location or position, the second is form or internal structure. In simplest fashion these two aspects emerge clearly when differences of scale are considered. On the atlas map towns are represented by conventional symbols and the main geographical implication is a concern with location, or with the town as a distributed feature. On maps of the scale of one inch or six inches to the mile, the town is no longer shown by conventional means but it is seen to have individual form or shape as well as internal structure, although this is, as yet, displayed only in a generalized way. On the scale of twenty-five or fifty inches to the mile, the internal structure becomes apparent in detail, in

---

[31] For a description see P. Hall (1966): *The world cities*, 95 (London).
[32] H. M. Mayer (1951): Geography and urbanism. *Scient. Mon.* **63**, 1. H. M. Mayer (1954): Urban geography; chapter 6 in Preston James and C. F. Jones, editors (1954): *American geography; inventory and prospect* (Syracuse, N.Y.).
[33] R. Hartshorne (1959): *Perspective on the nature of geography*, 21 (London).
[34] See chapter 2, below.

the form of streets, blocks and individual buildings, although still in an unreal, two-dimensional way. Finally on the ground, the real town is seen to be three-dimensional, for each building has height and this must be added to the geographer's appreciation. Indeed, the geographer, confronted with the town fabric, is also made to realize that the fourth dimension of time is involved, for many of the structures and much of the form are inherited from past periods. But this progress through the scales emphasizes the two main themes of study introduced at the outset, the town as a distributed feature and the town as a feature with internal structure, or in other words, the town *in* area and the town *as* area.

It is axiomatic that location can only be understood through function; what a town does, or did in the past, determines its location and controls its growth. It is possible to derive two associated concepts from the consideration of functions. These are:

1   *The nature of urban functions:* that is, we seek to answer the questions, What are the sorts of activities which dominate the whole range which towns perform? In particular, to what extent are specialized functions carried out and what are they?

2   *The stature (status) of urban services:* that is excluding specialized functions, we seek to answer the question: To what extent does the town take part in central place activities?

It is dangerous to confuse these two although they are so clearly bound together; we need a 'separate study of resource oriented functions and other activities whose location central place theory cannot explain and the subsequent superimposition of such functions on to the areal pattern of central places.'[35] Here therefore were two critical lines of investigation which are shown in figure 1−1.[36] The link between them is associated with accessibility and the transport role has, therefore, been isolated as a distinctive feature to be considered apart.

The morphology of towns, or the study of internal structure, is related to three variables. These are plan or layout, land-use or the function of buildings and the architectural style of buildings. These three vary independently and produce an infinite variety of urban scene. Each has to be considered separately and then the relationship between them demonstrated in a study of the whole townscape as shown in figure 1−1. This diagram is presented to indicate the relationship between the various areas of investigation which formed part of urban geography at that time.

The organizing concept behind figure 1−1 carries the implication that urban geography should be a unitary study. Function and morphology, the town in an area and the town as an area, it is suggested, should not be thought of as two clear-cut and distinct lines of investigation. They are closely linked: separation is only for convenience of analytical study, and it should be stressed that all these separate aspects, all these points of study,

[35]   W. Isard (1960): *Methods of regional analysis,* 227 (New York).
[36]   For another diagram in which a similar analysis is attempted, see: D. Thorpe (1966): The geographer and urban studies, *Dept. Geogr. Uni. Durham Occl. Pap. Ser.* **8,** 3.

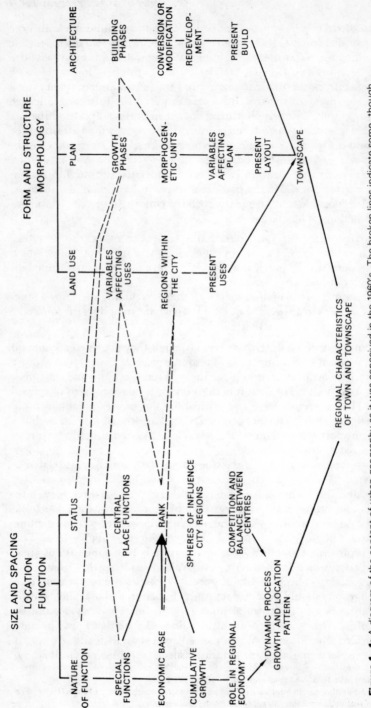

Figure 1–1: A diagram of the content of urban geography as it was conceived in the 1960's. The broken lines indicate some, though clearly not all, of the connections between the various aspects of study. They have been inserted as a rational representation of the complex way in which all the aspects that can be studied interact with each other. In all of these aspects three approaches can be identified: 1 Aggregate, locational analysis; 2 Disaggregated behavioural analysis; 3 Welfare analysis.

find their place in urban geography in so far as they build back into the general regional pattern of towns and townscapes. In this way the systematic study formed an essential part of the whole, which geography was seen to remain.

For some urban geographers this last sentence appeared either as a restriction or an irrelevance.[37] It seemed to imply that discrete areas of subject matter can be used to identify various disciplines rather than the methods they employ and in so doing initiates a later stage in the evolution of the geographer's concern with towns than that sketched at the outset of this chapter. This can be identified as the stage where the simplistic 'man in relation to his environment' was succeeded by 'the description and interpretation of the varying features of the earth's surface', or 'areal differentiation' in a shorter version. In relation to this newer theme the old phrase, 'but it's not geography', was still quoted and retained a relevance.

But if the emphasis is now to be on the way the geographer looks at things and not on the material studied then it is possible to transform the whole argument, as it has been so far outlined, so that the *subject matter* becomes the phenomenon of urbanism and the process of urbanization and *the approach* is geographical in so far as it is concerned with spatially distributed aspects; what distinguishes the geographer is the way he thinks about urbanism, not any specially segmented section of it. It follows that figure 1−1 might be of interest in that it depicts the various fields in which geographers worked during the immediate post-war period but at the same time it is misleading in so far as a scheme for urban geography should demonstrate the value and significance of method in the study of urbanization, and not be so overtly dominated by the concern for a holistic and discrete 'subject' geography which has been abandoned by many as not academically and intellectually viable, or indeed worthwhile.

The conceptual framework for a study of urban geography ought, therefore, to be concerned with 'urbanization' and not 'Geography'. At this point it is perhaps worth mentioning that urban history has faced precisely the same problems and most urban historians have come to the same conclusions. But to establish a framework common to all who are interested in urbanism presents severe problems. Nevertheless, at least one partially successful attempt has been made by Foley and it is significant that it was derived from a planner's attempt to show the way planning interests related to urbanism, or at least to metropolitan structure.[38] His scheme, he claims, was developed about a common conceptual framework and a common language for exchanging ideas.

In figure 1−2, which depicts Foley's basic notions, the vertical distinction is between those aspects which are aspatial, and where there is no concern

---

[37] A book which covers much of the field conventionally ascribed to urban geography is entitled *Geographic perspectives on urban systems*. Making due allowance for jargon the implications are clear: the subject is 'urban systems' which can be considered from a number of perspectives, one of which is 'geographical'.

[38] D. L. Foley (1964): An approach to metropolitan spatial structure; in M. Webber *et alia* (1964): *Explorations into urban structure*, 21−78 (Philadelphia).

	A ASPATIAL ASPECTS	**B** SPATIAL ASPECTS
I NORMATIVE OR CULTURAL ASPECTS	Social values: Culture patterns: Norms: Institutional setting: Technology:	Spatial distribution of culture patterns and norms: Values concerned with qualities and determination of spatial patterns of activities, population and physical environment:
II FUNCTIONAL ORGANIZATIONAL ASPECTS	Division and allocation of functions: Interdependence: Activity systems— persons and establishments in their functional-role sense	Spatial distribution of functions and activities: Linkages—spatially conceived: Spatial pattern of establishments, by functional type
III PHYSICAL ASPECTS	Physical objects: The Geographical environment: Man-developed improvements: Population	Spatial distribution of physical objects: Patterns of land forms, building, roads, people

Figure 1–2: Selected aspects of metropolitan structure: a conceptual view. *After D. L. Foley (1964).*

with location or distribution, and those where it is the dominant concern. The horizontal divisions are concerned with the different aspects which can be considered, and these are threefold. The first is concerned with the values of the social group and is termed cultural; the second is concerned with the functions and roles of people and institutions within the social group and is called the functional or organizational aspect; the third relates to visible physical objects in the city including buildings and people. All these have spatial consequences which are indicated under column **B**. In the organization of the scheme, functional organization occupying a middle position is seen as mediating between the norms and values of a population, which are culturally derived, and the physical reality of the city on the earth's surface.

The geographer's attention is clearly pre-empted by the spatial aspect but the framework emphasizes that this cannot be simply abstracted as 'urban geography', for there are vital derivations from aspatial aspects which first have to be understood. Within the scheme it is possible to indicate as examples the paths of controlling relations in retail location and housing type. The study of retail shops and their locations could be indicated by the first path shown on figure 1–3. The problem is rooted in the norms and

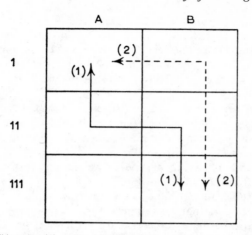

Figure 1–3: Retail location (1) and housing type (2) in relation to the conceptual scheme shown in figure 1–2.

patterns of shopping habits and in the technology of retailing. These in turn can be translated into terms of functional organization and structuring and these terms carry with them spatial implications which lead to the actual spacing of retail outlets within the city.

The second path indicates the relationship implicit in a study of a type of housing — for example inter-war semi-detached housing in Britain. Again the source of this housing character lies in the values and cultural norms of the population, how people see themselves in social terms determines the type of housing they will look for and where they will live. The phrase 'where they will live' shows that the move has been made into the 'spatial column'. Via a whole series of associations and linkages the pattern of housing types emerges in section 111B of the diagram. The movement is not a one-way process for the area and type of house can result in the acquisition of social values. Thus the techniques of social area analysis and the divisions they reveal are concerned with sections 1B and 11B but have a root relation with 1A and implications for 111B. The diagram can also be employed on an individualistic as well as an aggregative basis; the values and opinions of the person in a decision making context can be encompassed as well as the cultural norm and thus the framework can be adapted to a behavioural approach.

The scheme may also be extended in two ways. The first would be to cover both 'form' and 'process' where 'form' is taken to refer to the morphological or anatomical aspects and 'process' to functional or physiological aspects. Paths traced in this new structure become more complex and this is compounded when the second extension takes place, which is related to the time dimension so that a development sequence is brought in.

Each worker in the field of urbanization can place his work within this frame and here the urban geographer can see himself not as having concern with a chunk of subject matter but contributing his particular expertise to the problem of understanding the urban scene. If figure 1—1 has to be related to figure 1—2, then it will be seen to be mainly concerned with sections 11B and 111B. The relations via 1B and 1A are not encompassed and those with 11A are only implied. It is worthy of note that it is with the extension of enquiry in these directions that much of urban geography is now concerned.

As a result of such extension the structure of urban geography in the 1960's as represented in figure 1—1 has further severe limitations for process based studies have become dominant. Such new directions were derived from a lack of satisfaction with 'explanation' at the aggregate level. Thus, in relation to central places, theory moved further and further into abstract mathematical formulation on the one hand, a move which seemed to have little practical relevance, whilst on the other the replication of empirical studies added nothing but case examples which by their nature could do nothing to confirm or reject a theoretical formulation. Similarly in the field of social area analysis, the areas having been derived there seemed but little purpose other than to argue whether their patterning was concentric, sectoral or multi-nucleated.

The way forward was identified as lying in process or behavioural studies, where deeper rooted and more satisfactory explanations would be found. Central places, or shopping centres, obtained their statuses by the preferred behaviour of consumers and most certainly it could be demonstrated that such behaviour was not that predicted by central place theory. Likewise residential character was created through the locational choices of individual families, and in their perception of the qualities of areas and in their behaviour in choosing, more convincing insights into the creation of social areas were to be found. Urban geography moved into a predominantly behavioural phase when the literature was dominated by studies of consumer behaviour and residential choice, closely associated with investigations into people's perception of the townscape and the opportunities it offered.

In turn, dissatisfaction with behavioural studies has grown rapidly, largely because of the basic assumption of the unconstrained nature of choice. It was apparent that those with few resources to deploy had no choices to make, but were at the mercy of the 'system'. This awareness of deprivation was heightened by the actual physical process of inner city decay which characterized the western world, and also by the increasing impact of studies of the spontaneous settlement about the cities of the developing countries.

Urban geography in this way has become dominated by what can be called 'social conscience' studies which seek to identify the roots of spatial inequalities in urban terms. These can range from the relative deprivation of immobile residents of small country towns who are effectively isolated from standard urban services, to the limitations on life opportunities of those resident in the inner city. These sorts of people, it is contended, exercise little choice, for their life styles are dependent on the major public and private institutions which manipulate the space economy. Hence description of the patterns of deprivation has become associated with the analysis of the operation of those institutions which control the city. R.J. Johnston has effectively summarized these changes in relation to intra-urban structure: 'Three branches are identifiable in the current literature of urban geography. The first is a quantitative approach to description, based on a nomothetic philosophy in which the geographer's role is to document the spatial organization of society . . . . Second is the so-called behavioural approach . . . which proposed . . . the study of individual activities within their perceived worlds. Finally there is the approach variously termed 'radical' and 'structuralist' which stresses the constraints that society as a whole, and particularly certain groups within it, impose on the behaviour of individuals'[39].

Alongside these changing fashions in urban geography must be set a more revolutionary suggestion which looks to the abandonment of systematic studies, such as that of urban geography.

This has been effectively argued by Peter Gould in considering 'The open geographic curriculum'.[40] Such categories as urban geography, Gould contends, have outlived their usefulness, becoming limitations upon geographic instruction and pedagogic imagination. Thus Gould maintains that it is of little value to discuss tariffs in economic geography, administrative boundaries in political geography and housing constraints in urban geography, because the critical point is 'that there are barriers to all sorts of human flows across geographic space, including the barrier of distance itself, suitably warped and twisted by transportation and communications technology.' A modern geography should therefore be concerned with movement and barriers to movement, a higher order concept than the limitation to systematic divisions easily allows. This is a cogent argument but at this stage it is merely presented so that the reader can perhaps consider some of the 'higher order concepts' that might be implicit in the treatment of this conventional systematic study.

Although it has been shown as somewhat outdated, figure 1–1 is nevertheless adopted as the basic organizing structure of this book. On to that structure, however, is grafted the treatment of the material by three different but associated approaches:

1   The formal analysis of aggregate patterns, or the approach via locational analysis.
2   The analysis by disaggregated, process studies, or the behavioural approach.
3   The analysis of urban deprivation and the organizational structures which create it, or the institutional approach.

It would be possible to present the subject matter in a very different way taking one of the above approaches as the central theme, but the view taken

[39] R. J. Johnston (1977): Urban geography: city structures; *Progress in human geography* 1(i), 118–129 and 2(i), 148–152.
[40] Peter R. Gould (1973): The open geographic curriculum; in R.J. Chorley, editor: *Directions in geography*, 253–84 (London).

here is based on the principle of attempting to establish a viable and coherent urban geography deriving its structure from the central themes in its development over the last quarter of a century. The topic of urbanism is vast in scope and great in complexity and the range of any one book limited. Within those limitations it is hoped that something of the variety of concept and content in urban geography will be presented.

*Notes on further reading**

The general material which is usually covered by urban geography can best be appreciated by consulting the contents of some of the standard texts. Each of the following also has an introductory chapter which is relevant:

Beaujeu-Garnier, J. and Chabot, G. (1967): *Urban geography*, translated by Beaver, S. and Yglesias, G.M. (London).

Berry, B. J. L. and Horton, F. E. (1970): *Geographic perspectives on urban systems* (Englewood Cliffs, N. J.).

Johnson, J. H. (1968): *Urban geography: an introductory analysis* (London).

Jones, E. (1966): *Towns and cities* (London).

Murphy, R. E. (1966): *The American city* (New York).

Northam, R. M. (1975): *Urban geography* (New York).

Smailes, A. E. (1953) *The geography of towns*, first edition (London).

Scargill, D. I. (1979): *The form of cities* (London).

Yeates, M. H. and Garner, B. J. (1976): *The North American city* (New York) 2nd edition.

The main sources have been indicated in the footnotes and the most useful contributions are:

Foley, D. L. (1964): An approach to metropolitan spatial structure (see footnote 38).

Hauser, P. M. and Schnore, L. F. (1965): *The study of urbanization* (see footnote 26).

Thorpe, D. (1966): The geographer and urban studies (see footnote 36).

For a review of British and French urban geography during the period 1945–1975 see:

Carter, H. (1976): Urban Geography in Britain, 1945–1975 and

Dalmasso, E. (1976): La géographie urbaine en France depuis 1945, both in

Clarke J. I. and Pinchemel, P. (1976): *Human geography in France and Britain* (London), pp. 64–72 and 73–77.

An earlier French view of the field is:

Claval, P. (1968): La théorie des villes. *Revue Geographique de L'Est* 1–2, 3–56.

For a viewpoint contrasted to that presented in this book and which is sociological and marxist consult:

---

* These notes have been added at the end of each chapter as a brief guide. In general the footnotes which give reference to the major sources should be followed up for particular issues.

Castells, M. (1977): *The urban question. A Marxist approach* (London).

In order to keep abreast with the literature the following are of value:

Progress in Human Geography (London). Published four times a year and contains review articles of the field.

Hoare, R. and K. ed. (1966 – continuing): *Geo Abstracts C. Economic Geography* which contains a section on 'urban studies' and

Sheal, G. M. ed. (1966 – continuing): *Geo Abstracts D. Social and Historical Geography* which contains a section entitled 'urban'.

Both the above are published by the Univ. of E. Anglia at Norwich.

In a purely bibliographic context reference can be made to The Council of Planning Libraries Exchange Bibliographies (Monticello, Illinois). A very large number of bibliographies is available and many topics of direct interest to the urban geographer are covered.

A worthwhile addition to the urban literature has been the series of publications prepared for the Open University course entitled *Urban development* and published by the Open University Press at Walton Hall, Bletchley.

A series of volumes under the general title *Geography and the Urban Environment Progress in Research and Applications*, edited by Herbert, D. T. and Johnston, R. J. (London. Vol. 1, 1978 Vol. 2, 1979) contains miscellaneous papers.

A readable and low-priced review of urban problems can be found in:

Davies R. and Hall, P. (1978): *Issues in Urban Society* (London).

A book which attempts to present 'an outline theory based on structuralist principles' is:

Johnston, R. J. (1980): *City and society. An outline for urban geography* (London).

A book which reviews general theories of the city and is relevant to subsequent chapters (especially 2 and 17) is:

Smith, M. P. (1980): *The city and social theory* (Oxford).

2
The Process of Urbanization

1 Definition

The first and immediate problem that arises in the study of towns is that of their definition. What does the term 'town' or 'city' imply as against 'village' or 'hamlet' and what is the real nature of the distinction between that which is 'urban' and that which is 'rural'? The acceptance of a specialism entitled 'urban geography' implies that there is an area of study which is but part of 'settlement geography' and which is, in particular, contrasted with that of 'rural settlement'. In reality, the differences between 'urban' and 'rural', which are so easily made in an everyday way, become very difficult to portray in precise and scholarly terms. It is possible to identify three sources from which these difficulties arise.

a The Settlement continuum
The United Nations *Demographic yearbook* for 1952[1] was devoted to the problems of providing adequate data on the world urban population. It concluded that, 'There is no point in the continuum from large agglomerations to small clusters or scattered dwellings where urbanity disappears and rurality begins; the division between urban and rural populations is necessarily arbitrary.'[2] Thus as one goes down the scale from the largest metropolis, or indeed from megalopolis, to the single isolated farm it is impossible to identify a dividing line which is conceptually meaningful. This is reflected in the fact that there is a variety of names for the settlements near the assumed border. The oldest is 'suburb', although its original meaning was somewhat different, but in addition the terms 'sub-town', 'urban village' and 'rurban'[3] have been employed.

It follows from this that the most universal and apparently attractive method of defining a town by a fixed minimum population is unreal and that although the notion of size is involved it is difficult to translate it into specific terms. Apart from the fact that the figure used will be entirely dependent on arbitrary and often anachronous boundaries, the real range of minima employed in national censuses is ample testimony to this problem. This can best be seen in Annex II of the United Nations,

---

[1] United Nations (1955): *Demographic yearbook* 1952 (New York).

[2] United Nations (1955).

[3] The term 'rurban' was coined in one of the earliest of central place studies, C. G. Galpin (1915): *The social anatomy of an agricultural community*. (Agricultural experiment station of the University of Wisconsin) Res. Bull. **34**.

Department of Economic and Social Affairs publication, *Growth of the world's urban and rural population*, 1920–2000, which presents a 'List of definitions used in the estimation of "Urban" populations as nationally defined.'[4] An extract from this is reproduced in table 2–1. All countries without a city of at least 100,000 inhabitants in 1960 are omitted, but even so the minima range from 1000 (e.g. Canada) to 30,000 (e.g. Japan). The only solution proposed was that national data should be presented also according to a standard scale.[5]

The reasons for these differences lie in the differing cultural and economic situations involved. In Iceland, for example, a settlement of 300 or more people is normally concerned with urban functions, for the rural environment precludes such large agglomerations solely concerned in agricultural pursuits. In the south of Spain or of Italy rural settlement is basically agglomerated and 'villages' may reach totals of 8,000 to 10,000 population. This is due partly to the former insecurity of individual holdings because of banditry and partly to the whole nature of the economic organization of land-holding which has never suffered 'revolution' as in most of north-western Europe. This situation upsets both the layman's idea of towns as somehow being universally bigger than villages as well as the 'size density model' of more sophisticated treatments.[6] For it is also true that only some of the areas of high population density are also highly urbanized. Australia is one of the world's most highly urbanized countries but has a very low national population density; India is not highly urbanized but has a very high population density. It is an occidental thesis that high population density and urbanization are necessarily correlated.

In spite of this, however, it is difficult to reject the argument that urbanization as a process involves two elements: the multiplication of points of population concentration and the increase of the size of individual concentrations. But the technological, economic and sociological correlates of the process are crucial, rather than the nomination of particular sizes.

b The changing concept of urban character

The problem of identification of what is urban has been made all the more difficult by the fact that the concept and, indeed, the reality of what is urban are not static but are continually being changed by new conditions. In early times the town meant 'market town' and the legal possession of a market virtually defined a town. Often the town existed in sharp contradistinction to the surrounding countryside for the town walls were a tangible barrier between the urban and the rural. The growth of the suburb and the construction of several urban 'enceintes' were early to obliterate this ideal state

[4] United Nations (1969): Growth of the world's urban and rural population, 1920–2000. *United Nations, Department of Economic and Social Affairs, Population Studies* **44** (New York). An earlier publication with data for countries without cities of over 100,000 is (1950): *Data on urban and rural population in recent censuses* (New York).

[5] United Nations (1958): Principles and recommendations for national population censuses (New York), *Statistical Papers, Series M* **27**, 11.

[6] P. M. Hauser (1965): Urbanization: an overview; chapter 1 in P. M. Hauser and L. F. Schnore, editors (1965): *The study of urbanization*, 11 (New York).

table 2–1:

(a) Frequency of use of criteria in delimiting urban populations in national censuses.

Criteria	Frequency of use	
	Sole use	Used in conjunction with other criteria
1 Size of population	23	26
2 Density of population or of housing	1	10
3 Predominant type of economic activity	1	7
4 'Urban characteristics' other than (1) to (3) above, or unspecified 'urban characteristics'	3	13
5 Administrative function or structure, e.g., type of local government etc.	3	0
None specified*	56	0

* Note in relation to unspecified criteria. Considering that a criterion of administrative function is implicit where the area nomenclature is administrative centres of minor civil divisions, and a criterion of administrative structure can usually be assumed where the nomenclature is 'cities', 'towns' etc. with particular types of local administration, one can also say that the fifth criterion for the selection of urban units was implicit in sixty-seven censuses, and that no criterion was suggested in only twenty-nine censuses.

(**b**) Examples of minimum populations in national censuses.

France	1962	Communes containing an agglomeration of more than 2,000 inhabitants living in contiguous houses or with not more than 200 metres between houses, and communes of which the major part of the population is part of a multicommunal agglomeration of this nature.
Spain	1960	Municipios of 10,000 or more inhabitants.
East Germany		Communes of 2,000 or more inhabitants.
Belgium		Communes of more than 5,000 inhabitants.
Denmark	1960	Agglomerations of 200 or more inhabitants.
Canada	1961	Cities, towns and villages of 1,000 or more inhabitants, whether incorporated or unincorporated, including urbanized fringes of cities classed as metropolitan areas and other major urban areas. In 1961, also including urbanized fringes of certain smaller cities if the population of city and its urban fringe was 10,000 or more.
Japan		Urban municipalities (all shi and the ku of Tokyo-to) usually having 30,000 or more inhabitants and which may include some rural area as well as urban cluster.
Israel	1961	All settlements of more than 2,000 inhabitants, except those where at least one third of the heads of households, participating in the civilian labour force, earn their living from agriculture.
Mexico		Localities of 2,500 or more inhabitants.

but changes during the eighteenth and nineteenth centuries provided even greater difficulties.

Industrialization brought into being a large number of settlements which were certainly not villages, in the sense of being the nucleated settlements of agricultural populations, but neither were they market towns primarily serving the surrounding countryside. They were large tracts of bricks and mortar which broke across the old division. In Britain their status was significantly described under the Public Health Act of 1872 when they became 'Urban Sanitary Districts' and later 'Urban Districts', a term which did not disappear until local government reorganization in 1974. There is a wealth of implication in the contrast between a 'town' and an 'urban district'. This in turn has a bearing on the idea of the identification of towns by population size. Large these new agglomerations might be in numerical terms, but few other characteristics proclaimed them to be 'towns'. The situation has been further aggravated by the coming of the motor car and the rapid extension of surburbia. Very often vast areas of low density housing make up settlements in their own right. These have been categorized in subjective terms as 'sub-topia'[7] or in the case of Los Angeles as 'a hundred suburbs in search of a town';[8] but even an advanced statistical analysis ends by introducing a category called 'sub-urban type towns'![9]

In an academic context the way out of this situation has been to reinterpret the concept of 'market' town by an examination of the functions which the town performs for the surrounding countryside for, it is argued, a town is distinguished by its role as the central place for a tributary area. The rural countryside needs a focal point to which its produce can be sent for export and from which its needs can be distributed. 'It is in the cities that the geographies of production and consumption interlock.'[10] This general role is represented in the town by shops, banks and offices and similar institutions and a summation of these should be a measure of urban character. Even the small village has a general shop which carries out these functions so that there is no question of mere 'presence' or 'absence' of a function, but there could be a distinctive 'trait complex' of functional institutions which characterize the town and which signify an urban rather than a village situation.

Berry, looking at the system of central places in south west Iowa, stated, 'Centres are scaled into five sizes (hamlets, villages, towns, cities and the regional capital) according to the levels or steps of the central place hierarchy.'[11] Yet this is a completely arbitrary application of nomenclature to the ranks identified and presents no evidence for a conceptual break at the village-to-town level; this is only another step in the hierarchical scale and no more. It would be better, therefore, to call these levels Grade 1, Grade 2 and so on rather than give them the overtones involved by using long established names in general currency. This situation is made more complex by the existence in some countries of periodic markets and fairs, some of

---

[7] I. Nairn (1958): *Outrage* (London).

[8] Usually ascribed to J. B. Priestley.

[9] G. A. Moser and W. Scott (1961): *British towns; a statistical study of their social and economic differences* (London).

[10] B. J. L. Berry (1967): *Geography of market centres and retail distribution*, 2 (Englewood Cliffs, N. J.).

[11] B. J. L. Berry (1967), 14.

which are held in open and isolated areas with no settlement associated at all.

It follows that studies of the ranking of settlements according to central place functions have little *direct* contribution to make on the subject of urbanization and do not provide a universal tool for the study of the urban process. The idea of a certain minimum collection of functions defining what is urban is, therefore, no more helpful than the adoption of a minimum population figure.

It might well be argued that by the latter half of the twentieth century the distinction between urban and rural, town and country, is in any case unreal. The development of massive urban aggregations, reflected in the successive introduction into the literature of the terms conurbation, metropolis and megalopolis, has meant that few parts of highly developed countries are out of the range of urban influences and most parts are saturated by them. The result of this, in academic terms, is to associate urban and regional studies, for regionalism becomes urban based. The consequent study is of a scope considerably larger than that envisaged as urban geography in chapter 1.

c The inadequacy of official designation

This third area of difficulty follows from the first two, for if identification of what is urban is difficult in academic terms then the practical solutions adopted by governments are bound to be *ad hoc* and unsatisfactory. Most countries do have a formal means of identifying what is urban and this is sometimes based on legal title and is neither statistical nor functional in a commercial sense, though somewhat vaguely linked to both. In older countries many towns which have long decayed retain their former status and chartered rights and fight energetically to maintain them; likewise newly grown towns find it a lengthy and cumbersome process to obtain the articles of recognition.

On most counts, therefore, the official designation of the urban-rural dichotomy is pragmatic, anachronistic and not helpful. In most cases governments are looking to the evidence of students of urbanization in order to revise the system of government of which this rural-urban break is one feature.

2 Measurement

The first problem which arises from the discussion of definition is a practical question of procedures for measurement. This has already been partly considered in the criticisms offered concerning the definition of the urban proportion in various countries. The whole situation was well illustrated by Meuriot[12] in the early part of the century. However the figures in table 2−2 are analyzed, the conclusion is inescapable — Vienna was growing the faster. This is the exact reverse of the anticipated movement in light of historical

[12] P. Meuriot (1911): De la mesure des agglomérations urbains. *Bull. Inst. int. Statist.* **19**, 158.

table 2—2: A comparison of the populations of Vienna and Berlin, 1900 – 1910.

	Population 1900	Population 1910	Increase
Vienna	1,674,000	2,030,000	356,000
Berlin	1,888,000	2,070,000	182,000

table 2—3: A comparison of the populations of Vienna and Berlin in similar areas, 1900 – 1910.

	Urban area in hectares	Population 1900 in comparable areas	Population 1910	Increase 1900 – 1910
Vienna	17,000	1,674,000	2,030,000	356,000
Berlin	6,000	2,460,000	3,315,000	855,000

and political trends of the period. A close scrutiny of the data is therefore required. This reveals the situation in table 2 – 3 where the relation between the two cities is reversed.

This problem is usually stated in terms of 'under-' or 'overbound' cities.[13] In the underbounded city, the administratively defined city is smaller than the physical urban aggregate. In the overbounded city the administrative city is larger than the physical urban aggregate. The true bounded city, however, is virtually identical with the urban aggregate.

It follows that any measure of urbanization based upon census data is liable to marked error dependent on the under- or overbounded characteristic. Attempts to avoid this can be made in two ways:

(*i*) *The use of detailed rules for the definition of areas.* The most detailed survey of these problems occurs in *The delimitation of urban boundaries* by G. J. R. Linge[14] where the general problems are set out and proposals are made for the definition of the urban areas of Australian towns. Here it will suffice to point out that the Census Bureau of the USA[15] not only identifies 'standard metropolitan statistical areas', which are essentially city regions, but also 'urbanized areas' where a more limited definition of the settlement itself is attempted. For the 1966 census the 'urbanized areas' were based on enumeration districts which were usually no larger than one square mile and had no more than fifteen dwellings. The urbanized area then consisted of a central city which had a population of 50,000 together with:

1 Incorporated places with 2,500 inhabitants or more.
2 Incorporated places with less than 2,500 inhabitants, provided that each had a closely settled area of 100 dwellings or more.

[13] International urban research (1959): *The world's metropolitan areas*, 6–7 (Los Angeles).
[14] G. J. R. Linge (1965): The delimitation of urban boundaries. *Australian National University, Department of Geography Publication* **G/2** (Canberra).
[15] United States of America Bureau of the Census (1960). *US census of population 1960. United States summary* PC-1A.XIII. For an attempt to apply the definition of the SMA to extra-USA areas, see footnote 13 above.

3   Enumeration districts in unincorporated territory with a population density of 1,000 inhabitants or more per square mile (land devoted to such purposes as railway goodsyards, cemeteries, etc., being excluded).
4   Enumeration districts with less than 1,000 persons per square mile if they:

    a   eliminate enclaves;
    b   close indendations in the urbanized area of one mile or less across the open end;
    c   link outlying enumeration districts of qualifying density that were no more than one and a half miles from the main urbanized areas.

When Linge begins to make proposals for the Australian case, he immediately becomes involved in a set of rules which take some twenty-six pages of foolscap text to enunciate.[16] But there is little point in multiplying detail in this context other than to point out that the situation in England and Wales is the least satisfactory, for urban areas were defined purely in legal, administrative terms (county boroughs, municipal boroughs, urban districts) and the identification of conurbations is even less satisfactory, for though there is a vague background to ideas concerning circulation and association, the actual limits are arbitrarily identified and based on informed local opinion.[17]

All this indicates that extreme caution is needed when examining figures which purport to show a percentage of the population called 'urban' and that most solutions to this difficult problem are based on a series of empirically derived regulations.

(*ii*) *The use of population densities.* K. G. Gryztzell[18] has presented a method which can be used in comparative studies and is based on population densities alone. He argues that fair comparisons can only be made when the densities involved are similar. He therefore attempts to delineate areas, using the smallest administrative unit, where minimum densities can be equated. He identifies these smallest units and calculates their population densities. He then works outward from the large city until points are reached where the densities fall below a given figure, say 100 per km².

Although a degree of generalization is involved, this process allows a line to be drawn around the city so that all areas with a density which is over the given figure are included. For convenience sake Gryztzell terms this, if it were determined in relation to London, London 100. In fact, in south-east England the continuous area most easily defined is bounded by a lowest density of 104·9 per km²; this he calls London 104. He then argues that this area contains a total population that can be meaningfully compared with

---

[16] G. J. R. Linge (1965), 64–90.
[17] Registrar General: Census of England and Wales (1952): *London and five other conurbations* (London).
[18] K. G. Gryztzell (1964): The demarcation of comparable city areas by means of population density. *Lund Stud. Geogr., Series B, Hum. Geog.* **25**.

that of a similar density ring of 104 per km^2 which can be drawn around say Stockholm or Copenhagen. A series of rings of different density values can be identified and used in this way for comparative purposes. This overlaps with the formal definitions in relying on population density as a criterion and although interesting is no solution to the problem.

The two procedures which have been outlined above do not successfully separate urban from rural (nor are they primarily intended to do so), but they clearly do bear a significance for the measurement of urbanization when it is defined either as the proportion of the population living in towns or in towns of a given size. The intention of these procedures is to enable meaningful statements to be made in this context: it is evident that at the moment they are far from satisfactory.

Having considered the operational problems of definition and measurement three further issues arise for discussion. These are:

The facts of urbanization.
The causes of urbanization.
The problems of urbanization.

Although these can only be considered in a brief and introductory manner, it is appropriate that an outline sketch of each should be presented.

3 The facts of urbanization

The hard data in relation to urban populations have been admirably set out by Kingsley Davies.[19] The United Nations publication 'Growth of the World's Urban and Rural Population, 1920–2000' is a further essential source.[20] From these, three tables (Tables 2–4, 2–5 and 2–6) are presented which epitomize the major trends and on these a number of comments can be made.

a The recency of urbanization

In historical terms urbanization on any scale is essentially recent, a feature of the last one hundred and fifty years. It has been estimated that before the start of the nineteenth century only some 3 per cent of the world's population lived in towns of over 5000. By the present this has risen to near 40 per cent. Expressed in a different way, the world's population increased threefold between 1800 and 1960, the world's urban population increased thirty-fold. Between 1950 and 1970 the world's urban population rose from 28·2 per cent to 38·6 per cent.

[19] Kingsley Davies (1972): *World Urbanization 1950–1970*. Vol. 1: *Basic data for cities, countries and regions*; Vol. 2: *Analysis of trends, relationships and development* Berkeley: University of California, Population Monograph Series, 4 and 9.

[20] United Nations (1969): *Growth of the world's urban and rural population 1920–2000*. United Nations, Department of Economic and Social Affairs, Population Studies 44. An earlier publication with data for countries without cities of over 100,000 is: (1950): *Data on urban and rural population in recent censuses* (New York).

table 2–4 Distribution of the World's Population According to Size of Place

Size Category	Populations (000's) 1950	1960	1970	Percentage of World Total 1950	1960	1970
16,000,000	– –	– –	16,077	– –	– –	0·4
8,000,000	22,724	34,751	85,235	0·9	1·2	2·3
4,000,000	47,004	76,136	89,504	1·9	2·5	2·5
2,000,000	38,937	70,523	111,303	1·6	2·3	3·1
1,000,000	72,970	100,798	146,205	2·9	3·3	4·0
500,000	73,023	98,107	123,227	2·9	3·3	3·4
250,000	63,180	91,727	131,907	2·5	3·0	3·6
125,000	65,501	94,867	126,313	2·6	3·1	3·5
100,000	22,679	25,319	34,093	0·9	0·8	0·9
50,000	67,666	91,576	130,409	2·7	3·0	3·6
25,000	67,327	90,905	128,745	2·7	3·0	3·5
20,000	25,714	35,015	46,483	1·0	1·2	1·3
10,000	62,930	85,348	110,070	2·5	2·8	3·0
5,000	51,728	68,146	83,429	2·1	2·3	2·3
5,000	25,000	30,500	36,000	1·0	1·0	1·0
Rural	1,795,511	2,018,941	2,229,000	71·8	67·0	61·4
WORLD TOTAL	2,501,894	3,012,659	3,628,000	100·0	100·0	100·0

Source: K. Davis (1972): World Urbanization 1950–70. Volume 2. *Analysis of Trends, Relationships and Developments*

table 2–5 Percentages of total population in localities with 20,000 or more inhabitants in the world and major areas, 1920–1960

Major area	1920	1930	1940	1950	1960
World total	14	16	19	21	25
More developed major areas	30	33	37	40	46
Europe	35	37	40	41	44
Northern America	41	46	46	51	58
Soviet Union	10	13	24	28	36
Oceania	37	38	41	46	53
Less developed major areas	7	8	10	13	17
East Asia	7	9	12	14	19
South Asia	6	7	8	11	14
Latin America	14	17	20	25	33
Africa	5	6	7	10	13
More developed regions[a]	29	33	37	40	46
Less developed regions[b]	6	7	9	11	15

a Europe, Northern America, Soviet Union, Japan, Temperate South America and Australia and New Zealand.
b East Asia without Japan, South Asia, Latin America without Temperate South America, Africa and Oceania without Australia and New Zealand.
Source: United Nations (1969): *Growth of the World's Urban and Rural Population, 1920–2000.*

b The dominance of urbanization

'The most conspicuous feature of today's accelerated world population growth is its even greater rapidity of urbanization. In many periods of history, populations and cities have grown, but the tempo and dimensions of recent years have never been equalled'.[21] It follows that urbanization is the dominant process in the spatial organization of the world's population.

[21] United Nations (1969), 1.

table 2–6 Growth of the World's Total, Rural, Urban, and City Populations: 1800–1970

Population (millions)	World Total	Rural	Urban	Places 20,000 +	Cities 100,000 +
1800	978	948·7	29·3[1]	23·5	16·6
1850	1,262	1,181·2	80·8[1]	54·3	29·0
1900	1,650	1,425·6	224·4[1]	151·8	90·8
1950	2,502	1,795·5	706·4[2]	566·7[3]	406·0
1960	3,013	2,018·9	993·7[2]	809·7[2]	592·2
1970[4]	3,628	2,229·0	1,399·0	1,169·5	863·9
Per Cent Growth per Decade					
1800–1850	5·2	4·5	22·5	18·2	11·8
1850–1900	5·5	3·8	22·7	22·8	25·6
1900–1950	8·7	4·7	25·8	30·1	34·9
1950–1960	20·4	12·4	40·7	42·9	45·9
1960–1970	20·4	10·4	40·8	44·4	45·9

[1] Places of 5,000 or more inhabitants.
[2] Urban according to the definition of the country concerned.
[3] Estimated.
[4] Projected.

Source: K. Davis (1972): World Urbanization 1950–70. Volume 2. *Analysis of Trends, Relationships and Developments.*

Ethnocentric westerners, aware of the great changes brought about by industrialization in the last century, often regard that period as marking the peak of urbanization. This is not so, for present trends far outstrip those of nineteenth century change. The result is that whereas urban growth reached about 23 per cent per decade between 1850 and 1900, it achieved over 40 per cent between 1960 and 1970.

c The location of urbanization
The association of industrialization with urbanization in the west conceals the fact that urban growth is most conspicuous in developing countries. Indeed, the areas of massive contemporary urbanization lie predominantly in the developing parts of the world. This is most simply expressed by the gradual southward movement of the mean latitude of the largest cities. In 1921 the mean latitude of the 24 cities with a population of over one million was 44°30' north. By 1941 there were 41 such cities and the mean latitude was 39°20', whilst by 1961 the number of so-called 'millionaire cities' had increased to 113 and the mean latitude changed to 35°44'.[22] This progress south of the mean latitude epitomises both the extent (in the numbers involved) and the regional change in large scale urbanization.

d The size scale in urbanization
It is apparent from the difficulties set out in defining and measuring the city and its size that any comment on relative changes in the sizes of individual cities will rest partly on definition, whilst the notion of megalopolis makes

[22] D. L. Linton (1958): Millionaire cities today and yesterday. *Geography*, 43(4), 253–258.

the measurement of the size of individual agglomerations irrelevant. Even so, it is possible to make a number of propositions:

1   The size of urban agglomeration is increasing and there seems to be no limitation on urban growth.
2   The largest urban agglomerations are growing the fastest. In the words of the United Nations study, 'As can be seen from the comparison of estimates for 1920 and 1960, successive size groups of agglomerations accumulated population with successively greater rapidity'.[23]
3   In the industrialized countries there is a major restructuring of the population distribution taking place by which the inner cities are showing a loss of population and the outer suburbs substantial gains. Dependent on the definition of areas such a situation can show absolute losses by some major cities. This process of internal transformation, however, pushes the resident population further and further out, especially as rapid transit systems become more effective. This is the way in which megalopolitan structures are created. Table 2−7 illustrates these features.

table 2–7: U.S.A. Population by Type of Residence, 1970–974

Type of Residence	Percentage Change 1970–74
U.S.A. Total	4·1
Metropolitan Areas	3·6
Central cities	−1·9
Suburban Rings	8·4
Counties designated Metropolitan since 1970	10·4
Non metropolitan counties	4·2

Source: Sternlieb and Hughes (1975): *Post-Industrial America*

It is particularly significant that the greatest percentage increase was in counties taken into metropolitan areas after 1970, that is, in the outermost suburban areas.

4   Some of the oldest metropoles are showing overall decline. The prime examples are those of New England in the north-east of the U.S.A. where table 2−8 shows a considerable loss by outmigration which was not offset by the natural increase in the population.

table 2–8: Population Change in the Metropolitan Areas of 1−3 million of the Northeast Region of the U.S.A.

	1960−1970	1970−1973
Population Change	+1·0	−0·8
By Natural Increase	+7·8	+1·1
By Migration	−6·8	−1·9

Source: Sternlieb and Hughes (1975): *Post-Industrial America*

[23]   United Nations (1969), 32.

4 The causes of urbanization

It is possible to suggest three groups of causes which have precipitated the rapid urbanization of the present.

a Economic development

This relates to 'the movement of people out of agricultural communities into other and generally larger non-agricultural communities. This conception gives primary recognition to the differential ordering of occupations . . . within a given territorial space'.[24] The crux of this approach is a direct correlation of economic development with urbanization and it is usually couched in the form of the identification of phases of economic development each of which is associated with a degree of urbanization. Many interpretations of urban origins are set out in this way. Childe,[25] when discussing this subject in *The urban revolution* postulates a number of features which distinguish the new towns from the older settlements and foremost among these is the beginning of specialization in economic activity. No longer had craftsmen to be itinerant and by virtue of their skill detach themselves from the group. By the use of the surplus of production they could become a specialized section of the new urban society. The emergence of an administrative class (made up of king and priest), the keeping of records, the development of the arts, the extension of trade and the localization of special skills are all part of the same urban process.[26] Urbanization is seen therefore as a product of increasing economic specialization and advancing technology. The only way it is possible to advance from a subsistence basis is by specialization of economic activities. The linkages between specialisms necessitate the accumulation of people and this is the process of urbanization.

Two examples of this form of analysis can be considered briefly. The first of these was developed by Brian Berry who proceeds from the assumption that 'associations exist between the level of economic development of a country and the degree to which the country is urbanized'.[27] A principal component analysis using 43 indices for 95 countries revealed that four factors accounted for 90 per cent of the variance. In many ways this was hardly surprising for Berry puts into his matrix variables which are essentially economic or demographic in context and in some cases almost tautologous. Thus, railroads per unit area in kilometres and also per capita are used as well as roads and motor vehicles, also per unit area and per capita. Other variables relate to foreign trade, export and energy consumption.

[24] E. E. Lampard (1965): Historical aspects of urbanization; Chapter 14 in P. M. Hauser and L. F. Schnore, editors (1965): *The Study of urbanization* (New York), 520.

[25] V. G. Childe (1950): The urban revolution. *Town Planning Review* 21, 3.

[26] For an extended discussion see: H. Carter (1977): Urban origins. *Progress in Human Geography* 1(1), 12–32.

[27] B. J. L. Berry (1962): Some relations of urbanization and basic patterns of economic development, in F. R. Pitts, editor (1962): *Urban systems and economic development*, 12, (Eugene, Oregon).

There is a range of demographic variables, including population density and birth and death rates. In unsophisticated, perceptive terms, the variables are associated in nature. That his components are economic or demographic in nature and only a few account for a large proportion of the total variance was determined at the outset of the exercise. The first of the components was related to technology since it was associated with transport, communications, trade, energy production and consumption, national product and public services. The second factor was termed demographic. These two components were associated in the evaluation of a scale of economic development when they showed a high positive correlation with urbanization.

This led Berry to support Lampard's view that 'city growth is simply the concentration of differentiated but functionally integrated specialisms in rational locales. The modern city is a mode of social organization which furthers efficiency in economic activity'.[28] This argument in turn is developed in an evolutionary context and Berry parallels this idea with Rostow's 'stages of economic development'.[29]

b Agglomeration economies

To an extent this overlaps with economic development but rests more on the argument that growth is cumulative and cyclical. Once a large city is created then the attractions it offers in terms of supplies of labour and capital, as well as the build up of infrastructures, will of themselves promote growth so that a rising spiral of development is set in motion. This partly lies behind the fact that the largest cities tend to experience greatest growth. It is dealt with further in chapter 3.[30] The consequences are considerable. The Canadian Minister for Urban Affairs widely traced these for his country in 1974: '. . The hiving of most of Canada's population into the regions around Montreal, Toronto and Vancouver is continuing at a rate that is far too rapid for effective, planned response. Already these three centres claim a quarter of Canada's population. By the year 2000, one third of all Canadians could live in three urban regions. . . . We are over three quarters urban now. The proportion will climb to over 90 per cent if current projections hold up. And that urban population will be standing on less than two per cent of the Canadian land mass'.[31]

c Political and Social Change

Leonard Reissman[32] has developed an extended critique of most theories of urbanization but when he proposes his own organizing theory it is much in the same vein as that developed by Berry. However, he applies his ideas to 'the industrial city' only, thereby excluding 'all earlier cities—the medieval

[28] E. E. Lampard (1955): The history of cities in economically advanced areas. *Economic Development and Cultural Change* 3, 92.

[29] W. W. Rostow (1963): *The stages of economic growth* (Cambridge).

[30] See pp. 54—5.

[31] B. Danson (1974): *Notes for remarks to the annual conference of the Canadian Real Estate Association. Sept. 20th.* p. 2. Ministry of State. Urban Affairs Canada.

[32] L. Reissman (1964): *The urban process*, 16 (New York).

city, the city of antiquity, the Sumerian city . . . because the industrial city was a radical break from earlier urban history.'[33] Four urbanization variables are put forward as parts of his theory of urbanization. The first is 'urban growth' itself and this is measured by the percentage population in cities of over 100,000. The second is 'industrialization' which, he argues, 'applies to the whole process of change and its accompanying consequences, as a society moves from an agricultural to an industrial economy; from a small, rural homogeneous society to a large, metropolitan, heterogeneous massing.' This is measured by the percentage of national product derived from manufacturing. But technical change does not occur other than in a sympathetic social climate; in particular it does not occur without the 'human catalysts' to set it going. Consequently the third variable is an attempt to assess the restructuring of power relations within a society so that the move to industrialism can begin. The actual criterion used is the emergence of a middle class measured by per capita income. The last variable is the rise of nationalism—'a pivotal element in the social transition being analyzed' for it 'supplies the ideology that can command loyalties, motivate action and legitimate the changes to be effected'. This is measured by the percentage of literacy among the population over the age of fifteen.

A ranking of the countries of the world on each variable is constructed and each is broken into quarters. These quartile positions are then used to construct a typology of 'countries at different stages of urban industrial development, but also to emphasize the sequence countries follow in that development'. Reissman argues that it is evident that not all countries move in the same direction or in the same manner to urbanization; some countries begin with industrialism but others experience city growth first and industrialism follows. Other countries begin the process by the creation of nationalistic ideologies and then move to urbanization and industrialization. Reissman therefore presents a typology of urbanization couched in developmental terms (table 2−9).

table 2−9: The urban process. *After L. Reissman (1964)*

Stage I	Underdeveloped societies	e.g. Congo[x]
	Nationalizing societies	Turkey
	Industrializing societies	India
	Urbanizing societies	Egypt
Stage II	Transitional societies	Mexico
	Industrial societies	Greece
	Unbalanced urban societies	Panama
Stage III	Urban transitional societies	None
	Rural balanced societies	Ireland
	Urban industrial societies	Italy
	Industrial balanced societies	France
Stage IV	Unbalanced metropolitan societies	Chile
	Metropolitan societies	USA UK

[x]Note: This was the Congo as at the date of Reissman's book.

[33] L. Reissman (1964), 204.

This is wider in scope than Berry's analysis presented in *a* above and attempts to achieve a larger significance than is implied by the restrictive context of Rostow's 'stages of economic development'. But at root it is an economic study in spite of Reissman's argument that it is primarily social for it is constructed around the concept that cities are 'the centres of specialized economic activity'.

Reissman's study, however, emphasizes the significance of political and social change which in the developing world have generated an urbanization without industrialization. The simple notion that such less developed countries are now experiencing a process that went on in the industrialized countries of the West in the nineteenth century is simply not tenable. Even the rates of growth are different, for whereas for nine European countries in the nineteenth century at the time of fastest growth the average annual gain in urban population was some 2·1 per cent, at present in the less developed countries it is nearer 4·5 per cent.[34] It has already been indicated in the review of Reissman's analysis of the urban process that industrialization is not the sole trigger of urban growth and this is particularly relevant to much of the less developed world.

In many cases the most active process is the penetration of a peasant society by a capitalist system and this induces a geographic mobility without social mobility. Towns exert a psychological pull and the peasantry moves to the city seeking the products and standards presented by the new capitalist order. Again, the concentration of land ownership in a few hands and lack of locally orientated rural development provides no hold on the migrant. Political unrest and population growth itself add to the influx,[35] while the lack of changing standards means that natural increase of population remains high in the city. Thus McGee argues that 'at least one element of Western theory should be discarded when investigating the Third World city. This is the view that the city is an inducer of change.'[36] The result is that urbanization proceeds, if not without industrialization, at a pace which the industrial base cannot absorb,[37] and although there is a rapid and symptomatic increase in tertiary services, the consequences are extensive under-employment and unemployment. Translated into the actual and spatial manifestations in the city the process that has been outlined produces the shanty towns or bidonvilles at the margins and the extremes of poverty in the centres of the large cities.[38]

This last section immediately raises the associated issue of urban problems.

---

[34] Kingsley Davies (1969): The urbanization of the human population; in G. Breese, editor (1969): *The city in newly developing countries*, 5–20 (Englewood Cliffs, N. J.).

[35] M. Santos (1971): *Les villes du tiers monde*, 31–33 (Paris).

[36] T. G. McGee (1971): *The urbanization process in the third world*, 31 (London).

[37] G. Rowley (1973): Urban growth within developing countries. *Geoforum* 13, 69–74.

[38] D. J. Dwyer (1975): *People and housing in third world cities* (London).

5 The problems of urbanization

The wide ranging and infinitely complex problems of urban environments cannot be easily or simply summarized. The following, however, is a selection from some of the critical issues.

a Anomie and alienation

The most well known introduction to this concept is in Louis Wirth's seminal paper *'Urbanism as a way of life'*.[39] Rejecting simple measurements of size, density and occupational structure or administrative status as denoting anything fundamental, largely on the bases which have so far been outlined in this chapter, Wirth formulated a theory of urbanism based on existing knowledge of interrelations among social groups. The size of the aggregated population will affect relations between members, increasing the process of differentiation which ultimately leads to segregation. 'The bonds of kinship, of neighbourliness, and the sentiments arising out of living together for generations under a common folk tradition are likely to be absent, or at best, relatively weak in an aggregate, the members of which have such diverse origins and backgrounds. Under such circumstances competition and formal control mechanisms furnish the substitutes for the bonds of solidarity that are relied upon to hold a folk society together'.[40]

Urban dwellers meet in segmented roles and face to face relations are impersonal and superficial. In consequence of the 'superficiality, the anonymity and the transitory character of urban social relations'[41] the individual becomes alienated from his folk or rural background; a sense of belonging to an integrated community is no longer held and this leads to the state of 'anomie', of being lost in 'the lonely crowd'. Density also adds to diversification and gives rise to characteristic urban contrasts of wealth and poverty. In addition 'the close living together and working together of individuals who have no sentimental and emotional ties fosters a spirit of competition, aggrandisement and mutual exploitation. Formal controls are instituted to counteract irresponsibility and potential disorder. Without rigid adherence to predictable routines a large compact society would scarcely be able to maintain itself. The clock and the traffic signal are symbolic of the basis of our social order in the urban world'.[42] But diversification means heterogeneity and this breaks down caste boundaries and gives the individual a fluctuating status determined by his own ability and effort rather than by his birth. A social role is not given to the urban dweller by the social order into which he is born; rather it is achieved and during this process a series of different roles will emerge, the result of his relations with fellow workers, with managers, with officials. This can lead to a state of role confusion where the various parts to be played will conflict.

The consequences of the above rural-urban contrasts have been described

[39] L. Wirth (1938): Urbanism as a way of life. *Am. Journ. Sociol.* 44. For an extended critique see R. N. Morris (1968): *Urban Sociology* (London).
[40] L. Wirth (1938), 11.
[41] L. Wirth (1938), 12.
[42] L. Wirth (1938), 16–17.

as a 'rural-urban dichotomy'. There are two ideal constructs of the social situation, one urban, one rural — hence the generic name, 'theories of contrast'. Redfield,[43] basing his argument on work in Mexico, introduced a further element by suggesting that these two opposites were but polarizations of a successive pattern of change through which the folk society became urbanized. He therefore introduced the notion of a 'folk-urban continuum' and contended that the epitome of the urbanization process was a transformation of the social situation of the individual in relation to the trends outlined above.

These ideas have generated a very large literature. No sooner are they eroded by criticism than they are once more revived. Thus for example Ronald Frankenberg in his study *Communities in Britain*,[44] published in 1966, after examining a number of separate pieces of social research, proceeds to align them along what he terms a 'morphological continuum', and develops 'a theory of social change, a progressive and historical development from rural to urban, mediated by industrialization, division of labour and role differentiation'.[45] This means that the urban dweller is in terms of role theory — 'role confused'; 'in terms of Durkheim's division of labour — 'anomic'; in terms of Marxian proletarianization — alienated'.[46] Frankenberg then isolates and lists twenty-five themes in which this urban-rural dichotomy is revealed.[47]

Criticism of these ideas has been continuous since they were first put forward, yet their survival alone suggest that there is much of value in them. It is true that they maintain something of the earlier idea of the 'noble savage' and of even earlier preaching against the evils of the 'cities of the plains'. But most modern objection is associated with the fact that in extra-western areas large cities are found to be without the consequences set forth by these writers and that this transformation of social values is not a universal process but solely one related to a particular cultural context. The city must be considered as a dependent, not an independent, variable; that is, the urban process in this circumstance is dependent upon the larger social or cultural order in which it occurs and does not operate independently of that order. Likewise it is argued that any theory of change implies that these processes have operated historically. Early urbanization should have entailed the same transformation: yet Sjoberg has demonstrated that this was not so.[48] It is apparent that these ideas of social change have too much relevance to be rejected although they cannot be accepted as universal or as defining and explaining alone the urban-rural break. One of the real problems is that the whole concept is reductivist and is not amenable to

[43] R. Redfield (1941): *The folk culture of Yucatan* (Chicago).

[44] R. Frankenburg (1966): *Communities in Britain: social life in town and country* (London).

[45] R. Frankenburg (1966), 275.

[46] R. Frankenburg (1966), 276.

[47] R. Frankenburg (1966), 285—92.

[48] G. Sjoberg (1960): *The pre-industrial city* (New York).

quantitative evaluation.[49] The relevance of the rural-urban continuum thus becomes a matter of assertion rather than of proof. As Miner pointed out, Redfield stated his argument in such a way that there was neither a clear measure of the variables nor of their relation one to the other. No scientific testing was therefore possible.

More relevant criticism in the context of the large modern city is to be found in Harvey Cox's book *The secular city*,[50] where each of the 'losses' consequent upon urbanization is shown to have a compensating gain. For example, the anonymity of the city releases the individual from the claustrophobic constraints of custom and sets him free to experiment so that the city becomes the centre of innovation; it is both humanizing and liberating.

In the end, however, the notion of alienation becomes a powerful concept in the interpretation of urban ills. It can be seen to produce vandalism of property and violence to persons as the purposelessness of city life brings about an unconscious reaction and as the only producers of social cohesion are football clubs and street gangs.[51] Those who opt out become alcoholics or drug addicts if they remain in situ, or the members of communes if they seek the lost rural setting. In the close, rural society the community provided a safety net for those who could not cope; in the city the substitute welfare services are imperfect, inadequate and impersonal.

b Urban blight and poverty
In the discussion of the general field of human geography it was shown that concerns with social justice have become a major contemporary theme. There are two situations where such concerns find foci. These are:

1   The decaying inner city areas of western cities
2   The peripheral slums or 'bidonvilles' of the cities of developing countries.

Both these issues will be dealt with at a later stage but must be recorded here as being generated by the urbanization process with which this chapter is concerned.

c Transport systems
It can be argued that by providing diurnal mobility, traffic systems created the modern large city. They also created one of its greatest problems by allowing the rich to escape to the suburban periphery, the rural fringe, leaving the poor behind in the inner city. The preservation of that mobility for the better off, or its increase, provides further critical problems. New urban throughways are immensely costly and consume land and destroy or blight housing, but without them congestion and delay increase. The solutions which are so frequently discussed of either taxing or prohibiting the

[49]   But for a testing of Wirth's basic hypothesis see: C. S. Fischer (1973): On urban alienations and anomie: powerlessness and social isolation. *American Sociological Review* 38, 311–326.
[50]   H. Cox (1965): *The secular city*, Chapters 2 and 3, 38–84, New York.
[51]   D. Ley and R. Cybriwsky (1974): Urban graffiti as territorial markers. *Annals Assoc. Amer. Geogrs.* 64(4), 491–505.

entry of private cars beyond a fixed cordon will remain politically unacceptable until crisis brings its own conviction.

d Pollution

Many of the major nineteenth century problems have been solved by the provision of water and sewerage. In most countries Clean Air Acts have cut down pollution by smoke and industrial emissions. This is still a residuum of serious problems. Waste or garbage disposal becomes increasingly difficult, whilst air pollution from the exhausts of automobiles is far from fully solved. Noise pollution has been barely touched, although its most widespread manifestation in the flight paths about airports is a topic of widespread public interest. The combination of depressing urban environment and affluent mobility extends this problem beyond the conventional limits even of megalopolis. Saturated National Parks and the clashes consequent upon second homes are both the consequences of urbanization. The very notion of seasonal suburbanization as a description for the week-end retreat or the summer cottage emphasizes their urban roots.

e Vulnerability

The size of the modern large city and especially the intricacy and interconnectedness of the mechanisms which sustain it, make it excessively vulnerable. This can be elaborated on three scales. At the technical level any failure, however minor, can lead to paralysis. The classic case is that break down in the electricity supply to New York in 1965. The huge urban demand for water creates a situation where many communities have very little margin. The second scale is partly technical and partly political. The more complex the structure the more easy it is to disrupt, that is technical 'failures' can be brought about by strike action. Small groups of the population are in this way given immense leverage on their fellow citizens without any assurance that it will be used with discretion and responsibility. Finally at the wholly political scale the largest metropoles are extremely vulnerable to open violence, the urban guerilla is a classic feature of the late twentieth century metropolis. In the anonymity of the great city a few determined individuals can exercise enormous influence. In turn police forces, stretched as they are to contain violent and serious crime, become helpless to combat burglary and senior police officials have had to suggest that the citizen might have to defend his own possessions as law and order disintegrate.

f Finance

Faced with the problems set out so far, the city has to undertake vast expenditure simply to keep itself going. But this is at a time when the exodus of the high socio-economic status groups to the peripheral suburbs takes them and their tax or rate paying capacity beyond the city bounds. One set of figures from the U.S.A. is sufficient witness to this problem. 'The aggregate income in 1973 of families and unrelated individuals who moved out of cities between 1970 and 1974 was about $55·3 billion while that for families and unrelated individuals who moved into cities during this period was about \$25·7 billion.'[52] This means that cities lost the tax and other claw-backs on some \$29·6 billion of income in 1974. The near bankruptcy of New York, the greatest of the metropoles, is a sufficient symbol of the financial problem.

As these urban problems have been discussed the essential geographic perspective has been considerably diminished. It is against this background of crisis, however, that the subsequent rather more limited analysis should be set and it is to those crises that the material dealt with should be related.

Notes on further reading
Two broad treatments which have both general and regional sections are:

Jones, R. ed. (1975): *Essays on world urbanization* (London).
Alam, S. M. and Pokshishevsky, V. V. (1976): *Urbanization in developing countries* (Hyderabad).

As far as definition is concerned the following should be consulted:

Freeman, T. W. (1959): *The conurbations of Great Britain* (Manchester).
International Urban Research (1959): *The world's metropolitan areas* (see footnote 13).
Linge, G. J. R. (1965): The delimitation of urban boundaries (see footnote 14).
United Nations (1969): Growth of the world's urban and rural population, 1920–2000 (see footnote 4).

The definition of S.M.S.A.s can be referred to in:

U.S.A. Bureau of the Budget (1964): *Standard metropolitan statistical areas* (see footnote 15).

On the urbanization process the following are a sample of the range of work which followed from Wirth's paper (see footnote 39) in 1938:

Berry, B. J. L. (1961): Basic patterns of economic development; in Ginsburg, N., editor (1961): *Atlas of economic development* (Chicago).
Dewey, R. (1958): The rural urban continuum: real but relatively unimportant. *Am. J. Sociol.* **64**, 152.
Duncan, O. D. and Reiss, A. J. (1956): *Social characteristics of urban and rural communities* (New York).
Frankenberg, R. (1966): *Communities in Britain: social life in town and country* (see footnote 44).
Freeman, L. C. and Winch, R. F. (1957): Societal complexity: an empirical test of a typology of societies. *Am J. Sociol.* **62**, 61.
Hauser, P. M. (1965): Observations on the urban-folk and urban-rural dichotomies as forms of western ethnocentrism; chapter 13B in

[52] G. Sternlieb and J. W. Hughes (1975): *Post-industrial America: metropolitan decline and inter-regional job shift.* 54 (Rutgers, N. J.).

Hauser, P. M. and Schnore, L. F., editors (1965): *The study of urbanization* (New York).

Kolb, W. L. (1954): The social structure and function of cities. *Econ. Dev. and Cult. Change* **3**, 30.

Lewis, O. (1951): *Life in a Mexican village; Tepoztlan restudied* (Urbana, Ill.).

Lewis, O. (1952): Urbanization without breakdown: a case study, *Sci. Month.* **75**, 31.

Lewis, O. (1965): Further observations on the folk-urban continuum and urbanization; chapter 13A in Hauser, P. M. and Schnore, L. F., editors (1965): *The study of urbanization* (New York).

Miner, H. (1952): *The folk-urban continuum. Am. Soc. Rev.* **17**, 529.

Morris, R. N. (1968): *Urban sociology* (London).

Redfield, R. (1941): *The folk culture of Yucatan* (Chicago).

Redfield, R. (1947): The folk society. *Am. J. Sociol.* **52**, 293.

Reissman, L. (1964): *The urban process* (see footnote 32).

Schnore, L. F. (1961): The statistical measures of urbanization and economic development. *Land Econ.* **37**, 229.

Schwirian, K. P. and Prehn, J. W. (1962): An axiomatic theory of urbanization. *Am. Soc. Rev.* **27**, 812.

Stewart, C. R. (1958): The urban-rural dichotomy: concepts and uses. *Am. J. Sociol.* **64**, 152.

Tisdale, H. (1942): The process of urbanization. *Social Forces* **20**.

The most useful summary volume is that by L. Reissman whilst an extended critique of Wirth is presented by R. N. Morris.

For data on urbanization see:

Davies, Kingsley (1972): *World urbanization* 1950–1970. Volumes 1 and 2 (see footnote 19).

For data on the relative sizes of cities over an extensive historical time span see:

Chandler, T and Fox, G. (1974): *3000 years of urban growth* (New York).

Useful volumes for consideration of urbanization in less developed countries are:

Breese, G. editor (1969): *The city in newly developing countries* (Englewood Cliffs, N. J.).

Dwyer, D. J. (1975): *People and housing in Third World Cities* (London).

McGee, T. G. (1971): *The urbanization process in the third world* (see footnote 36).

Santos, M. (1971): *Les villes du tiers monde* (see footnote 35).

A more general overview can be obtained from Polish Academy of Sciences (1979): *The national settlement systems*. Institute of Geography and Spatial Organization (Warsaw), 3 vols.

A recent popular treatment of the urbanization process is:

Wilsher, P. and Righter, R. (1975): *The exploding cities* (London).

3

Urban Functions and the Functional Classification of Towns

Any advance which is made from a self-contained subsistence economy can only be effected by specialization. In this context, the town is a point of specialized activity carrying out tasks which are best performed either at central, accessible places or where a high degree of population concentration is economically necessary. The former can be regarded as co-ordinating activities, the latter as productive. A third activity can be added to these, that of the organization of the intermediary, long distance transport, so that the following can be regarded as characteristically urban functions.[1]

1 Central place functions, or general services, which are carried out for a more or less extensive but contiguous area;
2 Transport functions, which are carried out at break of bulk points along the major lines of communications;
3 Special functions, which are carried out for non-local, non-contiguous areas. These could include extractive and manufacturing industries with world wide markets, or indeed minor industries whose distributive areas are smaller than the general service area.

It is often stated that the essence of urban character is service for a tributary area and the study of central place functions has become a highly developed and specialized field which will be dealt with in the next chapter. But problems arise if such central functions are not clearly seen in their relation to the other two types described above. This is simply apparent in the consideration of the population total of a town, which is an unsatisfactory measure because it is inclusive and indivisible. It in no way measures the *centrality* of a town in relation to the surrounding countryside and Christaller was at pains to distinguish between the importance of a town, which could be measured by its population size, and the centrality, which required a different and more appropriate measure.[2]

Before centrality can be considered, therefore, it is necessary to consider those aspects of a town's activities which are not directly related to it. This involves a separation which is artificial but necessary, and most enlightenment will be derived from a separate study of resource-orientated functions and other activities whose locations central place theory cannot explain and

[1] *Vide* Chauncy D. Harris and E. L. Ullman (1945): The nature of cities. *Ann. Am. Acad. polit. soc. Sci.* **242**, 7.
[2] W. Christaller (1933): *Die zentralen Orte in Suddeutschland* (Jena); translated by W. C. Baskin, 1966: *Central places in Southern Germany* (Englewood Cliffs, N. J.).

the subsequent superimposition of such functions and activities on to the areal pattern of central places.[3]

It also follows that if a town owes its being, or its growth, to such specialized or resource-orientated functions, the complete investigation of the nature and degree of specialization is essential for the light it will throw on three related aspects of urbanism. These are:

1   The urban role in the national or regional economy.
2   The particular aspects of urban society which correlate with types of specialism.
3   The relation between function and locational patterns which is at the heart of the geographer's interests.

The procedure for this investigation has been based on processes of classification. 'In the earth sciences, as in the astronomical ones, the most notable advances are almost invariably associated with the construction of a theoretical model which, in a particularly symmetrical and harmonious manner, seems to embrace a large section of observed reality.'[4] Such model building characterizes central place theory, but in the analysis of specialized functions such a procedure is hardly developed. The construction of models often 'results from a backlog of accumulated information, although every such accumulation does not inevitably lead to such a construction and attempts are made then to digest the material by means of classifications, rather than by integrated models.'[5] Further 'scientifically, classification is of the utmost importance because of the empirically established fact that it is possible to set up certain classes in such a way that mere membership in the class renders highly probable the possession of attributes other than those needed to define the class.'[6]

Criticisms of such procedures have been made by numerous writers mainly on the grounds that most functional town classifications are seen as isolated exercises having no theoretical basis and often little practical purpose for classes distinguished are not shown to have other associated attributes. Nearly all these critics having made these points put forward their own classificatory system often without meeting the weaknesses they have identified elsewhere, so that a very large literature has developed.[7] Robert Smith, in reviewing this situation, puts forward two spatial characteristics that can be associated with town functions:[8]

1   There should be distributionnal characteristics of towns in similar functional classes that are peculiar to those classes.
2   Different functional classes ought to be associated with different types of hinterland areas.

[3] W. Isard (1960): *Methods of regional analysis* (New York) 227.
[4] R. J. Chorley (1963): Diastrophic background to twentieth-century geomorphological thought. *Bull. geol. Soc. Am.* **74**, 953.
[5] R. J. Chorley (1963).
[6] M. Cohen and E. Nagle (1934): *Introduction to logic and scientific method* (London).
[7] For a convenient review of various classifications see R. H. T. Smith (1965): Method and purpose in functional town classification. *Ann. Assoc. Am. Geogr.* **55**, 539.
[8] R. H. T. Smith (1965), 546−7.

This restates the point that has already been made, that any explanation of town distribution cannot solely rely on methods related to central place analysis but needs to be integrated with interpretations derived from specialized activities. The procedure lies within a long tradition and can be given a clear purpose even if it does not have a distinctive theoretical orientation.

1 Systems of classification

From earliest times, chorographical works have included descriptions of town functions and have carried the implication that towns fall into classes or groups by virtue of the functions they perform. The simple designation 'market town' or 'seaport' is a form of functional classification. With the increasing diversity of town function that followed the industrial developments of the eighteenth and nineteenth centuries, such descriptive classifications became more frequent and more elaborate. In Britain the Committee on the Health of Towns which reported in 1840[9] found that a prerequisite of their work was some orderly arrangement of the towns to be considered. Accordingly, they proposed five groups which were:

1   The metropolis.
2   Manufacturing towns.
3   Populous seaport towns.
4   Great watering places.
5   County and other considerable inland towns not being the seats of particular manufactures.

Here the distinction is made between central place cities (5) and special activity cities (2, 3, and 4) and the variable of size is clearly included in the words 'populous', 'great' and 'considerable'.

Since the time of this classification, attempts to suggest groups of towns linked by common functions have become more elaborate and statistically more sophisticated. At the same time, greater efforts have been made to understand the logical bases of classification and the nature of town function. It can be suggested that these attempts can be arranged in a progression from the simple general statement to the contemporary multivariate analysis. In general, this is a chronological arrangement and one in which statistical analytical tools become increasingly used.

a General description

This is the earliest stage in the analysis of town functions. Classes are established in descriptive terms only and towns are allocated to a class on a subjective basis. There are innumerable schemes of this sort appearing at the most elementary level but they all owe a great deal to one of the earliest of such classifications to appear in a geographic context. This was included by M. Aurousseau in his paper 'The distribution of population: a

---

[9] (1840): *Report of the select committee on the health of towns* (London) iv.

constructive problem'.[10] The scheme recognized six classes of active towns which were then subdivided (table 3−1).

Criticisms of these classes are not hard to find. There is a confusion of functional and locational terms; for example, 'tidal limit town' cannot in any way be a functional term; it is descriptive of a location which may or may not result in certain definable functions. The group labelled 'Communications' seem oddly elaborate compared with the other groups; moreover, its constitution appears open to criticism, for it includes two of the three basic types of urban activity identified earlier. 'Market towns' and 'Mining towns' are hardly of the same functional order and the promotion, at least, of the three sub-groups to major groups would seem logical and necessary.

Aurousseau's scheme, although subject to criticism, marks an important stage in the development of functional study. It brought together many diverse ideas into one comprehensive scheme which was at once the climax of a long period of purely descriptive work and the springboard for new methods.

b Statistical description

This stage in the consideration of town functions introduces objective, statistical material into the problem of classification. The most consistently used data have been occupation or employment ratios. There is a clear link between an employment group and a town's function. Numbers employed are not immediately important, but rather the proportional place which an

table 3−1: A classification of cities. *After M. Aurousseau (1921).*

Class I Administration	Class II Defence	Class III Culture
Capital cities	Fortress towns	University towns
Revenue towns	Garrison towns	Cathedral towns
	Naval bases	Art centres
		Pilgrimage centres
		Religious centres

Class IV Production	Class V Communication		
Manufacturing towns	a Collection	b Transfer	c Distribution
	Mining towns	Market towns	Export towns
	Fishing towns	Fall line	Import towns
	Forest towns	towns	Supply towns
	Depot towns	Break-of-bulk	
		towns	
		Bridgehead towns	
		Tidal limit towns	
		Navigation head	
		towns	

Class VI Recreation
Health resorts
Tourist resorts
Holiday resorts

[10] M. Aurousseau (1921): The distribution of population: a constructive problem. *Geogrl. Rev.* **11**, 563.

employment group takes in the whole range of groups in the town. If mining employs 30 per cent of the total occupied population in a town, then this is a clear diagnosis of an important mining function and such figures can be referred to as the diagnostic ratios. But there are difficulties which arise in the equation of employment category and town function.

The first is the obvious problem of reducing the many thousands of occupations into a limited number of significant groups.[11] In this process, a large number of arbitrary decisions are made, which the classifier has to accept on the principle that all his results will be similarly affected. The second major problem is that the same occupation group can mean different things in different places. To cite a simple example, in the British census the group titled 'Personal service', including hotel and café proprietors, barmen and domestic servants, is usually taken to be diagnostic of a resort function. But if the occupation structure of Oxford[12] is examined it will be found that the largest single group is 'Personal service' accounting for some 14·6 per cent of the total. The next highest group is 'Metalworking and engineering' employing nearly 13 per cent. The conclusion, that Oxford is a resort with an important engineering sector, might have an uncomfortable element of the truth, but it is hardly the whole truth. The source of error is the substantial employment by the Oxford colleges of those in occupations grouped under 'Personal service'. This is an obvious example, but much more subtle confusions can arise and the data have to be handled with care.

Studies based on the principle of statistical description can be found in the earliest stage of urban geography[13] as for example in Olinto Marinelli's 'Dei tipi economici dei centri abitati a proposito di alcune citta italiane ed americane.'[14] But the most widely quoted example is that put forward in 1943 by Chauncy D. Harris in which a functional classification of the cities of the USA was outlined.[15] Eight classes of towns were recognized: manufacturing, retail, wholesale, transport, mining, university, resort and retirement, and diversified. One example will be sufficient to indicate the principle used. Transport centres are defined as towns where 'Transportations and communication contain at least 11 per cent of the gainful workers and workers in tranportation and communication equal at least one third the number in manufacturing and mechanical industries and at least two thirds the number in trade'.[16] This example illustrates the problem of diagnosis. 'Communications' should include workers engaged in telephone and telegraph services (in Britain it includes lift attendants), and yet the class 'transport centre' seems to imply something rather more limited.

---

[11] A brief consultation of the volume of the 1951 census (1956): *Classification of occupations* (London) will reveal the complexity of this problem.

[12] Census of England and Wales 1951 (1956): *Occupation tables* (London).

[13] For a review of early work see M. Aurousseau (1924): Recent contributions to urban geography: a review. *Geogrl. Rev.* 14, 444.

[14] O. Marinelli (1916): Dei tipi economici dei centri abitati a proposito di alcune citta italiane ed americane. *Riv. geogr. ita.* 23, 413.

[15] Chauncy D. Harris (1943): A functional classification of cities in the United States. *Geogrl. Rev.* 33, 86.

[16] Chauncy D. Harris (1943).

If the criteria for the definition of this town type be considered, two bases for recognition are apparent:

1   A certain minimum proportional employment, the diagnostic ratio, in this case of 11 per cent.
2   A certain degree of dominance of this group, measured by comparison with other groups.

Both these criteria were set up by simple empirical means. The experience of the classifier is used to assign towns to groups which are then converted into functional classes by means of a definition which fits with a minimum degree of disturbance, that is with a minimum number of accessions or deletions. This is a logical step forward from Aurousseau's system for the groups there defined are now given precise statistical definitions. But these definitions are the result of subjective decision, and although dispersion graphs and other aids may be used, the decision is still personal.

This is clearly accepted in another classification which has some parallel features. Duncan and Reiss in their book *Social characteristics of urban and rural communities* include a large section dealing with 'functional specialization'.[17] In this, the lowest value of upper decile or quintile groups is used as a criterion of definition, although this is varied in application. For specialization in transport, the definition is derived thus: 'Since the distributions of places by the percentage of persons employed in transport are quite leptokurtic, although positively skewed, the upper decile was taken as the criterion.'[18] This gives a ratio of between 8 and 12 per cent dependent on size, for allowance is made for different size classes in the classification, with the comment at one point that, 'the choice of the quintile as a cutting point, of course, is somewhat arbitrary'.[19] The name given to these sorts of classification is 'statistical description'.

c Statistical analysis

The next step in functional classification is linked with the attempt to offset criticism of the sort directed at Harris's scheme. This means that the classes recognized have to be derived statistically from the raw material. When it is stated that an employment of 11 per cent of the labour force in transport and communication is the diagnostic ratio, then is is implied that it is only above this level that employment become distinctive when compared with other towns. Webb's contrast between 'isolated urban society' and 'integrated urban society' is here relevant.[20] In the first case, as in the city in Von Thünen's isolated state, specialization can only be identified and measured by comparing one employment sector in the city with another sector, in the same city, in relative terms. In the second case an employment

---

[17] Otis D. Duncan and Albert J. Reiss (1956): Functional specialization of communities. Part IV of *Social characteristics of urban and rural communities*, 215 (London).
[18] Otis D. Duncan and Albert J. Reiss (1956), 244.
[19] Otis D. Duncan and Albert J. Reiss (1956), 223.
[20] See chapter 6, pp. 133–4. J. M. Webb (1959): Basic concepts in the analysis of small urban centres of Minnesota. *Ann. Assoc. Am. Geogr.* **49**, 55.

sector can be compared with the same sector in other cities, either in absolute or in relative terms, or with the means for the whole group. In many cases methods do not clearly distinguish between these two bases of comparison and indeed in many cases they are both used, but without clear comprehension of the implications.

In Harris's scheme there is an implied and subjective comparison of the particular city with the average city in order to derive a critical figure. This process becomes the basis of many schemes of statistical analysis, where local conditions are compared with national average conditions. A good example of such a procedure is in the calculation of location quotients[21] which measure the local significance of an industry by relating the ratio of its local employment to the national average.

In 1953, L. L. Pownall attempted to use this concept in a study of 'The functions of New Zealand towns'.[22] The mean employment was calculated for seven different size groups of towns and then within its appropriate group a town was examined for positive deviation from the mean 'The positive deviations from these national averages are taken here as criteria expressing the relative importance of six different functions: manufacturing, building and construction; primary industry; transport and communications; distribution and financial; hotel and personal service; administration and professional service.'[23] The seventh class, that of residential function, was based on the ratio between total population and population gainfully employed. Any town could be specialized in more than one function and a discussion of the seven classes followed. Pownall's groups are clearly too dependent on the occupational groups for 'building and construction' is a universal within which specialization is incidental rather than fundamental. Again, a residential function is far better expressed as either 'resort function' or 'retirement function' or both combined since it is not easy to distinguish them.

A more fully developed and more logical scheme is that of H. J. Nelson who in 1955 set out 'A service classification of American cities'.[24] Nelson poses the question, 'How large a percentage of the labour force must be employed in a particular service to make the performance of the service far enough above normal to warrant separate classification?' In his answer, he defines 'normal' as mean or average for the whole country and the degree above normal he defines by use of the standard deviation, a measure of the departure from the mean condition of any member of a series.[25]

Diagnostic occupational groups are selected from the census returns. These relate to manufacturing; retail trade; professional service; transportation and communications; personal service; public administration;

[21] See for example West Midland Group (1948): *Conurbation* (London) 105.

[22] L. L. Pownall (1953): The functions of New Zealand towns. *Ann. Assoc. Am. Geogr.* **43**, 332.

[23] L. L. Pownall (1953), 334.

[24] Howard J. Nelson (1955): A service classification of American cities. *Econ. Geogr.* **31**, 189.

[25] For the explanation of these methods see S. Gregory (1963): *Statistical methods and the geographer* (London).

wholesale trade; finance, insurance and real estate; mining. For each occupational or diagnostic group the standard deviation from the mean for all towns is calculated. Any town which then shows a percentage employment of more than mean plus one standard deviation is said to be significantly characterized by the function diagnosed by the occupation group. This is further developed by recording how many times the employment ratio in one town is above the mean for all towns in terms of the standard deviation.

Thus, the mean for employment in mining in all urban areas of the USA is 1·62 per cent and the standard deviation (SD) is 5·01 per cent. This means that the diagnostic ratio for a mining town would be 1·62 + 5·01 = 6·63 per cent. Degrees of specialization can now be measured by mean + twice the standard deviation (1·62 + 10·02 = 11·64) and mean + three times the standard deviation (1·62 + 15·03 = 16·65). Since the standard deviation is properly only a valid measure when distribution about the mean is normal, no more than three standard deviations are measured, so that Butte, Montana, with 32·1 per cent in mining would be characterized as Mi3, indicating that it is a mining town with an employment proportion over three standard deviations above the mean.

R. S. Dick working in Queensland, Australia,[26] adopted a similar technique but expressed his results more completely by including the percentage employment as well, so that Butte would have been shown as $Mi32^{+3}$, indicating a total employment of 32 per cent as well as the three standard deviations above the mean. This procedure emphasizes that no exclusive classes result from this form of statistical analysis. Any town could have a number of different groups over 'mean plus standard deviation' or indeed, it could have no group over the appropriate diagnostic ratios and to meet this problem Nelson had to add a further functional class called 'diversified'. The forcing of multi-functional towns into unifunctional classes is of necessity an unsatisfactory process which Nelson and Dick avoid, but at some sacrifice of simplicity, for the purpose of classification is partly, at least, the reduction of complexity to a comprehendible form.

Two further points need to be added here. The functional classes are determined by the occupational groupings of the census. Thus, in Britain, it would be impossible to recognize, as does Nelson, a wholesale function, for no appropriate occupational group is recognized in the census of occupations. In addition, diagnostic ratios will vary considerably with the sample of towns taken. Thus, in Wales, the mean employment in mining is 7·7 per cent and the standard deviation 11·96 per cent so that mean plus standard deviation is 19·66 per cent, a very different figure from that for the USA given above. It might be argued that here the comparisons are not proper for the above example equates a very much larger country with but part of the United Kingdom.

Even so this objection emphasizes the problem in that diagnostic ratios must be related to the particular circumstances and the character of the

---

[26] R. S. Dick (1961): Variations in the occupational structure of central places of the Darling Downs, Queensland. *Univ. Queensland Pap.* **1**, 2.

areas being investigated. They cannot be put forward as of universal application. International comparability is still far off.

d Urban economic base studies
These studies have developed during the whole of the period covered by the classifications reviewed and indeed, there is an overlap between the two. In practice, the studies introduce little that is very different, but there is a more extended background of principle.

A review of principle could start with Chauncy D. Harris's classification already considered. Under that classification, transportation centres are defined as having 11 per cent of their gainful workers employed in transport and communications. If this is analyzed, it means that Harris regards 11 per cent as the critical value at which transport employment becomes diagnostically significant in terms of the country as a whole. But this is not necessarily a useful measure, for what is required is some estimate of the point at which employment in transport becomes critical in the life of the town, not merely keeping it going but making a distinctive and generative contribution to its economic well being. This is the essence of the concept of the 'economic base', around which an elaborate theory has accumulated[27] and which seems to offer at least the possibility of model building.

The earliest suggestion of the concept appears to have come in 1902, when W. Sombart in *'Der moderne Kapitalismus'*[28] identified a dual function in towns which he characterized as 'stadegrunder', or basic; and 'studefuller' or complementary or non-basic. These concepts have come into English mainly via the work of planners, particularly in the USA. In a work published in 1928,[29] Robert M. Haig distinguished between 'primary occupations', or the producing of goods for external purposes, and 'auxiliary occupations', or the producing of goods and services for the convenience of the primary group. This concept was developed, and the terminology of the economic base was introduced by Homer Hoyt in 1939.[30] Here the idea is propounded in its modern form. Economic activity can be broken down into two components:

1   That which meets non-local demand: this   Basic or city forming
     is the contribution to the national economy.
2   That which meets local, internal demand: Non-basic or city
     this keeps the city going but makes no   serving
     contribution to the national economy:
     'We cannot live by taking in each other's
     washing.'

It follows from the above definitions that the basic component is 'city forming' because it induces growth. It creates a centripetal flow of income

[27] The most convenient source for consulting material on this topic is Ralph W. Pfouts (1956): *The techniques of urban economic analysis* (West Trenton, N.J.).

[28] W. Sombart (1902): *Der moderne Kapitalismus*, volume 2 (Leipzig).

[29] Robert M. Haig (1928): Regional survey of New York. *Major economic factors in metropolitan growth and arrangement*, volume 1 (New York).

[30] See A. M. Weimer and H. Hoyt (1939): *Principles of real estate* (New York).

into the city which is available for distribution and circulation. But some qualification is necessary. The dictum quoted in 2 above, 'We cannot live by taking in each other's washing', is only partly true. By extending the boundaries of the unit for which the economic base study is to be made, one eventually arrives at an area where there is no export of goods or services at all, at which point all activities would, by definition, be non-basic. Such a unit would be hard to find, but nation states might approach the condition in varying degrees. Nevertheless within the limited unit of the city, it is argued that if it is possible to isolate the basic component of a city's economy, then we have isolated the growth-inducing or 'city forming' element. This is the obvious key to the study of locational advantages and growth, and should be the basis of classification.

The practical problem remains in the method by which this basic component is to be isolated. Hoyt himself proposed a cumbersome procedure by which local and non-local destinations of goods and services sold were determined by questionnaire, and the trade and professional population apportioned to basic or non-basic activities by using the proportion of the national income obtained by the city.[31] Any such procedure is clumsy, unreliable and hardly practical when a large number of towns is being considered. Most methods subsequently proposed have aimed at simplification and have fallen back on the old idea of comparing local with national, particularly with mean or some other condition. The national proportion employed in any occupation is obtained and the number expected to be so employed in a town of any size is calculated. If the actual employment when compared with this expected total shows a surplus, then this represents basic employment. This is the principle used in the clearest statement of this concept by J. M. Mattila and W. R. Thompson who proposed an 'index of surplus workers'.[32]

$$S = ei - \frac{et}{Et} Ei$$

where ei = the regional employment in the industry concerned;
et = the total regional employment in all industries and economic activity;
Ei = the national employment in the industry concerned;
Et = the total national employment in all industries and economic activity.

This index can be used in a classification of towns by the following procedure. The index is calculated for all occupational groups in the town and all positive values are totalled giving an aggregate of surplus workers for the town. The percentages of the aggregates formed by each occupational surplus are calculated and ranked. These rankings are then used as a basis for functional classification. An application of this Index of Surplus

[31] A. M. Weimer and H. Hoyt (1939).
[32] J. M. Mattila and W. R. Thompson (1955): The measurement of the economic base of the metropolitan area. *Land Econ.* **31**, 215.

Workers can be examined in *Provincial metropolis*[33] where it was used in the study of the economic base in south-east Lancashire.

A somewhat different approach was that of G. Alexandersson in a study of the industrial structure of cities in the USA.[34] The problem as he states it remains the same—'to identify the value above which employment is significant.'[35] In this case, the value attempts to answer, the question 'What ratios in different industries are a necessary minimum to supply a city's own population with goods and services of the type which are produced in every normal city?' The clear difference between the term 'normal city' and the idea of a 'national average' is at once apparent. The use of national average does not measure an economic base and, insofar as such figures are used, as in the Index of Surplus Workers, these methods are little different from those of Nelson *et alia* described in the previous section.

Alexandersson, therefore, asks the more pertinent question in terms of economic base analysis. Accordingly, he ranks the employment ratios in each industry for all the towns he is considering and constructs a cumulative distribution diagram of percentage of cities against percentage employment (figure 3−1). By empirical means two points (K_1 and K) were chosen, 1 per cent and 5 per cent from the point of origin, and employment structures set up using these values to provide a diagnostic employment ratio.[36] That is, in a sample of 500 cities, the 5th and the 25th would be chosen and in Alexandersson's 864 cities of over 10,000 population in the USA, the 9th and the 43rd cities respectively were chosen. In the final analysis the 5 per cent point was selected so that for any functional category employment in the 43rd city in rank order from the minimum became the diagnostic proportion and these proportions were used to set up a 'normal' city with a balanced occupational structure. Specialization was then measured by proportional employment above the K value.

This scheme has the merit of using an established normal structure rather than an 'average' structure, but the setting up of this normal structure is marked by empirical decisions, while a very large sample is needed to make it worth employing.

Perhaps the logical conclusions of these analyses is reached in the suggestion by Ullman and Dacey[37] whose work, in principle, parallels that of Alexandersson. They argued that the *minimum* percentage employed in any city provides the non-basic ratio since this must identify the smallest proportion for a viable city. This is an argument clearly open to serious challenge. Indeed the use of minima had been considered and rejected by Alexandersson on the grounds that anomalous cases would become the decisive ones. His choices of the K point was specifically made to avoid that

[33] L. P. Green (1959): *Provincial metropolis*, 43 (London).

[34] G. Alexandersson (1956): *The industrial structure of American cities* (Lincoln, Nebraska, and Stockholm).

[35] G. Alexandersson (1956).

[36] G. Alexandersson (1956), 17.

[37] Edward L. Ullman and Michael F. Dacey (1962): The minimum requirements approach to the urban economic base; in K. Norborg, editor (1962): *Proc. Lund Symp. urb. Geogr. 1960*, 121.

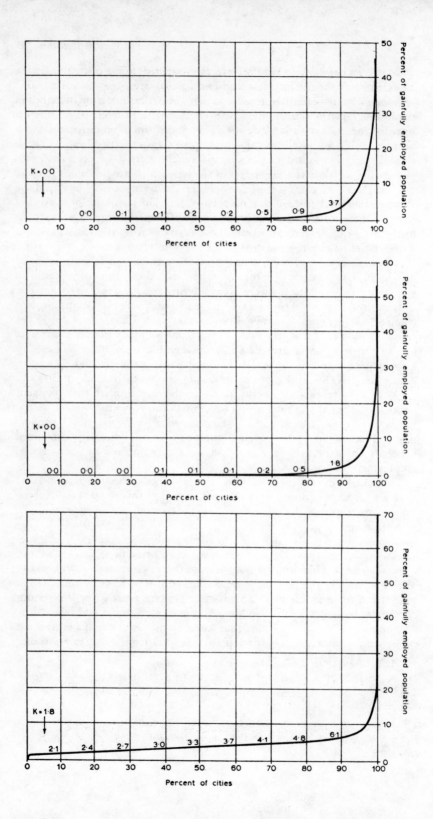

problem. To some extent Ullman and Dacey minimize the difficulties since the variation of the minimum with city size is taken into account. This non-basic ratio is subsequently used to classify cities not by comparing one employment sector with another but by measuring the extent to which a city departed from the various minima, thus providing an Index of Diversity (D) where:

$$D = \Sigma i \left[\frac{(Pi - Mi)^2}{Mi} \right] \Big/ \frac{[\Sigma iPi - \Sigma iMi]^2}{\Sigma iMi}$$

where i = each of employment groups.
      Pi = percentage employed in each of i groups.
      Mi = minimum requirement for each group.
      Σi = the sum of all the groups.

The higher this Index the more specialized is a town, the lower, the more diversified. It is apparent that this Index demonstrates how statistical measures are increasingly employed and how the study of the ways in which towns differ from each other is the real basis of classification. This leads on to the last group of classifications.

e Multivariate analysis
One of the major criticisms of all the systems so far described is that they rely on one set of data only. It is true that a number of measures have been proposed for the economic base including wages and salaries, value added and production, but the sheer difficulty of obtaining and using data has confined schemes to employment figures. By using multivariate techniques, it is possible to examine how towns are related to a series of variables.

Perhaps the best example of this is in *British town: a statistical study of their social and economic differences* by Moser and Scott.[38] The reasons for and the objectives of this work are succinctly stated. It is contended that 'no systematic and general research has been done into ways in which British towns differ or resemble one another', therefore the authors try to assemble

---

[38] G. A. Moser and Wolf Scott (1961): *British towns; a statistical study of their social and economic differences* (London). For an updating of this work see: D. M. Grove and C. A. Roberts (1980): Principal Component and cluster analysis of 185 large towns in England and Wales *Urban Studies*, 17, 77–82.

Figure 3–1: Cumulative distribution diagrams of employment in selected occupations in U.S.A. cities. *After Alexandersson (1956).*

The top diagram shows employment in mining which is revealed as a very atypical urban occupation so that K = 0·0.

The middle diagram shows employment in automotive manufacturing which is also revealed as an atypical (specialized) activity due to its concentration about Detroit and its neighbouring towns. Again K = 0·0.

The lower diagram shows employment in medical services. These are much more ubiquitous so that K = 1.8 and only one highly specialized town emerges, Rochester, Minnesota.

and collate material relevant to this purpose and then to classify towns on the basis of their social, economic and demographic characteristics. They confine their work to towns of over 50,000 population and for these assemble a total of 57 variables generally grouped under the headings Population Size and Structure, Population Change, Households and Housing, Economic Character, Social Class, Voting Characteristics, Health and Education. Only a selection of towns is analyzed, the selection being based on the variable of size which is, unfortunately, later found to have little correlation with the other variables. Also this is a very much broader study of difference in which not only characteristics other than function are introduced, but by using changes between 1931 and 1951, a dynamic element is brought into what has been in all other classifications a static situation.

Nevertheless, the volume leads up to the last chapter entitled 'A classification of towns', and, since this is expressed in functional terms, it cannot be disregarded. The procedure is that a correlation matrix is established by using the product moment correlation coefficient[39] for all the variables taken in pairs.

It follows on *a priori* grounds that there is likely to be some systematic variation, but in this complexity dependent variation will not be a fruitful line to follow—hence the need to evaluate independent variation or 'the relationship of a set of variates among themselves no one being selected as special'. The investigation now leads to a component analysis, that is a study of how much of the total variation can be accounted for by a small number of independent variates, called components. These are purely mathematical artefacts, not individual members of the original series of variables and it is found that a good deal of the total variation is accounted for by the first four components. It is possible, however, to associate these components with certain of the variables and to give them some general meaning. In this case the associations were as follows:

Component 1   Social class.
Component 2   Population growth 1931–1951.
Component 3   (a) Development after 1951.
               (b) The working population in 1951.
Component 4   Housing conditions.

These are taken to be parameters of difference among the towns of England and Wales and a process of classification is set up based on the weightings recorded on the first two components with the additional evidence of the next two used when needed. The scheme aimed at producing groups of at least ten towns and ended with fourteen groups. From these London and Huyton were excluded since they were 'too different from other towns to be included in any group'. This is an allocation based not on simple function, but on a large number of criteria. Nevertheless, the final groupings accentuate a functional description. In outline, the scheme is given in table 3–2.[40]

[39] S. Gregory (1963): *Statistical methods and the geographer* (London).
[40] G. A. Moser and W. Scott (1961), 17–8; 80–93.

table 3–2: Classification of British towns: classes identified by G. A. Moser and W. Scott (1961).

Mainly resorts, administrative and commercial towns
   1 mainly seaside resorts,
   2 mainly spas, professional and administrative centres,
   3 mainly commercial centres with some industry.

Mainly industrial towns
   4 including most of the traditional railway centres,
   5 including many of the large ports as well as two Black Country towns,
   6 mainly textile centres in Yorkshire and Lancashire,
   7 including the industrial towns of the north-east seaboard and mining towns of Wales,
   8 including the more recent metal manufacturing towns.

Suburbs and suburban type towns
   9 mainly 'exclusive' residential suburbs,
   10 mainly older mixed residential suburbs,
   11 mainly newer mixed residential suburbs,
   12 including light industry suburbs, national defence centres and towns within the
       sphere of large conurbations,
   13 mainly older working class and industrial suburbs,
   14 mainly newer industrial suburbs.

Not allocated: London and Huyton.

It is interesting to compare these results with the initial identification of urban functions which was suggested at the beginning of this chapter:

1   *Central place activities* are directly comparable with the 'mainly admin-istrative and commercial towns' which Moser and Scott identify as Group 3. But the Resorts which they also include (Groups 1 and 2) would have to be placed with the Special Activities and it is unfortunate that this major class straddles distinctive central place and special functions.

2   *Transport activities* are not directly shown to produce a distinct set of towns, though Groups 4 and 5 in the classification are identified broadly in these terms. But these groups include other towns as well with no dis-tinctive transport function.

3   *Special activities* include the remaining groups, although 'suburbs' have no distinctive functional connotation. They are parts of larger units which appear in the classification due to the use of local government units.

This detailed investigation can be effectively compared with Aurousseau's scheme for it is particular to an area, precise in definition and 'the criteria of classification emerged from the analysis itself'.[41]

Another attempt at investigation into urban character was made by Hadden and Borgatta[42] in relation to American cities. Sixty-five variables were used and separate analyses for different city sizes were carried out.

[41] G. A. Moser and W. Scott (1961), 18.
[42] J. K. Hadden and E. F. Borgatta (1965): *American cities; their social characteristics* (Chicago).

From the matrix sixteen factors were extracted and the first of these, socio-economic status', was the same as that in the British study. The second, third and fourth factors however, were linked to 'non-white population', 'age composition' and 'education'. Subsequently the factors were used to select variables in order to construct a profile for each city by a simple decile division and though this does not provide a classification as such, it does provide a socio-economic profile (table 3–3).

table 3–3: Sample profiles of American cities. *After J. K. Hadden and E. F. Borgatta (1965).*

Profile item	New York	Chicago	Cincinnati	Arcadia
Total populations 000s	7781	3550	0502	0041
Per cent single dwellings	0	0	0	0
Density	9	9	7	3
Median income	4	7	3	9
Deprivation index	7	7	7	0
Per cent non-white	7	8	8	0
Per cent foreign born	9	8	3	5
Median age	8	7	6	9
Per cent population increase 1950–1960	1	1	1	8
Per cent same house 1955–1960	8	4	3	3
Per cent migrants	2	0	1	4
Education centre	6	3	7	5

Arcadia (Calif.) is included as a small town example.

This however carries the problem away from that posed at the outset which related economic function to the broader issues of urban character.

2 Summary

Five broad methods have been surveyed forming a progression from simple description through classification by one criterion to elaborate statistical processing. At this point, some review of these methods is appropriate. Any system of taxonomy is arbitrary and this arbitrariness becomes emphasized when variates rather than attributes form the basis.[43] The whole system established can only be judged in the light of the particular purpose in hand, for all.classifications of the order discussed here are only more or less satisfactory methods of associating like things so that understanding becomes easier. The main purpose of classification is to provide a rational framework for description and to lead toward a developed analysis of location. Aurousseau, as a preface to his scheme, wrote: 'When we examine the idea of position in an abstract way, it is at once evident that function is the driving force in the life of towns.'[44] Position or location can only be understood through function. Of itself a location is meaningless and, as is true of all

[43] See Harold M. Mayer and Clyde F. Kohn (1959): *Readings in urban geography*, 127–8 (Chicago).
[44] M. Aurousseau (1921), 569.

resources, only gains meaning through use. The type of use is shown quite clearly in both Harris's and Nelson's classifications and, from the viewpoint of the simplest needs of the urban geographer, this form of classification is acceptable.

It is true that only the crudest and most elementary insight is given into the complex working of the urban economy. It is to further this insight that economic base studies have grown. 'Properly speaking there is no single criterion for using the base concept. Any urban investigator is free to use the base for whatever purpose he has in mind . . . this is merely another way of saying that the urban base approach is a framework of analysis. . . . Its advantage over the other frameworks is that it points up the interactions of the local economy in a meaningful manner.'[45]

Base studies are, therefore, likely to be worth while when a more detailed investigation of the urban economy over an area is required. In addition, such studies do attempt to provide some limited form of conceptual basis for comprehension, as well as a classification for description.[46]

Finally, multivariate analysis is of a different order for it is itself a measure of the degree of difference between towns and not of special functions. However, classes, given descriptive names, have been derived from the known character of the members of 'urban profiles' have been constructed. Moser and Scott make the revealing statement that 'It is gratifying that the final classification corresponds so well to one's common-sense knowledge of British towns. It is clearly more satisfactory to have a group of towns which can reasonably be labelled . . . than a group which contains diverse elements.'[47] This means little more than that the investigation confirmed the standard but simple classifications of the type proposed by Aurousseau. There would be considerable food for thought were it otherwise. The simple forms of analysis are perfectly satisfactory and adequate for many geographic purposes, but the direction of further progress undoubtedly lies in the more sophisticated forms of regional analysis.

In considering the problem of 'hierarchies' in *Locational analysis in human geography*, Haggett looks upon all the specialized centres as being merely discordant elements in an otherwise ordered situation.[48] The analysis of this discord involves basic-non basic studies, distortion due to agglomeration and to resource localization including the whole nexus of Weberian location studies. To append these as mere distortions of the central place order is disingenuous for what is required is the integration of these great ranges of studies. This task Isard attempted in part in his massive work *Methods of regional analysis* but the final synthesizing channels are left as conceptualized but not operational. If, therefore, the goal is made more modest, it is possible to carry out a meaningful analysis of town location

[45] Charles M. Tiebout (1956): The urban economic base reconsidered. *Land Econ.* **32**, 95.
[46] For critical evaluations of the 'economic base' concept see Part II of Ralph W. Pfouts, editor (1956).
[47] G. A. Moser and Wolf Scott (1961), 89–91.
[48] P. Haggett, A. D. Cliff and A. Frey (1977): *Locational analysis in human geography*, 2nd edition. (London).

through such classificatory procedures as have been advanced in this chapter; the complex is not necessarily the best.

At this stage, however, it is necessary to reinforce the notion of the influence of specialized functions on urban growth and to demonstrate them as something more than a mere distortion of a basic regularity. Perhaps the simplest model of these influences has been put forward by Pred,[49] although his work owes something to the earlier schemes of 'cumulative causation' put forward by Myrdal[50] in his studies of economic growth on a regional basis.

Pred concerns himself more directly with the growth of American cities between 1860 and 1910 and proposes a model of 'the circular and cumulative process of industrialization and urban-size growth'. If the introduction of factory industries into a mercantile city is envisaged then the chains of reaction illustrated in figure 3–2 are evoked. 'New manufacturing functions, whether or not they primarily serve local markets, will have an

Figure 3–2: The circular and cumulative process of industrialization and urban-size growth. *After A. R. Pred (1966).*

initial multiplier effect',[51] that is new services will be demanded, while linked industries will be encouraged. The result will be 'an alteration of the city's occupational structure (with a more even balance struck between the industrial sector and the wholesaling-trading complex), an increase in population, or growth in urban size, and the probable attainment of one or more new local or regional industrial thresholds'.[52] This attainment of new thresholds will, in turn, support new manufacturing functions and encourage invention and innovation, and so the whole circular and

    [49] A. R. Pred (1966): *The spatial dynamics of the US urban-industrial growth 1800–1914: interpretative and theoretical essays* (Cambridge, Mass.).

    [50] For a review of Myrdal's ideas see D. E. Keeble (1967): Models of economic development; chapter 8 in R. J. Chorley and P. Haggett, editors (1967): *Models in geography*, 243–302 (London).

    [51] A. R. Pred (1966), 25.

    [52] A. R. Pred (1966), 26.

cumulative process continues, until interrupted or impeded by diseconomies or by competition from other growing centres.

To some extent Pred's work is a more sophisticated interpretation of the old elementary notion of 'geographical inertia', for which he provides a convincing rationale. Nor has Pred been alone in attempting to suggest generalizations of this sort. Smolensky and Ratajczak[53] have proposed a sequence of three stages which they call 'elemental settlement', 'conforming city' and 'urban agglomerate'. The 'elemental settlement . . . originates because of economies of specialization in performing what would otherwise be ubiquitous economic activities'.[54]

This explanation is directly in line with central place theories. Such a settlement 'becomes a "conforming city" when a factor specific to that site, giving an absolute cost advantage to entrepreneurs locating in that town, becomes economically relevant to profit-maximizing entrepreneurs'.[55] This implies the sort of transformation suggested by Pred which initiates cumulative growth.

Wilbur R. Thomson has also proposed what he calls 'stages of urban growth'[56] beginning with the 'stage of export specialization' where the local economy is dominated by a single industry or even a single firm. Presumably one could envisage this as equivalent to the town in former times, when it was dominantly a defensive, military strongpoint. This is followed by a 'stage of export complex' where a broadening of the local economy takes place possibly by extending forward or backward stages in production or by adding suppliers or consumers of intermediate products. Presumably in the parallel quoted above this stage would be achieved by the broadening of primarily military functions into commerce and administration. Thompson next proposes a 'stage of economic maturation' or 'local service sector puberty' where local activity replaces imports with its new 'own use' production and business and services are expanded. This leads to the final 'stage of regional metropolis', where the local economy is seen as a node connecting and controlling neighbouring cities, once rivals but now satellites. It is interesting to observe that Smolensky and Ratajczak envisage a regular pattern of 'elemental' settlements transformed by the discriminating advantages of particular site characteristics, while Thompson seems to think in terms of an initial stage where site characteristics discriminate transformed to one where the regional metropolis 'organizes' its satellites. These notions have some relevance to the problems to be discussed in chapter 6.

One phrase used by Pred can here be isolated. The changes which have been contemplated are accompanied by 'an alteration in the city's occupational structure' and this has been the concern of the present chapter.

[53] E. Smolensky and D. Ratajczak (1965): The conception of cities. *Explor. entrepr. Hist.*, *Second ser.* **2**, 90–131.

[54] E. Smolensky and D. Ratajczak (1965), 90–1.

[55] E. Smolensky and D. Ratajczak (1965), 91.

[56] W. R. Thompson (1965): *A preface to urban economics*, 15–16 (Baltimore). W. R. Thompson (1968): Internal and external factors in the development or urban economics; in H. S. Perloff and L. Wingo, editors (1968): *Issues in urban economics*, 43–63 (Baltimore).

Industrialization, or the growth of any special functions, affects urbanization and vice versa, so that the size and spacing of cities is in part the product
of the way in which the specialized tasks which cities perform — mining coal,
making cars or providing rest and relaxation — are carried out. This means
that consideration of these roles has to be married with that of general
regional functions in any total explanation of the urban pattern.

It is, however, apparent that the larger the city, or the more advanced the
economy in terms of western industrial capitalism, then the more multi-
functional the city becomes. One of the more recent attempts at the sort of
classification discussed in this chapter is that by B. J. L. Berry considering
what he terms the latent structure of the American urban system.[57] A factor
analysis with a varimax rotation was carried out of a 1762 (cities) by 97
(variables) data matrix. The factors abstracted are shown in table 3—4. The

table 3—4: Latent dimensions of the American urban system in 1960. *After B. J. L.
Berry (1972).*

Factor no.   Factor description
1	Functional size of cities in an urban hierarchy.
2	Socioeconomic status of the city residents.
3	Stage in family cycle of the city residents.
4	Nonwhite population and home ownership.
5	Recent population growth experience.
6	Economic base: college towns.
7	Population proportion foreign born or of foreign stock.
8	Recent exployment expansion.
9	Economic base: manufacturing.
10	Extent of female participation in the labour force.
11	Economic base: specialized service centres.
12	Economic base: military.
13	Economic base: mining.
14	Extent to which elderly males participate in labour force.

conclusions from this exercise suggest that if the factors are uncorrelated
then the economic base of urban centres tends to act independently of other
urban structural features. As multifunctional towns lose distinction in
economic specialization it is the broader socioeconomic dimensions which
emerge as bases of contrast. The distinctive towns specialized by their
economic bases are small and unimportant. 'It follows that the traditional
economic approach to city classification is of minimal and declining
relevance.' The one exception is the market-orientated activities, for every
urban system is hierarchically structured, the structure resting on aggregate
economic power, and, as Berry concludes, the functional size of centres in
an urban hierarchy is a universally latent dimension. Two conclusions
follow:

1   Into the patterns of urban growth so far set out needs to be added a
process of functional change by which, as divergences of economic base

[57] B. J. L. Berry (1972): Latent structure of the American urban system; in B. J. L. Berry,
editor (1972): *City classification handbook: methods and applications,* 11–60 (New York).

are progressively diminished, contrast is developed in the general and separated contexts of socioeconomic status and life cycle stage, and possibly a racial or ethnic characteristic as the society becomes culturally heterogeneous.

2 The one exception is the universal size dimension and it is to the consideration of this and its hierarchical structuring that this study must now turn.

Notes on further reading
There is an extensive, if somewhat repetitive, literature on the functional classification of towns. The most useful and incisive contribution is Smith's paper:

Smith, R. H. T. (1965): Method and purpose in functional town classification (see footnote 7).

His scheme for Australian towns should be consulted; it also contains a bibliography.

Smith, R. H. T. (1965): The functions of Australian towns. *Tijd. voor Econ. en Soc. Geog.* **56**, 81.

'A review of classificatory schemes' is included in chapter 2 of:

Hadden, J. K. and Borgatta, E. F. (1965): *American cities. Their social characteristics* (Chicago).

The most useful summary of schemes using economic base notions is in:

Alexandersson, G. (1956): *The industrial structure of American cities* (see footnote 34).

Studies further to those mentioned in the text are:

Ahmad, Q. (1965): Indian cities: characteristics and correlates. *Univ. of Chicage, Dept. of Geog., Research papers* **102**.

Carriére, C. and Pinchemel, P. (1963): *Le fait urbain en France* (Paris): Livre IV, Les fonctions urbaines, 243–304.

Hance, W. A. (1960): The economic location and function of tropical African cities. *Human Organization* **19**. 135.

Harris, C. D. (1945): The cities of the Soviet Union. *Geog. Rev.* **35**, 107.

Hart, J. F. (1955): Functions and occupational structure of cities of the American South. *Ann. Assoc. Am. Geogr.* **45**, 269.

Lal, A. (1959): Some aspects of functional classification of cities and a proposed scheme for classifying Indian cities. *Nat. Geogr. J. India.* **5**, 12.

Mints, A. A. and Khorev, B. S. (1959): An economic geographic typology of Soviet cities. *Voprosy Geografi.* **45**, 72, in Russian but see also — R. J. Fuchs (1964): Soviet Urban Geography: an appraisal of post war research, *Ann. Assoc. Amer. Geogr.* **54**, 282.

Sandru, I., Cucu, V. and Poghirc, P. (1963): Contribution géographique à la classification des villes de la Republique Populaire Roumaine. *Ann. de Geog.* **72**, 162, 185.

Steigenga, W. (1955): A comparative analysis and classification of Netherlands towns. *Tijd. voor Econ. en Soc. Geog.* **46**, 105.

Trewartha, G. T. (1952): Chinese cities: origins and functions. *Ann. Assoc. Am. Geogr.* **42,** 69.

Watanabe, Y. (1961): An analysis of the function of urban settlements based on statistical data. A functional differentiation vertical and lateral. *The Science Reports of Tôhoku University* (7th Series), *Geography* **10,** 63.

A most useful volume with wider applications is:

Berry, B. J. L. (1972): *City classification handbook: methods and applications* (see footnote 57).

For a more recent thorough treatment of one country see:

Pumain, D and Saint Julien, T. (1978): *Les dimensions du changement urbain. Evolution des structures socio-économiques du système urbain français de 1954 à 1975.* (Paris).

For an analysis of British towns see:

Grove, D. M. and Roberts, C. A. (1980): Principal components and cluster analysis of 185 large towns in England and Wales. *Urban Studies,* 17, 77–82.

A classification of Russian towns (in Russian) is provided in Medvedkova, O. L. (1979): Structural peculiarities of cities as multifunctional centres. *Izvestiya Akademi Nauk SSR, Seriya Geograficheskaya,* 1, 53–71.

A wider review of the Canadian system is:

Simmons J. W. (1979): The Canadian Urban system. *Univ. of Toronto, Centre for Urban and Community Studies, Research Paper 104.*

4

Central Place Functions and Central Place Theory

In the last chapter means were suggested by which the special functions which towns perform could be identified and evaluated. In order to introduce some clarification into this process, systems of classification were proposed. These make it possible if only in general terms, to isolate those functions which are only found in *some* towns and leave remaining those functions which are common to *all* towns. Every town (in some measure) acts as a focus for the surrounding countryside and it is from this role that the general functions are derived. Since in acting as a focus the town functions as a central place, the term 'central place functions' is commonly used and from this, central place theory has developed.

No consideration of central place theory can proceed far without introducing the name of Walther Christaller whose work *Die zentralen Orte in Suddeutschland (Central places in southern Germany)* was published in 1933[1] and it as well to begin an analysis of central place theory[2] with Christaller's ideas. He divided his book into three parts. The first, called the Theoretical Part, was concerned with the setting up of the theory; the second, the Connecting Part, considered practical methods whereby the theory could be tested in the real world; in the last part, the Regional Part, southern Germany was examined, and the methods devised in the second part were employed to substantiate the theory. The practical methods devised were not very successful and have not been used subsequently and it follows that the regional application is also of limited value. It is the theoretical part which is of greatest interest and worthy of close attention.

The introduction to the theoretical part of Christaller's book is entitled 'Are there laws which determine the number, distribution and size of towns?' and the major theme of the first part is contained in this title, for the aim of the author is to establish a deductive theory which reveals the 'Ordering principle' in the distribution of towns. Christaller justifiably set his ideas alongside those of Von Thünen in relation to agricultural production[3] and

---

[1] W. Christaller (translated by C. W. Baskin), (1966): *Central places in southern Germany* (Englewood Cliffs, N.J.).

[2] B. J. L. Berry and A. Pred (1961): Central place studies: a bibliography of theory and application. *University of Pennsylvania, Regional Science Research Institute, Bibliography Series* 1. Supplement published in 1965. This is the major source for material relative to central place theory. It contains a useful introductory review. A further supplement has been added: H. F. Andrews (1970): Working notes and bibliography on central place studies, 1965 – 1969. *University of Toronto, Dept. of Geography, Discussion Pap.* 8.

[3] J. H. Von Thünen (1826): *De isolierte Staat in Beziehung auf Landwirschaft and Nationalokonomie* (Hamburg).

Weber in relation to industrial location.[4] It cannot be overstressed that Christaller was seeking to elaborate a deductive theory and that deductive reasoning more and more occupies the heart of science. 'The more advanced a theory is, the more its exposition assumes deductive form . . . an advanced science is an immense system of interconnected facts, new discoveries are fitted into the system even if at times the system must be modified to accommodate them.'[5] The system in turn 'guides us to further experimental observations; finally it shows us what are the right questions to ask if we seek to understand the world in which we live.'[6]

Christaller's initial procedure, therefore, is to outline what he calls 'fundamental meanings', that is, the assumptions on which his argument is based. These assumptions are the *a priori* foundations of the whole construct. If they can be shown to be manifestly untrue then the model itself, however meticulous and valid its internal logic, will not truly generalize the real world and will be at odds with empirical findings. When a model such as this seems not to be confirmed by investigation of the real world it may be due to:

1   Faulty logic in the building of the model.
2   The inclusion of an inadequate array of variables.
3   Untrue assumptions.

Foremost among Christaller's assumptions is the one that towns act as central places for the countryside, that they come into being to carry out at a central accessible place the tasks which the life of the countryside creates. Christaller acknowledges that this basic assumption is derived from previous workers; as early as 1916 Gradman[7] had contended that the distinctive role of a town was 'to be the centre of its rural surroundings and mediator of local commerce with the outside world',[8] collecting and exporting the local products, importing and distributing the necessary goods and services which the countryside demands.

The significance of this role cannot be measured by the population of a town for whereas size might be a measure of 'importance', it is not a measure of centrality. Indeed it includes in an indivisible total the population due to those special functions which we have been at great pains to exclude. Centrality, the degree to which a town serves its surrounding area, can only be measured in terms of the goods and services offered. There are variations in quantity as well as in quality, there are different orders of goods and services for some are costly and purchased or needed infrequently and will need large populations to sustain them; others are everyday needs and will require small populations. From this two concepts emerge:

[4] A. Weber (edited by C. J. Friedrich) (1929): *Theory of the location of industries* (Chicago).
[5] S. Stebbing (1943): *Modern Elementary logic*, 183. This is a quotation from Einstein.
[6] S. Stebbing (1943), 184.
[7] R. Gradman (1916): Schwäbische Städte. *Z. Ges. Erdk.* (Berlin).
[8] R. Gradman (1916), 427.
[9] For this see B. J. L. Berry and W. L. Garrison (1958): A note on central place theory and the range of a good. *Econ. Georg.* 34; and, Recent developments of central place theory. *Pap. Proc. Reg. Sci. Assoc.* 4, 107.

1 *Threshold population.*[9] Christaller did not use this term but the concept is implied in his construct. The threshold is defined as the minimum population that is required to bring about the offering of a certain good for sale or to sustain any service; in economic terms this means the minimum demand to make such an offering viable. Assuming uniformity of income, consumption and taste it can be measured in terms of population numbers. In a concrete way this concept is easily demonstrated by the minimum varying population required to maintain successively a district nurse, a doctor, a specialist doctor such as a paediatrician, a general hospital and a specialized eye hospital. To evaluate these minima is much more difficult.

2 *Range of a good or service.* This is the maximum distance over which people will travel to purchase a good or derive a service offered at a central place; at some range from the centre the inconvenience of travel measured in time, cost and trouble will outweigh the value or need of the good, or an alternative nearer centre becomes available. Again this can be visualized in the length of journey to buy bread, which is likely to be very small and hence there will be very frequent trips, as against a journey to buy a fur coat, where in relation to the value of the article and the infrequency of demand a much longer trip would be tolerated. If a sick and dying person can only obtain remedial treatment in one place in the world, then the range of the service could be extended to its absolute maximum measured in miles. Again there are severe practical problems in that most journeys have multiple purposes, one can buy the bread and the fur coat on the same trip, but these are excluded from the present theoretical consideration.

It is possible from the above to isolate two limits in relation to each good or service; one can be called a lower and the other an upper limit (figure 4−1).

Upper Limit or Range. At this point journey to centre is not worth while in relation to need for good or service. Cost or inconvenience outweigh need or alternative centre becomes available

Lower Limit or Threshold. A population of this size (area x density of population) is required to sustain a good or service

Figure 4−1: The lower limit (Threshold) and the upper limit (Range) of a good from a central place.

The lower limit is determined by the minimum demand necessary to ensure a commodity or service is offered, that is, the threshold; the upper limit is that beyond which a good will no longer be obtained from a centre, the range.

If these principles are now applied as controls to the development that would take place on an isotropic surface, that is, a flat uniform plain of equal population density and with no variation in wealth or income, then it is possible to derive a model of town distribution.

At this point a word on nomenclature must be interposed. Christaller designated the various ranks of settlements by using the initial letter of the different orders of settlements as they could be identified in southern Germany. They are listed in table 4−1 and used in this discussion. To continue the argument, a settlement given the rank '*B*' is postulated. This serves the surrounding area and if one of the goods which it offers, number 21, can be given the upper limit, or range of 21 kilometres, and if the lower limit or threshold is such that it can only be offered at *B*, then it will be supplied over an area of 21 kilometres radius about *B*. Now if the next central good, number 20, has a range of 20 kilometres, then there will emerge a ring one kilometre wide which cannot be served from *B* with that good. Further centres are therefore presupposed and if the lower limit, or threshold, is sufficiently elastic, then these must be of the same *B* order. But they must be equidistant from *B* in terms of all the presupposed conditions and if the most closely packed equidistant distribution of settlement points is adopted, there will be six of these on a ring about *B* (figure 4−2).

Christaller gives the distance between these centres as 36 kilometres although the justification of this is provided later and such arithmetical

table 4−1: The orders and arrangement of centres.

Type of centre i.e. rank of order	Number of places	Number of complementary regions	Range of region in Kilometres
M (Marktort)*	486	729	4·0
A (Amtsort)	162	243	6·9
K (Kreisstadt)	54	81	12·0
B (Bezirksstadt)	18	27	20·7
G (Gaustadt)	6	9	36·0
P (Provinzstadt)	2	3	62·1
L (Landstadt)	1	1	108·0

*The terms used in this table are the ones most frequently employed in an English context, the first part referring to administrative areas, such as Gau or Kreis, and the 'stadt' meaning city. The longer terms used by Christaller were Marktflecken (Market locations), Amtsstädchen (Office towns), Kreisstädtchen (County seats in the American meaning of the term), Bezirkshauptorte (main district or regional centres), Gaubezirkshauptorte (Gau centres), Provinzialhauptorte (provincial capitals), Landeszentralen (major regional centres). Christaller also added Reichsteilstadte, or RT, for those cities which were more than major regional centres, but not national capitals, with populations of about 1 million, and Reichshauptstadte or R (world cities or national capitals with a population of over 2 million). (*Source:* C. W. Baskin (1957): *A critique and translation of Walter Christaller's 'Die Zentralen Orte in Suddeutschland'.* University of Virginia: unpublished Ph.D. dissertation, 345−52.)

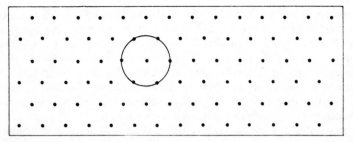

Figure 4–2: The most closely packed equidistant distribution of points (settlements) and the smallest association of centres.

distances should not properly be part of a deductive structure. For still lower order goods the next locations will be those at the centres of equilateral triangles joining the *B* centres (figure 4–3); at these points *K* centres will

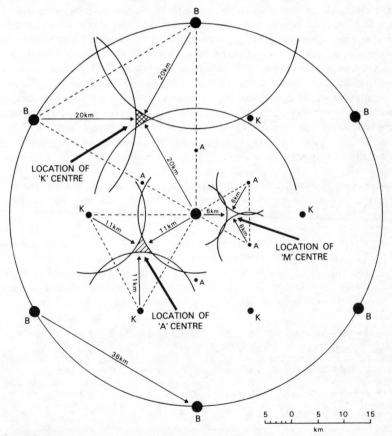

Figure 4–3: The derivation of the urban hierarchy after Christaller (1966). For explanation see text. This diagram comes from: C. R. Lewis (1977): Central Place Analysis. Unit 10, Fundamentals of Human Geography, Open University.

emerge. Now goods numbers 19, 18, 17, 16, 15, 14, 13 and 12 with ranges of 19, 18, 17, 16, 15, 14, 13 and 12 kilometres can be offered effectively at the *B* and *K* centres, but good number 11 cannot, for once more the unserviced one kilometre ring will emerge; a futher series of lower order service centres has to be introduced. In this way, a whole hierarchy of central places emerges with towns of equal rank equidistant from each other. Christaller called the area which a town served the 'complementary region' and under the conditions above, these regions were circular. However, to avoid overlap, and to match the densest distribution of settlement points, the circular regions were transformed into hexagons.

If there are further goods for which the threshold population required is greater than that provided by the *B* system, then one place alone from that system may be sufficient and it accordingly will acquire higher value as a central place and is given the designation of a '*G*' centre. It will have a range of 36 kilometres as suggested above, for it is now apparent that it is at a value three times the next lower range limit that transition from one rank of central place to another becomes necessary. New and higher order centres will therefore be found with ranges of 62 kilometres and 108 kilometres. At each of these distances new types of goods can be offered because the range, and thereby the threshold population, is increased. Each central place is able to offer all the goods of lower order centres and, in addition, a distinctive range of goods related to the increased size of its hinterland. On this basis a distinctive series of ranks emerges which is referred to as the urban hierarchy. The pattern finally produced is shown on figure 4 – 4 and in table 4 – 1.

It should be apparent, however, that the threshold and range of any one good or service will be an arbitrary figure and consequently it is possible that each one will demand a different hierarchical structure. Christaller understood this to some extent and was aware that throughout the theoretical part he was describing a special case. In the case demonstrated above, there is a strict ordering whereby each settlement serves its own hinterland and an area/population equivalent to the hinterlands of two other settlements in addition, hence it has been called 'the rule of threes', or, using the constant *k* to express this, then *k* = 3 (figure 4 – 4). But still retaining the hexagonal structure of basic settlements Christaller realized that two other situations were possible where *k* = 4 and *k* = 7 as shown on figure 4 – 5. In order to

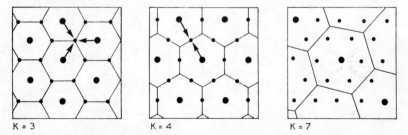

K = 3   K = 4   K = 7

Figure 4–5: The central place system: the three smallest systems. K = 3, K = 4 and K = 7. *After P. Haggett (1977).*

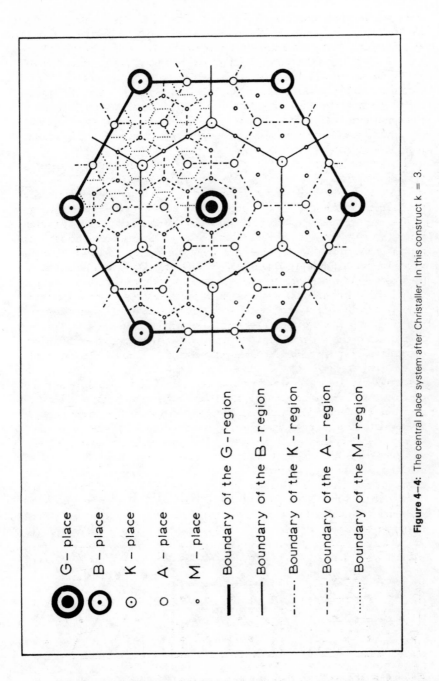

G – place

B – place

K – place

A – place

M – place

Boundary of the G – region

Boundary of the B – region

Boundary of the K – region

Boundary of the A – region

Boundary of the M – region

Figure 4–4: The central place system after Christaller. In this construct k = 3.

MARKETING   PRINCIPLE   K = 3

ADMINISTRATIVE   PRINCIPLE   K = 7

TRANSPORTATION   PRINCIPLE   K = 4

Figure 4–6: The three controlling principles, identified by Christaller, corresponding to the three smallest systems in figure 4–5.

resolve this problem Christaller associated a controlling principle with each of the three arrangements (figure 4−6).

1 *The marketing principle: k* = 3. All areas are served from a minimum set of central places.
2 *The transport principle: k* = 4. There, the distribution is such that as many places as possible lie on main transport routes connecting the higher order centres.
3 *The administrative principle: k* = 7. Efficient administration is the control in this case and this will demand a clear separation of all complementary regions for they cannot be shared administratively.

However, these three principles of arrangement do little to offset the major problem. Christaller presents no argument to justify giving every good the same threshold and range, or a multiple of these basic measures, so that although his theoretical framework is sustained by these means its relation to reality is made more remote.

Much detail has been omitted, yet the preceding paragraphs give the core of Christaller's ideas. In a situation not without precedent, another worker was arriving at similar conclusions virtually at the same time. This was August Lösch whose *Economics of location* was first published in 1939.[10] Lösch was concerned with the central problem of the location of economic activity and particularly with the creation of economic regions. His emphasis was, therefore, like Christaller's on economic factors as against what he termed the 'natural' or 'political'; raw materials were to be equally dispersed over a flat plain characterized by a pattern of self-sufficient farms equally spaced in the densest possible manner. Spatial differences would emerge from this postulated initial situation owing to the forces of concentration brought into play by the possibility of specialization and of the operation of economies of scale, although there would be limiting forces in the form of transport costs and the benefits of diversified production.[11] Lösch outlined the situation of one of the farmers who set out to produce beer, a secondary productive activity, it should be noted, and not a tertiary service. The size of his market can be determined from the relations implicit in the normal individual demand curve (figure 4−7).

If *OP* is the brewery price, the individual will buy *PQ*. But away from the centre of production, *P*, the priced will increase due to transport costs until at *F* beer is so expensive that it cannot be sold. *PF* is the extreme range and total sales will be the volume of the cone, formed by rotating *PFQ* around *P*, multiplied by a factor representing population density. So far a constant price has been assumed, *OP*, but that price will vary with the total sold, that is with the economies of scale that can be introduced as production increases. A new curve, therefore, is drawn based on the volume of the demand cone calculated for a series of arbitrary prices, that is, it represents total demand as a function of brewery price (△, △′). On this is

[10] A. Lösch (1954): *The economics of location* (New Haven). This is an English translation by W. H. Woglom. The German edition first appeared in 1939.
[11] A. Lösch (1954), 105.

Figure 4–7: Lösch's derivation of the market area and demand cone from the demand curve for a product as a function of distance. For explanation see text. *After A. Lösch (1954).*

superimposed a planning curve, the smallest average cost at which any amount can be produced (π). These must intersect before any beer can be sold, for if they do not, the costs of production exceed the price which sufficient people will pay. On the graph (figure 4–8), MN will be the total that can be sold and MF the maximum shipping distance, that is the range over which beer can be sold. But the output of the brewery can be reduced and production still be profitable until the two curves are tangential (see broken line on figure 4–8). Thus M_1F is a measure of the minimal area needed before beer can be produced and if this be multiplied by a factor representing population density, then the minimum number of people required to sustain the brewery is obtained. To translate this into terms already used, this is the 'threshold population'.

It will be apparent that we are here very close to Christaller. MF is the upper limit and M_1F the lower as defined above. The two authors have similar fundamental ideas but they have couched them in different arguments.

Lösch proceeds to demonstrate that his analysis will result in a series of

Figure 4–8: Demand curves (l) – quantity demanded as a function of price – and Planning curve (p) – smallest average cost related to quantity produced. For explanation see text. *After A. Lösch (1954).*

circular market areas but in order to cover the territory most economically these are converted into hexagons and a proof provided that this is justifiable. The hexagonal structure is dependent on the number of farms required to institute the production of a commodity and this number will vary considerably from commodity to commodity. Lösch, unlike Christaller, allows for this fact and adapts it into his structure. Given the closest packed distribution of farms and hexagonal market areas the smallest number of farms which can be served is three as in figure 4−5. This is the minimum threshold and thereafter the succession continues through four and seven (figure 4−5). This is in accord with the argument developed by Christaller, but Lösch continues the logic of this procedure for there is a whole series of succeeding arrangements out of which Christaller only isolated the three smallest cases. The whole series continues 3.4.7. 9.12.13.16. etc. Lösch proceeds to consider the *ten* smallest areas and tabulates the relations between them (figure 4−9 and table 4−2).

Figure 4−9: The ten smallest possible market areas. *After A. Lösch (1954).*

table 4–2: The ten smallest possible market areas.

Area no.	No. of settlements completely supplied	Distance between centres	Range
1	3	$a\sqrt{3}$	a
2	4	$a\sqrt{4}$	a
3	7	$a\sqrt{7}$	a
4	9	$a\sqrt{9}$	$a\sqrt{3}$
5	12	$a\sqrt{12}$	2a
6	13	$a\sqrt{13}$	$a\sqrt{3}$
7	16	$a\sqrt{16}$	2a
8	19	$a\sqrt{19}$	2a
9	21	$a\sqrt{21}$	$a\sqrt{7}$
10	25	$a\sqrt{25}$	$a\sqrt{7}$

As intimated earlier, every good sold, every service offered will have a different lower and upper limit, a different threshold and range and indeed, could be offered at a variety of different points. There is no reason therefore why a chaos of different meshes should not occur thrown over the supposed uniform plain. Some order can be introduced by arbitrarily centering all the meshes on one point, which is *ipso facto* made the metropolis. Further, by rotating the various nets about this point city rich and city poor sectors can be produced with a maximum degree of coincidence. But it must be emphasized that only by excessive and unreal simplification, so that a uniform structure is presupposed with a fixed k, can Christaller's model be derived. Under Lösch scheme a hierarchy *in the strictest sense of the term*, that is with an equal and regular addition of the number of subsidiary places served, does not emerge. But distinctive groupings of the subsidiary places can be found and hence distinctive ranks identified. The confusion here is possibly semantic but clear comprehension is essential if empirical studies are to be properly conducted and interpreted. 'To conclude, therefore, it must be admitted that whilst the functional array of services does fall into distinct groupings in all cases, it is only when a fixed k is assumed that a strict hierarchy in the Christaller sense is obtained.'[12].

At this stage, it is appropriate to introduce another interpretation of city size: this is the Rank-Size Rule for Cities. The basis of the 'rule' was originally put forward by Felix Auerbach in 1913,[13] but its development and popularization is associated with George K. Zipf[14] in a volume published in 1941 and entitled *National unity and disunity*. In loose terms the 'rule' states that if the population of a town is multiplied by its rank, then this will equal the population of the largest and highest ranked city. It is often stated as

$$R^n S_R = M$$

where R = the Rank of a city, S_R = the Population of a city of rank R, and M and n are constants.

[12] W. K. D. Davies (1964): *The hierarchy of commercial centres; a case study in South Wales*, 2 – 10 (University of Wales: unpublished Ph.D. thesis).

[13] F. Auerbach (1913): Das Gesetz der Bevolkerungskonzentration. *Petermanns Mitt*, **59**, 74.

[14] G. W. Zipf (1941): *National unity and disunity* (Bloomington, Ill.).

But where R is 1, whatever the value of n, S equals M so that the constant M is the population of the largest city. It is also less reliably argued that in western industrial countries the constant n is equal to unity so that the descriptive version given above holds good (figure 4−10).[15]

Superficially the rank-size rule seems to contrast with the conclusions of Christaller and Lösch in nearly every aspect. It is supposedly an observed fact, and not a deductive model. It is true that Zipf saw it as part of a broader theory in which any economy was subject to two forces. The one moved towards diversification where a large number of communities benefited from being located near to raw material sources and minimized transport-costs. The other force was one of unification where a small number of large communities minimized movement of finished goods to the consumer. From these opposing conditions a balance emerged which was reflected in the rank-size rule.

It is apparent at a superficial level that if the rank-size relationship implied in the rule is accepted as an accurate finding, then it completely contradicts the hierarchical situation derived from deductive argument. Christaller postulated a stepped and ranked distribution of size classes; Zipf's finding shows a smooth relation where no distinctive classes can be identified. Insofar as Zipf's work is empirical then its introduction into this chapter concerned with model building is perhaps, unjustified, but the rank-size rule has become such a well-known statement that its conflict with Christaller's ideas needs to be noted. But the conflict has been considerably exaggerated and, at this stage, there is no need to accept the view that the rank-size rule undermines the idea of a hierarchy.

Attempts have been made to show that the two concepts are not incompatible[16] even when applied to the same data and indeed, the very meaning of the word 'hierarchy' needs clear and precise definition in this context. This has not gone without challenge[17] but there are more cogent and simpler bases for no undue disturbance being generated by the introduction of Zipf's work. The factual truth of the Rule has been challenged and certainly, it has been shown that it applies only to large areas.[18] It measures size by population totals and not centrality as envisaged by Christaller and in consequence, it embraces not only central place functions but special functions as well, those special functions which need to be examined separately from central place functions as the last chapter demonstrated. When *all* urban functions are massed together then it is perfectly possible that the wide range of other functions, over and above central place functions, can transform a ranked hierarchial array into a continuous rank-size relation. The empirically observed rank-size rule need not therefore deter us as this stage from

[15] B. J. L. Berry (1961): City size distributions and economic development. *Economic Development and Cultural Change* **9**, 573 − 88. See also the same author's (1971) Urbanization and national development (New York).

[16] B. J. L. Berry and W. L. Garrison (1958): Alternate explanations of urban rank-size relationships. *Ann. Assoc. Am. Geogr.* **48**, 83.

[17] M. F. Dacey (1966): Population of places in a central place hierarchy. *J. Reg. Sci.* **6**(2), 27.

[18] Charles T. Stewart (1958): The size and spacing of cities. *Geogr. Rev.* **48**, 222.

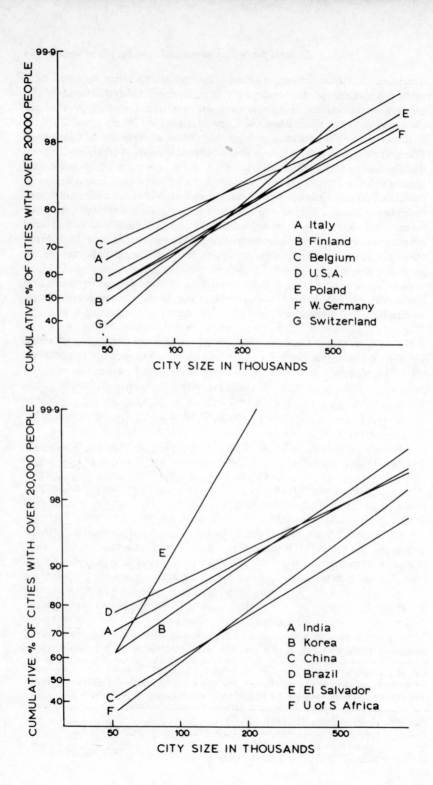

accepting the theoretical constructs of Christaller and Lösch.[19]

At this stage some brief review of the argument is needed. Models of the distribution of central places have been deduced and these hold good under the condition that special functions are excluded, or severely limited, and that service for a contiguous surrounding area is assumed as the sole urban role and that the earth's surface is a flat, homogeneous plain with an even distribution of resources and population. That empirical study, or indeed 'common sense', might show no such pattern as that envisaged in theory to exist is of no consequence. The point at issue is whether these models are logical constructions which, although isolating only a limited number of factors operative on town distribution and postulating unreal conditions, nevertheless give insight into the nature of town distribution. Moreover, these concepts point in the right direction for they demonstrate the search for unified principles rather than continue the description of individual towns. They connect what had hitherto been isolated fact and they lead to further experimental observation by indicating the most pertinent questions we can ask.

The clearest exposition of the implications of a Christaller type hierarchy has been given by John Marshall.[20] He argues that the diagnostic criteria of hierarchical structuring are:

1 *Spatial interdependence of the centres.* This means that there is a network of relationships between the centres represented by physical flows of goods and people. This network focuses on the hierarchically superior town.
2 *Functional wholeness of the system.* This is perhaps the most important criterion. It implies that any abstraction from the real world for study must consist of a 'whole' system. To an extent this is an impossibility since no system is discrete in an absolute sense but certainly the consideration of arbitrarily defined tracts of territory makes no sense in central place terms.
3 *Discrete stratification of centres.* This needs little comment. Stratification has to be demonstrated in objective terms.
4 *Interstitial placement of orders.* This is a spatial requirement in accord with Christaller's notion that lower order towns will occur at intermediate places between the next superior order towns. Whereas this is a conditional of the spatial arrangement, it is difficult to see why it should

[19] B. J. L. Berry (1967): Modern theoretical departures; chapter 4 of *Geography of market centres and retail distribution* (Englewood Cliffs, NJ). This chapter, which is concerned with mathematical formulation of central place theory, forms an appropriate continuation to the argument presented here.

[20] J. U. Marshall (1969): *The location of service towns. An approach to the analysis of central place systems.* University of Toronto, Dept. of Geography, Research Pubs. (Toronto).

Figure 4–10: Countries with lognormal (rank-size) distributions of urban populations. The upper diagram consists of what are generally regarded as developed countries while the lower diagram shows that this condition is also found in countries generally regarded as underdeveloped. *After B. J. L. Berry (1961).*

necessarily be a condition of hierarchical structuring. Thus in a valley re-entrant into a thinly peopled highland mass town rank will increase down valley as successive streams of population meet. A hierarchical structure, dependent on threshold and range can emerge without this particular form of interstitial placement.

5   *Incremental baskets of goods.* This condition means that each rank can be distinguished by characteristic assemblages of goods, the thresholds of which mean they can only enter at a particular level.

6   *A minimum of three orders.*

7   *A numerical pyramid in order membership.* These last two are self-evident.

At the same time there are many difficulties which have already arisen in considering the central place model:

1   Christaller's presentation clearly involved excessive simplification and the concept of market, transport and administrative systems appears as an unconvincing attempt to sidestep the difficulties which accumulate about this simple model. The adoption of Lösch's approach seriously modifies the notion of a clear-cut, unequivocal hierarchy.

2   At least two other ways of ordering towns in a system have been propounded from an inductive, empirical basis and there appears a marked unconformity between these observations and theoretical models. These are:

a   Rank-size distribution.
b   Primate city distribution.

The rank-size relationship has already been discussed (p. 70) but the notion of the primate city needs brief comment. It was formulated by Mark Jefferson as long ago as 1939 in a paper entitled '*The Law of the Primate City*'.[21] Jefferson propounded the view that 'the largest city shall be super-eminent and not merely in size, but in national influence'. On an intuitive level this type of dominance of the whole economic cultural and political scene by one city is associated with what is sometimes called 'The Great Tradition' or with a 'primary ortho-genetic city' where all these definitions refer to a situation where the peoples who made up the pre-civilized folk matrix more or less shared a common culture which was the matrix of the urban culture which developed from it.[22]

This situation has clearly perplexed research workers on central place theory. Not only was there the problem of the way in which such a city system as envisaged by central place theory had emerged, if the concept has any meaning other than as a purely static and unreal postulate, but further, an observed and contrasted situation was proposed in the dominance of the primate city. Berry turned to this problem in a

[21]   M. Jefferson (1939): The law of the primate city. *Geogr. Rev.*, **29**, 227.

[22]   M. Jefferson (1939). See also, Clyde E. Browning (1962): Primate cities and related concepts, in F. R. Pitts ed. (1962): Urban systems and economic development (Eugene, Oregan), 16.

statistical exercise in which he measured economic development on a multivariate basis, and concluded that 'primacy as measured by the importance of a single primate city tends to decline as one ascends the development scale, and as the size of the country increases.'[23] These ideas lead directly to the situation postulated by Hoselitz, who maintained that 'a comparative analysis of central places might show . . . the degree to which a rationalized western system of economic organization and activity had penetrated a given country and might be a fairly good measure of the breadth on which the economic development of a country has taken place.'[24] And again Hoselitz writes, 'The development of a given system of cities is related to processes of economic growth . . . such a theory is as yet non-existent but it is possible that further study and refinement might lead to one.'[25] The same idea is implicit in Berry's study of urban development in the Ashanti area of Ghana[26] although nowhere does a detailed study of the processes of development precisely depict the stages of change.

Linsky devoted a paper to testing a set of hypotheses concerning primate cities[27] but apart from a strong negative relation with areal extent of dense population, the degree of association with the other variables 'was disappointingly small'. He concluded that the 'concept of development (of primacy) implies an historical process. It suggests the need for studies systematically relating changes in degree of primacy with changes in the social, economic and geopolitical conditions within countries.'[28]

It is apparent that little progress has been made towards explanatory generalization in this area of investigation, possibly because open enquiry is hampered by the necessity of deploying a central place scheme at one end of economic development and a primate city scheme at the other, in spite of the fact that analyses have shown this to be inappropriate.

3   The brief venture into the discussion of change underlines the extent to which the approach through the models of Christaller and Lösch is a static one. Christaller, it is true does consider 'dynamic factors' but there is but little opportunity in his approach to encompass the obvious known facts of town growth and decay.

There are further problems but these can best be introduced in the next stage of analysis when empirical verification for central place notions is sought. Verification involves the development of techniques for the ranking of towns and the identification of spheres of influence. These form the next area for consideration.

[23] B. J. L. Berry (1962): Some relations of urbanization and basic patterns of economic development, in F. R. Pitts ed. (1962), 12.
[24] B. Hoselitz (1955): Generative and parasitic cities. *Econ. Devel. and Cult. Change*, 3, 278.
[25] B. Hoselitz (1955), 278.
[26] B. J. L. Berry (1962): Urban growth and the economic development of Ashanti, in F. R. Pitts ed. (1962), 53.
[27] A. S. Linsky (1965): Some generalization concerning primate cities. *Ann. Assoc. Amer. Geogr.*, 55, 506.
[28] A. S. Linsky (1965), 511.

Notes on further reading

Christaller's work is now easily accessible in translation, and this and Lösch's contributions are the major works which should be read:

Christaller, W (1966): *Central places in southern Germany* (see footnote 1).

Lösch, A (1954): *The economics of location* (see footnote 10).

Two clear introductions to central place ideas are:

Berry, B. J. L. (1967): *Geography of market centres and retail distribution* (Englewood Cliffs, N. J.).

Marshall, J. U. (1969): *The location of service towns. An approach to the analysis of central place systems* (see footnote 20).

A detailed critique and reinterpretation is presented in:

Beavon, K. S. O. (1977): *Central place theory: a reinterpretation.* (London).

The bibliographies mentioned in the text are essential and should be consulted for some guidance into the large amount of literature on central place studies:

Andrews, H. F. (1970), Working notes and bibliography on central place studies, 1965–1969 (see footnote 2).

Berry, B. J. L. and Pred, A. (1961): Central place studies: a bibliography of theory and application (see footnote 2).

An interesting and valuable study of early ideas akin to Central Place Theory is to be found in:

Dawson, J. (1969): Some early theories of settlement location and size. *J. Tn. Plan Inst* **55**, 444.

A more advanced and very useful discussion of the 'theory of the distribution of city sizes' is to be found in:

Richardson, H. W. (1973): *The economics of urban size* (Farnborough), Chaps 11 and 12, 139–70.

A fascinating, if idiosyncratic, book on the notion of centrality is:

Bird, J. (1977): *Centrality and cities* (London).

A volume which contains general papers which reassess the contribution of Lösch and review central place theory is:

Funck, R. and Parr, J. B. (1978): *The analysis of regional structure: essays in honour of August Lösch.* Karlsruhe Papers in Regional Science.

A further general review volume in German is:

Heinritz, G. (1979): *Zentralität und Zentralen orle. Eine einführung* (Stuttgart).

A recent discussion of the rank-size rule is undertaken in:

Beguin, H. (1979): Urban hierarchy and the rank-size distribution. *Geogl. Anal.* **11**, 149–164.

Whilst the relationship between Christaller's and Lösch's constructs are considered in:

Marshal, J. U. (1977): Christallerian networks in the Löschian economic landscape. *Prof. Geog.* **29**, 153–59.

5

The Ranking of Towns and the Delimitation of Spheres of Influence

There have been a considerable number of empirical studies in which the central place model has been tested[1] in the real world but it has been shown that many of these must be of local and limited value[2] since:

1   In many cases there is no precise statement of what is being measured and in some, no attempt is made to formulate definitions of the terms used.
2   The methods of identifying town ranks vary considerably from study to study. This is partly a consequence of the varying availability of data but it precludes easy comparability.

1 Definition of terms

Even many of the statistically more sophisticated works often fail to define the terms adequately and waver between claiming to be studies of 'towns' and studies of certain aspects of towns, that is, of tertiary services. At the outset, therefore, what is being measured must be identified in three contexts.

a The aspect of the town as central place being studied

Attempts to measure centrality have been couched in different terms and at a number of different levels. Some have dealt exclusively with the functions the town performs for the tributary area as measured by physical establishments such as shops and offices; others have simply used size as measured by population totals. Christaller, although he later ascribed population ranges to his ranks of towns, initially differentiated between the 'centrality of a place' and the 'size of a town'[3] choosing the words deliberately and thereby introducing the terminology of central place theory. The importance but not the centrality of a town could be measured by its population. It is true that given the conditions of classical central place theory there is an absolute correlation between population and centrality but in the real world the large

---

[1] For a listing of these studies consult the bibliography in B. J. L. Berry and A. Pred (1961): Central place studies: a bibliography of theory and applications. *University of Pennsylvania, Regional Science Research Institute, Bibliographic Series* 1 (Supplement, 1965).
[2] W. K. D. Davies (1966): The ranking of service centres: a critical review. *Trans. Inst. Br. Geogr.* **40**, 51.
[3] W. Christaller (translated by W. C. Baskin, 1966) (1933): *Central places in southern Germany*, 17–18 (Englewood Cliffs, NJ).

range of non-central place functions adds to the population. This is universally recognized though it has not inhibited analyses based on population totals. In addition there is the further difficulty already discussed in chapter 2 of defining urban populations, for numbers can vary with the area taken.[4]

There is a further problem even if some more direct measure of service to the surrounding area is taken. Towns serve these areas as administrative and social centres as well as economic centres and there is no need whatsoever for these non-economic services to be located on an economic basis. Indeed in Britain, it is fairly evident that social services, such as hospitals and schools for example, could not be provided in thinly peopled rural areas at an economic level and they are subsidized by inputs from the central government. The examination of rate support grants[5] to local authorities will amply illustrate this point. It follows that two different principles based on the need for profitability in the one case and the provision of a needed social service on the other are operative. Stated in another way, one situation demands that the threshold value holds; the other does not, so that in this latter case the whole concept of economic threshold is rejected in favour of social need.

b   The unit of study adopted
There are three levels at least at which an investigation can be carried out:

1   *The towns.* This includes all the nominated services within the town area, using an administrative or census definition and including subsidiary shopping centres.

2   *The commercial core.* This concentrates on the central area but includes all commercial (i.e. economic) services such as offices and theatres as well as shops.

3   *The retail centre.* In this case the count of establishments is limited to retail shops in the central area or CBD which in turn poses problems of definition. Thus in their study in southwestern Iowa, Berry, Barnum and Tennant define a business district as 'a group of spatially contiguous establishments less than 300 feet from each other, and either separated from other establishments by more than 300 feet or if in a continuous shoestring of business, falling into "peaks" or "ribbons" of land values'.[6]

c   The level of generalization at which the study is being made
Here again a series of levels can be recognized and this difficulty can be

---

[4] See page 20 *et seq*.

[5] These are the grants made by the central exchequer to supplement local finances derived from local sources. For an example of the extent of these grants see. P. R. Mounfield and H. D. Watts (1968): Mid-Wales: prospects and policies for a problem area; chapter 11 in E. G. Bowen, H. Carter and J. A. Taylor, editors, *Geography at Aberystwyth* (Cardiff). Fig. xi–2(a) is a map of the proportion of expenditure met by rate deficiency grants in England and Wales. These are now called 'Rate Support Grants'.

[6] B. J. L. Berry, H. G. Barnum and R. J. Tennant (1964): Retail location and consumer behaviour. *Pap. Reg. Sci. Assoc.* **9**, 68.

equated with that of weighting for size of a facility or establishment by number of employees, size by floor space or some other measure. In retail trade these problems emerge more clearly and it is possible to conduct a count on the following bases.[7]

1 *Establishments*. In this case one shop is taken at its elementary value and counted as a single unit. It is in this form that most census data are available.

2 *Functions*. Here each type of outlet is counted regardless of the association in establishments.

3 *Functional units*. This would imply a count of the total number of outlets regardless of type.

An example may clarify these possibilities.[8] There are three shops *A*, *B* and *C*. *A* is a grocer, greengrocer and off-licence wine and spirit retailer; *B* is a greengrocer and fishmonger; *C* is a grocer and butcher. Thus a count would reveal three establishments (*A*, *B* and *C*), five functions (grocer, greengrocer, off-licence wines and spirits, fishmonger, butcher) and seven functional units (two groceries, two greengroceries, and one each fishmonger, wines and spirits, butcher).

If the example quoted is referred to all three units of study then it will be seen that one person making a field survey in which retail functional units in the retail centre of a town are being surveyed will be working on very different figures from someone using the administrative area of the town and counting all retail, service, social and administrative establishments. Above all, elaborate and sophisticated methods of statistical analysis are of little value if imprecise and ill-considered data are employed.

2 Methods of ranking towns

In chapter 3 it was shown that classification of towns by functional character has become more objective as methods were refined. This is also true of attempts at town ranking. In this case, however, the early purely descriptive stage does not exist, other than in the use of size classes of towns, and it is possible to recognize two major phases, the first in which subjective identification dominated and a second in which objective, statistical investigation of the hierarchy was introduced. A further problem exists in that direction of emphasis has stressed now the internal characteristics of the town, now its external relations.

The earliest attempts at the empirical identification of the hierarchy of towns which Christaller's logic proposed were based on the *a priori* assumption that a distinctive ranking could be found. This was based upon the analyst's perception that such an ordering existed and the task was not to provide the means by which the existence of a hierarchy could be tested but rather the basis for the identification of ranks of towns which were assumed to exist. There are many examples of this type of analysis but perhaps the

[7] H. A. Stafford (1963): The functional basis of small towns. *Econ. Geogr.* **38**, 165.

[8] W. K. D. Davies (1966), 52.

most widely known and quoted are those of A. E. Smailes in Britain[9] and J. E. Brush in the United States.[10]

Smailes worked on the basis that 'any grading must in some measure be arbitrary . . . yet the indefiniteness of boundaries does not warrant denial of the reality of stratification.'[11] He was intuitively aware of the existence in Britain of what he called 'the fully fledged town' which was identified as a distinctive stratum in the settlement pattern. Moreover, he also argued that this level was characterized by the occurrence together of certain key features which made up a 'trait complex'. This was made up of:

	A	Branches of three of the five major banks together with a Woolworth's store
diminishing to	A^1	three branch banks
and	A^{11}	two branch banks
	B	Grammar school and hospital
diminishing to	B^1	only one of the above
	C	Cinemas
diminishing to	C^1	only one cinema
	D	Publication of a local newspaper

The complete 'trait complex' derived from the above was $ABCD$ but Smailes accepted as the minimum qualifications for this level $A^1B^1C^1D$ or A^1BC. 'Sub-towns' which did not meet these requirements were identified and, by using additional criteria, major towns, cities and major cities were introduced to give a complete ranking of the urban settlements of England and Wales.[12]

There is an immediate methodological comparison between this attempt to rank towns and that by Chauncy D. Harris to classify them referred to in a previous chapter.[13] Both procedures were descriptive but both employed a numerical element to give a validity to the categories that were identified by the insight and experience of the classifier. Smailes's scheme was equally important in that it brought the notion of central place before a wide geographical field and that was a first approximation to a ranking scheme. Moreover it had a certain element of balance in that retail and commercial activities were represented by Woolworth's and the banks, social services by schools and hospitals, entertainment by the cinema and regional association by the local newspaper.

But it was also weak on a number of vital points. The grounds on which the criteria were selected were nowhere made explicit and the choice can only be interpreted as arbitrary. Even with this arbitrary basis no attempt is made to justify the definition of the grades; again, it is not demonstrated that they emerge from the data used. 'The symbols of urbanism' may 'hang

---

[9] A. E. Smailes (1944): The urban hierarchy of England and Wales. *Geogr.* **29,** 41.
[10] J. E. Brush (1953): The hierarchy of central places in southwestern Wisconsin. *Geogr. Rev.* **XL,** 380.
[11] A. E. Smailes (1944).
[12] A. E. Smailes (1946): The urban mesh of England and Wales. *Trans. Inst. Br. Geogr.* 87.
[13] See page 41.

together in a trait complex' but there is no proof of this other than the author's assertion. Lastly, the large scale on which this ranking was applied (the whole of England and Wales) meant that a large variety of situations was being forced into the mould of the scheme and many of the real difficulties were avoided in this process.

These criticisms were equally applicable to a similar study by John E. Brush of 'The hierarchy of central places in southwestern Wisconsin'.[14] Brush maintained that the status of trade centres was determined by the functions they perform, by the combination or association of distinctive sets of functional units (i.e. a trait complex) and he then proposes that although clear-cut breaks cannot be recognized, nevertheless 'a threefold classification becomes apparent — hamlets, villages and towns.'[15] This classification is then demonstrated by reference to the presence or absence of key establishments related to a range of central functions: retail trade, wholesale trade, finance, trade and personal service, amusements, transportation, communication, utilities, manufacturing, professional services and government. There are clear parallels with Smailes's procedures both in their strength and weaknesses and also an indication of the direction of future work. Many interested in the concept of town rank were fully aware of the technical drawbacks to the work of Smailes and Brush and accordingly a series of schemes were advanced to offset them.

a The inclusion of all city facilities rather than an arbitrary selection
This is implicit in the very extended list of facilities used by Brush but the attempt to be totally inclusive presented great difficulties in terms of data collection. At the same time problems of equivalence presented themselves for in any unweighted count of retail facilities a large central jeweller could be equated with a corner newspaper shop as just one retail establishment. Floor space and turnover which can be used for weighting are rarely available in the detailed form that would make them valuable.[16] The compacting of shops into groups, as for example 'convenience goods' and 'shopping goods' can offset this to some extent, but again a series of arbitrary decisions has to be made in the process.

b More rigorous procedures in the identification of ranks
The first stage was that the identification of ranks was made more objective by the awarding of points for certain facilities present so that a score was obtained for each town. These scores were then analyzed to identify groupings that might occur. However, in most cases the groupings were defined arbitrarily with little attempt being made to identify linkages or to compare in-group or between-group distances.

The main exception to this was the work of Mauri Palomäki[17] in the South

[14] J. E. Brush (1953).
[15] J. E. Brush (1953), 385.
[16] W. K. D. Davies (1967): Centrality and the central place hierarchy. *Urb. Stud.* **4**, 63.
[17] M. Palomäki (1964): The functional centres and areas of South Bothnia, Finland. *Fennia* **83**, 1.

Bothnian area of Finland. Centrality was measured in two ways. The first was in *quantitative* terms 'simply on the basis of the number of types of central function occurring in' the towns.[18] For this, the totality of functions was broken down into separate elements, thus administrative, wholesale, retail, medical and public health activities were examined separately. For each, number of functions per settlement was plotted against each settlement and by inspection groupings were identified; these are called indicator groups. 'The internal uniformity of the indicator groups is estimated by calculating the standard deviation and the variation coefficient, first within the group from its mean value and then from the mean of the indicators left in between the means of consecutive groups.'[19]

In *qualitative* terms an attempt is made to determine the extent to which central functions belong to the same indicator group by computing coefficients of common occurrence.[20] The degree of correlation between the occurrence of functions is used not to show the interdependence of pairs of functions but rather 'the dependence of various institutions on the abstract centrality of central places'.[21] Thus, for example, in medical and public health activities, the indicators of the second class of centre are:

Physician	communal home	$= +0.75$
	dentist	$= +0.82$
	health clinic	$= +0.66$
	veterinarian	$= +0.73$
	local hospital	$= +0.62$

where the correlation with the typical central function (physician) is given.[22] From this the lower correlates, the clinic and the hospital, are dropped and the remainder taken as diagnostic.

After this procedure has been followed for each activity, the results are combined in a 'partial synthesis' from which a final ranking is derived. Palomäki's work is interesting in that his indicators are very similar to Smailes's 'trait complex' but they are derived for a series of grades not merely for a preconceived fully-fledged town. At the same time the analysis is much wider ranging and a real effort is made to examine critically both in-group nearness and between-group distance. But from the brief outline it will be evident that, throughout, a number of subjective decisions are made which determine the result.

In 1958 Berry and Garrison prefaced an examination of the functional bases of the central place hierarchy with the statement that 'there has been no satisfactory evidence provided that would suggest that a hierarchical class-system of centres does indeed exist'[23] and in the light of the foregoing

---

[18] M. Palomäki (1964), 21.
[19] M. Palomäki (1964), 47.
[20] M. Palomäki (1964), 21. This is the standard correlation coefficient.
[21] M. Palomäki (1964), 21.
[22] M. Palomäki (1964), 110.
[23] B. J. L. Berry and W. L. Garrison (1958): Functional bases of the central place hierarchy. *Econ. Geogr.* **34**, 145.

consideration this was an appropriate comment. They therefore set out to conduct a rigorous test for the ranking of towns in Snohomish County, Washington. All the central place functions were considered which could be identified, though they were dominantly commercial in character. These were divided into variates, of which there could be more than one in each centre, and attributes where by definition, there *could* only be one e.g. public library. Each of the variates was analyzed by means of a scatter diagram of number of shops against population. Best fitting exponential curves were fitted to each diagram so that it was possible to identify the population necessary for each type of shop to appear. In the terms of the last chapter, the threshold populations were identified. These threshold populations were then tested for randomness by a χ^2 test and shown to be more even than random. Then, using the criterion that every member of a group should be closer to some other member than to any other outside the group, three groups of functions were identified. The attributes were analyzed by calculating correlations with population totals of the centres in which they were found and then ranking them in ascending order of these coefficients. Test of significant differences between these coefficients revealed that all but one fell into three groupings. Finally the two sets of threefold groupings were shown to be associated so producing three classes of central place.

Berry and Garrison claim that their method is capable of being reproduced in other areas and at levels of the central place hierarchy other than the universe of small centres considered. But difficulties arise if this is attempted.

The use of centre population rather than tributary area population will only work in a rural area where there are no disturbing elements. The thresholds identified are not *real* thresholds in any sense since the populations of the surrounding rural areas are excluded. It would be difficult to envisage this method being applied to a heavily industrialized area for the central place equipment of a settlement is related to the total tributary population, not the population of the centre itself and in an area where the population is distributed unevenly between the two at different places then real problems will arise. As it is, and even in this selected area, the paper ends with explanation of some marked deviants because of such difficulties. Likewise where large towns are involved, the simple enumeration of stores becomes a large task and problems associated with what is being counted occur; this is the establishment-unit-outlet dilemma which has already been outlined. Berry and Garrison's work in Snohomish County was of real importance in that for the first time a rigorous, objective analysis of well defined data showed that distinctive hierarchical levels did occur. But the extension of this method to other areas presented problems which meant that little duplication has taken place to provide a series of comparative studies.

Subsequent refinement of techniques has, in this sphere, as in that of functional classification, involved the use of multivariate techniques.[24] A

---

[24] See B. J. L. Berry, H. G. Barnum and R. J. Tennant (1964). Also B. J. L. Berry and H. G. Barnum (1962): Aggregate relations and elemental components of central place systems. *J. Reg. Sci.* **4**, 35.

good example is the work of Abiodun on Nigeria.[25] She includes all settlements in her study, not a preconceived selection which has been designated urban. These are assembled into an array of settlements against numbérs of central functions, which are arbitrarily weighted, and this is converted into a correlation matrix of the occurrence of each of the functions against all the others where 1 is self correlation or complete correlation and 0 mutual independence. From this, and by means of high correlation, the elements of a 'trait complex' could be identified by abstracting those functions highly correlated. In order to examine whether such parsimony is possible this matrix is then subjected to a principal component analysis in which the first component accounts for 52·735 per cent of the variation and the second 15·279 per cent, so that some 68 per cent of the variation is accounted for by the first two components.

The very real problem in this sort of analysis is however to interpret the derived component in terms of the original variables. In this case there is no simple solution since none of the variables loads strongly on the first component which is consequently interpreted as giving weight to the overall general importance of settlements. The second component gives greatest weight to economic and administrative functions. The process is continued by the abstraction of successive components which are then used as a basis for grouping.

One of the most valuable aspects of component analysis is that it is possible to obtain assessments of each of the original units of measurement, i.e. the settlements, on scales of scores for each of the derived components. To these an objective grouping procedure is adopted which purports to measure 'functional distance' between settlements or, in different terminology, to identify a hierarchy, if it exists. It is not clear whether the number of groups was derived from the data or predetermined,[26] for the significant statement is made: 'a good knowledge of the area under study greatly facilitates such an identification.'[27] One wonders why this is so if all the procedures are impersonal; such a statement could well have been written into Smailes's 1946 paper. Mrs. Abiodun eventually identifies five distinct levels of settlement in her study and therefore supports the concept that towns are sorted into distinct grades by the way in which they serve the surrounding area.

It is not improper at this stage to question whether the application of these complex procedures, possible only with the use of modern high speed computers, is fully justified. However collected, the data tend to be crude and very variable in form. Thus Abiodun writes, 'the data on urban retail shops are not available and are very difficult to collect . . . the distribution of representative retail company stores has been used.'[28] Thus not only are the data preselected but the use of the word 'representative' emphasizes the point — by whom are these thought to be representative and on what grounds? Again an arbitrary weighting device for the services used in the study is introduced to be a measure of quality rather than quantity (see Palomäki, page 82). It is argued that there is no reason, with or without this, 'why the same order of hierarchy should not reproduce . . . the choice of a measure will however affect the ease with which groups of the hierarchy are identified.'[29] This immediately indicates that a hierarchy is to be derived and will be better defined if such a device is used; we are back to the arbitrary subjective decision for which Smailes was criticized in 1946.

Given the consistent problem of subjective decision there is much to be said for a simple but effective measure such as that used by Davies in South Wales.[30] A location coefficient of a single outlet of any functional type was determined by the formula:

$$C = \frac{t}{T} \, 100$$

where C was the location coefficient of function t, t was one outlet of function t and T was the total number of outlets of t in the whole system. 'Multiplication of the relevant location coefficient by the number of outlets of each functional type present in a settlement gives the degree of centrality (centrality value) imparted to each settlement for every different type of function. A functional index is derived by the addition of all the centrality values attained by any settlement.'[31] Thus if there are 200 grocers in the area examined, the location coefficient is:

$$C = \frac{1}{200} \times \frac{100}{1} = 0 \cdot 5$$

If there are 23 grocers in settlement A then the centrality value for this function in the settlement is $0 \cdot 5 \times 23$ or $11 \cdot 5$. If there are only two large department stores in the area then $C = 50 \cdot 0$ and if one of these is in A then the centrality value contributed is $50 \cdot 0$. The total of the centrality values, that is $11 \cdot 5 + 50 \cdot 0 + n$, gives the functional index which is used as the basis for ranking.

A weighting for numbers of employees or floor space can be introduced to allow for variation in size of outlet. This process is fairly simple and gives the basis for an effective study of grouping. Its main drawback is that it presupposes a closed system which is clearly not the case, not even where it is used in a South Wales mining valley, where owing to physical conditions there is a high degree of isolation.

While attempts at identifying the hierarchy of towns through their establishment or facilities were becoming increasingly sophisticated, a similar process was characteristic of attempts to examine the ranking of towns not by direct but by 'indirect' means. If the status of a town were a reflection of its dominance over the surrounding area, then it could be argued that the degree of dominance could best be measured by some assessment of the

[29] J. C. Abiodun (1967), 354.
[30] W. K. D. Davies (1967) Centrality and the central place hierarchy. *Urb. Stud.* **4**, 61.
[31] W. K. D. Davies (1967), 63.

strength of the area-town link. Indeed, Christaller adopted this interpretation in his measure of centrality:[32]

$$Z_z = T_z - E_z \; \frac{T_g}{E_g}$$

where T_z = number of telephones in the central place; E_z = population of the central place; T_g = number of telephones in region; E_g = population of region. So that $T_g:E_g$ is the ratio of telephones to population in the region which, multiplied by the population of the central place, gives an expected total if the distribution of telephones was even. This subtracted from the actual central place total gives a measure of centrality (Z_z) which is the relative concentration of telephones in the central place. It is true that Christaller used the physical presence of an instrument and not the number and direction of calls, so that he was measuring a ratio of appliances rather than communication flows but it was an apt choice at an early period and one when the telephone was not as ubiquitous as it is at the present time.

The concept of flows between town and country had been at the core of the earlier pre-Christaller work of Galpin[33] and Kolb[34] but it was taken up mainly by Green[35] and Carruthers[36] in Britain. In the first instance, it was mainly concerned with defining spheres of influence[37] but subsequently Carruthers produced a ranking of towns based on the operation of motorbus services. It was argued that 'bus traffic is especially useful as a means of giving some indication of the nodality of any centre. The bus operators have discovered "by a process of trial and error where the majority of persons wish to make the majority of journeys".'[38] A diagram was constructed of 'total number of buses on market days or Saturdays' entering a centre against 'percentage of those buses serving smaller places exclusively'. Towns were located on this and a classification into grades developed by inspection.

This was a crude and unsophisticated method but it was a precursor of the present interest in graph theory as a means of ranking centres. This has been developed by Nystuen and Dacey[39] who argue that 'a hierarchy of cities may be reduced to an abstract network of points and lines. The points represent the cities while the lines represent the functional associations. Though a myriad of lines exists in the network, there is present a basic structure of strongest associations which creates the nested nodal regions and the

[32] W. Christaller (1966), 143–50.

[33] C. J. Galpin (1915): The social anatomy of an agricultural community. *Univ. Wis. agric. Exp. Stat. Res. Bull.* **34**.

[34] H. J. Kolb (1923): Service relations of town and country. *Univ. Wis. agric. Exp. Stat. Res. Bull.* **58**.

[35] F. H. W. Green (1950): Urban hinterlands in England and Wales. *Geogr. J.* **116**.

[36] I. Carruthers (1957): A classification of service centres in England and Wales. *Geogr. J.* **123**, 371.

[37] See page 91.

[38] I. Carruthers (1957).

[39] J. D. Nystuen and M. F. Dacey (1961): A graph theory interpretation of nodal regions. *Pap. of Reg. Sci. Assoc.* **7**, 29.

hierarchy of cities.'[40] The basic principle is that 'functional association' may be measured by flows between centres (of people, or communications of any form). These can be assembled into a matrix as illustrated below in figure 5–1A, from which the nodal structure can be abstracted (figure 5–1B). This structure can be used to distinguish groups of cities that have maximum direct linkages and the rank order of these cities can be calculated.

The extension of graph theory to *indirect* associations involves further adjustments of the raw data matrix but once this is done, it is possible by these techniques to 'divide a set of cities into sub-groups which specify a central place and its subordinate hierarchy'.[41] The data most easily accessible and used in this context are telephonic communication data and this reversion to Christaller's original choice of data field is both interesting and significant. An example showing this worked out for Wales by Lewis and Davies[42] is illustrated in figure 5–2.

Matrix of number of messages between city-pairs
To City

		a	b	c	d	e	f	g	h	i	j	k	l
	a	0	**75**	15	20	28	2	3	2	1	20	1	0
	b*	69	0	45	50	58	12	20	3	6	35	4	2
	c	5	**51**	0	12	40	0	6	1	3	15	0	1
	d	19	**67**	14	0	30	7	6	2	11	18	5	1
	e*	7	40	48	26	0	7	10	2	37	39	12	6
From	f	1	6	1	1	10	0	**27**	1	3	4	2	0
City	g*	2	16	3	3	13	31	0	3	18	8	3	1
	h	0	4	0	1	3	3	6	0	12	**38**	4	0
	i	2	28	3	6	43	4	16	12	0	**98**	13	1
	j*	7	40	10	8	40	5	17	34	98	0	35	12
	k	1	8	2	1	18	0	6	5	12	**30**	0	15
	l	0	2	0	0	7	0	1	0	1	6	**12**	0

Column
Total 113 337 141 128 290 71 118 65 202 311 91 39
Largest flows bold. Largest flow determined by the number of out-going messages.

*Largest flow from these cities is to a 'smaller' city where 'size' is determined by the column totals.

Figure 5–1A: In the matrix of messages the total in-message flow, the column totals, is a measure of centrality and can be used to rank the centres. The rows indicate flows from centres. A centre is independent if its 'largest' flow is to a smaller centre. Using this property, and the principles of transitivity (if a city *a* is subordinate to a city *b* and *b* is subordinate to *c* then *a* is subordinate to *c*) and that a city cannot be subordinate to any of its subordinates, a graph can be constructed as below.

[40] J. D. Nystuen and M. F. Dacey (1961), 31.

[41] J. D. Nystuen and M. F. Dacey (1961), 41.

[42] W. K. D. Davies and C. R. Lewis (1970): Regional structures in Wales: two studies of connectivity; chapter 2 in H. Carter and W. K. D. Davies, editors (1970): *Urban essays: studies in the geography of Wales*, 22–48 (London). For a more detailed analyses see; D. Clark (1973a): Urban linkage and regional structure in Wales: an analyses of change 1958–68, *Trans. Inst. Brit. Geogrs.* 58, 41–58, and (1973b): The formal and functional structure of Wales, *Ann. Assoc. Amer. Geogrs.*, 63, 71–84.

Figure 5–1B: Graph of a nodal structure of a hypothetical region. *After J. D. Nystuen and M. F. Dacey (1961).*

It will be apparent from the foregoing discussion that nothing like consensus exists as to *the* method for examining whether a hierarchical structure exists and for the identification of city ranks. As with the analysis of town functions the use of component analysis has made a significant advance possible in objectivity and it would seem that for the moment in that area together with the use of graph theory, that most promise lies.

There are three perspectives from which the elements of urbanism can be viewed. The first of these is the static structure and, to a large extent, this has been the concern in this chapter, for a ranking of towns reveals a static structure of graded nodes. The third perspective, dynamic process will be described later in chapter 6. The second perspective is that of the connectivity of the parts or of the movements and flows of people and goods between the nodes which has already been partially introduced into the problem of ranking the nodes. This immediately leads to the notion of the 'field' within which these flows are taking place and so to the problem of what Christaller called the 'complementary region', but which is now usually termed the 'urban sphere of influence'.

Figure 5–2: The nodal structure of Wales from trunk telephone call data. *After C. R. Lewis, in Carter and Davies (1970).*
In this figure the ranks are based on the maximum outgoing calls, a centre being ranked above those centres which are subordinate and below the centre to which its calls are directed. Thus chains of call links can be traced from the lowest ranked centres, through the intermediaries to London. Aberystwyth, however, stands outside this linked system and is therefore ranked as a first order centre. This is a particularly interesting indication of the small discrete area on the west coast and confirms the anomalous ranking given to the town intuitively by Smailes in 1946. Compare the situation of centres e and g in figure 5–1B. The data are only for non-contiguous telephone areas in the Wales and Border region, so that cities outside the area are greatly under measured, only their links with Wales being included, e.g. Liverpool.

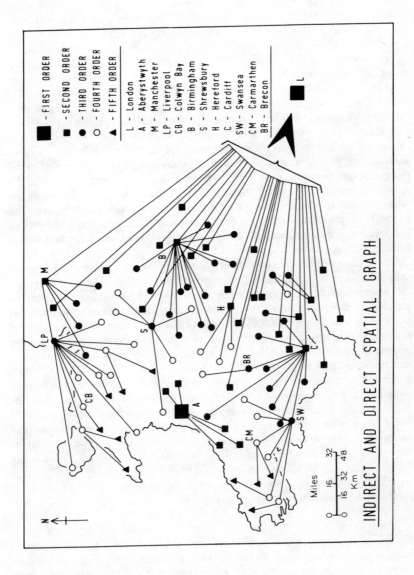

INDIRECT AND DIRECT SPATIAL GRAPH

■ – FIRST ORDER
■ – SECOND ORDER
● – THIRD ORDER
○ – FOURTH ORDER
▲ – FIFTH ORDER

L – London
A – Aberystwyth
M – Manchester
LP – Liverpool
CB – Colwyn Bay
B – Birmingham
S – Shrewsbury
H – Hereford
C – Cardiff
SW – Swansea
CM – Carmarthen
BR – Brecon

At this point it should be emphasized that no town has '*a*' sphere of influence for in reality every good and service offered will attract purchasers from different areas. The assumption is required that certain functions will become associated in distinctive complexes, each complex in turn associated with a fairly clearly marked grade or rank in the hierarchy, for the concept of a sphere of influence to become meaningful. Even so a town will have many spheres of influence, each corresponding to levels in the hierarchy at and below that of the level of the town concerned. In the characteristic American sequence of hamlet, village, town, the town will have its own sphere of influence together with the spheres where it functions at the lower level of village and hamlet.

All this is implicit in the theoretical discussion in chapter 4, but it does need repetition in the light of many studies which claim to delimit *the* sphere of influence of a town. No such thing exists without appropriate qualifications as to the level at which it is being considered. Some problems associated with central place theory and consumer behaviour will be considered in the next chapter, but it must be briefly noted here that the whole notion of the sphere of influence rests on the assumption that people will travel to the nearest place at which a good or service is available, whereas the increasing mobility of populations has made them much more footloose. Spheres of influence are generalizations of movement not neat, compact and determining bounds.

There have been two approaches to the identification of urban spheres of influence. The first has looked outward from the town in order to identify the various areas which are served by it. The second has looked inward from the countryside and has been more concerned with consumer behaviour and the way in which people use the various centres. Given the general trend of interest in central place studies toward consumer behaviour the second approach has become dominant, but a brief review of the earlier method can be considered first.

Early attempts at defining urban spheres of influence were closely associated with Smailes's 'trait complex' for if the elements of that complex defined a 'fully-fledged' (i.e. a particular rank or grade of) town, then the areal extent which those elements dominated, delimited the urban sphere of influence.[43] Moreover, if they were associated within the town then the areas over which they extended their influence should also coincide. 'It is usually found that the fields shown by various indices group themselves sufficiently to allow broad recognition of composite fields at a series of functional levels which correspond to the more clearly defined ranks of the urban hierarchy.'[44]

The procedure, therefore, was to plot the areas which the selected criteria covered, for example the area from which a bank drew its customers, a hospital its patients, a cinema its clients, a school its pupils and a local newspaper its readers. An example of this method is given in figure 5–3 where

---

[43] A. E. Smailes (1947): The analysis and delimitation of urban fields. *Geogr.* **32**.
[44] A. E. Smailes (1947), 151.

the boundaries of seven selected functions exercised from Aberystwyth are indicated. It would be meaningless to resolve these lines into *one* sphere by any such method as identifying a median between the maximum and minimum areas, for at least two spheres are identifiable, an inner intensively dominated one and an outer extensive sphere with a possible intermediary area between, indicating the town operating at three hierarchical levels.

This method was and is a quick and useful one but it is open to the same sorts of criticism as the selection of the indices for a 'trait complex'; the choice is arbitrary and often an ill-considered rag-bag of areas is assembled. It would be no easy task to justify the seven criteria chosen for the map of Aberystwyth and a selection of seven others might possibly present a very different picture. The resolution of all or some of the variations into one median line, to imply a sphere at a selected level, has no logical basis, for it quite unjustifiably assumes that a certain selection of lines has some form of real association, which in turn rests on the fact that they are related to the operation of a town at that level which has already been partly predetermined by the choice of criteria.

Since the sphere of influence is established about the town, one might well argue that the approach to its definition must be the reverse of that of ranking the town and, therefore, the attempt at defining the sphere from within the town is an indirect method. More profitable has been the second group of methods which have sought to identify areas within which movement to centres is taking place. Here the earliest methods were by examining the physical movement of vehicles, particularly buses.[45] A flow diagram of bus services produced a visual pattern of movement into (and out of) a centre and by inspection, a sphere of influence could be delimited. Apart from the fact that the private car now carries a large share of this movement, the crudity of the method meant that while quick and easy, it was not acceptable at a rigorous level of investigation.

Most contemporary work uses a method which is a variation on that introduced by Bracey in 1953.[46] A questionnaire is drawn up which aims to elicit the usual place at which a standard array of goods and services is obtained. Three difficulties immediately arise, all of which are implicit in the last sentence:

1   How is the sample of population to answer the questionnaire chosen?[47] There is little doubt that consumer behaviour will vary with such characteristics as income, social class, possession of a private car and place of work. Properly the sample should be stratified according to characteristics such as these, but since basic data are lacking it is seldom possible to do this in a systematic way, although questions as to

[45] F. H. W. Green (1950). See also S. Godlund (1956): Bus services in Sweden. *Lund Stud. Geogr. Series B: Human Geography* **17**.

[46] H. E. Bracey (1953): Towns as rural service centres. *Trans. Inst. Br. Geogr.* **19**, 95.

[47] For some comments on the construction of questionnaires in geography see S. R. Cowie (1968): Question construction for behavioural research; in IBG urban studies group: *Techniques in urban geography*, 1 (Salford conference).

1 ————————————
2 —·—·—·—·—·—
3 ×××××××××××
4 ············
5 —··—··—··—
6 —ı—ı—ı—ı—
7 —▾—▾—▾—▾—

Miles
0   3   6   9
0   3   6   9   12
Km

ABERYSTWYTH ●

B

Miles
1 0   3   6   9
1 0   3   6   9   12
km

97
119   133
116   126
133   144

ABERYSTWYTH ●

143   144   143
139   140
143
142   136   134   110
83   73
64   54   44   77   84   97
       13   18   32   25
26 15   6
8   3   4   10   10
     8   3   6
0   0   3   ● LAMPETER   1
0   0   1   0   1
0   0   2
0   2
0
0

ABERAERON ●

● TREGARON

occupation of household head and possession of a car and so on can be asked and used later as variables. The selection of respondents is usually, therefore, quite arbitrary, but with an attempt to obtain a fairly uniform ground coverage. Rowley[48] in a study in Wales obtained five completed questionnaires from each quarter kilometre grid square on the British Ordnance Survey map. If an adjustment to population is made, so that a given percentage sample is obtained, then the task is very great indeed, and also very monotonous. There are inherent problems in selecting respondents even from electoral registers or other lists and these are seldom overcome, except in very small scale studies where the behaviour of specific groups is the prime purpose.

2   How is the standard array of goods and services determined? C. R. Lewis[49] in a study of only the small towns of mid Wales identified 157 different functions. To put all these on a questionnaire, which is to be completed by large numbers of people, is not practicable and some selection *has* to be made. Rowley[50] in the study noted above used 20 goods and services, and attempted to range these over high order and low order categories. But whatever is done the selection remains subjective and arbitrary.

3   What is meant by 'usual place of purchase'? Attempts can be made to refine this by defining it as the place at which the largest expenditure was incurred over the period of a week or longer, or just the last place of purchase can be recorded. Again a measure of vagueness can creep in where the respondents are faced with providing an instant answer from recollected actions.

There is a solution to the last two difficulties and this is to have selected respondents keeping a complete account of the place and amount of all

[48] G. Rowley (1967): *The middle order towns of Wales* (University of Wales: Unpublished Ph.D. thesis).
[49] C. R. Lewis (1970): The central place patterns of mid-Wales and the middle Welsh borderland; chapter 10 in H. Carter and W. K. D. Davies, editors (1970), 228–68.
[50] G. Rowley (1967).

Figure 5–3: The urban sphere of influence of Aberystwyth as revealed **A:** by an arbitrary array of criteria and **B:** by questionnaire survey.

In the upper map the criteria are
1.   An Insurance Company's Office Area
2.   Baker's Delivery Area
3.   Agricultural Co-operative Delivery Area
4.   Bank Area
5.   School Catchment Area
6.   Postal District
7.   Veterinary Surgeon's Area

On the lower map of the area of maximum purchase for twelve goods and services was asked of twelve people randomly selected for each kilometre grid square of the British Ordnance Survey map. The replies nominating Aberystwyth were summed for each square and used as spot heights in drawing isopleths. Note that although the bases were very different there is a correspondence between the two maps.

purchases over a given period, a complete diary of expenditure. This solution increases the difficulties of selecting the sample to an enormous extent and can only be used when answers to specific hypotheses as to consumer behaviour are required, and not a general interpretation of urban spheres.

Once the questionnaires have been completed the procedure is straightforward. For each of the central places a point is awarded each time it is nominated as the place of purchase of a good or service. Each questionnaire cannot be treated as an isolated spot score since individual eccentricities have to be eliminated. A number of questionnaires are, therefore, totalled, for a given grid square on a map, for an administrative area or for an arbitrarily defined settlement. In Rowley's study five questionnaires for every quarter kilometer square meant that, with 20 goods and services on the sheet, a total of 100 answers was obtained each nominating a centre used. In this case these could be treated directly as percentages and these scores can be used to denote the patterns of affiliation. Isopleths can be interpolated and it can be maintained that:

1   The 50 per cent isopleth for any centre will indicate the point at which a settlement loses dominance.
2   The bunching of isopleths at any point will indicate a sharp change of gradient and the limit of a sphere of influence related to a bundle of functions at a given rank in the hierarchy.
3   The 1 per cent isopleth will mark the absolute limit of a settlement's influence.

An example of this sort of exercise is given in figure 5−4.

To some extent the problems inherent in formulating a questionnaire with an array of goods and services can be offset by a less discriminating but simpler method. This is to find out the frequency of visits to shop at the various centres ranged on a standard scale (such as weekly, monthly and less frequently than monthly) or absolutely over a given period. These data can then be plotted directly (see figure 5−4B) or can be used to identify an ordering of flows. Davies and Lewis[51] have presented a study in this form where the raw data were aggregated to give flows from each settlement to Swansea in the two weeks previous to the survey. The flows were ranked in relation to the centres receiving them. First order and second and third order flows to Swansea were in this way identified and mapped (figure 5−5A & B, see pages 96−7) and from these patterns it is possible to demonstrate Swansea's sphere at two levels, the metropolitan level, where it dominates a well defined city region, and a 'town' level, where it functions at a rank comparable with its largest neighbours, such as Llanelli or Neath.

Much more sophisticated methods of analyzing these sorts of data have now been developed reliant on multivariate statistical techniques. It is possible to convert an origin-destination matrix of flows (of goods, people or messages) between places (as in figure 5−1) into a Q-mode similarity matrix which can be subject to factor analysis. The factors pick out clusters of towns

[51] W. K. D. Davies and C. R. Lewis (1970), 36−7.

Figure 5–4: A: Maximum and fifty per cent areas for towns in southwest Wales. The initial letters refer to the centres. **B:** the fifty per cent trade areas and areas visited for weekly shopping. *After G. Rowley (1967).*

Figure 5-5A

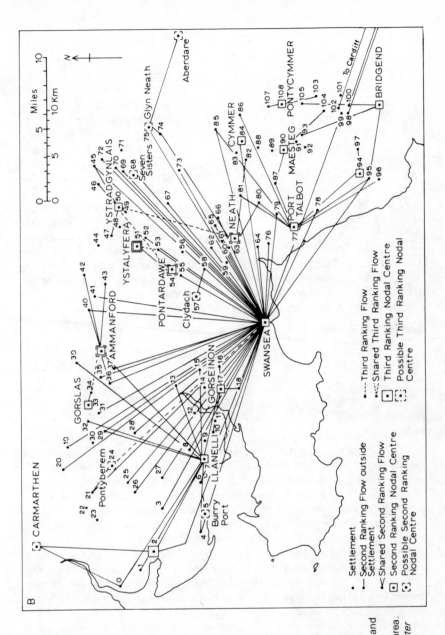

Figure 5–5: A: First ranking and **B:** Second and third ranking connections in the Swansea area. *After W. K. D. Davies, in Carter and Davies (1970).*

Legend:
- Settlement
- Second Ranking Flow outside Settlement
- Shared Second Ranking Flow
- Second Ranking Nodal Centre
- Possible Second Ranking Nodal Centre
- Third Ranking Flow
- Shared Third Ranking Flow
- Third Ranking Nodal Centre
- Possible Third Ranking Nodal Centre

with similar linkage patterns and the factor scores measure the importance of a place as a destination. 'If there is a spatially structured pattern of (telephone) calls each factor will have one dominant factor score, signifying a dominant destination, and the towns linked to this destination are identified by high factor loadings on the axis'[52]. In his study of telephone calls in Montana[53] W. K. D. Davies was able to establish the pattern of connectivity between places and resolve this into a system of central places and linkages in a map resembling those in figures 5–5A & B. The abstraction of higher order factors (see p. 274) enabled the mapping of second and third order regions of increasing generality.

One last point needs to be added at this stage. The exercises above present the most general of pictures and conceal the great variations in consumer behaviour. A brief example may be cited. Nader in a study in Durham investigated shopping habits in Penshaw, a former mining settlement some five miles from Sunderland.[54] Within Penshaw he contrasted the shopping orientation of households on a new private housing estate with that of the remainder of the ward. The results of the enquiry into the purchase of weekly groceries is shown in table 5–1.

table 5–1: Purchases of weekly groceries. *After G. A. Nader (1968).*

Place of purchase	Per cent purchased Penshaw estate	Rest of ward
Sunderland	34·6	2·9
Local	53·0	76·4
Mobile shop	2·7	10·7
Other centres	9·7	10·0

They show markedly the different orientation which, apart from relations with income and occupation, is linked to such variables as previous place of residence of households, the working status of the wife and the workplace of working wives. This brief consideration of shopping habits indicates that in reality the situation is far more complex than even the most complex interpretation of an urban hierarchy and spheres of influence indicates, and that it is the way people perceive the environment, in terms of town centres, that determines the pattern, and not necessarily the other way round. Classical central place theory often gives the impression of a deterministic, rigid structure, established on the day of creation, to which mere mortals have no option but to conform, but on the other hand a given system exists to be perceived in a variety of ways. This introduces qualifications which can be set aside to the next chapter.

One further matter needs to be considered at this stage. Although many investigators have sought by the complex methods here set out to rank towns into hierarchies, there has been a sad lack of the adaptation of these

[52] W. K. D. Davies (1979): Urban connectivity in Montana. *Annals of Regional Science*, 13, 32.

[53] W. K. D. Davies (1979), 29–46.

[54] G. A. Nader (1968): Private housing estates. The effect of previous residence on workplace and shopping activities. *Tn Plann. Rev.* 39, 65.

methods for the analysis of historical data, and until this is done one could well argue that studies of dynamic process in the city system are all inadequately based. It is not without a degree of amusement that one notes the abandonment of very elaborate ranking procedures immediately the past is considered and the use of simple population totals. Either the sole use of population figures is totally inadequate in historical contexts or a great deal of time and effort is being wasted at the present! Fortunately, there are examples of studies which attempt to establish hierarchies in past times by using data which are usually gathered from contemporary directories.[55]

In a British context, however, these do not become available until the end of the eighteenth century and before this there is little that can be used other than the descriptive accounts of travellers[56] or, reverting to population totals, the sorts of figures that can be derived from the hearth tax. Lucy Caroe has presented an attempt to employ 'association analysis' on nineteenth-century East Anglian data.[57] This work effectively displays how contemporary quantitative analyses can be employed in considering historical data. But the real problem arises in converting this static analysis of 1846 information into a series of analyses over time. Here the functional index devised by Davies is simpler and has many advantages.

The real problems that remain are best revealed by C. R. Lewis in a study of mid Wales.[58] Owing to variations in information available different sets of towns have to be taken into account at each date so that it is necessary to recalculate centrality values and functional indices for different sets of towns at every date so that effective comparison becomes possible. Lewis converts the functional index for each settlement into a percentage figure of all the settlements of the whole area so that he obtains a measure of how all the towns shared the total 'servicing' of the region between them at different dates. It follows that meaningful comparisons of the centrality of different centres over time can be made. The urban hierarchy can in this manner be seen not as a static thing but as comprising relationships between towns that are constantly fluctuating and a sounder basis can be given to earlier studies which attempted to investigate this feature.[59]

It is similarly possible to identify spheres of influence for past periods, but here the data are so severely limited that one is bound to work from the city outwards. At the same time, material of very varying character has to be used as it becomes available. Rodgers has used the location of the outburgesses on the Burgess Rolls of 1542 to 1602 in order to derive the market

[55] W. K. D. Davies, J. A. Giggs and D. T. Herbert (1968): Directories, rate books and the commercial structure of towns. *Geogr.* **53**, 41.

[56] H. Carter (1955): Urban grades and spheres of influence in south-west Wales. *Scott. Geogr. Mag.* **71**, 43.

[57] L. Caroe (1968): A multivariate grouping scheme: 'association analysis' of East Anglian towns; in E. G. Bowen, H. Carter and J. A. Taylor, editors (1968): *Geography at Aberystwyth*, 253 (Cardiff).

[58] C. R. Lewis (1970), 228.

[59] H. Carter (1955). Also H. Carter (1956): The urban hierarchy and historical geography, *Geogr. Stud.* **3**, 85; reprinted in A. R. H. Baker, J. D. Hamshere and J. Langton, editors (1970): *Geographical interpretations of historical sources*, 269 (Newton abbot).

area of Preston in the sixteenth and seventeenth centuries.[60] Newspaper advertisements have also been used as well as administrative areas for, after all, the very way in which many English counties were named after the central town indicates the use of the concept of a sphere of influence in very early times. Again the charters which were granted to medieval towns often specify the area within which people were to use the market of the chartered town and this also gives some indication of very early spheres of influence.[61] At a later date the journeys of carriers to market,[62] or of stage coaches, provide an equivalent of bus route analysis.

It is apparent that a wide range of material is available for the geographer investigating the past. This material is fragmentary and there are very many difficulties in its employment, but a good range of preliminary work exists in considering the developmental process in the city system.

In terms of an effective academic enquiry a stage has now been reached where the results of experimentation can be assessed. In chapter 4 a number of assumptions were presented which sought to establish that certain regularities exist in the way in which cities are disposed on the earth's surface; the models of Christaller and Lösch are, therefore, hypotheses as to what will be found in reality. The physical scientist sets up his equipment to carry out the experiments relative to a hypothesis. This chapter has been concerned with a similar process in the social sciences. We do not set up equipment but it is essential to devise procedures so that a hypothesis can be effectively tested. This is by no means easy and indeed it is possible to present a case that the basic tenets of central place *theory* were established in 1939; the subsequent decades have been devoted largely to the devising of effective techniques to test the theory in the real world and that with only a modicum of success.

Notes on further reading

The essential material is in the bibliographies cited in footnote 2 (p. 59) of the previous chapter. A paper of particular value is:

Davies, W. K. D. (1966): The ranking of service centres: a critical review (see footnote 2).

The book referred to in the notes on further reading on p. 76:

Funck, R. and Parr, J. B. (1978): *The analysis of regional structures: essays in honour of August Lösch*

should also be consulted especially:

Klemmer, P., Methods for the determination of centrality, pp. 84–61.

A further paper is:

Bennison, D. J. (1978): The measurement of settlement centrality. *Prof. Geogr.*, 30(4), 371–376.

[60] H. B. Rodgers (1956): The market area of Preston in the sixteenth and seventeenth centuries. *Geogr. Stud.* **3**, 45. Reprinted in A. R. H. Baker *et al.* (1970), 102.

[61] H. Carter (1969): Caernarvon; in M. D. Lovel, editor (1969): *Historic towns; maps and plans of towns and cities in the British Isles, with historical commentaries, from earliest times to 1800*, 5 (Oxford).

[62] H. Carter (1955); also P. R. Odell (1957): Urban spheres of influence in Leicestershire in the mid-nineteenth century. *Geogr. Stud.* **4**, 30.

6

Some Problems Associated with Central Place Theory and the Distribution of Towns

1 Problems derived from empirical studies

Christaller's study of central places in south-west Germany[1] was aimed at answering the question whether there were general laws which governed the size and spacing of towns. His model was designed to provide an affirmative answer by revealing the underlying regularity in town distribution. As chapter 5 has demonstrated, most early attempts at empirical investigation accepted Christaller's thesis as proven, and questioning neither his assumptions nor the logic of his argument, they set out to show its applicability to the real world. But these somewhat uncritical studies were soon to be paralleled by others which found little of the regularity which Christaller's model predicted.

The first challenge was directed at the point where central place theory seemed clearly inapposite. A cursory inspection of the distribution of towns in most areas of the world reveals no sign of a hexagonal lattice. If, obeying the demands of threshold and range, particular grades of towns were marked by characteristic assemblages or bundles of functions, they seemed most certainly not to display any regularity in distribution. The time lag before any serious work on this aspect of central place theory was undertaken was partly due to the fact that many investigators assumed it was self-evident that no such spatial arrangement appertained, and partly to the lack of adequate techniques for examining the distribution patterns.

These were eventually derived from the investigations of plant ecologists, and a series of papers by Dacey[2] applied nearest neighbour analysis[3] to town (central place) distributions. 'The central concept of nearest neighbour analysis is randomness. When there is complete absence of a systematic pattern of points in a specified region, the distribution of points is called random. A pattern that is not random is either more clustered than random

[1] W. Christaller (translated by C. W. Baskin) 1966: *The central places of southern Germany* (Englewood Cliffs, NJ).
[2] M. F. Dacey (1962): The analysis of central place and point patterns by a nearest neighbour method; in K. Norborg, editor: *IGU symp. Urb. Geogr. Lund 1960*, 55.
M. F. Dacey (1960): The spacing of river towns. *Ann. Assoc. Am. Geogr.* **50**, 59.
M. F. Dacey (1964): Modified poisson probability law for point patterns more regular than random. *Ann. Assoc. Am. Geogr.* **54**, 559.
M. F. Dacey (1967): Some properties of order distance for random point distributions. *Geogr. Annlr.* **49**(b), 25.
[3] For a comment see W. Porter (1960): Earnest and the Orephagians: a fable for the instruction of young geographers. *Ann. Assoc. Am. Geogr.* **50**, 297−9.

or more uniform than random.[4] Christaller's thesis unequivocally implies that the distribution of central places is uniform and that a situation 'more uniform than random' should be shown regardless of rank if all the central places of an area are analysed. Dacey demonstrated that, using Brush's data for southwestern Wisconsin,[5] the system most closely approximated a random condition. From this three implications were drawn:

1 There *was* a hierarchy of central places in the area but the spatial distribution did not conform to central place theory.
2 A hierarchy did exist but had not been properly defined.
3 Central place theory did not apply to market towns in southwest Wisconsin.[6]

Taking into account the inadequate diagnostic basis of Brush's ranking, the third implication was at least possible. Later work by L. J. King[7] was no more successful in identifying uniform lattice patterns. Using the nearest neighbour statistic (Rn), with $Rn = 0$ *indicating a clustered situation*, $Rn = 1$ a random situation and $Rn = 2 \cdot 15$ a uniform lattice, King examined twenty sample areas and found that his results showed a range of $Rn = 0 \cdot 7$ for an area in Utah to $Rn = 1 \cdot 38$ for part of Missouri. Although a claim was made that some of the samples, such as the Missouri one quoted above, could be classified as 'approaching uniformity'[8] the general conclusion must be that these patterns approximate to a 'random' condition. There have been later attempts to rescue an element of regularity from these apparently random distributions, such as that of Medvedkov using the concept of entropy.

Entropy is a notion borrowed from the statistical theory of information. Entropy helps to measure disorder in settlement patterns, so that the random and uniform components are effectively separated and measured.[9] This means that any settlement pattern is assumed to have a regular and a random component and the calculation of the entropy value is designed to disentangle these two parts, indicating the degree of disorder. This seems of comparatively little value, and of questionable validity, in relation to a static distribution but may possibly be useful in assessing whether a distribution is becoming more uniform with time. But it is possible to conclude that in few areas can any element of regularity in town distribution be discerned. The concept of the hexagonal lattice therefore holds little value to the student of the real world whatever may be its attraction to the student of social and economic geometry.

[4] M. F. Dacey (1962).   [5] M. F. Dacey (1962).
[6] W. Porter (1960).
[7] L. J. King (1962): A quantitative expression of the pattern of urban settlements in selected areas of the USA. *Tijdschr. econ. soc. Geogr.* 50, 1. L. J. King (1961): A multivariate analysis of the spacing of urban settlements in the United States. *Ann. Assoc. Am. Geogr.* 51, 222.
[8] L. J. King (1962).
[9] Y. V. Medvedkov (1967): The regular component in settlement patterns as shown on maps. *Soviet Geogr.* 8, 50. Y. V. Medvedkov (1967): The concept of entropy in settlement pattern analysis. *Pap. Reg. Sci. Assoc.* 18, 165. For a brief study using the concept of entropy in which the procedure for its calculation is given see R. K. Semple and R. G. Golledge (1970): An analysis of entropy changes in a settlement pattern over time. *Econ. Geogr.* 46, 157.

At the same time the idea that ranks of towns universal to the western world were to be recognized, an implicit tenet of a paper by Brush and Bracey,[10] was also becoming less tenable. Philbrick had attempted to demonstrate a seven-stage hierarchy of nested functions which was equated with seven broad categories of functional roles.[11] These provided the base pattern of areal organization as shown in figure 6−1A, B, & C. Carol used this same system in considering the central place system in its internal city context[12] although this involved the telescoping of three of Christaller's ranks into one called 'middle order'. This presumably corresponded with Philbrick's 'third order'.

The detail of these schemes is not important here, but rather the idea that all settlements in all countries would neatly drop into their appropriate slots.

Figure 6−1 A, B & C: Functional organization in the north-east United States. *After A. K. Philbrick (1957).*

These maps indicate centres of progressive importance from the second order to the seventh order, which is New York. The individual pattern about a fourth order city. South Bend is shown in figure 6−1B. There is a pyramical structure leading to the largest city at the apex. This is one of the basic principles of areal functional organization and carries the implication that a similar seven ordered structure can be identified outside this area and considered as universal.

[10] J. E. Brush and H. E. Bracey (1966): Rural service centres in south-western Wisconsin and southern England. *Geogrl. Rev.* **45**, 559.

[11] A. K. Philbrick (1957): Principles of areal functional organization in regional human geography. *Econ. Geogr.* **33**.

[12] H. Carol (1960): The hierarchy of central functions within the city. *Ann. Assoc. Am. Geogr.* **50**. See p. 107.

Figures 6–1B and 6–1C

But any attempt to define these 'slots' reveals the complete lack of agreement among the many empirical studies. After considering a summary statement in graphical form (figure 6–2)[13] of some of these schemes one is forced to recall the conclusion of Lukermann that the result was a multiplicity of taxonomies rather than explanatory generalization.[14] Moreover in the background of these classificatory studies was the 'rank size rule'[15] which states that empirical investigation in reality revealed not a stepped but a log-normal relationship between size of town (measured by population) and rank in the system. (See p. 70)

This situation was greatly disturbing to urban geographers who in the early days had seen central place as a universal theory of town location. Berry, along with other authors, turned to these problems first showing that the rank size relation and a hierarchical structuring were not incompatible[16] and could be subsumed under the same system. The result depended largely on the analytical approach for, by adjustments, either situation could be revealed. Moreover it was argued that any system was composed of two parts, one called *aggregative*, the other *elemental*.[17] 'At the aggregative level the blending of many varying, but locally homogeneous areas leads to

Figure 6–2: Comparative population sizes for various orders of central places: some early studies. *After W. K. D. Davies (1964).*

[13] W. K. D. Davies (1964): *The hierarchy of commercial centres: a case study in South Wales* (University of Wales: unpublished Ph.D. thesis). See volume **2**, figure 3–1.

[14] F. Lukermann (1966): Empirical expressions of nodality and hierarchy in a circulation manifold. *E. Lakes Geogr*, **2**, 20.

[15] G. K. Zipf (1941): *National unity and disunity* (Bloomington, Ill.).

[16] B. J. L. Berry and W. L. Garrison (1958): Alternate explanations of urban rank-size relationships. *Ann. Assoc. Am. Geogr.* **48**, 83.

[17] B. J. L. Berry and H. G. Barnum (1962): Aggregate relations and elemental components of central place systems. *J. Reg. Sci.* **4**, 35.

the emergence of a continuum of centres. Within each small local area, the levels of the hierarchy are clearly represented. The theoretical postulate is that the levels of centres are a function of the grouping requirements of certain bundles of central functions. Or, in other words, that classifications of centres and functions exist in which interaction effects are highly significant.'[18] The last part of this statement is nothing more than a direct repetition of the argument by Smailes for the 'trait complex' though the statistical procedures in identification are objective and rigorous. But if the merging of these locally homogeneous areas is one reason why the hierarchy is obscured it also means that a clear limit is set to the universality of any ranking for it will be a product of the particular economic, social and spatial conditions of individual areas.

Berry takes this problem further.[19] At the outset it can be demonstrated, as implied in the last paragraph, that local environmental constraints will act upon the system. Thus, for example, there is no direct relation between size of area and population density nor a simple expansion of area to compensate for falling density. It was observed that areas do expand as the density falls, in keeping with threshold demand, but the areas do not expand as fast as the densities fall so that the size of the population served falls. As a result, under these conditions, functions with the greatest threshold requirements at any level of the hierarchy move up to the next level; there is what Berry terms a phase shift.

If these several limitations are considered, it is apparent that the notion of a series of universal levels was over-optimistic and that the ranking of places is most meaningful within limited and local areas. To rank the towns of England and Wales is a useful descriptive device but has little meaning in central place terms because of the enormous variety of environmental conditions (using the word 'environment' in its widest and proper sense). The concepts of central place theory are invaluable in the analysis of the size and spacing, that is in the distribution, of cities but the uniform deterministic setting in which they are implied to operate bears little relation to actuality.

2 The problem of the intra-urban hierarchy

So far in this chapter it has been assumed that a hierarchical structuring is only applicable to discrete settlements, but it is apparent that all large cities, and indeed some small towns, will have not one *central* business district but also one or more subsidiary districts.

The earliest studies made of subsidiary business districts were not linked with central place ideas but were derived from empirical observation of city structure. The most widely known were by M. J. Proudfoot who identified five types of retail structures within the cities of the United States.[20] These he

[18] B. J. L. Berry and H. G. Barnum (1962), 46.

[19] B. J. L. Berry (1967): *Geography of market centers and retail distribution.* (Englewood Cliffs, NJ).

[20] M. J. Proudfoot (1937a): City retail structure. *Econ. Geogr.* 13, 425–8. (1937b): The outlying business centers of Chicago. *J. Ld. Pub. Util. Econ.* 13, 57–70.

defined as:

1 The CBD.
2 The outlying business district.
3 The principal business thoroughfare.
4 The neighbourhood business street.
5 The isolated store cluster.

Proudfoot noted that these displayed a 'progressive change' clearly indicating that he was identifying a ranked structure although making no link with the then nascent and little known central place theory. Similar empirical studies continued to be made with ranked structures generalized from the observed situation in the real world. Thus W. Burns in his book *British shopping centres*[21] published in 1959 outlined a similar structure which he described as 'commonly accepted' at that time and called a four tier system, excluding 'the corner shop'. This was:

1 The town centre (the equivalent of the CBD).
2 District centre.
3 Neighbourhood centre.
4 Subcentre.

In addition Burns introduced a diagram (figure 6–3, page 110) which clearly indicated a nesting arrangement. His main concern was to further reduce the complexity of this by advocating a three tier system and, although without demonstrating any real understanding of the operation of threshold and range controls, Burns based his work on the arguments commonly employed in central place studies. He saw convenience as the major control and interpreted it through frequency of visits, contrasting frequent or daily needs with periodic or weekly needs and special or less than weekly needs. Also considered was 'selectivity' by which the individual exercised choice by other than 'convenience' measures, involving personal characteristics such as cleanliness or willingness to offer credit or status value. Burns in this way included those aspects of consumer behaviour which have only more recently been considered in a central place context.

Given the rapid development of central place notions, the growing number of empirical works being published and the existence of studies which identified ranks of business districts within the city, it was inevitable that the two lines of research should be brought together and the attempt made to see in the types of business districts the equivalence of ranks in the general urban hierarchy. Hans Carol writing of his work on Zurich claims, 'When this survey was begun in 1952, it was, to my knowledge, the first attempt to use the central place concept for analysing the pattern of central functions within the city'.[22] Carol recognized that distinctions in level were not simply related to numbers of shops but also to the variety of goods available for sale at a centre and the quality (price) range within each good (figure 6–4A and B). The extent of the service area was also considered.

[21] W. Burns (1959): *British shopping centres*. (London).
[22] H. Carol (1960): The hierarchy of central functions within the city. *Ann. Assoc. Am. Geogr.* **50,** 419.

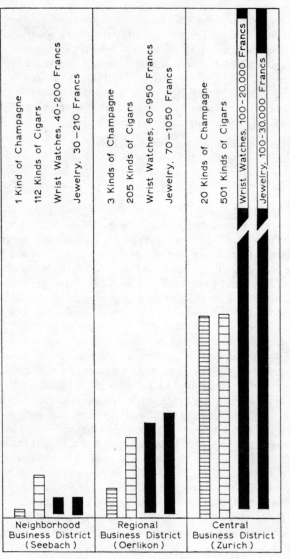

Neighborhood Business District (Seebach)	Regional Business District (Oerlikon)	Central Business District (Zurich)
1 Kind of Champagne	3 Kinds of Champagne	20 Kinds of Champagne
112 Kinds of Cigars	205 Kinds of Cigars	501 Kinds of Cigars
Wrist Watches, 40-200 Francs	Wrist Watches, 60-950 Francs	Wrist Watches, 100 - 20,000 Francs
Jewelry, 30—210 Francs	Jewelry, 70—1050 Francs	Jewelry, 100 - 30,000 Francs

Figure 6—4A: The range of goods in business districts at three different levels. This indicates the variation in the range and quality of similar goods at different levels of the hierarchy.

Figure 6–4B: The percentage of shopping trips made by persons residing in a Zurich suburb (Schwamen dingen) to three levels of business district. This indicates the differing orders of goods which are brought at the differing centres. *After H. Carol (1960).*

DISTRICT CENTRE

NEIGHBOURHOOD CENTRE

SUB-CENTRE

Figure 6–3: The four-tier system of intra-urban shopping centres. *After W. Burns (1959).*

From a survey of three centres of different 'levels' a hierarchical classification was derived which recognized four ranks of centre:

1   *CBD.* Serving the whole city.
2   *Regional business district.* Offering middle order goods (see figure 6–4A and B) and serving some 90,000 to 100,000 population.
3   *Neighbourhood business district.* Offering low order goods, frequently needed and with a very limited range of higher order commodities. Such districts were usually situated towards the periphery of the city and served some 5,000 to 10,000 people.
4   *Local business district.* 'A cluster of a few round-the-corner shops.'

In spite of the differences in nomenclature there is a clear equivalence to the four tier system which Burns discussed but with the beginnings of some rigour being injected into the study of these various levels. This was further advanced in the work of W. Garrison and others.[23] In this it was pointed out

[23] W. Garrison *et alia* (1959): Empirical verification of concepts of spatial structure. Chapter 4 in *Studies of highway development and geographic change*, 67–99 (Seattle).

that much of the existing work was intuitive and based on the conventional distinction between 'convenience', 'shopping' and 'speciality' goods. A survey of definitions indicated the variety of different bases used to identify the ranks of centre which have been so far indicated in this chapter. In addition Garrison emphasized the additional problem of string streets which were much more apparent in an American context. A study of Spokane, in which 49 business types located in 285 business centres were identified, was undertaken by means of a 49 × 49 correlation matrix of business types. By means of linkage analysis a series of nine groupings of businesses was derived and linkage analysis again applied to a 9 × 9 matrix of the average correlation for each group of business types. The result was a clear distinction of a nucleated component made up of three groups, which were given no distinctive names, and an arterial component with an automobile set, a supplies set and a string street set.

This was undoubtedly the first study to demonstrate the contrasting characteristics of these subsidiary business districts in statistical terms and also to make the link with a wider country area. 'It is readily evident both empirically and theoretically that nucleated shopping centres *within* urban areas (densely built-up areas with concentrated purchasing power) and alternate nucleated urban centres (nucleations in the otherwise more sparsely populated areas of less concentrated purchasing power) are of the same nature.'[24] It also follows that intra-urban business districts are not only to be found within large metropolitan centres. If a small town has a central shopping array equal to that of the neighbourhood business district using Carol's terminology then it will be possible to identify local business districts, at the lowest level, within the urban area. The intra-urban arrangement of business districts is not a problem related solely to the large city.

The reference above to Carol's terminology indicates one of the problems in these studies, the variety of nomenclature employed for the subsidiary districts. To a large extent this has been solved by the summary work of Brian Berry who, drawing on work such as Garrison's, has outlined a complete typology of the commercial characteristics of American cities outside the CBD[25] (figure 6−5). This is based on a threefold division of these areas into:

1	A hierarchy of business centres.	Centres.
2	Highway-oriented commercial ribbons and urban arterial commercial developments.	Ribbons.
3	Specialized function areas.	Specialized areas.

The hierarchy of centres includes four ranks below the CBD, thus adding one to the pattern already identified, largely it would seem by splitting the regional level into two and calling the lower segment the 'community centre'. This presumably provides a parallel to the five ranks of town within

---

[24] W. Garrison *et alia* (1959), 99.

[25] B. J. L. Berry (1962): *The commercial structure of American cities; a review.* Community Renewal Program (Chicago); see also Berry's (1967): *Geography of market centers and retail distribution,* 46 (Englewood Cliffs, NJ).

Figure 6–5: A typology of business districts. *After B. J. L. Berry (1962).*

a central place system which Berry indicates—hamlet, village, town, city and regional capital. Indeed Carol set out this equation quite clearly (table 6–1).[26]

Under the broad heading of 'ribbons' a number of differing types is identified. The first is the well established shopping street which usually leads from the nucleated centre or is substituted for the lower order centres. The second is the highway-oriented ribbon which is ubiquitous in the USA but very much less common in Europe largely due to a less intensive use of the automobile and the more effective application of planning controls. It consists of a characteristic and garish assembly of motels, filling stations and restaurants. The third type, the urban arterial locations, is made up of stores with excessive space requirements, such as furniture or appliance stores, building and lumber yards. They rely on special purpose trips and can concentrate on providing easy access along the arterials together with good parking facilities, rather than associating with other business in the central area. The specialized areas are often closely associated with the nucleated business district and provide grouped but specialized services, such as medical districts with associated doctors, dentists, opticians and pharmacists.

It would seem that although there is some discrepancy between the five ranks of business district and the ranks of city often identified, nevertheless here is a definitive statement of typology. Unfortunately there are two difficulties which arise once a locational study of these centres is considered. The first of these is derived from social contrasts within the city. These mean that purchasing power is not evenly spread over the city and consequently demand generated is also not evenly spread. At the same time population densities vary as do shopping habits. In a 'working class' area in Britain, where the family does not own a car or a refrigerator, purchases will tend to

26 H. Carol (1960).

table 6-1: Hierarchies of centres. *After Carol (1960)*.

USA	Switzerland	Centres of Zurich	Centres—American cities
Hamlet	Dorf	Local business district	Local centre
Village	Markt-Ort	Neighbourhood BD	Neighbourhood centre
Town	Stadt	Regional BD	Community centre
City	Grosse Stadt		Regional centre
Metropolis	Metropole (Zurich)	CBD of Metropole	CBD of metropolis

be frequent and the 'corner shop' an important element. In the well-to-do suburbs of American cities where car owning is universal and refrigerators and deep freezes ubiquitous, shopping habits will be very different and most convenience goods will be purchased at the weekly visit to the supermarket, so that the corner shop will not exist.

The whole situation is further complicated by the fact that the pattern of nesting with discrete tributary areas which is implied by theory is not borne out in practice. People shop around and for a variety of reasons will not necessarily use the nearest centre. This was demonstrated by H. R. Parker[27] in Liverpool in 1962 where the detail of bus routes controlled shopping rather than simple physical proximity. Again Ronald Jones has shown that even in a new town, with planned neighbourhoods with their appropriate shopping centres, people do not hold to the anticipated patterns but will move to centres outside their own neighbourhoods.[28] All these factors make neat typologies somewhat suspect, other than as very general subjective guides to the basic structure.

Two studies can be considered in elaboration of the difficulties outlined in the last paragraph. One of the most detailed studies of intra-urban retail nucleations is that by Barry Garner using the area so often worked over in urban studies—Chicago.[29]

Garner faces the first problem of how these nucleations are to be defined in areal terms and proposes an objective method based on land-value profiles which are constructed along the streets which meet at the peak land value intersection. 'The zone of transition between nucleated and ribbon functions is identified on each profile as the point where the curve levels off to form the ridge of value associated with the ribbon'[30] (figure 6-6). For each of the nucleations identified the relations between number of establishments, floor space and number of business types were examined by means of scattergrams. This provided an initial problem in that there were clear

[27] H. R. Parker (1962): Suburban shopping facilities in Liverpool. *Tn. Plann. Rev.* **33**, 197.
[28] R. Jones (1969): Geographical aspects of behaviour within the framework of neighbourhood units in East Kilbride. In *Processes and patterns of urbanization*, IBG Urban Studies Group.
[29] B. J. Garner (1966): The internal structure of retail nucleations. *Northwestern Univ. Stud. Geogr.* **12**.
[30] B. J. Garner (1966), 191.

Figure 6–6: A method of areal definition of subsidiary business districts. *After B. J. Garner (1966)*. The criterion used is land values and the point of marked fall off away from the centre is identified on each side of each street.

deviant cases from regression lines drawn to show relations between pairs of the variables. The location of these deviants suggested an association with the socio-economic status of different parts of the city reflecting basic contrasts in purchasing power.

Accordingly Garner was forced to divide his nucleations into two, one associated with low income areas, which he termed 'workingmen's areas' and the other with remaining areas, which he termed 'the rest of the city'. The hierarchy of nucleations was then determined by analysis of the relation between the number of occupied establishments and the number of business types (figure 6−7). This produced three levels which were identified as:

Figure 6−7: The hierarchy of retail nucleations in Chicago, 1961 *After B. J. Garner (1966).* For comment on the levels identified see text page 116.

1   Regional centres.
2   Community centres.
3   Neighbourhood centres.

in line with the outline proposed by Berry and excluding the lowest order at the 'street corner' level. In the workingmen's areas the equivalent scattergram did not reveal clear classes and observations clustered about the regression line. By employing nearest neighbour techniques two classes were eventually identified, termed 'workingmen's major' and 'workingmen's minor'. Garner makes the interesting comment that 'the classification offered . . . is not the only possible allocation of retail nucleations to various levels or orders in a hierarchy. Rather, it may be considered one of several other systems which are dependent upon the methods of analysis and purpose of study'.[31] This would seem to suggest that the ordering of the centres is a matter of simple convenience rather than of inherent character. His next step is to analyse the spatial distribution of these centres and he concludes that there is little regularity to be found. 'In general, nucleations of the same order are not uniformly spaced throughout the study area. This is to be expected from the marked unevenness of the population distribution and purchasing power.'[32] A relation to a $K = 4$ network is suggested but is so tentative as to be of little use. To a large extent this sort of conclusion reflects problems inherent in central place studies in that location patterns tend simply to reflect the distribution of population.

R. J. Johnston in an analysis of an intra-metropolitan central place hierarchy in Melbourne[33] related the range of centres (he identified *eight* grades) to three factors. These were variations in residential density, the socio-economic status of the population and the age of development of an area. These are clearly not independent variables for there is a close association between them. Melbourne was divided into seven areas (area 4 being subdivided in 4a and 4b to distinguish an older and a newer area) on the basis of socio-economic status. The areas are shown on figure 6−8 and the results are indicated in table 6−2.

This evidence confirms the hypotheses advanced by the author[34]:

1   Isolated establishments are highly concentrated in the older high density, low status parts of the city. This is for the reasons indicated already.
2   Lowest order centres are most common in areas of high population density and adjacent to those parts with an excess of isolated establishments.
3   With increasing status and decreasing population density centres of the lower orders become less frequent.

[31] B. J. Garner (1966), 49.
[32] R. J. Garner (1966), 50.
[33] R. J. Johnston (1966): The distribution of an intrametropolitan central place hierarchy in Melbourne. *Aust. Geogrl. Stud.* **IV**, 17−33.
[34] R. J. Johnston (1966), 21−4.

Figure 6—8: The social areas of Melbourne. *After R. J. Johnston (1966).* This division was based on proportion aged 15—20 in full time education. Six sectors were defined and the largest subdivided to recognize older and newer suburbs. The social rank is generally in descending order, 4A, 6, 4B, 2, 5, 3, 1, 7.

4 High status sectors have a top heavy hierarchy.
5 Low status sectors have a bottom heavy hierarchy.
6 The central areas show the most balanced situation.

At this point it is worth considering a further study, made of Edinburgh by Ronald Jones.[35] Again a careful method of delimiting centres was employed and a classification derived by a scattergram of total floor space in each centre against the number of selected non-convenience types of shop. Four grades (below the Edinburgh CBD) were identified and Grades, I, II

[35] R. Jones (1967): Central place theory and the hierarchy and location of shopping centres in a city: Edinburgh. Inst. Br. Geogr. Study Group in Urban Geography. *Aspects of central place theory and the city in developing countries.*

table 6–2: Distribution of Melbourne's hierarchy. *After R. J. Johnston (1966).*

Sector	1	2	3	4A	4B	5	6	7	Total
Nucleated centres									
1·1	1	–	2	2	1	2	–	3	11
2	9·1	0	18·2	18.2	9·1	18·2	0	27·3	100
2·1	2	4	4	9	2	8	13	10	52
2	3·8	7·7	7·7	17·3	3·9	15·4	25·0	19·2	100
3·1	3	2	1	7	3	3	7	2	28
2	10·7	7·1	3·6	25·0	10·7	10·7	25·0	7·1	100
4·1	3	–	10	19	3	9	7	10	61
2	4·9	0	16·4	31·2	4·9	14·7	11·5	16·4	100
5·1	3	2	9	8	6	2	6	–	36
2	8·3	5·6	25·0	22·2	16·7	5·6	16·7	0	100
6·1	7	4	11	8	5	8	8	10	61
2	11·5	6·5	18·1	13·1	8·2	13·1	13·1	16·4	100
7·1	18	4	36	17	17	22	24	19	157
2	11·5	3·5	22·9	10·9	10·9	14·0	15·3	12·1	100
8·1	50	12	75	23	40	37	35	40	312
2	16·0	3·9	24·0	7·4	12·8	11·9	11·2	12·8	100
Isolated									
1	182	48	225	82	32	92	98	584	1343
2	13·5	3·6	16·8	6·1	2·4	6·8	7·3	43·5	100
Percentage of total	13·0	3·7	18·1	8·5	5·3	8·9	9·9	33·9	100

Note: For each grade of centre row 1 gives absolute frequencies; row 2 gives percentages.

and III were subdivided into groups *a and b* (figures 6 – 9 and 6 – 10). In considering the distribution of these centres Jones notes the way in which the higher grade centres cluster around the CBD. This he argues reflects far more of the city's population distribution of 40 years ago and illustrates the significance of inertia as a factor. The retail distribution has not been adjusted to suburban extension and this is possibly related to the nature of that extension itself by private developers and municipal authorities. This means that in Edinburgh the hypotheses put forward by Johnston as to the distribution of high and low order centres in relation to the city centre do not apply.

Jones concludes, 'In terms, therefore, of central place theory, it is difficult to discern any extensive fit between what might theoretically be expected and the actual distribution and hierarchical structure of suburban retail facilities in the city body.[36] Moreover he goes on to question whether this is likely to be the case in Britain and introduces the problem raised by Parker that movement is related to the vagaries of the bus service rather than to simple distance. Moreover given the convergence of public transport towards the city centre then the only location where high grade subsidiary business districts can survive is precisely where they are located in

[36] R. Jones (1967).

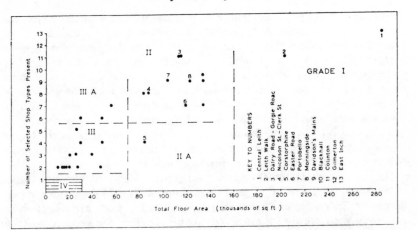

Figure 6–9: The identification of subsidiary business districts in Edinburgh. *After R. Jones (1962)*. The basis is a scattergram of selected non-convenience shopping facilities against floor area. The grades identified are shown. Leith Walk (No. 2) is given the grade 1A to separate it from Central Leith. The Edinburgh CBD is excluded.

Edinburgh, where the incoming flows begin to converge at these minor, inner nodes. The large outer suburban shopping centre is the product of the privately owned car and a footloose population.

The conclusion from all these studies is not an easy one. The notion of subsidiary business districts conforming neatly to the ranks of the urban

Figure 6–10: The hierarchy of suburban shopping centres in Edinburgh. *After R. Jones (1967)*.

hierarchy and disposed according to a hexagonal central place net has clearly to be abandoned. Every study which has been carried out carries the same conclusion and this applies not only to western cities but to non-western examples also, as in the study of Calcutta by A. K. Dutt. 'In contrast to Christaller's seven levels of central places, only four such levels exist in Calcutta . . . The norm of central places in Calcutta is 1:4:18:36 which does not conform to any uniform ratio.'[37] The procedure of analysis by ranking of these districts, however, is clearly one to be adopted, but the explanation of the patterns is likely to be found in the complex of city growth, the segregation of its social areas and in consumer evaluation of the costs and means of travel and of the cheapness or prestige of shops.

Garner has also demonstrated that owing to the standard forces operative in competition for central land, the shops selling higher order goods dominate the centre and those selling lower order goods are relegated in turn to successively distant zones[38] (figure 6−11). This is in keeping with the analysis which will later be considered on urban land used in general.

3 The problems of cultural and behavioural variations

Further limitations of the notion of the hierarchy itself have been forthcoming largely through investigations in the field of market research. Here the viewpoint has been that of the individual consumer as opposed to the aggregate or bundle of establishments at a centre from which consumer behaviour has been extrapolated.

Donald L. Thompson has maintained that all the geographical analyses, such as those discussed in this chapter, have a basic assumption which is 'that the decision maker corresponds to the "economic man" in that an objective analysis of revenues and costs, satisfactions and dissatisfactions, utilities and disutilities and the maximization of the differences between the two lies at the heart of any decision to patronize one retail store rather than another.'[39] Thompson then argues that the sorts of phenomena which are to be explained, such as the distribution of retail sales, are 'the result of the summed reactions of many individuals, each free to make his decision as he sees fit given the perceived and real constraints with which he may find himself faced'. Then, referring to Lynch's work on *The image of the city*[40] which demonstrates the way in which perception of the urban environment varies between individuals, Thompson goes on to argue that the real key in retail research lies in behavioural studies: 'the fundamental factor affecting the geographic distribution of retailing is the manner in which consumers organize their perceptions of the external environment with which they are faced.'[41]

[37] A. K. Dutt (1969): Intra-city hierarchy of central places: Calcutta as a case study. *Prof. Geogr.* 21, 18−22.
[38] B. J. Garner (1966), 97−124.
[39] D. L. Thompson (1966): Future directions in retail area research. *Econ. Geogr.* 42, 1.
[40] K. Lynch (1960): *The image of the city* (Cambridge, Mass.).
[41] D. L. Thompson (1966), 17.

Figure 6–11: The structure of intra-metropolitan business districts. *After B. J. Garner (1966).* The three graphs are equivalent to those which are used in figures 8–6 and 8–7 on pages 190–1. In these cases *A, B* and *C* represent Regional, community and neighbourhood business types respectively. The presence and distribution of businesses of these various orders is shown by *R, C* and *N* respectively on the diagrams which represent the regional, community and neighbourhood levels.

Two studies can be quoted which have illustrated this point. The first is that of Murdie, significantly titled 'cultural differences in consumer travel'.[42] Murdie studies consumer travel in an area of southwestern Ontario where there are two contrasted groups which he calls old order Mennonites and modern Canadians. The old order Mennonites form a relict element, equivalent to the Amish or Pennyslvania Dutch peoples of the United States. They are the strictest preservers of the traditional ways.

In a standard analysis in central place terms a series of regression analyses is carried out where the dependent variable is distance travelled to first choice centres and where a series of independent variables is considered such as the number of central functions in the first and second choice centres, frequency of purchase, etc. The major explainer of distance travelled is the number of functions in the first choice centre in accordance with classical central place theory, but there are considerable differences between the two groups which are best illustrated by figures 6−12 and 6−13 showing contrasts in travel for purchases of clothing and yard goods. Here, whereas the outer range of modern Canadians increases with the size of centre visited, for the Mennonites it does not for the outer range is fixed at six miles. The old order Mennonites still wear the same clothes as their ancestors who came to the country. They have no interest in fashion. They buy their clothes, therefore, locally at the nearest point. New fashions coming into an area reach the regional capital first and are thence diffused down the hierarchy so that the first contact of the countryside with the new fashions is in the largest city. But this whole process is meaningless to the Mennonite people. One could argue that their cultural inheritance has transformed a good from a high to a low order or 'one may conclude that the central place importance has virtually no effect on distance travelled by the old order Mennonites for these goods'[43] and that 'socio-economic influences on relative mobility, as these are reflected in differences in the levels of space preferences attained by different consumers, must be considered in more heterogeneous areas.'[44] Or, in other words, the perception of the consumer is a vital factor.

This idea has been best developed in a series of papers by Rushton and others.[45] An investigation into the dispersed farm population of Iowa[46] was designed to consider the spatial behaviour of consumers by examining the assumption, implicit in central place theory, that people will travel shorter distances for those goods and services which occur with the greatest frequency. It is argued that the above assumption, together with the hypothesis that many goods and services have similar thresholds and ranges (i.e. trait

[42] R. A. Murdie (1965): Cultural differences in consumer travel. *Econ. Geogr.* **41**, 211.
[43] R. A. Murdie (1965), 232.   [44] R. A. Murdie (1965), 233.
[45] R. G. Golledge, G. Rushton and W. A. Y. Clark (1966): Some spatial characteristics of Iowa's dispersed farm population and their implication for the grouping of central place functions. *Econ. Geogr.* **42**, 261. See also G. Rushton (1966): Spatial pattern of grocery purchases by the Iowa rural population. *Univ. Iowa Stud. Bus. Econ., New Series* **9**.
[46] R. G. Golledge, G. Rushton and W. A. Y. Clark (1966).

complexes occur), is the rationale for inferring behaviour from the distribution and frequency of occurrence of central place functions. This in turn is the basis for the ranking of goods and services into district grades.

The study deals with two sets of data, the distance of travel for maximum purchase and nearest purchase of thirty three goods. A considerable degree of flexibility in the purchase characteristics of some goods was shown by analysis of standard deviations from mean distances travelled, but the crux of the study was a rank correlation between order of entry of goods by distance to maximum purchase centre and by distance to nearest purchase town (table 6–3). The correlation coeffificients derived were 0·23 and 0·32, neither of which were significant at the 0·01 level of confidence. It is apparent from this result that Iowans do not always make their maximum

table 6–3: Rank correlation of functions by order of entry, distance to maximum purchase town and distance to nearest purchase town. Iowa data. *After R. G. Golledge, G. Rushton and W. A. Y. Clark (1966).*

Function	(a) Rank by order-of entry	(b) Rank by distance to max. purch. town	(c) Rank by distance to nearest purch. town
Car service	1	2	1
Food & drink away from home	2	5	5
Groceries	3	3	3
Church	4	1	2
Barber	5	4	4
Appliances	6	20	20
House fuel	7	6	6
Furniture	8	24	23
Variety	9	22	17
Building services	10	11	10
Drugstore	11	8	8
Physician	12	16	15
Car sales	13	23	24
Shoe repair	14	13	11
Dry cleaning	15	15	14
Movies	16	21	21
Food locker	17	7	12
Women's clothing	18	19	22
Dentist	19	18	16
Jewelry	20	17	19
Men's clothing	21	10	9
Repairs to T.V. & appliances	22	9	7
Children's clothing	23	14	18
Sporting goods	24	12	13

	a & b	a & c
Kendall's Tau	.23	.32

Figure 6–12: Cultural determinants of the journey to retail centres. The journey to shop for clothing and yard goods. **A:** Modern Canadians. **B:** Mennonites. *After R. A. Murdie (1965).*

REGIONAL CAPITAL
CITY
TOWN
VILLAGE
HAMLET

0   2   4   Miles
0   2   4   6   Km

Figure 6–13: Cultural determinants of the journey to retail centres. The journey to shop for shoes: **A:** Modern Canadians. **B:** Mennonites. *After R. A. Murdie (1965).*

REGIONAL CAPITAL

CITY

TOWN

VILLAGE

HAMLET

0   2   4 Miles
0   2   4   6 Km

purchases at the nearest available location. A further attempt to group 'functions' by distances travelled for maximum purchase using standard statistical grouping procedures produced seven 'ranks' which did not provide a means of distinguishing the conventional functional contrast of the village, town and city.

The conclusions of the study are that detailed information on expenditure patterns deduced from the occurrence of functions, does not agree with direct interview results, and that 'the grouping of central place functions on the basis of travel behaviour produces a different ordering of functions than grouping on the basis of occurrence of functions.'[47] This type of study leads to the sort of impasse with which the preceding chapter concluded. Rushton writes 'Central place theory is only one of the many areas of human geography where assumptions about the spatial behaviour patterns of individuals are incorporated in explanations of spatial structure.'[48] This is a 'chicken and the egg' type of problem; which comes first the city system or the patterns of behaviour of individuals?

At this point it is worth introducing the work that has been carried out to place the definition of shopping trade areas, or urban spheres, on a basis more in line with consumer behaviour. The earliest attempts were simply deterministic and formulated in the terms of gravity models. The most well known is Reilly's Law of Retail Gravitation which is usually given in the form:

$$Bb = \frac{Dab}{1 + \dfrac{Pa}{Pb}}$$

Where Bb is the break point between city A and city B in miles from B, i.e. B's sphere of influence; Dab is the distance between A and B in miles; and Pa, Pb are the populations of A and B respectively. Huff was responsible for restating this in probabilistic terms on the basis that the likelihood of a consumer going to any centre is based on the number of items required and the effort and expense which has has to make. From these two variables Huff derived an expression:

$$P\ (Cij) = \frac{\dfrac{Sj}{Tij^\lambda}}{\sum\limits_{j\ =\ i}^{n} \dfrac{Sj}{Tij^\lambda}}$$

Where $P\ (Cij)$ is the probability of consumer at a given point of origin i travelling to a given shopping centre j; Sj is the area of selling space devoted to the sale of a particular class of goods by shopping centre j; Tij is the travel

[47] R. G. Golledge, G. Rushton and W. A. Y. Clark (1966).
[48] G. Rushton (1969): Analysis of spatial behaviour by revealed space preference. *Ann. Assoc. Am. Geogr.* **59**, 391. For the comments that follow see D. L. Huff (1963): A probabilitic analysis of shopping centre trade areas. *Land. Econ.* **39**, 81.

time involved in getting from a consumer's travel base *i* to shopping centre *j*; and λ is a parameter to be estimated empirically to reflect the effect of travel time on various kinds of shopping trips. If P (Cij) is calculated for a series of points of origin (i) then isopleths, or equiprobability contours, can be drawn for each of the centres (j). A trade area can be identified by isolating points where the same equiprobability contours from different centres intersect.

4 Problems derived from extended approaches

But these attempts to move from deterministic to probabilistic interpretation although taking in consumer behaviour still assume the given pattern of central places and indeed make assumptions, such as the relevance of travel time or distance, which seems not to be confirmed by Rushton's work. Thus we are brought back to the problem of behaviour in relation to central places. One cannot assume that either one came first for behaviour patterns and the distribution of places are fundamentally interdependent and 'in the context of ongoing spatial processes, behavioural changes may call forth structural changes, as well as the converse.'[49] This situation creates critical problems for investigations which view central place systems independently of consumer behaviour, but equally it presents problems to investigations of consumer behaviour which accept a given distribution of central places in relation to which behaviour patterns are described.

The two elements which have been introduced into this chapter have provided the bases for much of the work, derived from central place ideas, which has exercised geographers in recent years. These elements are the extension of the retail gravity concept to provide basic models for regional planning and the ever-deepening concern with a behavioural approach as explanation is sought by moving from the aggregate scale of central place theory to the level of the individual and the way he perceives and uses the city system. These two developments are briefly discussed below, although it must be recorded that each has an extensive literature which is outside the scope of this volume to explore.

a Aggregate models derived from central place principles

Regardless of the divergence of individual actions from those predicted by the central place model, orders of towns can be effectively identified and the operation of the constraints of threshold and range remains meaningful at the general scale. At such a scale, therefore, the tenets of the model may be used for prediction and hence for planning, much of which has to remain at an aggregate level. Lakshamanan and Hansen's retail potential model[50] is presented here in the form set out by the UK Department of the

---

[49] B. J. L. Berry (1968): A synthesis of formal and functional regions using a general field theory of human behaviour; part IV, chapter 3 of B. J. L. Berry and D. F. Marble, editors (1968): *Spatial analysis*, 420 (Englewood Cliffs, NJ).

[50] T. R. Lakshamanan and W. G. Hansen (1965): A retail market potential model. *J. Amer. Inst. Plnnrs* 31, 134–50.

Environment.[51] The problem is to estimate the durable sales potential of a shopping centre. This is taken to be a function of its own size, the size and prosperity of its population catchment and its spatial relation to competing shopping facilities. In this context the size modified by income levels to give deployable expenditure can be equated with the threshold principle while competition from other centres represents the idea of range. The basic formulation is that of the gravity model with the region divided into a number of arbitrary zones as opposed to spheres of influence:

$$SAL_j = \Sigma RSP_i \; \frac{\dfrac{ATR^b_j}{Tij^a}}{\displaystyle\sum_\kappa \frac{ATR^b_k}{Tik^a}}$$

Where SAL_j represents durable sales at centre j; RSP_i, the retail spending power in zone i; ATR_j, ATR_k, the attraction indices for centres j and k; T_{ij}, T_{ik}, the interzonal travel time between zone i and centre j and zone i and centre k; and a, b are constants.

Before this can be run the various terms need to be defined; for example a measure of the attraction index has to be devised and travel times determined. The problems these cause will not be discussed since the concern here is with the nature of the concept rather than the technical problems of making it operational. Moreover, to a large extent the area of enquiry moves into that of regional planning rather than urban geography (although the boundaries between the two are more arbitrary than meaningful). Again, the introduction of this model is not a point of departure for embarking on the provision of a text in the building, calibration and operation of planning models, an obvious task in itself,[52] but rather to indicate one of the ways in which central place theory has played a part in generating models basic to contemporary regional planning.

b Consumer behaviour

If the planner has made considerable use of models derived from central place theory the geographer seemed at one stage to have reached an impasse: most central place studies were regarded simply as descriptive and not as explanatory. The discrepancy between action as predicted by central place theory and behaviour in the real world situation provided the basis for the resolution of this impasse. The work of geographers such as Murdie and Rushton (see pp. 122 ff.) backed by a major change in human geography itself towards a behavioural approach,[53] has generated a considerable range

---

[51] Department of Environment (1973): *Using predictive models for structure plans* (London: HMSO).

[52] See, for example, G. Chadwick (1971): *A systems view of planning* (London); and I. Masser (1972): *Analytical models for urban and regional planning* (Newton Abbot).

[53] K. Cox and R. G. Golledge (1969): Problems of behavioural geography. *North Western Univ., Dept. of Geogr. Res. Series*, 17 (Evanston, Illinois). For a much earlier statement at the beginning of this development see W. Kirk (1952): Historical geography and the concept of the behavioural environment. Indian Geographical Society. *Silver Jubilee Souvenir and N. Subrahmanyam Memorial Volume.*

of studies in consumer behaviour. This has meant a fundamental change in the scale of analysis from the city in the region to the individual in his 'environment': the new approach is usually called 'cognitive behavioural'.

'The cognitive behavioural approach to location theory and consumer behaviour is a synthetic framework, starting with the individual decision maker as the basic unit of analysis. The individual's behaviour is viewed as a function of the environmental situation and the decision-making processes with respect to the environment. In contrast to the deterministic location theory framework which makes a set of assumptions that factors out the processes of human decision making, the cognitive behavioural approach specifically focuses upon the nature of the decision-making process and the parameters which determine its outcome.'[54] The long quotation from R. M. Downs can be used to isolate four aspects of this approach which although separated are closely interlinked and overlap.[55] These are:

(*i*) *Motivation, goals and attitudes.* The whole question of what motivates the shopper is paramount for this determines consequent attitudes and goals. If the individual seeks to minimize costs then time will be spent 'shopping around' to find the cheapest source of goods. On the other hand a wealthy, or lazy, shopper might be content with the nearest source. Yet another person might look on shopping as a basis for socializing and choose the friendliest shop. In more general terms it is possible to adopt Wolpert's conclusion that the concept of the spatial satisficer appears more descriptively accurate of the behavioural patterns of the sample population than the normative concept of economic man. The individual is adaptively or intendedly rational rather than omnisciently rational.[56]

(*ii*) *Decision-making and preference studies.* The motives and attitudes of the consumer have to be translated into action and this is done via a decision-making process in which various desiderata are played off against each other. In short, each shopper will have a preference structure derived from basic attitudes and this can be represented by a series of cognitive categories such as cost (cheap – dear); distance (near – far); variety (good range of goods – poor range of goods); and so on.

(*iii*) *Perception.* Between the preference structure of an individual and the actual choice in the real world will intervene the individual's perception of the various shopping centres. This will depend not simply on abstract preferences but on a whole range of other influences including past experience.

(*iv*) *Search procedures and learning processes.* No individual will have

[54] R. M. Downs (1970): The cognitive structure of an urban shopping centre. *Environment and Behaviour* 2(1), 13–39.
[55] I would like to thank Dr. N. J. Williams for help in preparing this material.
[56] J. Wolpert (1964): The decision process in a spatial context. *Ann. Assoc. Am. Geogr.* 54, 558.

perfect knowledge of an area on which to base decisions. There will be rather a continuing process of learning and of comparing centres. During this phase successive searches will probably be made to find those shops or centres most in accord with preferences.[57] Here the problem is that such a process will culminate in habit which might become out of phase with changing reality, and, until it is complete or rigidified into habit, the actual behaviour of the individual may not be a confirmation of the preferences held.

Given the four aspects of a cognitive behavioural approach it will be increasingly apparent that the critical issue becomes the techniques of measurement which have to be devised in order to evaluate behaviour. An example from Downs will serve as an illustration of this sort of work.[58] A real difficulty is that as deeper comprehension of complex behaviour is sought so investigation merges into the work of the psychologist concerned with human motivation and choice. The basic problem presented by Downs was to access the image of a shopping centre held by a group of shoppers, the hypothesis to be tested in more general terms relating to the way a segment of the spatial environment was evaluated.

In order to achieve this Downs made use of the semantic differential devised by C. Osgood to measure the connotative meanings of concepts in what he termed 'semantic space.'[59] In its application in this case it operates by asking respondents to assess the shopping centre in relation to a series of bipolar attributes. Nine cognitive categories were hypothesized with four attributes in each category giving a total of thirty six in the total scale. The nine categories were: price; structure and design; ease of internal movement and parking; visual appearance; reputation; range of goods; service; shopping hours; atmosphere. The breakdown of one of these categories into the four attributes can be given as an example:

Structure and design

well designed	badly designed
simple layout	complicated layout
designed with shopper in mind	not designed with shopper in mind
wide pavements	narrow pavements

Each respondent was asked to assess the centre on a seven point scale ranged between the two extremes thus:

well designed ⎣__⎣__⎣__⎣__⎣__⎣__⎦ *badly designed*
    1   2   3   4   5   6   7

Respondents placed a mark at what they thought to be the appropriate

[57] R. G. Golledge and L. A. Brown (1967): Search, learning and the market decision process. *Geografiska Annaler, Series B* **49**, 117–24.

[58] R. M. Downs (1970).

[59] C. Osgood, G. Suci and P. Tannenbaum (1957): *The measurement of meaning* (Urbana, Illinois).

point. A mark between 2 and 3 would indicate that the centre was adjudged to be only fairly well designed. Each response was given a value and accordingly means and standard deviations for each attribute were calculated. In addition the total responses for each scale were correlated with the total responses for all other scales and a 36 × 36 matrix compiled. Downs then factor-analyzed the matrix to give the principal factors contained — that is, how the image of the shopping centre was structured. Reviewing these findings Downs concluded that the image of a downtown shopping centre is composed of eight cognitive categories which, arranged in order of descending importance, are:

1   Service quality.
2   Price.
3   Structure and design.
4   Shopping hours.
5   Internal pedestrian movement.
6   Shop range and quality.
7   Visual appearance.
8   Traffic conditions.

He then divided these into those related to the retail establishments themselves (1, 2, 4 and 6), and those related to the structure and function of the shopping centre (3, 5, 7 and 8). There is here a most significant movement from the simplistic assumptions of central place theory to the derivation of the base on which people behave. Even so there is a considerable way to go beyond this. The image needs to be collapsed in terms of social groups, age groups, type of residence and all the various characteristics of the population. Nader concludes a paper on socio-economic status and consumer behaviour, by demonstrating differences in expenditure pattern to type of house and the ownership of a car.[60]

In order to avoid one of the major problems of the semantic differential — the arbitrary selection of categories by the investigator, — it is possible to employ personal construct theory.[61] Very briefly, in this sort of operation the respondent is given three towns or shopping centres and asked to nominate the two most similar. The criterion of differentiation is then ascertained and built into the semantic differential so that the categories are constructed from the experience of people rather than imposed by the preconceptions of the investigator.

The introduction of personal construct theory implies that Downs's problem was relatively simple in that he was concerned with the evaluation of attitudes to one centre only, whereas in most investigations the task is to unravel the attitudes which led to the decision to select one out of a number

[60] G. A. Nader (1969): Socio-economic status and consumer behaviour. *Urban Studies* 6, 235−45.
[61] G. A. Kelly (1955): *The theory of personal constructs* (London); also D. Bannister (1962): Personal construct theory: a summary and experimental paradigm. *Acta Psychologica* 20, 104−120; and J. Harrison and P. Saare (1971): Personal construct theory in the measurement of environmental images. *Environment and Behaviour* 3, 351−74.

of possible centres. To achieve this geographers have resorted to attitude tests which were initially derived for work in social and educational psychology. The scaling of attitudes is usually accomplished by means of Likert or Thurstone scales based on the expression of agreement or disagreement to prepared statements. But this is a complex technical area and reference to appropriate literature is the only course here.[62]

This discussion has been directed towards indicating the nature of work in the field of consumer behaviour and the nature of the techniques which have been employed. The geographer faces very severe problems in this area for as the scale is enlarged to become that of the individual consumer so the study becomes more psychological than spatial.[63] Nevertheless the implications of the cognitive-behavioural approach to traditional geographical problems are far-reaching. 'There is no doubt that as a general framework it will aid us immensely in the search for lawfulness and regularity underlying shopping patterns . . . and it will be of fundamental importance in constructing theories about spatial behaviour. It will, however, take a very long time to reach this level of sophistication.'[64] It is the aggregate of multiplicity of individual decisions which underpins the patterns of central places: as is so often the case, the geographer's basic dilemma is one of the scale at which he wishes to work; his difficulty is to reconcile work at a variety of scales on the same problem.

If central place studies are beginning to consider consumer behaviour, there is as yet little attention devoted to the behaviour of the entrepreneur. Lewis[65] has attempted demonstrate how entrepreneurial interpretation of opportunities available can be seen in the context of part time operation of functions. Barton has approached the same problem in a different way by examining the development of the central place system or the creation of centrality. She concludes the 'exchange and the entrepreneurial role are basic features of the achievement of centrality. The entrepreneur occupies an institutional niche created by the existence of comparative advantages and imperfect competition. As a result, places achieve excess importance, or centrality, by virtue of capturing a role in exchange'.[66]

Certainly if the geographer is going to involve himself in studies of the way the whole central place system is perceived by the individual consumer, he

---

[62] The two key works are: R. Likert (1932); A technique for the measurement of attitudes. *Archives of Psychology* 140; L. Thurstone and E. Chave (1929): *The measurement of attitude* (Chicago). For a text in behavioural research see: F. N. Kerlinger (1969): *Foundations of behavioural research* (London).

[63] For an indication of work by psychologists see: H. M. Proshansky, W. H. Ittelson and L. G. Pivlin, editors (1970): *Environmental psychology: man and his physical setting* (New York), and for an example of the architects' interest see J. Lang, C. Burnette, W. Moleski and D. Vachon, editors (1974): *Designing for human behavior: architecture and the behavioral sciences* (Stroudsburg, Pennsylvania).

[64] B. J. Garner (1970): Towards a better understanding of shopping patterns; in R. H. Osborne, F. A. Barnes and J. C. Doornkamp, editors of *Geographical essays in honour of K. C. Edwards* (Nottingham).

[65] C. R. Lewis (1970). See also T. L. Bell, S. R. Lieber and G. Rushton (1974): Clustering of services in central places. *Ann. Assoc. Am. Geog.* **64**, 214–25.

[66] B. Barton (1978): The creation of centrality. *Ann. Assoc. Amer. Geogr.* 68(1), 44.

must also develop studies, on the lines of those concerned with the policy of firms in industrial location, which take account of the decisions by entrepreneurs to develop types of establishments in particualar towns.

5 Problems of historical change and the central place system

There is another series of problems that is associated with central place theory as the model Christaller presented is a deterministic economic model and allows for very little historical variance to be introduced. The material considered in this chapter might well lead to one of the dangers noted at the outset, for towns are not places solely for the satisfaction of economic demands. There is a wide variety of other demands, administrative, social, cultural, all of which have an influence on location and size. Many of these are derived from the past, a feature self-evident in such centres as Florence or Canterbury but also applicable on a minor scale. Even without these marked examples the evolutionary element has to be built in and a chance or random process substituted for the simple determinism of Christaller. To some extent this has been envisaged by a change to the employment of a probability (stochastic) approach to the generation of settlement patterns,[67] though the 'explanatory' element in these studies remains slight.

The actual process by which the city system is built up, however, is an area of enquiry which appears to offer a fair possibility of generalization once these inhibiting conditions are removed. In most cases it can be argued that at an early stage in the development of a city system, the competition and interaction between the centres, which is postulated as a necessary condition of central place systems, did not obtain. What did rule was the principle of separation whereby each centre served a surrounding area but lack of communications prevented competition and each centre was at a similar level.

Guttenberg has characterized this as a situation with 'distributed facilities',[68] that is, where the various urban facilities are distributed according to population in a system where little interaction takes place. This same situation has been envisaged by Webb[69] who postulated two theoretical viewpoints under which the phenomena of urban function may be developed. These he termed 'isolated urban society' and 'integrated urban society'. In the first, there are differentiated functions but no contact; in the second, full communication and free exchange of goods. As an example of the first condition, Von Thünen's isolated city is used and it is suggested that if this is cut off from all others then each city would of necessity duplicate the same services, all other things being equal. Attempting to cite an example, Webb takes up pre-industrial western society and maintains that 'existing in

[67] R. Morrill (1962): Simulation of central place patterns over time; in K. Norborg, editor (1962): *IGU symp. urban geogr. Lund 1960*, 109. R. Morrill (1965): *Migration and the spread and growth of urban settlement* (Lund). G. Olsson (1967): Central place systems, spatial interaction and stochastic processes. *Reg. Sci. Assoc. Pap.* **18**, 13.

[68] A. Z. Guttenberg (1960): Urban structure and urban growth. *J. Am. Inst. Plann.* **25**, 104.

[69] John W. Webb (1959): Basic concepts in the analysis of small urban centres of Minesota. *Ann. Assoc. Am. Geogr.* **49**, 55.

comparative isolation one from the other, there was often little contact of economic significance between the urban places of medieval Europe.'[70]

But even if economic organization was rudimentary, there was still a need for political and administrative control which in a 'pre-industrial' stage was usually dominant over economic relations. This political control was often exercised from a single centre which was the epitome of the folk culture and which thus attained a pre-eminence above a multiplicity of cities of the same low order; that is, it occupied a primate position. But economic development, the thickening of the whole web of economic activity which accompanies the process of urbanization, together with advances in communication techniques, led to interaction between these distributed points and to the possibility of a selected few being vested with higher order services by virtue of their nodality.

At this point one can introduce the ideas of primary and secondary urbanization. It is possible that this move towards discrimination between centres had already been partly anticipated by the creation of hierarchy of administrative centres related to the primate capital and the two emergent town systems, one based on economic activity, the other on political organization, do not mesh. The result is a haphazard system of towns, 'rotten boroughs' and 'ancient cities', with important administrative but negligible economic functions, and large 'urban areas' important economically but not otherwise. Further developments result in a sorting out of this situation, mainly, but not solely, in economic terms, though nearly all countries show that this sorting is far from complete.

This analysis is in line with that of Guttenberg who argues that transportation is the means by which the distributed features become 'undistributed' or related to a different ordering principle. Transportation decisions 'will result in a constantly changing structure with the emphasis shifting along the continuum between the situation with highly distributed centres to the situation with one major undistributed function.'[71] Lukermann argues in a similar way, identifying three elements in urban systems analysis: hierarchy, nodality and circulation. Nodality is identified as 'a behavioural act of man, not simply a geometric point or a circulation intersect. In behavioural terms a nodal location is that place where the individual has the greatest freedom to interact. Such a definition involves both population density and areal accessibility, as well as functional availability. Expressed in locational terms, nodality and hierarchy are conceptually analagous. A spatial hierarchy is the specification of a nodal system.'[72]

In the above 'the greatest freedom of the individual to interact' is very near to many of the ideas in the aspatial concepts of the process of urbanization already considered in chapter 2, and the two aspects are thus brought together. The generalized pattern is revealed as a series of isolated centres being brought into interaction through the operation of the circulation

[70] John W. Webb (1959), 56.
[71] A. Z. Guttenberg (1960), 109.
[72] F. Lukermann (1966), 22.

manifold and from that interaction a hierarchical situation appears.

This is in line with the present author's work in Wales.[73] There the Anglo-Norman conquest introduced the castle town or bastide into a non-urbanized folk society where the move towards urbanization was but incipient. There was no primary urbanization, no epitome of the folk culture, but only secondary urbanization and this created a series of military centres isolated amid an alien population and in an area of fragmented topography. But with the breakdown of isolation through the increase of transport facilities, differentiation became apparent. At first, this is represented in administrative terms, for government was the prime urban function and a hierarchy of administrative centres emerges, but one clearly reflecting the older military situation rather than the newer evolving economic one. The result is a period of transition or change until, by the end of the eighteenth century, a sorting out has taken place and a discernible 'economic' hierarchy is present.

It is clear that this process of development is seldom uninterrupted and complete, and any nation or area can go through the same process more than once. Thus in Wales a degree of equilibrium had barely been attained before the beginnings of iron working and coal mining in the mid-eighteenth century (or, to put it another way, the beginning of the Industrial Revolution) resulted in the generation of a whole new series of unifunctional settlements. The mining village is the epitome of the unifunctional 'node' dominated by the principle of separation. But interaction was now quicker and the patterns of circulation exercised a discriminatory influence on these nodes, creating the degrees of nodality which have resulted in a hierarchical arrangement of contemporary centres, that is one where towns can be ascribed to fairly clearly stepped grades or ranks.

The present urban system of Wales is a complete mix, resultant from the partial integration of two phases of development, neither of which has been completely consummated, worked out in terms of contemporary technological, economic and social characteristics. But if the complexity be disregarded, then the basic sequence can be understood in the terms outlined above. In this context the 'primate situation' is not regarded as inherent in the scheme: at no time in Wales has there been a primate city. It is, however, interesting to speculate that the tendency to equilibrium which is envisaged in the climax phase need not lead to a situation exclusively hierarchical in terms of the definition given above, and depending upon economic and cultural conditions, one could envisage the process leading to an arrangement in accord with either the 'law of the primate city' or the 'rank-size rule'. This would depend on the exact nature of the interaction between primary and secondary urbanization and between the developmental sequence outlined above. The aim here is not to postulate an abstract but unreal situation but to generalize the processes that have produced the wide range of variant conditions which now obtain.

The failure of an orthogenetic city to emerge in Wales and the complete

[73] H. Carter (1965): *The towns of Wales; a study in urban geography* (Cardiff). H. Carter (1970): *The growth of the Welsh city system* (Cardiff).

dominance of secondary urbanization is simply revealed in the fact that Wales had no capital city until 1955 when the opposition of the folk-culture was finally overcome by the reality of the present economic situation.

A situation has now been reached where it is possible to suggest the main controls of urban location as they have been set out in the last four chapters.

The accompanying diagram (figure 6–14) attempts to portray a conceptual framework which summarizes the various influences on the locational pattern. The urban system (S) is conceived as being created at time t_1 through a phase of genesis (P_1). The system itself becomes rapidly composed of two elements, one a set of towns owing their origin to special functions with peculiar locational demands, the other a set of towns owing their growth to central place functions derived from general regional demand. These are intimately related for their complex interaction produces an urban set (S_1). This net is then itself subject to the continuing

Figure 6–14: The growth of a system of cities.

modification brought about by two sets of influences. The first of these is the economic, technological and organizational changes which progressively bring new pressures to bear. Thus changes in transport techniques or the productivity of agriculture will influence the system. The second set of influences are closely related and could be included under the same general heading. These are the series of minor exogenous influences which, except in very unusual cases, continually affect the system.

The system therefore, is never a closed system but remains open (S_2). The minor or long term slow changes can be absorbed into the system without signs of discontinuity but in most areas there occur major changes and hence major exogenous interpolations which are clearly related to specific new urban roles with specific and new locational demands. This can involve the creation of an unconformable urban net (P_2). There follows a period of rapid adjustment with marked fluctuations in the rank position of towns in the system until, through the revised pattern of regional demand, a modified system (S_3) is produced. Once more this is subject to minor interpolations and will react to technological and organizational change. The present city system, therefore, is seen as a momentary still in a moving picture in the true context of 'sequent occupance'. It is the product of the interaction of a series of time and place related acts of growing and declining towns.

There are other theoretical formulations which can be linked with the scheme outlined. The whole process of town founding can be conceived as an innovation and the subsequent development as a diffusion process. Hägerstrand's three stages in the process[74] are very similar to the stages of 'town genesis', 'transition and sorting', and 'climax' that have been outlined for the Welsh system and indicated in more generalized form on figure 6–14. Each major phase has many analogies with the way in which the available space and economic potential are eventually taken into the urban service network and the way in which this network increase in density. Again the patterns of urban-industrial growth in a cumulative fashion set out by Pred,[75] and considered earlier, can be associated with the way in which the initial creations of a genetic phase can effectively remain the major foci by the positive influence of self-sustaining growth rather than by the sole operation of external circulation.

Lampard[76] in considering urban systems introduces the two notions of morphostasis and morphogenesis. Morphostasis represents the result of 'deviation-counteracting feedback networks' or 'a most probable state under constraint'. Morphogenesis is a deviation amplifying process, giving an open-ended development with no evident tendency to entropy. Lampard quotes Maruyama[77] as concluding that every system, including city systems,

[74] T. Hägerstrand (1952): The propagation of innovation waves. *Lund Stud. Geogr. Ser. B. Human Geography* **4**, 16–17.

[75] See chapter 3, page 54.

[76] E. Lampard (1968): The evolving system of cities in the United States; in H. S. Perloff and L. Wingo, Jr., editors (1968): *Issues in urban economics*, 98–100 (Baltimore).

[77] M. Maruyama (1963): The second cybernetics: deviation amplifying mutual causal processes. *Gen. Sys.* **8**, 233–41.

is made up of sub-systems variously manifesting deviation-correcting or amplifying processes whose prevalent effect will either tend to return the whole to morphostasis or transform it by morphogenesis. To some extent the genetic phase, the major exogenous interpolations, envisaged in figure 6–14 represent transformations by morphogenesis, the emerging city systems within phases of transition represent morphostasis. Generalizations which argue for increasing entropy in a city system — that is the movement of the system to a more uniform and less random form — are only acceptable for certain selected phases or periods; no universal process can be isolated.

The conclusions set out above are, to a degree, confirmed by Robson in his book *Urban growth*. After examining the growth of British towns during the nineteenth century, Robson concludes 'the details of the spatial patterns can only be interpreted in terms of the particular factor endowments and historical events which underlaid the growth of certain towns and the decay of others.'[78] These endowments and events epitomize the consequences of major exogeneous interpolation into the system of cities. The remainder of Robson's book seeks to demonstrate that 'the diffusion of entrepreneurial innovations through a set of nineteenth-century cities may well be characterized by a simultaneous process of hierarchical space jumping from larger to smaller cities and of localized spread outwards from regional centres.'[79] In essence this is a version of the cumulative character already considered as part of the way in which the city system grows. Robson's study adds both depth and elegance to previous work but provides no novel basis for synthesizing urban growth.

6 Conclusion

The situation, whereby classical central place concepts are increasingly revealed as inadequate, which has been sketched in this chapter may now be summarized as follows:

1   Hexagonal lattices have nowhere been convincingly demonstrated and even regularities have only been tentatively demonstrated.
2   A hierarchical structuring holds good only over limited and homogeneous areas; the aggregation of areas masks this structuring.
3   Studies of the perception and use of centres by individuals have not demonstrated that their behaviour is in accord with that predicted by theory.
4   The economic deterministic character of central place theory, just as it takes no account of individual perception, allows no room for the random disturbances brought into play in the historical past and which are still relevant to modern conditions.
5   The restriction of central place analysis solely to economic tertiary services represents an abstraction from the reality of city locations where a wide variety of other activities are performed and exert a marked influence.

[78] B. T. Robson (1973): *Urban growth: an approach* (London), 126.
[79] B. T. Robson (1973), 186.

To a large extent the changes in the nature of urban geography identified in Chapter 1 have, over the last decade, directed interest away from conventional central place studies. Modern urban geography when it emerged in the late 1950's and in the 1960's was dominated, virtually created, by central place theory. In 1962 Bunge could write, 'if it were not for the existence of central place theory, it would not be possible to be so emphatic about the existence of a theoretical geography . . . this author is of the opinion that the initial and growing beauty of central place theory is geography's finest intellectual product . . .'[80]. But now very little research takes the theory as its major theme. It was, of course, very much part of the quantitative, empirical, positivist tradition which has waned over and against both behavioural approaches and welfare orientated investigation, and indeed against what is called 'applied geography'. It is possible, therefore, to identify three offshoots of the central place tradition in urban geography:

1 *Marketing geography*. This is the main areas of 'application' where most studies have to take into consideration the central place system, and where some are based on it[81]. Certainly in this chapter the development of supermarkets and hypermarkets has not been considered although they are how critical elements in the retail system and have considerable impact on the internal patterning of the city (see Chap. 12 p. 319).

2 *Rural deprivation*. The academic identification of hierarchical levels or continua has given way to the measurement of deprivation created by differential access to goods and services which are only available at aggregated places. The more specialized the good or service the more distant it becomes to peripheral populations or, in central place terms, range increases as higher thresholds have to be attained. This is then exacerbated by disadvantage. The traditional ecological structuring elements of society, socio-economic status, life cycle and ethnicity, accentuate disadvantage. Thus the poor, immobile elderly suffer greatest from lack of access to essential services. This becomes an urban feature, too, as the intra-urban system of central places discriminates to the same degree as the inter-urban system. This problem is taken up again in chapter 15.

3 *Optimization studies*. The applied aspect of revealed deprivation appears in studies designed to optimize the distribution of goods and services to a given population[82]. Many problems which exercise welfare

---

[80] W. Bunge (1962): *Theoretical geography* (Lund), 129.

[81] R. L. Davies (1976): *Marketing geography* (London).

J. A. Dawson (1979): *The marketing environment* (London).

J. A. Dawson and D. A. Kirby (1979): *Small scale retailing in the U. K.* (Farnborough).

[82] For a general review see: D. M. Smith (1977): *Human geography: a welfare approach.* Chap. 11, Location and allocation problems: what should go where.

For some specific studies see: G. W. Shannon et al. (1969): The concept of distance as a factor in accessibility and utilization of health care. *Medical Care Review*, 26, 143–161.

G. W. Shannon et al. (1975): A method for evaluating the geographic accessibility of health services. *Professional Geographer*, 27, 30–36.

geographers, and those, too, who are more generally concerned with welfare, arise out of the management of the central place system and the pay-offs between range and threshold. The viability of rural schools, access to special hospitals, the variations in the prices of goods; all these are, at least in part, problems of the central place system.

Notes on further reading
The main references on consumer behaviour are included in the footnotes but the following are most useful:

Davies, R. L. (1973): Patterns and profiles of consumer behaviour. *Univ. Newcastle on Tyne, Dept. Geogr., Res. Series* **10.**

Davies, R. L. (1976): *Marketing geography with special reference to retailing* (London).

Downs, R. M. (1970): The cognitive structure of an urban shopping centre (see footnote 54).

Williams, N. J. (1979): The definition of shopper types as an aid in the analysis of spatial consumer behaviour *Tijdsch. voor econ. en soc. geog.*, 70, 157–163.

More general works are:

Cox, K. and Golledge, R. G. (1969): *Problems of behavioural geography* (see footnote 34).

Downs, R. M. (1970): Geographic space perception: past approaches and future prospects; in *Progr. in Geogr.* **2** (London).

Foxall, G. R. (1977): *Consumer behaviour* (Cambridge).

Gold, J. R. (1980): *An introduction to behavioural geography* (Oxford).

The study of Welsh towns by the author attempts to outline the growth of a system of cities:

Carter, H. (1969): *The growth of the Welsh city system* (Cardiff).

Morrill's study of part of Sweden should also be read:

Morrill, R. L. (1966): Migration and the spread and growth of urban settlement. *Lund Stud. Geogr. Series B Hum. Geogr.* **26.**

Robson's study is now the best complete work on city growth:

Robson, B. T. (1973): *Urban growth: an approach* (see footnote 78).

Other relevant studies are:

Lampard, E. (1968), The evolving system of cities in the United States (see footnote 76 and further studies across p. 141).

Madden, C. H. (1956): Some spatial aspects of urban growth in the United States. *Econ. Devel. and Cult. Change* **4,** 386.

Thompson, W. R. (1965): *A preface to urban economics* (Baltimore); chapter 1, Economic growth and development: processes, stages and determinants.

The most useful study utilizing the notion of entropy in settlement systems is:

Semple, R. K. and Golledge, R. G. (1970): An analysis of entropy changes in a settlement pattern over time. *Econ. Geogr.* **46,** 157.

Studies of intra-urban business districts are:

Berry, B. J. L. (1962): *The commercial structure of American cities: a review* (see footnote 25).

Carol, H. (1960): The hierarchy of central functions within the city (see footnote 22).

Dutt, A. K. (1969): Intra-city Hierarchy of central places: Calcutta as a case study (see footnote 37).

Garner, B. J. (1966): The internal structure of retail nucleations (see footnote 13).

Johnston, R. J. (1966): The distribution of an intra metropolitan central place hierarchy in Melbourne (see footnote 33).

Jones, R. (1967): Central place theory and the hierarchy and location of shopping centres in a city: Edinburgh (see footnote 35).

For a study which argues for a continuum in shopping centres see:

Beavon, K. S. O. (1972): The intra-urban continuum of shopping centres in Cape Town. *South African Geog. Jnl.* **54**, 58–71.

A succinct statement of a typology of business centres is given in:

Berry, B. J. L. (1967): *Geography of market centres and retail distribution* (see footnote 25) 42–58, 'The urban case'.

A general overview with a good bibliography is to be found in:

Mills, E. (1974): *Recent developments in retailing and urban planning.* Prag Technical Papers TP3

A paper which considers the entrepreneurial attitude in consumer behaviour is:

Blommestein et alia (1980): Shopping perception and preferences: a multi-dimensional attractiveness analysis of consumer and entrepreneurial attitudes. *Econ. Geog.*, 56(2), 155–174.

Two studies which review aspects of the evolution of the city system in the United States are:

Conzen, M. P. (1977): The maturing urban system in the United States 1840–1910. *Ann. Assoc. Amer. Geogrs.*, 67(1), 88–108.

Meyer, D. R. (1980): A dynamic model of the integration of frontier urban places into the United States system of cities. *Econ. Geog.* 56(2), 120–140.

Whilst a classic overview of the evolution of the American city system was set out by:

Borchert, J. R. (1967): American metropolitan evolution. *Geogr. Rev.* 57, 301.

A book of readings contains the usual varying value gathering of papers

Bourne, L. S. and Simmonds, J. W. eds. (1978): *Systems of cities: readings on structure, growth and policy.* (Oxford).

but the most extensive review of the development and present characteristics and trends of settlement systems is to be found in the work of the International Geographic Union's Committee on National Settlement Systems:

Polish Academy of Science (1979–80): *The national settlement systems* (Warsaw), 3 vols.

7

The Analysis of Town Plan

The distribution pattern of towns and the complex flow of goods and people within that pattern have been represented in the preceding chapters as constituting a grand unity or, if the term is preferred, a system. But for purposes of examination that unity has been broken and the whole divided into a number of aspects which could be separately considered. In examining the *internal* characteristics of towns, as against their external relations, the same general structuring can be proposed, for at the most complete and complex end of the scale there is the 'townscape'. This term 'townscape' is given different emphasis dependent on the particular discipline in the context of which it occurs, but in urban geography it is taken to mean the whole objective visible scene in the urban area, or the total subjective 'image of the city'.[1]

This totality can again be envisaged as a system made up of a complex of interrelated parts. It also follows that there are comparatively few studies of 'townscape' because of the very intricacy of the problem, although a wide new field of enquiry is being opened by studies of perception which, instead of accepting an all-embracing objective interpretation of the townscape, are concerned to evaluate what elements are perceived by the individual and in what way this perception is related to behaviour and hence to activity systems within the city.[2] But if this aspect of perception, whereby the individual reduces the city to the level of his own needs and operations, is left aside until later (chapter 14) the more formal interpretation is left.

It has now become a convention to break down the complexity of townscape into three component parts; street plan or layout, architectural style or build, and function or land-use. These are closely interrelated and indeed their separation in academic studies has led to gross distortions of reality. Most economic theories of land-use ignore the fact that a town is made up of three-dimensional structures and assume the spread of uses over an even, undifferentiated surface. But for analytical purposes, and with the same principle in view as was evident in the analysis of urban functions, of advancing comprehension by the simplification of reality, it is preferable to adopt this standard breakdown in the first place and consider each of the three components of townscape separately.

The first of the three is town plan, the analysis of which has the anomaly of

---

[1] K. Lynch (1960): *The image of the city* (Cambridge, Mass.).
[2] F. Stuart Chapin (1965): *Urban land use planning*, second edition, 221 *et seq.* (Urbana, Ill.).

being one of the oldest and most widely known aspects of urban geography and, at the same time, the one in which comparatively little progress has been made. At the Lund Symposium on Urban Geography in 1960, Garrison maintained that in urban morphology 'the studies we are now making are no richer than the studies we were making twenty or thirty years ago'[3] and blamed this on the lack of development of general theory and the failure to use good measuring devices. The intervening decades have seen very little change in this situation. Students of town plan have had no Christaller to follow and consequently have tended to work within traditional lines. These traditions have been made up of two sorts of analysis, the one mainly concerned with shape, the other with the historical components of the plan.

The analysis of the shape or form of the town plan has long generated a terminology which has become part of everyday vocabulary. The most common of all these terms is the 'grid plan' or 'chequer board'. Strictly speaking this means a layout in which every street crosses another at right angles and at the same interval. Looser use of the term has, however, reduced it to mean any sort of rectangular arrangement of streets. In contrast with the true grid is the completely irregular layout, while the radial-concentric plans form a third group. Radial-concentric is a self defining term where properly a number of roads radiate from a centre and are successively cut by a series of concentric circular roads, the centre of the radials and the circles being common. But again this term has been debased and is used generally for any street layout which has a strong circular, or indeed nuclear element.

Debasement was to a large extent inevitable for few cities show a street plan which meets the precise demands of the true grid or radial-concentric schemes and the terms have therefore become little more than a conventional descriptive shorthand. Nevertheless, attempts have been made to erect rich classificatory structures on these rather inadequate foundations. Dickinson has proposed what he terms 'basic systems of urban ground plan'.[4] These are defined as follows:

1   *Irregular plans.* When the conditions are strictly interpreted the streets in this group are haphazard in width and direction and there are no dominant through routes or points. There would be few true examples although Dickinson points to the Moorish towns of Spain and some older sections of North African towns.

2   *Radial-concentric plans.* The term has been defined above. In so far as progressive outward growth from a nucleus, such as church or market place, is envisaged Dickinson is inclined to look upon these plans as the result of natural growth, rather than as necessarily planned forms.

3   *Rectangular or grid plans.* Again these have already been defined. A progressive modification of the true grid to the generally rectangular can be included under this omnibus description.

[3] K. Norborg, Editor (1962): Symposium discussion. *IGU symps. in urban georg.*, Lund 1962. 463.
[4] R. E. Dickinson (1950): *The west European city* (London).

This outline is a useful, though not very penetrating, descriptive or classifying device in approaching the study of plan. Most towns fall into none of these categories neatly and accordingly further elaboration has been attempted. The sterility of this approach can be illustrated by considering a scheme proposed by Tricart[5] which is given in table 7−1 in outline and should be read with the appended notes.

The other traditional approach to the study of town plan has been

table 7−1: Tricart's (1954) scheme for the analysis of town plan

```
1   Homogeneous towns, i.e. towns with a unified structure[1]
    a Planned towns[2]      (1) Rectangular plans
                                 i Linear
                                ii Ribbed
                               iii Parallel
                                iv Grid
                            (2) Radial concentric plans
                                 i Star[3]
                                ii Circular[4]
    b Unplanned towns, i.e. towns of natural growth[5]
                            (1) Fortress towns[6]
                            (2) Star shaped towns[7]
                            (3) Irregular plans[8]

2   Heterogeneous towns, i.e. towns with a complex structure[9]
    a Replanned towns[10]
    b Polynuclear towns[11]
    c Net pattern towns[12]
    d Globular towns[13]    (1) Concentric
                            (2) Radial
```

1 The essential feature is that the town is made up of a simple plan unit, a situation which is unlikely in any area of strong urban growth.
2 Allowance has to be made for alteration of the planned core by later growth under changed conditions.
3 The radials dominate.
4 The concentric roads dominate.
5 These displays less systematic forms but possess a homogeneity often dependent on continued adaptation to a dominant feature either physically derived, such as an aspect of site, or culturally derived from the past.
6 This is an odd class since it is designated by function rather than by shape. The implication is that form is dominated by a strong focal point.
7 Created by free outward growth, particularly where there have been no walls.
8 Irregularity of plan is often a consequence of site conditions but the same conditions mean that the town develops as one unit.
9 In this major category the towns are made up of more than one plan element giving a richer and more varied class but one which Tricart argues is not as numerically dominant as might be expected. A transitional class is suggested where a town is made up of a series of clear geometrical elements but which have no relation to each other; Los Angeles is the example proposed.
10 A new planned section is often added to an older irregular core.
11 Made up of juxtaposed but contrasted elements, such as ex-colonial towns with their European compounds contrasted with the native quarters. (See pp. 386−90)
12 This is near to the original meaning of 'conurbation', being made up of a series of separate nodes connected by transport lines. A mining area is suggested but presumably the classic 'dispersed city' would be of this form.
13 The diverse elements here show one of the emphases noted in 3 and 4 above.

through the identification of major growth phases. Towns, it is argued, seldom grow slowly and gradually but are characterized by periods of still-stand and periods of rapid growth. The periods of extension provide the successive plan elements, and it is possible to isolate them and then to interpret them by reference to the general history of town development.

In chapter 6 where the urban growth process was examined it was noted that a distinctive aspect of this process was physical extension and it was also noted that there were a large number of studies devoted to this aspect of urbanization. These are the standard works, such as *Town building in history*[6], which isolate and examine each dominant phase in the history of town design. Examples of these books range from Lavedan's classic *Histoire de l'urbanisme*[7] to the recent fine work by Reps, *The making of urban America*.[8] There is little point here in attempting to present a review of phases of town development in this tradition for any selected area. The standard works are easily accessible and an attenuated outline of no value. In the geographical context of plan analysis, for most of the above works are historical in concept, the main purpose of such an approach is to establish the generality of urban extension in an area. The way in which any town has grown and the successive phases identified can then be interpreted in relation to the general pattern.

The key to this sort of approach is the conventional growth plan which has played such a major role in urban geographical studies. Figure 7−1 shows the growth to 1900, of the small town of Aberystwyth on the west coast of Wales. The dates selected are such as to isolate the three major periods when rapid extension took place so that the block structure of the medieval town, the grid of the early nineteenth-century extensions beyond the walls and onto the common lands of the borough, and the linear extensions of the latter part of the century, are clearly established. Three growth phases are thus linked with three types of layout. In turn each layout can be interpreted as a characteristic product of its age. Thus the early nineteenth-century development is in many ways a characteristic extension which has found its apotheosis in the westward extension of London. Figure 7−2 shows the way in which London had grown rapidly in the late seventeenth and particularly in the late eighteenth century and the early nineteenth by the development of a whole series of squares and terraces on what had once been aristocratic estates. Sir John Summerson's *Georgian London* provides a study of this process, constituting a detailed investigation, therefore, of one of these growth phases.[9]

It is apparent that this process of plan analysis is essentially historical and provides little of the theory or measurement which it is claimed are needed to put geographical studies on a more respectable plane, or at least to substitute generality for the scholarly study of the unique.

[5] J. Tricart (1954): L'habitat urbain. *Cours de géographie humaine*, Fasc. 2 (Paris).
[6] F. R. Hiorns (1956): *Town building in history* (London).
[7] P. Lavedan (1926−52): *Histoire de l'urbanisme*. 4 volumes (Paris).
[8] J. W. Reps (1965): *The making of urban America* (Princeton).
[9] J. N. Summerson (1946): *Georgian London* (London).

Figure 7–1: Growth plan of Aberystwyth. *After H. Carter in E. G. Bowen (1957).*

This is a standard growth plan in which medieval nucleus, early nineteenth-century rectangular extra-mural extension and late nineteenth and early twentieth-century ribbon development are apparent.

Certainly some advance in this respect has been made by M. R. G. Conzen who has attempted to establish 'some basic concepts applicable to recurrent phenomena in urban morphology'.[10] There is, however, a considerable conceptual gap between the isolation of 'recurrent phenomena' and the 'provision of a theoretical basis yielding concepts of general application' and whereas Conzen undoubtedly provides a major step forward both in concept and meticulous analysis of plan, his work hardly provides a *theoretical* basis. Conzen's main contribution, the admirable detail of analysis excluded, would seem to lie in the way in which the interaction between phases of extension is introduced, whereas often in previous studies bits of plan have been merely tacked on successively. He demonstrates at the outset that the major townscape aspects—plan, build and land-use—react at different

[10] M. R. G. Conzen (1960): Alnwick: a study in town plan analysis. *Trans. Inst. Br. Geogr.* **27**.

Legend:
- Medieval Nuclei
- Regular development in small units chiefly late 17th and early 18th centuries
- Irregular development in small units chiefly late 17th and early 18th centuries
- Regular development in large units the West End Estates
- Scattered development of suburban land in units of varying size Dotted squares indicate villa development
- Ribbon development

Figure 7–2: The growth of London up to 1830. *After J. N. Summerson (1945)*

A growth plan on a very different scale from that in figure 7–1. Here the major elements in London's growth are clearly depicted. The medieval city is surrounded by irregular close development, which by the nineteenth century was mainly manufacturing in function and working class in character. The regular development of the western areas about the medieval nucleus foreshadows the regular development of estates. Some detail has been omitted from the original.

rates to the forces of change brought to bear on them. Land-use is the most volatile and can respond rapidly. The buildings themselves can be adapted to alternative uses without replacement, and the capital invested in them means that this takes place so that change is less rapid than with land use. But the layout of a town, the streets themselves, cannot be destroyed and rebuilt as easily as single buildings, and hence remains relatively permanent. The result, Conzen argues, is that plan is the most conservative aspect of townscape and hence demands a historical approach.

At the outset, therefore, his work is conventional insofar as it involves the identification of growth phases. It is only within this approach that some fundamental concepts are introduced which it is claimed have significance beyond the simple case under consideration.

Good examples of these concepts are the ideas of 'the fixation line' and 'the fringe belt'. Conzen criticizes many of the traditional growth plans, stating that the phases mapped are haphazardly chosen and are seldom related to real structural features in the plan itself. But such structural features can be identified, for the plan is not made up by a simple process of addition. Thus in the growth process certain limits are established which by their significance act as fixation lines. These lines structure the plan which grows in annular fashion in relation to them in a series of fringe belts, so that the whole plan can be conceived as being given form by the interaction of successive fixation lines and fringe belts. In the case Conzen analyses, the small town of Alnwick in Northumberland, the medieval wall is considered as constituting a fixation line. In relation to it two processes develop, repletion within the wall and accretion outside it. Accretion takes place within the fringe belt through the development of the open fields which lay outside the fixation line. The fringe belt itself is composed of two sections, the proximal or inner margin where development is closer and more continuous, and the distal or outer margin where growth is more sporadic and the development more dispersed in character. Ultimately the fringe belt plots can be *preserved*, that is they remain as open ground within the urban area, or they can be *translated*, that is used for special purposes. Thus one can conceive of many urban parks and gardens as 'preserved fringe belt plots'. The general outline of the situation is illustrated in figure 7−3.

The above summary is but an outline of one of the concepts introduced into his analysis by Conzen. The approach he adopts clearly goes beyond the descriptive account of growth phases and digs down into the structure of town plan. Indeed the very notion that plan has such a structuring is a notable advance on the idea that it merely consists of adding successive pieces together. But valuable as this is, the claim that a theory is being developed is not justified. The approach is not theoretical-deductive but essentially empirical-inductive and it is on the empirical approach that emphasis is ultimately placed. When Conzen identifies 134 plan elements in a small town (population 7,500) then it is evident that immense local complexity has overtaken generality. As a work of intense scholarship and one which adds notably to the conventional growth plan study, Conzen's book is distinctive.

Figure 7–3: The fringe belts of Alnwick in 1851. *After M. R. G. Conzen (1960).*

This is a summary map which omits much of the detail of the original. The fixation line marks the former town walls; the inner fringe belt represents development upon the 'tails' of the former burgage plots; the extramural belt represents more spacious development on the land outside the walls. These are the structuring elements in the evolving plan.

A series of papers by Whitehand has developed some of the implications of Conzen's work.[11] In particular he has effectively demonstrated the operation of a process of competition for fringe belt sites between the institutions that are particularly characteristic of these areas — for example, the parks and gardens noted above — and residential uses, which can compete effectively in times of economic and housing boom. Whitehand writes, 'Institutions originally located at some distance from the edge of the built-up area, on what were submarginal sites for the house builder, may be

[11] J. W. R. Whitehand (1967): Fringe belts: a neglected aspect of urban geography. *Trans. Inst. Brit. Geogr.* **41**, 223–33; (1972): Building cycles and the spatial pattern of urban growth. *Trans. Inst. Brit. Geogr.* **56**, 39–55; (1974): The changing nature of the urban fringe: a time perspective; chapter 3 in J. H. Johnson, editor: *Suburban growth* (London).

surrounded by new residential development by the end of a housing boom. Thus we must envisage a situation in which, by the end of a boom period, a zone of housing will have been added to the built-up area, but, scattered beyond it and sometimes lying within it, will be the sites of institutions. During a housing slump, while the house builder is largely inactive, institutions will develop the majority of the most accessible sites which, added to what were outlying institutional sites created during the previous housing boom period, will form a zone with a strongly institutional character. Repeated cycles of booms and slumps are likely to result in a series of alternating zones characterized by different proportions of institutions and housing.'

This research is most significant because the investigation of morphology via the fringe belt is integrated with that of land-use patterns and is therefore relevant not only to the chapters which follow on urban land-use and the rural-urban fringe, but especially to that most important area of the integration of morphological and functional studies.

There are two aspects of mathematical geography which would seem to have some relevance to the problem of town plan. The first of these is the analysis of shape as proposed by Bunge.[12] Since descriptions of plan are often couched in the terminology of shape—star shaped or globular for example—then it would seem that the overall shape of towns could be analyzed in this fashion. At the moment, however, the theoretical basis is hardly established firmly and the complexity introduced—for the overall shape also possesses an internal structure (streets and blocks)—would seem to indicate that although there may be a future line of development, it is as yet too tentative to be explored here.

The second aspect is the development of theoretical work on the description of line patterns. The network of city streets is, *par excellence*, a line pattern and it would seem that any statistical descriptive device would enable a more relevant and measured comparison to be made of street patterns. A study which might well be appropriate is that of Dacey on line patterns;[13] but the ultimate grouping of such patterns into random, grouped and non-random, in the same way as point patterns are analyzed by nearest-neighbour methods, seems far too restricted as far as town plan analysis is concerned.

A further area of investigation could well be associated with the dimensional analysis of linear networks. A town plan is a linear network and it would seem that all the techniques which are appropriate to this sort of problem could equally be applied to town plans. If rail networks in countries can be analyzed then there seems no reason why street patterns in towns cannot, although a major problem does occur in the definition and identification of the networks.[14]

[12] W. Bunge (1962): *Theoretical geography*, 73—87 (Lund).

[13] M. F. Dacey (1967): Description of line patterns; in W. L. Garrison and D. F. Marble, editors (1967): *Quantitative geography*, Part I, 277 (Evanston, Ill.).

[14] P. Haggett, A. Cliff and A. Frey (1977): *Locational analysis in human geography*, 2nd edition, 468—70 (London); P. Haggett and R. J. Chorley (1969): *Network analysis in geography* (London).

The total length of the street system (L) related to area (A) might provide a beginning where L/A gives a measure of street density, and the variance of street density over the urban area would be an interesting aspect of plan.[15] The shape of the network, an aspect of graph theory as proposed by Kansky, is less easy to derive since this involves the concept of diameter, or the shortest distance between the most distant vertices of the plan.[16] If the total city plan is broken into convenient smaller units in order to identify internal variation, then 'diameter' can have no real meaning. It is unfortunate in this respect that the rich resources of graph theory cannot easily be brought to bear. Perhaps the simplest measure would be merely to find the mean angle at which streets intersect in each small unit and this, together with the street density and a measure of linear grouping into random, non-random and grouped patterns, might be utilized to associate similar plan areas. The result would be a breakdown of the total city layout into 'plan regions' based on objective and measurable criteria. The interpretation of this regional pattern would then be the basic purpose of plan analysis.

This introduction of 'purpose' immediately raises the need to consider plan contrasts from some more relevant standpoint than the traditional historical view. The foundation already exists if Stanislawski's study of the grid pattern town is examined.[17] In a paper which is primarily concerned with the evolution of the grid pattern, he derives certain general conditions which are necessary for such a plan to be adopted. That is, Stanislawski presents an argument that, independent of particular historical circumstances, a grid will emerge given certain conditions. There are five conditions proposed:

1 A new town, or a new part of a town is in question.
2 There should be centralized control.
3 Very often the new town has colonial status.
4 There should be a measured disposition of available land.
5 There should be a knowledge of the grid.

Inspection of these will reveal that, excepting the last, they can be reduced to the single notion of the operation of centralized political control in a colonial or quasi-colonial situation. But it is possible to carry the argument further. The rigidity of the grid demands centralized political control. In more general terms, uniformity of plan (though this may take a wide variety of forms other than the grid) reflects organized central control, so that contrasts in the uniformity of plans are a reflection of the degree of the concentration of power. This concentration can be interpreted via the decision-making process: thus when decision making is fragmented, plans are incoherent; when it is concentrated, plans are coherent. The merchants of medieval London built their houses where they wished and from this

[15] P. Haggett and R. J. Chorley (1969).

[16] K. J. Kansky (1963): Structure of tranport networks: relationships between network geometry and regional characteristics. *Univ. Chicago, Dept. Geogr., Res. Pap.* **84.**

[17] D. Stanislawski (1946): The origin and spread of the grid pattern town. *Geogr. Rev.* **36,** 105.

fragmentation an incoherent plan of streets and alleys resulted. The modern suburbs are laid out by a municipal authority and a coherent plan appears.

This particular line of argument may be contested, although it is more likely to be judged self-evident. But it is a line independent of *particular* historical input defining a unique situation. It suggests that if plan characteristics could be measured by such methods as those proposed above, then these could be set against a series of other variables, one of which would be a measure of the degree of concentration of the decision-making process. It is the essence of this argument that the variables which shape plan can be isolated independently of any one historical phase. It is possible to propose a list which would include, for example, political, economic, cultural and religious factors. These do not work independently, however, and most plan elements are a product of two or more, or indeed of all of them. In the present context they may be considered separately.

Under the heading political influences are included those forces which are related to the concentration of power either in the hands of a single person or a group of people. It has already been maintained that the conditioning forces of the grid plan as envisaged by Stanislawski nearly all pertain to the concentration of power. The same situation is seen in that phase of town building which is usually given the name Renaissance and Baroque. Mumford, outlining the controlling conditions of the new urban complex, writes, 'between the fifteenth and eighteenth centuries a new complex of cultural traits took shape in Europe. . . . The new pattern of existence sprang out of a new economy, that of mercantile capitalism; a new political framework, mainly that of a centralized despotism or oligarchy, usually embodied in a national state; and a new ideological form, that derived from mechanistic physics.'[18] Here Mumford associates three of the variables that have been isolated — economic, political and cultural — and from them derives urban form. *The city in history* is perhaps the outstanding study which sees plans as the product of such associated forces, although their analysis is confined to the usual historical progression. But in a section, headed appropriately 'The ideology of power',[19] Mumford derives the obvious parallel with a much earlier period, 'thus the baroque rulers reinstated all the institutions of the original urban implosion.'[20] But the comparison is not completely true for although the processional way of Ur might have been a response to the same basic forces as the avenues of Versailles, the residential areas were very differently disposed. The order and harmony of mechanistic physics had produced an emphasis on the complete balance and control of the whole plan, but such was certainly not the case at Ur where the detail of much of the city seems to have been the consequence of innumerable individual decisions. But it follows that the city plan is the reflection of the concentration of power and of the cultural forces at work.

Versailles has already been noted; Richelieu (figure 7–4) provides a

[18] L. Mumford (1961): *The city in history*, 345 (New York).
[19] L. Mumford (1961), 363–7.
[20] L. Mumford (1961), 367.

A Place du Marche
b Place des Religieuses
C Market Hall
D Church

Figure 7—4: Richelieu. This is a composite map which attempts to depict in diagrammatic form the layout of the town and the château and its grounds.

smaller but no less appropriate example and can indeed be regarded as the precursor of Versailles.[21] Cardinal Richelieu decided in 1625 to transform an old residence and convert it into a château fitting to his estate. The architect was Jacques Lemercier. The château was finished by 1635, but in 1633 royal permission had been obtained 'fair bâtir un bourg clos, avec pouvoir d'y établir des marchés et foires ayant pareils privilèges que celles de la ville de Niort et de Fontenay-le-Comte.' The whole layout displays that unity of design that comes from being built at one time and under the complete control of one hand. The aspects of design, which Lavedan in his *Histoire de l'urbanisme* carefully notes, are a consequence of that control. It is possible to discuss at length the aesthetic and planning principles of this case, but these details, such as the way the main squares are disposed, are a consequence of the design ideas of the time.

The same concentration of power, although in a somewhat different general context, led to the ground plan of Washington, appropriately a centre of federal government and the focal point of the political power of the United States. At the same time it had clear links with its European predecessors through L'Enfant as designer — who 'was the product of his age and the instrument through which certain principles of civic design that had

[21] For a description see P. Lavedan (1926—52): *Histoire de l'urbanisme; Renaissance et temps modernes*, 228—32 (Paris).

been developed in western Europe found expression on the Potomac river.'[22] The whole situation, however, in which these principles could be put into effect depended upon the unity of political control vested in the commissioners as the instrument of the president of the United States.

If, in contrast, one considers towns during the industrial period, two differing aspects appear. On the one hand the concentration of power led to the construction of company towns with very clearly marked rectangular patterns. But at the same time the freedom in many places from any controlling national or municipal authority led to the conditions of near anarchy under which planless agglomerations of poor cottages took place creating the feature so often associated with industrialization. Without prolonging the discussion, it is contended that studies of the way in which controlling power is distributed will give considerable insight into the degree of formality in town layout.

To a large extent in the above discussions a second variable has been introduced but not identified and this is the one which was initially called 'cultural'. This is the system of social values which underlies town layout. Perhaps an appropriate example is Philadelphia (figure 7−5). 'The dominant force in the shaping of Philadelphia,' writes A. N. B. Garvan, 'was the philosophy of William Penn.'[23] This can be applied to the layout as well as the general atmosphere of the early city. The charter which Penn obtained from Charles II in 1681 established him as governor and proprietor. Purchasers of a share in the province were also to be provided with a city plot within Philadelphia. The commissioners who accompanied the first settlers were given detailed instructions, dated 30 September, 1681, for the laying out of the new town, and the regularity of a somewhat unusual town was clearly provided for by Penn in the instructions. 'Be sure to settle the figure of the town so that the streets hereafter may be uniform down to the water from the country bounds; let the place for the storehouse be on the middle of the key, which will yet serve for market and statehouses too. This may be ordered when I come, only let the houses built be in a line, or upon a line, or as much as may be. . . . Let every house be placed, if the person pleases, in the middle of its plot, as to the breadth way of it, that so there may be ground on each side for gardens or orchards, or fields, that it may be a green country town, which will never be burnt, and always be wholesome.'[24]

Garvan points out that this implies a very unorthodox city since Penn 'neglected the urban centre for his gentlemen's seats. He visualized, not a city but a residential district of regularly arranged parks with uniform streets down to the water from the country bounds.'[25] The only commercial consideration is the 'place for storehouses'. The actual planning on the spot by Thomas Holme brought to bear some experience of town foundation in Ireland,[26] as well as much of the discussion of the reconstruction of London

[22] J. W. Reps (1965), 252.
[23] A. N. B. Garvan (1966): Proprietary Philadelphia as an artefact; in O. Handlin and J. Burchard, editors (1966): *The historian and the city*, 197 (Cambridge, Mass.).
[24] J. W. Reps (1965), 160.
[25] A. N. B. Garvan (1966), 190.
[26] A. N. B. Garvan (1966), 191.

Figure 7–5: Philadelphia in 1682.

after the Great Fire, so that eventually 'little remained of Penn's original plan and instructions. Instead an extremely interesting and complex plan evolved which owed little to the proprietor except the partial achievement of his intent. But nevertheless Holme firmly agreed with Penn's objectives to create a regional plan suitable for Quaker worship in which the proprietor's interests would be secure.' Garvan develops the contrast between Philadelphia and the New England settlements from which it had two major differences. The settlement was widely scattered and settlers isolated and the whole of the three counties was covered more or less at once: there was no moving frontier. Only a population predominantly free of dependence, either upon a fixed ministry or a place of worship, could make so rapid an advance. Friends free to workship with one another in their own houses found the scheme totally agreeable, while their contemporaries disputed in New England legislatures the precise location of Puritan meeting houses and adjacent home lots.[27]

It is also instructive to observe the consequences for the plan once the concentration of decision making in Penn's hands was broken. The American Revolution destroyed the proprietary, which was transformed into a 'political administration for the benefit of democratic voters and settlers'. The result was the substitution of a varied, haphazard 'control', in which individual speculation was a key factor. 'It would be at this point quite easy to condemn the *laissez-faire* city and point out that as an artefact of the mature philosophy of William Penn, Philadelphia's end was near.'[28] The point here is neither to condemn nor praise nor even to evaluate plan in such terms at all but to demonstrate the way in which the variables that have been isolated act in fact as a complex matrix. The single control of Penn represents the concentration of decision making already identified; the city he built was the creation of the cultural values by which he lived. As power was dispersed other values began to play their part, very different from the Quaker beliefs of Penn. The general layout of the whole area as well as part of the particular detail of the city of Philadelphia can however be fairly associated with the general cultural inheritance of the proprietor and his associates. In particular a contrast between the mode of settlement in the area and that of the Puritans in New England can be related to differences in the form of worship.

This aspect, of religious influence on plan, is one which deserves more attention than it has had. In extra-European areas cosmological forces have been particularly important and their significance within Europe has not been properly evaluated. Wheatley[29] in a critical review of Sjoberg's *Preindustrial city*[30] argues that Sjoberg 'does less than justice to a principle related to that of symbolic centrality, and that is the construction of the city as an *imago mundi*, with the cosmogony as paradigmatic model.' Wheatley further points out that southeast Asian capitals were often laid out as images of the universe and quotes Groslier's interpretation of the temple-city of

[27] A. N. B. Garvan (1966), 196.
[28] A. N. B. Garvan (1966), 198.
[29] P. Wheatley (1963): What the greatness of a city is said to be. *Pacific Viewpoint* **4**, 163.
[30] G. Sjoberg (1960): *The pre-industrial city; past and present* (Glencoe, Ill.).

Kambujadesa, 'un diagramme magique tracé sur le parchemin de la plaine' or 'an expression in plastic terms of Khmer cosmological concepts'.[31] The use of cardinal axes has been extremely widespread and even in terms of *cardo* and *decumanus* must preserve a basically cosmological purpose.

Perhaps the most intensive study of the religious influence on town lay-out is that by Rykwert on *The idea of a town* with the subtitle of the anthropology of urban form in Rome, Italy and the ancient world. He concludes, 'It is difficult to imagine a situation where the formal order of the universe could be reduced to a diagram of two intersecting co-ordinates in one plane. Yet this is exactly what did happen in antiquity: the Roman who walked along the *cardo* knew that his walk was the axis round which the sun turned, and that if he followed the *decumanns*, he was following the sun's course. The whole universe and its meaning could be spelt out of his civic institutions'[32].

Again the well-known example of Angkor Thom demonstrates 'the minutiae of cosmic symbolism'. 'The city was surrounded with a wall and moat forming a square almost two miles on each side, its sides being directed towards the four cardinal points. There are gates in the middle of each side and a fifth one on the East leading to the entrance of the royal palace. The towers above the gates are crowned with the same fourfold faces of Lokesvara as those of the central temple. Thus, that smaller world, the city of Angkor, and through its means the whole Khmer empire were put under the protection of the "Lord of the Universe".'[33]

In Burma the ancient city of Srikshetra (Old Prome) was, according to tradition, built by the Gods themselves as an image of Indra's city Sudarsana. The remains of the city in fact show a circular layout.[34] In this context perhaps one of the most fascinating instances of cultural change is in the squaring of Circleville, a town situated in the state of Ohio in the United States.[35] The original settlement was established in 1810 after the establishment of Pickaway County. The site selected on the Scioto river was occupied by a large circular Indian earthwork and the new settlement was adapted 'to the shape of the circular enclosure'. This produced Circleville (figure 7–6), a unique radial concentric scheme in the early town plans of America. Reps writes, 'while one is inclined to give credit to an unknown tribal chief or priest, the honours must surely go to Driesbach (the founder) for realizing the potentialities of the site.'

Here then the magico-religious significance of an Indian shape had been transformed into the layout of an American town. But by the time James Silk Buckingham visited the town in 1840 changes were in progress. 'So little veneration . . . have the Americans for ancient remains, and so entirely

[31] P. Wheatley (1963), 179.

[32] J. Rykwert (1976): *The idea of a town. The anthropology of urban form in Rome, Italy and the ancient world*, 202 (London).

[33] R. Heine-Geldern (1958): Conceptions of state and kingship in southeast Asia. *Southeast Asia Program, Department of Asia Studies, data paper number* **18**, 34 (Cornell University).

[34] R. Heine-Geldern (1958).

[35] This account is based on J. W. Reps (1965), 484–90.

1810

Feet
0   200 400

0   100
Metres

Figure 7—6: Circleville (Ohio) in 1810. *After J. W. Reps (1965).*

destitute do they appear to be, as a nation, of any antiquarian taste, that this interesting spot of Circleville, is soon likely to lose all traces of its original peculiarities. The centre of the town contained, as its first building, an octagonal edifice . . . and the streets beyond this were laid out in a circular shape. . . . But though the octagonal building still remains, the circular streets are fast giving way, to make room for straight ones; and the central edifice itself is already destined to be removed, to give place to stores and dwellings; so that in half a century or less, there will be no vestige left of that peculiarity which gave the place its name, and which constituted the most perfect and therefore the most interesting work in antiquity of its class in the country.'[36] Reps argues that the reasons for the change were that the lot shapes were awkward, that the central circle had soon degenerated and become unkempt and that the waste ground in the centre and at the angles where the circular section was joined to the surrounding grid could be profitably used. The result was the 'squaring of Circleville' between 1837 and 1849 as shown in figure 7—7. Although sound economic reasons can be advanced for this odd episode in the development of American town plans, nevertheless it is possible to speculate that at the root of the matter was the fact that radial-concentric plans were not consonant with the cultural background of the settlers. The grid was the form they knew and understood, and the symbolic preservation in the town form of the rites and usages of the Indians must have seemed particularly inappropriate. This seems to be at the basis of objections that the concentric scheme was a 'piece of childish sentimentalism' in the way it preserved the old tradition. It is certainly

[36] J. S. Buckingham (1842): *The eastern and western states of America,* **1,** 351 (London).

1837　　　　　　1838

1849　　　Feet　　　1856

```
0      500   1000  1 500
├───────┼──────┼──────┤      Feet
0      200       400
└───────┴────────┘
       Metres
```

Figure 7–7: The squaring of Circleville. *After J. W. Reps (1965).*

possible to regard the squaring of Circleville as an illustration of cultural forces at work and not merely as an economic exercise in convenience.

The last phrase 'an economic exercise in convenience' introduces the problem of 'economic' influences on town plan. These are comparatively easy to demonstrate in a general sense since town growth is largely the consequence of economic forces. Perhaps the most distinctive work in this context is that of Ganshof in his study of the growth of towns between the Loire and the Rhine in the Middle Ages.[37] His specific intention is to study the physical extension of towns, 'nous nous sommes proposé de retracer le développement des villes dans l'espace. . . .'[38] The key to the physical pattern is seen by Ganshof to reside in the 'pre-urban nucleus' which was a strong point, most often a Roman town or fort which survived the turbulent period of imperial collapse to provide a point of security in later times. 'Thanks to their fortifications, these *civitates* and *castra* played the role of pre-urban nuclei in the formation of medieval towns. In other words, it is around this pre-existing Roman element that the medieval town is formed.'[39] Other nuclei were found in the castles of the nobility, particularly in Flanders and

---

[37] F. L. Ganshof (1943): *Etude sur le développement des villes entre Loire et Rhin au moyen-âge* (Paris/Brussels).
[38] F. L. Ganshof (1943), 7.
[39] F. L. Ganshof (1943), 27.

Brabant, whilst a third type was found in the residences of the emerging ecclesiastic hierarchy.

All these had in common the offering of a degree of physical protection in a greatly disturbed world. But they were no more than *pre-urban* nuclei, the element generative of growth was the new merchant or commercial quarters which were added to them. Commercial activity revived after the disruptions of the 'Dark Ages' and as it did so, it needed security above all else. Revived commerce became attached to the earlier nuclei which could provide protection and added a new and growing quarter to the old settlements. These agglomerations or suburbs (sub urbium) had distinctive names, portus (poort), vicus (vik) or in France, burgus (bourg). Thus there emerges the fundamental and characteristic difference which can be found in French towns between *cité* and *bourg*, between the old protective core and the new quarter of the merchants, the bourgeoisie.

Figure 7−8 indicates the basic structure of Bonn in West Germany. The Roman castrum on the Rhine bank was followed by the bishop's seat which was established some distance to the west with the basilica of St. Cassius at the heart. Bonn had, therefore, two elements of the pre-urban triad of nuclei. The first fortification of the basilica was probably undertaken at the end of the eighth century. Subsequently, with commercial development, the market was established at a characteristic point in front of the gate of *Villa Basilicata*, the node about the basilica. Around this, the new plan element collected and, as in most cases, this was walled in 1244. Most often the market was at a focus·of tracks which by use became the main thoroughfares. Since the area was outside the close control of urban institutions, haphazard building led to plans which lacked regular form. At Bonn the

Figure 7−8: Bonn: the basic plan structure. *After F. L. Ganshof (1943).* For a commentary see text.

regularity of the Roman fort contrasts with the loose block pattern of the later mercantile town. Here the argument reverts to degree of political and institutional control, bringing back into play a variable already discussed.

Ganshof's study is a clear indication of the way economic factors generate physical growth in particular locational situations. But the conclusions are directed towards general areas of growth rather than plan, and although there are implications for layout they cannot be made explicit in the context of his study. It is apparent, though, that many of these new areas had little regularity in their layout, for it was not until an integrated combination of the fortified strongpoint and the centre of economic development was created in the *bastide* that once again the controlled chequer board layout was revived. This lapse of control is indeed mirrored in the way in which the later layout of Caerleon in Monmouthshire had deviated from the original Roman grid as the imperial control fell away and a period of local usage overlaid the older plan (figure 7–9).

It is perhaps in the context of circulation that economic influences on plan can best be made explicit. The basic function of the street system is to provide the most effective means of movement within the city. In nearly all cases, however, the present layout is inherited from a time when movement was on a very different scale and based on a completely different technology. It is from this that the traffic problems which now face all large cities result.

But these features are apparent at a very much earlier period. The simple way in which the grid of Greek colonial cities was laid down is related to the fact that no adaptation to site was necessary. At Miletus the simple plan outline does not show that the streets across the slope took in actuality the form of elongated staircases, an arrangement peculiar to a situation where wheeled vehicles were not dominant and much was carried by mules which could negotiate the stepped streets.

The distinction in medieval towns between street widths was often based on the function the streets were to perform. 'In larger towns, or in towns deliberately planned like the true batsides of southwestern France, the colonial towns of eastern Germany or Edward I's boroughs in Wales, it is generally not difficult to distinguish three functional types of streets, though frequently they are combined in varying degrees. Major traffic streets (Verkehrsstrassen, carrières at Montpazier) connecting the restricted points of exit from the walled town commonly had the greatest width. Residential streets (Wohnstrassen), carrying traffic to and from adjoining residential plots only, were often narrower. Occupation roads (Wirtschaftsstrassen) providing subsidiary access, were the narrowest type.'[40]

It follows from the close relationship between street layout and the functions which streets are called upon to perfom that one of the major themes of modern town planning should be 'traffic in towns'.[41] The whole engineering and planning process is concerned with the analysis of traffic generation through origin and destination surveys and then the manipulation of the

[40] M. R. G. Conzen (1960).
[41] Report of the steering group and working group appointed by the minister of transport (1963). *Traffic in towns* (London).

Figure 7–9: Roman Isca and medieval Caerleon. *After V. E. Nash-Williams (1954):* Roman frontier (*Cardiff*).

urban environment so that flows can be accommodated. This is not, therefore, a problem in street widening or reorientation, but involves the whole city complex. The minimization of travel by the compacting of such land-use categories as need constant physical interaction is a vital part of this process, but also the complete or partial restructuring of the street pattern can be involved.

One of the instances of this process which can usefully be cited is the study of Newbury (Berkshire), a market town of some 30,000 population, which occurs in *Traffic in Towns*.[42] The portion dealing with the town centre considers the relationship between accessibility and environment, an environment derived from the past and in which much of historical and architectural interest is retained. A series of proposals is made on an increasingly radical scale of development – minimal redevelopment, partial redevelopment, comprehensive redevelopment. These scales involve a successively greater alteration of the ground plan until at the comprehensive stage wholesale clearance and rebuilding is envisaged. 'The northern part of Northbrook Street is redeveloped with the whole of the ground level given over to parking and servicing with shopping and residential accommodation over. . . .'[43] The old layout under this scheme is virtually obliterated and a completely new plan comes into being in an attempt to combine 'highest standards of environment' with 'a very high level of accessibility'. The point at issue here is not concerned with planning principle or whether such a drastic remodelling of an old town will produce high environmental standards, that is to say, the concern is not with the merits of any form of plan but solely with the fact that the demands of modern accessibility can drastically reframe an old plan. Here then is another major variable which will determine the form of the town as it is on the ground and as it appears on the map.

Conclusion

This chapter on the study of town plan has necessarily striven to move away from the historical-descriptive orientation by which plan analysis has been dominated. There seems to be little point in including in this book a potted history of town-plan development; in doing this nearly all the standard texts become mirror images of each other. A review of the possibilities for future advance seems to indicate three directions. It would be neat if they could be associated with the three paradigms of modern geography, logical positivism, behaviouralism and phenomenology and radicalism, but although, as will become apparent, there is a relationship, it is certainly not of a direct nature.

1 *Shape analysis.* This is within the core of positivist tradition and based on the belief that a thorough, quantified analysis of shape will reveal the critical variables which determine that shape. It is an approach which

[42] Report of the steering group . . . (1963), 54, *et seq.*
[43] Report of the steering group . . . (1963), 72.

argues that a plan is in essence a network and, therefore, can be interpreted via network analysis. But it is doubtful whether refined description would add greatly to comprehension, and many of the variables seen as acting on shape would be difficult to define and quantify. There seems little hope of resorting to the geographers' standard solution, of feeding a large array of variables into a multivariate analysis in order to discern some prime component of variation. Attempts have been made[44] but there is no evidence of their building up into a significant research frontier; rather the opposite, the isolated attempts of the early 1970's[45] seem to have fallen away.

2　*Behavioural and decision making approaches.* It can be argued that the division of town plans usually made into 'planned' and 'unplanned' categories is pedagogically convenient but fundamentally false. All plans are the consequence of decisions by landowners (or squatters), developers and builders. All that varies is the scale of the decision making authority which can cover a whole town or city, or be confined to a small plot. It is the product of all these decisions which constitutes the town plan. Plan, in brief, is the outcome of the perceptions, principles and policies of those individuals or groups who can effectively exercise the necessary power, within any constraints operated by the larger society of which they form part. The present author has demonstrated how one family in the mid-nineteenth century could initiate, lay out and effectively control the ground-plan and built form of a nineteenth century seaside resort[46]. Urban historians, much more sensitive to the influence of individuals, and less concerned with theoretical viewpoints, have been made much more successful in demonstrating how the owners of large urban estates were able to determine the character of their development[47].

If contemporary geography seeks to identify the roles of decision making through the operation of effective economic and social power, then it is proper that the geographer of an urban form which is relict from past periods, should also attempt to identify the perceptions, motivations and decision which exercised the creators of plans. Perhaps the most useful exegesis has been made by George Gordon[48]

[44] S. Openshaw (1974): *Processes in urban morphology with special reference to South Sheilds.* Unpub. Ph.D. dissertation. Univ. Newcastle on Tyne. H. A. Millward (1975): *The convergence of urban plan features: a comparative analysis of trends in Canada and England.* Unpub. Ph.D. dissertation, Univ. of Western Toronto.

[45] H. A. Millward (1974): A comparison and grouping of ten Canadian cities with respect to their street-plan. Paper presented at the annual meeting of the *Canadian Assoc. of Geogrs* (Ontario Division).

[46] H. Carter (1970): A decision making approach to town plan analysis: a case study of Llandudno, in H. Carter and W. K. D. Davies eds. *Urban essays: studies in the georgraphy of Wales* (London), 66–78.

[47] D. Cannadine (1977): Victorian cities: how different? *Social History*, 4, 457–482.

C. W. Chalklin (1974): *The provincial towns of Georgian England* (London).

M. J. Daunton (1977): *Coal metropolis. Cardiff 1870–1914* (Leicester).

[48] G. Gordon (1980): *Urban Morphology — Structure and process.* University of Strathclyde, Dept. of Geography, Research Seminar Series No. 10.

who sees plan as consisting of:

a   Morphological elements: plots, buildings, use, streets, plans, townscapes

created by

b   Actors: landowners, developers, builders, investors, financiers, architects, planners, lawyers, local authorities, national government, purchasers

operating on

c   A stage: sites, site characteristics, land value surfaces, accessibility surfaces, innovations, regulations, controls and constraints.

But this anticipates the examination of the wider situation in which decisions are made.

3   *Fringe Belt Evolution*. Undoubtedly the most stimulating writing on an historico-geographical theory of urban form has been that by Whitehand[49], and in regard to his work it is perhaps unfair to use such a limiting heading as 'fringe belt evolution'. In a short space it is difficult to do justice to complex notions, but essentially Whitehand deploys his argument around two foci. The first is related to the way in which the built form, which includes style, material and function, evolves over time. This is identified with the processes of innovation and diffusion. The second is concerned more directly with amounts of building over time. Periodicities in both can be identified and then associated, although this is far from a simple operation. It is to this relationship of stylistic innovations and building cycles that the economic concept of the land-value gradient is added, giving the distinctive belt-like basis of extension. At this point it is possible to take up the notion of the fringe belt from an earlier part of this chapter. 'During a slump in house building land at the edge of the built-up area is generally relatively cheap and tends to be acquired by low-intensity users, such as various types of institution, for whom accessibility to the city centre is not a high priority. During a boom in house building similar sites are more expensive and tend to be developed intensively for housing, which has a greater need for accessibility: relatively low intensity users seeking to initiate developments are relegated to more remote sites'[50]. These booms and slumps are directly related to the amounts of building over time, that is to building cycles. Into this also can be fitted the innovation of building and planning styles and their diffusion. The result is a framework which 'offers at least a provisional reference point for analytical work on the relationship between social and economic events and townscape development'[51].

A good deal of empirical work needs to be done before these general notions can be converted into an acceptable theory of urban form[52]. But

[49] J. W. R. Whitehand (1977): The basis for an historico-geographical theory of urban form. *Trans. Inst. Brit. Geogrs.*, New Series, 2(3), 400–416.

[50] J. W. R. Whitehand (1977), 407.

[51] J. W. R. Whitehand (1977). 412.

[52] H. Carter and S. Wheatley (1979): Fixation lines and fringe belts, land uses and social areas: nineteenth century change in the small town. *Trans. Inst. Brit. Geogrs.*, 4(2), 214–237.

they have one critical aspect in their favour, they are concerned with the general structuring of towns and not with unique examples of historical narrative of plan development.

It would be too optimistic to suggest that in one of these three possibilities for the advance of plan studies, or indeed in all three integrated for that is a perfectly feasible expectation, there lies the basis of a burgeoning interest in plan analysis. Given present concern in urban geography with the immediacy of social relationships and of intra-urban inequalities, then plan is always likely to be a minority interest. Even so, the implications involved in how advantages were perceived by land-owners and how decisions were made in the context of the impact of new ideas on building style and the advantages of cashing-in on an upswinging building cycle, might provide significant insights into the social areas of cities. For after all, one is there only a step away from the concept of the acquisition of class monopoly rents[53].

Notes on further reading

The best introductions to contemporary work on the town-plan are to be found in the works of Whitehand, especially:

Whitehand, J. W. R. ((1977): The basis for an historico-geographical theory of urban form. *Trans. Inst. Brit. Geogrs.*, New series, 2(3) 400–416.

Although it has wider connotations than town plan, an excellent consideration of urban morphogenesis is:

Vance, J. E. (1977) *This scene of man: the role and structure of the city in western civilization* (New York).

There are many histories of town planning and studies of individual towns but few attempts at plan analysis. A standard history of town plan development is:

Lavedan, P. (1926–1952): *Histoire de l'urbanisme* (see footnote 7): **1:** *Antiquité;* **2:** *Moyen age;* **3:** *Renaissance et temps modernes;* **4:** *Epoque contemporaine.*

Useful volumes in English are:

Burke, G. (1971): *Towns in the making* (London.

Curl, J. S. (1970): *European cities and society* (London).

Hiorns, F. R. (1956): *Town building in history* (see footnote 6).

Morris, A. E. J. (1972): *History of urban form* (New York).

From a purely descriptive and gazeteer point of view, an interesting series is:

Gutkind, E. A. (1964 cont.) *International History of City Development* (London): **1:** *Urban development in Central Europe* (1964); **2:** *Urban*

[53] see p. 312.

development in the Alpine and Scandinavian Countries (1965); **3:** *Urban development in Southern Europe; Spain and Portugal* (1967); **4:** *Urban development in Southern Europe; Italy and Greece* (1969); **5:** *Urban development in Western Europe: France and Belgium* (1970); **6:** *Urban development in Western Europe: Great Britain and the Netherlands* (1971); **7:** *Urban development in East-Central Europe* (1972); **8:** *Urban development in Eastern Europe* (1972).

Another series dealing with a number of separate topics is:

Collins, G. R. editor (n.d.): *Planning and cities* (London).

Three books concerned with Britain are;

Ashworth, W. (1954): *The genesis of modern British town planning* (London).

Bell, C. and R. (1967): *City fathers; the early history of town planning in Britain* (London).

Lobel. M.D. editor (1969): *Historic towns; maps and plans of towns and cities in the British Isles,* (Oxford). This is a fine source of studies on individual towns, three volumes have been published.

Two books which deal with the U.S.A. are:

Tunnard, C. and Reed, H. H. (1955): *American skyline* (Boston).

Reps, J. W. (1965): *The making of urban America* (see footnote 8).

One of the few geographical works which deals with townscape as such is:

Johns, E. (1965): *British townscapes* (London).

An excellent example of a volume devoted to one particular form of town is:

Beresford, M. (1967); *New towns of the Middle Ages* (New York-Washington).

Some of the most stimulating writing on the religious element in town origins and layout is by Wheatley:

Wheatley, P. (1967): Proleptic observations on the origins of urbanism; in R. Steel and R. Lawton, Editors (1967): *Liverpool essays in geography,* 315 (London).

Wheatley's major work is:

Wheatley, P. (1971): *The pivot of the four quarters* (Edinburgh).

Another book which develops on a rich fashion the idea of the town as symbol is:

J. Rkywert (1976): *The idea of a town* (London).

In the context of plan and analysis itself the two early works by Conzen are essential reading:

Conzen, M. R. G. (1960): Alnwick: a study in town plan analysis (see footnote 10).

Conzen, M. R. G. (1962): The plan analysis of an English city centre; in K. Norborg, Editor (1962): *Proceedings of the I.G.U. symposium in urban geography,* Lund, 1960, 383 (Lund).

A further work which attempts to set up a framework for studing urban morphology is:

Badcock, B. A. (1970): A preliminary note on the study of intra-urban physiognomy. *Prof. Georg.* **22,** 189–96.

For further material on the origin and early development of English and European towns the most useful sources are:

Ennen, E. (1979): *The medieval town.* Europe in the Middle Ages. Selected Studies No. 15. (Amsterdam). Translated by N. Fryde.

Reynolds, S. (1977): *An introduction to the history of English medieval towns* (Oxford).

The above two volumes are essentially 'historical' in approach but topographical aspects are the main concern in:

Barley, M. W. ed. (1976): *The plans and topography of medieval towns in England and Wales.* C.B.A. Research Report No. 14.

Barley, M. W. ed. (1977): *European towns; their archaeology and early history* (London).

This last book is an important contribution to the study of the origin and early development of European towns. In it Chap. 11, K. Böhner, Urban and rural settlement in the Frankish kingdom, has a section on Bonn (pp. 196–198) which elaborates the material presented in this chapter.

The most detailed study of the plan evolution of an English city is contained in:

Barlow, F., Biddle, M. et alia (1976): *Winchester in the early middle ages. An edition and discussion of the Winton Domesday* (Oxford), Vol. 1.

For an excellent discussion of issues in townscape studies and urban morphology in relation to urban geography in the U.S.A. see:

Conzen, M. P. (1978): Analytical approaches to the urban landscape, in Butzner, K. W. ed. (1978): *Dimensions in human geography: essays on some familiar and neglected themes.* Univ. of Chicago, Dept. of Geog. Research Paper No. 168, 128–165.

For other American studies see:

Lewis, P. F. (1976): *New Orleans: the making of an urban landscape* (Cambridge, Mass.).

Zelinsky, W. (1977): The Pennsylvania town: an overdue geographical account. *Geog. Review,* 67, 127–147.

8

Urban Land-Use: General Problems

The range of studies, which is covered by the simple phrase 'urban land-use' is vast in the extreme and includes contributions from all the disciplines which conventionally fall within the social sciences. Many of these studies are basically aspatial in context and, therefore, would seem not to come within the purview of geographical investigation. But this distinction between work irrelevant and relevant to urban geography is difficult to sustain, for very often as the chain from a spatial location is traced back the beginnings are found in a concept which appears essentially aspatial. For example, 'social distance' is a sociological concept to be studied within the structural-functional context of that discipline. Laumann,[1] following the much earlier study of Bogardus,[2] defines subjective social distance as 'an attitude of ego toward a person (alter) with a particular status attribute';[3] this attribute in the study he presents is simply 'occupation'. But it is at once apparent that, in terms of the selection of a residential site, subjective social distance could be related to a physical distance and immediately an aspatial sociological concept becomes a spatial locational, that is a geographical, factor. It follows that at the outset it is essential to stress that the urban land-use pattern is the consequence of a large number of operative forces and that most generalizations attempt to ignore many of them.

The basic geographic interest is in land-use as a distributed feature or as an aspect of areal difference. But the approach adopted in this general chapter is to begin with the early attempts to survey the whole city structure as one unit in the search for an overriding explanation. This, it is true, was not part of the early geographical tradition which was much more concerned with the interpretation of the particular land-use map of one city as an exceptional or unique case.

However, the general schemes proposed by Burgess and his followers were rapidly adapted from the field of human ecology, in which they were proposed, into geographical studies and most works on particular cities concluded with a statement of the extent to which the town under consideration matched the generality of concentric zonal or other postulated patterns. As the ecological emphasis on sub-social processes of competition for space became marked there was an increasing trend toward the emphasis of

---

[1] E. C. Laumann (1966): *Prestige and association in an urban community* (Indianapolis, Ind.).

[2] E. S. Bogardus (1925): Measuring social distance. *J. appl. Sociol.* **9**, 299.

[3] E. C. Laumann (1966), 4.

economic variables and accordingly the more direct statement of land-use schemata was made in the context of the land market and economics; theory of urban land-use became an essential part of land economics. But the strong reaction to these mechanistic explanations clearly revealed that the abstraction of a limited set of economic variables from the whole complex set acting on land-use was an unsatisfactory procedure. Moreover, much of this tradition was derived from the geographer's land-use map, a statement of an aggregate situation.

As in other fields the most promising line of approach changed from the derivation of generalizations from the completed aggregate state to the analysis of individual personal or corporate need so that the total land-use was seen as the consequence of a very large number of separate activity systems, each having individual characteristics and reacting not in the abstract but in the context of a given set of structures which compose the actual city. From this summary it is possible to isolate three main approaches:

1　The ecological.
2　The economic.
3　Via activity systems.

These three approaches can be examined in terms of the overall land-use pattern and subsequently identified in a discussion of the various parts of the town as they have conventionally been isolated in land-use studies.

1　Human ecology and urban land-use

E. W. Burgess's thesis[4] that urban land-use tended to display a zonal organization concentrically arrayed about the city centre (figure 8−1A & B) has for the last forty years been the starting point for most considerations of the utilization of land in cities. Each succeeding author has outlined the concentric zone scheme, or theory as it is sometimes called, subjecting it to what is now a fairly standard critique. Since this process continues it seem that the concentric zone scheme must either present something of value or be the only generalized statement available, and is, therefore, presented *faute de mieux*.

Recent concern with model building in the social sciences has to some extent put Burgess's scheme upon a more elevated plane. It can quite justifiably be considered a normative model, 'a simplified structuring of reality which presents supposedly significant features of relationships in a generalized form'.[5] Comparison is at once suggested with Christaller's statement of central place theory[6] as another early model concerned with spatial and locational aspects within the social sciences. But here little progress can be

---

[4] E. W. Burgess (1925): The growth of the city: an introduction to a research project; in R. E. Park and E. W. Burgess, editors (1925): *The city*, 47 (Chicago).

[5] P. Haggett and Chorley, R. J. (1967): Models, paradigms and the new geography; chapter 1 in *Models in geography*, 22 (London).

[6] See chapter 6, page 59.

Figure 8–1A & B: The concentric zone scheme of urban land-use. *After E. W. Burgess (1925).* **A** indicates Burgess's detailed interpretation of Chicago while **B** is his generalization for all rapidly growing industrial cities.
C: The sector scheme of *H. Hoyt (1939):* **1:** CBD; **2:** wholesaling and light manufacture; **3:** low-class residential; **4:** middle-class residential; **5:** high-class residential. **D:** The multiple nuclei scheme of *C. D. Harris and E. L. Ullman (1945).* The areas numbered are as in **C** with the addition of: **6:** heavy manufacturing; **7:** outlying business district; **8:** residential suburb; **9:** industrial suburbs.

made, for Burgess does not deduce a structure from a series of initial assumptions. His model is explicitly inductive and presumably intuitively derived from the observation of a large number of American cities in general, and of Chicago in particular, though the process is not made clear in his chapter on 'The growth of the city: an introduction to a research project' in the book *The city* written with R. E. Park in 1925.

The scheme is baldly introduced. 'The typical process of the expansion of the city can best be illustrated, perhaps, by a series of concentric circles, which may be numbered to designate both the successive zones of urban extension and the types of areas differentiated in the process of expansion.'[7] Moreover, there is a strong historical element in the scheme, for when process is introduced (in terms of invasion and succession and concentration and decentralization) it is envisaged in the historical context of the growth of the American city and not in terms of contemporary forces creating by their interaction an equilibrium condition which is the land-use pattern. Nevertheless it is a model in the proper sense of the term. It was to Burgess 'an ideal construction of the tendencies of any town or city to expand radially from its central business district. . . . Encircling the downtown area there is normally an area of transition which is being invaded by business and light manufacture. A third area is inhabited by the workers in industries who have escaped from the area of deterioration but who desire to live within easy access of their work. Beyond this zone is the "residential area" of high class apartment buildings or of exclusive "restricted" districts of single family dwellings. Still further, out beyond the city limits, is the commuters' zone — suburban areas, or satellite cities. . . .'[8] This sketch of the concentric zones is immediately followed by a section which firmly links it with a historical process, 'the tendency of each inner zone to extend its area by the invasion of the next outer zone',[9] so that in the early history of Chicago all zones were included within the inner zone but have emerged as distinctive parts of the city during the process of growth and expansion. Undoubtedly Burgess's presentation was sketchy and muddled. The zones are related partly to generalization based on evidence from Chicago and other cities, partly to the processes of city growth, partly to the sub-social ecological forces of competition then dominating the thought of the 'Chicago School'.

Reactions to the concentric zone model can be considered under three headings. Most critiques contain elements of all three and the division is one of convenience of review. The divisions are:

1   Destructive criticism which rejects the thesis.
2   Criticism which lays emphasis on factors which were either excluded by Burgess or to which he gave little weight.
3   Attempts to exclude historical process and to evaluate the implicit assumptions on which the thesis is based and hence recast the whole argument in deductive form.

These can be considered in turn.

a   Rejection of the Burgess model
There are four closely related bases on which a direct rejection of the usefulness and validity of the model set up by Burgess has been proposed.

[7] E. W. Burgess (1925), 49.
[8] E. W. Burgess (1925).
[9] E. W. Burgess (1925).

(*i*) *Gradients as against zonal boundaries*. This line of criticism is usually linked to a paper by M. R. Davie, 'The pattern of urban growth'.[10] Beginning from the position that 'very often distorting factors so frequently disrupt or obscure the concentric circle pattern so as to make it useless as a tool for study', Davie goes on to introduce the notion of gradient, that is of the rate of change of any variable condition away from the city centre and toward the periphery. If a truly zonal situation is to be found then these gradients should show marked breaks at the successive zonal boundaries, much as in meteorology a 'front' marks the dividing line between two air masses of contrasted characteristics. Using a study of delinquency rates in Chicago, the city from which Burgess derived his model, Davie argued that although there was a decline from the city centre 'there is nothing which would suggest a combination into concentric zones.'[11] That is, although significant changes were associated with distance from the city centre, they did not show a grouping or greater rapidity of change at any zonal boundaries — or in terms of the simile used above, there were no 'fronts'.

There is some danger that this sort of criticism can fall into the rather arid 'core' versus 'boundary' argument so familiar in regional geography, but certainly gradient studies have failed to demonstrate the sharp changes which are implicit in the concentric zone model. These criticisms are perhaps more important in that they are closely associated with and lead into the second basis for rejection.

(*ii*) *Internal heterogeneity of the zones*. The notion of well defined boundaries around clearly distinctive ecological 'regions' is to some extent linked with Park's idea of the 'natural area'.[12] Hatt distinguished two emphases within this one concept: 'one of these views the natural area as a spatial unit limited by natural boundaries enclosing a homogeneous population with a characteristic moral order. The other emphasizes its biotic and community aspects and describes the natural area as a spatial unit inhabited by a population united on the basis of symbiotic relationships.'[13]

In both of these the words 'a spatial unit' emphasize the common core of the concept — the existence of well contrasted, discrete social areas within the city. But Hatt proceeded to demonstrate that such natural areas 'do not exist' and followed by making the distinction between 'natural areas as logical statistical constructs integrated with a plan for research' and the 'concept of natural areas as a series of spatial and social factors which act as coercive influences upon all who inhabit the geographically and culturally defined area.'[14] This latter view, Hatt argued, involved the 'reification' of a concept which was useful as a way of organizing data and in approaching the complexity of the city but useless and dangerous if it were elevated to a tenet

[10] M. R. Davie (1961): The pattern of urban growth. Reprinted in G. A. Theodorson (1961): *Studies in human ecology*, 77 (New York).

[11] M. R. Davie (1961), 79.

[12] R. D. McKenzie (1925): The ecological approach to the study of the human community; in R. E. Park and E. W. Burgess, editors (1925), 77.

[13] P. Hatt (1946): The concept of natural area. *Am. sociol. Rev.* **11**, 423.

[14] P. Hatt (1946), 427.

of faith and conditioned research direction. If the natural areas were considered in this lesser way as units for organizing data then there were clear implications for the concentric zones, for they were demoted from the 'natural' products of ecological processes to mere useful devices in statistical analysis, in the manner that examination of data by distance zones and directional sectors has often been used. Moreover that analysis would demonstrate the amount of internal difference . . . 'variations within the main zones of development were no less important than differences between them.'[15]

Seen as having no basic ecological justification and displaying much internal variation, the zones lost most of their significance. 'The theories of Burgess and Park may no longer be related to modern conditions and . . . a new framework is needed for the systematic study of the complexity of urban life. Some would even say that the situation is now so complex that it is impossible to devise an overall framework of any kind and that it would be better to concentrate on the study of a number of typical areas.'[16] This latter view is one of clear rejection, although how what constitutes a 'typical area' is to be isolated and defined is not made clear.

(*iii*) *The scheme is anachronistic.* It will be noted that in the quotation at the end of the above paragraph there occurs the statement that the theory under review 'may no longer be related to modern conditions.' Since Burgess's model was stated in a historical context this is a fair comment, and therefore, though the zonal scheme might have been apposite for the American city of the 1920s, it is certainly not useful for world wide application in the second half of the twentieth century (see figure 8–2).

(*iv*) *The scheme lacks universality.* It is only just to record that Burgess made no claim that the model had relevance other than to rapidly growing, industrialized American cities, but inevitably it has been taken as universally applicable to all cities. The examination of what he calls 'the pre-industrial city' by Gideon Sjoberg[17] effectively disposes of this extension. Sjoberg demonstrates that the city prior to industrialization, both in a historical and a spatial context, displays a structural pattern which is a negation of the concentric zone scheme in all ways. Three major aspects of this contrast are emphasized.

1   'The pre-eminence of the centre over the periphery especially as portrayed in the distribution of social classes.'[18] In this context of the 'pre-industrial' city the privileged classes, the elite, gather at the centre because of their need for the closest association with the governmental and religious buildings which physically and symbolically represent political power. 'Because political and religious activities in feudal cities have far more status than the economic, the main market though often

[15]   E. Gittus (1964): The structure of urban areas, a new approach. *Tn. Plann. Rev.* **35**, 7.
[16]   E. Gittus (1964).
[17]   G. Sjoberg (1965): *The pre-industrial city, past and present.*
[18]   G. Sjoberg (1965), 95.

Council

Private

—·— C.B.boundary

0 ½ Mile

0 ½ Km 1 1½

Figure 8–2: The distribution of municipal housing in Sunderland. *After B. T. Robson* (*1969*). Although the distribution is limited to the confines of the administrative area, it shows clearly the areas in which peripheral municipal housing has been located. This sort of decision, in essence part of political processes, undermines the simple notions of market forces as the creator of concentric zonal patterns of land-use.

set up in the central sector, is subsidiary to the religious and political structures there . . . the commercial structures in no way rival the religious and political in symbolic eminence; typically these tower above all others. . . . These land-use patterns refute the still widely accepted proposition of the Chicago School that the 'central business district' is the hub of urban living, a generalization fulfilled only in industrial cities.'[19]

2 'Finer spatial differences according to ethnic, occupational and family ties.'[20] There is a characteristic segregation along these various lines. A prime example is the ghetto of the medieval European city or indeed the monopolization of some areas by particular crafts which is still visible in the street or 'quarter' names of contemporary cities. It should be

[19] G. Sjoberg (1965), 97.
[20] G. Sjoberg (1965), 95.

stressed that in chart 2 of his chapter on the growth of the city, Burgess clearly showed a 'black belt' in Chicago which cut across the concentric zones. 'Wedging out from here is the black belt,' he wrote, almost using a sectoral terminology (figure 8–1A).

3   'The low incidence of functional differentiation of land-use patterns.'[21] The multiple use of single plots is a further characteristic of the pre-industrial city as for example in the use of church land for market places, even the use of the church yard itself; those who were buying and selling in the outer court of the Temple at Jerusalem were doing so in a typical location. Again, more often than not merchants and artisans live at their place of work in quarters above or behind their shops so that there is not that essential division of place of work and place of residence on which the concentric zone scheme is based. This, of course, is partly a consequence of a technology unable to provide the necessary rapid transport to make this feasible.

'To reiterate, the feudal city's land-use configuration is in many ways the reverse of that in the highly industrialized countries'[22] (figure 8–3). Although it is not necessary to accept Sjoberg's terminology his views have been expounded at some length since they so effectively demonstrate that Burgess's model depended not only upon those processes which human ecologists called sub-social (but which seem to have simply been economic competition for a scarce commodity, that is central city land) but also upon a whole array of social and technological conditions which were never made explicit and which were often ignored when the model was seized upon as being universally applicable.[23]

There is no need, however, to look at such widely diverging areas and times to make the point that Burgess's model is limited in universality. The location of British municipal housing estates (figure 8–2) shows that the simple notion of a rise in social status with distance from the city centre is not true. These estates are the consequence of an entirely different set of socio-political forces than those moulding the American city in the 1920s, when American municipal authorities were effectively not in the house constructing business. Once one moves outside the 'American culture province' and tries to interpret city patterns created by different social-economic-political-technological (i.e. cultural) conditions, then the applicability of American based concepts and models becomes less than complete.

The whole tenor of the four lines of criticism which have been outlined is to reject the Burgess model on two major grounds. First, it is limited

[21] G. Sjoberg (1965), 96.
[22] G. Sjoberg (1965), 103.
[23] For elaboration see page 184 *et seq*.

Figure 8–3: The social areas of Popayán, Colombia. This map clearly depicts the reversal of the concentric zone arrangement of urban land uses in a town of pre-industrial character. The central association of the 'upper-class' residential areas with the central institutions emerges clearly. *After A. H. Whiteford (n.d.):* Two cities of Latin America (*New York*).

historically and culturally to a particular situation at a particular time in a particular country, and, second, even then it quite arbitrarily emphasizes clear-cut boundaries which cannot be justified by gradient study and assumes a natural sorting of distinctive areas, whereas the city is in reality a most complex patchwork which defies the massive generalization. Many of these criticisms will be familiar to geographers, for fundamentally they question the existence as such, of natural areas (or regions) other than as the constructions of the investigator, and hence also the validity of the boundaries which demarcate them. To adapt a sentence critical of the regional geographer to apply to Burgess, he may be accused of 'drawing lines that don't exist around areas that don't matter.'[24] In some ways these various attacks make elaborate parade of a simple theme, that the model of concentric zones is too simple and too limited in historical and cultural application to carry one far into an understanding of land-use patterns. With this clearly understood the model remains useful as a first approximation and as a pedagogic device; it is no longer a springboard for research.

b Extension of the Burgess model
Since the concentric zone model excludes a wide variety of factors which affect urban land-use it is possible to introduce many of these in extensions of the model. Four of these can be considered here, the first and the last perhaps not standard inclusions but the middle two now invariably sketched alongside the Burgess model.

(i) The introduction of building height. There is an implication in the concentric zone model that the city is a two dimensional feature and little attention was paid in its formulation to the height of buildings and the variation of use with height. It is quite simple, however, within the overall limits of the model itself, to introduce this feature. Accessibility not only diminishes outward from the centre but upward from the ground. If the vertical changes in use are examined they are often found to parallel the horizontal changes. This is depicted in figure 8–4. Characteristically in the smaller town the ground floor retail shop has office space above, frequently occupied by legal or insurance firms, whilst above this is an apartment or maisonette. This parallels the horizontal sequence. Types of use which cannot effectively compete for a desired central location because of the high costs are relegated to the transitional or mixed fringe which surrounds the CBD *or* they are relegated to the upper floors of centrally located buildings.

The whole model can, therefore, be thought of as a flattened dome reaching its highest point at the peak land value and with a series of bands of land-use taking off progressively from the outer edges, thinning markedly towards the centre where they overlay each other at the central vertical axis.[25] Thus logically the outermost commuter zone, where there are the

[24] G. H. T. Kimble (1951): The inadequacy of the regional concept; in D. Stamp and S. W. Wooldridge, editors (1951): *London essays in geography* (London).
[25] It will be seen that this is in fact a very different shape from that which is given by the analysis of urban land values or indeed from that of the average city with its tall central

Figure 8–4: The relation of land-use to building height. The upper diagram shows a more simplified form of the larger diagram. These are only generalized sketches to demonstrate the principle of the way in which each zone of the concentric scheme in fact overlies the other at the city centre.

most valued residential locations, would form the uppermost layer of the dome at the centre where it is found in the form of penthouse flats and apartments. This extension into the vertical has only been sketched here and would involve a number of problems if strictly interpreted. It suggests, however, an area of extension of the model in need of more thorough and logical exposition.

This brief presentation illustrates the way in which extensions *can* be made. Some of these have reached absurdity, as in the one that suggests the model should consist of squares rather than circles since most American cities are built on a grid plan.[26]

(*ii*) *The emphasis of sectors.* The earliest constructive criticism of Burgess was best presented in a volume by Homer Hoyt published in 1939 by the United States Federal Housing Administration and entitled *The structure and growth of residential neighborhoods in American cities.*[27] After conducting a factual examination of residential rent patterns in twenty-five widely distributed cities in the USA, Hoyt concluded that 'there is, nevertheless, a general pattern of rent that applies to all cities. This pattern is not a random distribution. It is not in the form of sharply defined rectangular areas, with blocks in each rental group occupying completely segregated segments. It is not in the form of successive concentric circles. . . . Even when the rental data are put into a framework of concentric circles there is revealed no general gradation upward from the centre to the periphery. From the evidence presented, therefore, it may be concluded that the rent areas in American cities tend to conform to a pattern of sectors rather than of concentric circles.'[28] (See figures 8−1C and 8−5.)

Thus Hoyt presented what has been called the 'sector theory'. As the title of the volume where it appeared suggests, he was concerned primarily with residential uses and the key to the sector arrangement was to be found in the location of the high quality areas. These, Hoyt maintained, 'do not skip about at random in the process of movement − they follow a definite path in one or more sectors of the city';[29] that is they are extended outward along communication axes thus producing the sector; they do not encircle the city as its outer limits. In this process certain features exercise a dominant influence. These are, in addition to communication lines, high ground free from flood danger, open country with no physical barriers, the homes of community leaders, the attraction of office blocks and stores which also move, established outlying business centres and the operation of real estate promoters. At the same time, as is evident from the foregoing list, some land-uses will attract each other, as in the move of quality residence to outlying business centres, while some will repel each other. Thus heavy industry

buildings. But there is no basis (keeping within the context of Burgess's arguments) to make it other than the shape indicated.

[26] E. Bergel (1955): *Urban sociology*, 109 (New York).
[27] H. Hoyt (1939): *The structure and growth of residential neighborhoods in American cities* (Washington).
[28] H. Hoyt (1939), 73−6.
[29] H. Hoyt (1939), 114.

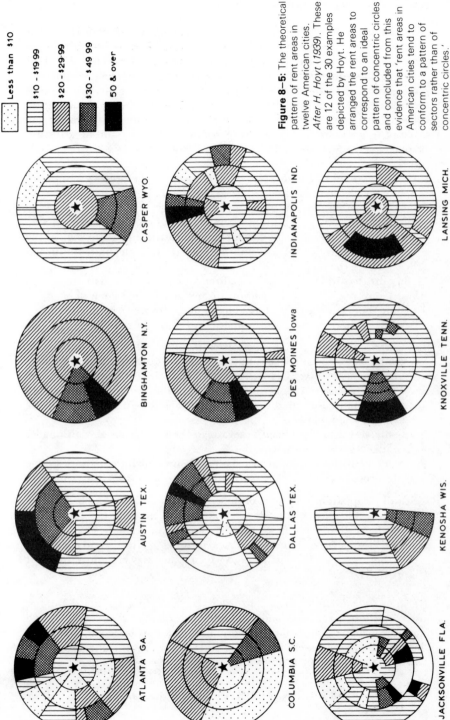

Less than $10
$10 - $19.99
$20 - $29.99
$30 - $49.99
$50 & over

CASPER WYO.

INDIANAPOLIS IND.

LANSING MICH.

BINGHAMTON N.Y.

DES MOINES Iowa

KNOXVILLE TENN.

AUSTIN TEX.

DALLAS TEX.

KENOSHA WIS.

ATLANTA GA.

COLUMBIA S.C.

JACKSONVILLE FLA.

Figure 8–5: The theoretical pattern of rent areas in twelve American cities. *After H. Hoyt (1939).* These are 12 of the 30 examples depicted by Hoyt. He arranged the rent areas to correspond to an ideal pattern of concentric circles and concluded from this evidence that 'rent areas in American cities tend to conform to a pattern of sectors rather than of concentric circles.'

will also probably extend along a line of communication, be it railway or waterway, and also occupy a sector — but one which due to repulsion will be located directly away from the high quality residential sector (figure 8−1C).

Essentially, therefore, the *directional* element will control land-use contrasts rather than distance, and accordingly the city structure becomes sectoral in character. Hoyt did not discount the distance variable but rather added the further directional element which he considered vital in any attempt to give more reality to Burgess's model: he was adding a further degree of verisimilitude at the expense of simplicity.

(*iii*) *The emphasis of multiple nuclei.* A model made up of a number of separate nuclei was proposed by C. D. Harris and E. L. Ullman.[30] It was conceived as a further move away from the massive generalization and toward reality. It is an observed fact that many towns and nearly all large cities do not grow simply about a single central business district but are formed by the progressive integration of a number of separate nuclei into the urban fabric — hence the suggestion of a multiple nuclei model. These nuclei, and further districts which become specialized and differentiated in the growth process, are not located in relation to any generalized zone or distance attribute, but rather are they bound by a number of controls which produce a pattern of characteristic associations between the nuclei. These are:

1   Certain activities require specialized facilities. Thus the retail district demands maximum accessibility, something quite different from geometrical centrality.

2   Like activities group together since they profit from association, hence the specialized legal districts or theatrelands. In short, there are external economies.

3   Some activities repel each other, as in the separation of high quality residences from industry.

4   Some activities cannot afford the high rents which the most desirable sites, relative to their interests, demand.

It will be apparent that none of these was very new (they had been noted by Burgess and Hoyt), but Harris and Ullman argued that during the historical growth process these influences would condition the emergence of separate areas, neither zones not sectors, forming in effect a patchwork but where there were clear controls as to which 'patches' were joined together (figure 8−1D).

(*iv*) *The introduction of a size variable.* In presenting his model Burgess used the words 'great cities' and 'our largest cities' and he clearly had in mind a process which applied to the largest cities. But how large are 'great' and 'largest'? Burgess himself stated that all the zones were contained in one when Chicago was but a small and primitive settlement. The concentric

---

[30] C. D. Harris and E. L. Ullman (1945): The nature of cities. *Ann. Am. Acad. pol. Sci.* **242,** 7.

zone model does not apply to the large metropolis where the simple concept of a CBD has fragmented into a large number of specialized tracts — financial, legal, retail, theatre areas to identify only the beginnings of specialization.

The conclusion from this is that if the evolution of the zones from a 'primitive cell' to a great city can be traced historically, then this same process should be identifiable at the present moment by examining different size classes of town. It should be possible to trace a progression from the smallest settlement where there was no apparent differentiation of uses, to the next class where a fairly well defined residential ring has become segregated and surrounds a core of mixed but mainly non-residential uses. The next size class is characterized by the crystallization of a retail core with a mixed surround which is partly the product of the expulsion of non-retail uses as the core developed and their taking over of premises in the first residential ring. And so on through to the metropolis. It must be emphasized that these are identified as the characteristics of size classes, not stages in the growth process.

Nevertheless this immediately brings to mind the attempt by Griffith Taylor to formalize the sorts of contrasts which have been outlined. His scheme recognized:

Infantile towns	Haphazard distribution of shops and houses, no factories.
Juvenile towns	Differentiation of zones begins, shops are separated.
Adolescent towns	Scattered factories, but no definite zone for first-class houses.
Early mature towns	A clear segregation of first-class houses.
Mature towns	Separate commercial and industrial areas, four zones of houses, ranging from mansions to shacks.

This is an inadequate table[31] in almost every way. The use of terminology adapted from the cycle of erosion as propounded by W. M. Davis is ill considered and completely inappropriate; above all it is unnecessary since the characteristics outlined are correlates of size and possibly of economic base.

Indeed Taylor wrote size into the text indicating, for example, that the population of the 'juvenile town' would be about 20,000 but then arguing, with some justification but little proof, that 'stage' and 'population' need not be closely associated. There are problems; in its early stages a crude mining town may have a large population yet remain still little more than a 'camp', but these are problems partly associated with the 'economic base'. The progressive differentiation of uses in Taylor's 'cycle' is but thinly indicated and not rigorously pursued. His identification of 'the various ages of towns' is, therefore, not very impressive and is seldom quoted in the literature of urban geography, but it pointed in the right direction and posed questions which have yet to be effectively answered. If the appearance of segregated land-uses is part of the urban growth process, at what town sizes or at what

[31] G. Taylor (1949): *Urban geography*, 421–3 (London).

hierarchical grades and in what manner does this differentiation take place and under what functional conditions? Perhaps it is sufficient here merely to point out that Burgess's model clearly involved a size variable which was barely considered, although held constant by implication, let alone worked out in detail.

This brief review of models which have aimed at generalizing the total land-use pattern of a city has demonstrated some of the ways in which Burgess's original scheme has been extended. These extensions are the product of an inductive approach, the thesis being that knowledge of land-use in a large number of cities will show that there is little correspondence between model and reality. If, therefore, further variables are introduced — size, height, axial growth, multiple nuclei — then progress will be made by making the generalization 'more real'. But as this is done so too some of the grand simplicity of the original is lost. Indeed one questions whether the 'multiple nuclei' model can rightly be so called. It is based on well-known statements regarding uses and makes no marked contribution to their complex association in area in a locational sense.

At an earlier stage a quotation from Hoyt was introduced denying that land-uses formed a patchwork; multiple nuclei theory argues that they do and because of this ought perhaps to be associated with the destructive criticisms rather than those which modify. Perhaps it is worth repeating that Burgess's original formulation of a concentric zone model remains as still providing stimulating insight into land-use patterns and if it has lost the relevance to the formulation of research projects and designs which it had in the 1920s, it is still a most useful pedagogic device for approaching the complexities of the problem it seeks to illuminate. Perhaps this is why the more frequently it is dismissed as no longer of relevance, the more consistently it appears in texts such as this.

c The presentation of the Burgess model in the form of a deductive theory
As dissatisfaction with the concentric zone scheme of urban land-use grew, so, sometimes explicitly, sometimes implicitly, attempts were made to reframe the model as the end product of a deductive argument. In this process a statement of premises becomes essential, making the assumptions on which the model rests the subject of elaboration. The clearest exposition of these assumptions is that by Leo F. Schnore[32] who lists five:

1   Assumption of heterogeneity. This is a restatement of Quinn's argument that widely contrasted population types are a prerequisite. Quinn envisaged contrasts in race and in degree of cultural assimilation as well as in social class and occupations.[33] This would hardly seem essential, particularly if the model were only to take in 'large' western cities when occupational and class differences are implicit.

[32] L. F. Schnore (1965): On the spatial structure of cities in the two Americas; chapter 10 in P. M. Hauser and L. F. Schnore, editors (1965): *The study of urbanization*, 353 – 4 (New York).
[33] J. A. Quinn (1950): *Human ecology*, 120 (New York).

2 Assumption of an economic base. Certainly a mixed industrial-commercial city was implied by Burgess, but a much greater clarity is to be obtained if a certain economic functional character is specified.

3 Economic and cultural assumptions. Burgess assumed those conditions which were appropriate in the America of the 1920s, such as private ownership of property, economic competition and efficient transport, equally easy, rapid and cheap in all directions.

4 Assumptions as to the geometry of space. Schnore adds this to the earlier listing by Quinn. He maintains that it is necessary to assume a single centre (hence disposing of the multiple nuclei problem) and that physical area increases as the square of radial distance and consequently that space is in shortest supply at the centre. In addition there is the further necessary condition that central areas are most highly valued by virtue of short supply and accessibility to all other areas. Competition for these central locations leads to a 'sifting and sorting' with physical positions largely determined by economic ability to compete for space.

5 The assumption of occupancy patterns. Schnore argues that for the Burgess model it is necessary that social classes with superior economic status will be able to pre-empt the newer and more desirable areas, or will at least have a high degree of freedom of choice as against a very restricted choice for the poor.

But even starting from this list comparatively little progress has been made in the presentation of a convincing argument. Schnore proceeds to list variables rather than deduce an urban arrangement. To some extent this somewhat limp end is partly bound up with the development of human ecology itself in this particular context.

The classical ecologists had been concerned to demonstrate parallels with plant ecology and hence they looked upon urban land as subject to competition from rival interests carried on at a 'sub-social' level. 'The basic process in human relationships is competition largely involving a struggle for space.' In this process 'human society was seen as organized on two levels: the biotic and the cultural. The biotic level involves basic, non-thoughtful adjustments made in the struggle for existence. The level is regarded as sub-social. . . . The cultural level is seen as a superstructure and excluded from human ecology.'[34] This framework might be applicable to the study of diseases or the spatial arrangement of a primitive population but if the land-use pattern is to be interpreted in this way two problems immediately arise:

1 The more the concept of sub-social competition for a scarce resource is examined and refined the more the ecologist is taken directly into the field of land economics, and this is particularly so when a deductive model of the city is desired excluding those cultural and social influences which the ecologist eschewed. When Quinn writes 'Ecological interaction underlies many aspects of community life. Merchants who want strategic commercial sites at the heart of the city compete for the

---

[34] G. A. Theodorson (1961): *Studies in human ecology*, 3 (New York).

limited supply of land in this location',[35] and then goes on to argue that urban residents 'bid for the limited supply of residential space', one is forced to conclude that 'sub-social' is merely another term for 'economic' for he is making a straightforward statement which is almost a definition of economics — the allocation of scarce resources to alternative ends. It follows that the vigorous attempts to present a theory of urban land-use have passed to the land economists and that the stream of work started by Burgess while still of value in its empirical side has not been a source of rich theoretical construction.

2   The clear rejection by the classical human ecologists of social and cultural influences while making for simplicity in terms of economic theory, has led to severe criticisms in the inductive sphere for, as the economic implications of competition became apparent, it was only to be expected that protest would arise against these mechanistic theorems.

Two such protests can be noted:

(*i*) *Sentiment and symbolism as ecological variables.* In a paper with this title Walter Firey[36] called attention to the difficulty outlined in the last paragraph — 'A different order of concepts, corresponding to the valuative, meaningful aspect of spatial adaptation, must supplement the prevailing economic concepts of ecology.' Firey made his objection to the classical position on two grounds arguing that there were two kinds of human adaptation to the urban environment.

The first he called 'volitional adaptation' since 'values which express primarily the identity or solidarity of a small cultural system may acquire spatial articulation.' His work on central Boston emphasized, for example, the value system derived from a cultural heritage, which gave Beacon Hill its distinctive character and determined its residential status unrelated to any distance or directional controls. This objection may be restated in the form that culturally rooted values exert a 'causative' influence on urban land-use patterns.

The second sort of adaptation was termed 'rational', since 'interests dominate the spatial adaptation of certain social systems.'[38] This is nearer the economic approach of his precursors in human ecology but even so Firey argued 'these interests come directly from broader and larger cultural systems.' This objection to economic determinism may be stated in the form that market forces themselves stem indirectly from larger cultural controls; they are not self-generated.

(*ii*) *The place of social power in the determination of land-use.* This aspect

---

[35] J. A. Quinn (1939): The nature of human ecology: re-examination and re-definition. *Soc. Forces* **18**, 166.

[36] W. Firey (1945): Sentiment and symbolism as ecological variables. *Am. sociol. Rev.* **10**, 140.

[37] W. Firey (1947): *Land use in central Boston*, 34 (Cambridge, Mass.).

[38] W. Firey (1947).

of land-use determination was earliest stated by W. H. Form.[39] He prefaced his case with a plea for models which consider social reality and not solely economic abstraction. In particular he argued that it is necessary to discard the idea of a free unorganized market in which individuals compete impersonally. This done it becomes imperative to identify who are the largest consumers of land, which organizations deal in land, and which associations mediate conflicts of land-use.

He identifies four organizational complexes which are dominant: the real estate and building businesses; larger industries, businesses and utilities; individual home owners; local Government agencies. The problem then becomes the exposure of the resources or influence which each of these can deploy, their functions in terms of the land-use market, the nature of their internal organizations, the accountability of the groups and the 'image of the city' within which each group works and the 'values' they consider paramount. Finally it is necessary to consider the relations between them much as one would study a collective bargaining process in industry. This provides a very different view of the sorting process from that of the classical ecologists. It is further developed in chapter 11.

In conclusion to this section dealing with human ecology and land-use it would seem reasonable to infer that work on ecological lines has reached an impasse. Its predominant economic bias has little to offer besides the more rigorous theoretical constructs of the thorough-going economist, whilst its rejection of cultural and social influences has hampered a vital line of enquiry. More recently the main trend has been to enumerate the variables which influence land-use in order to define an 'ecological complex'. These in themselves have become more elaborate, although generally in agreement. The framework outlined by Schnore[40] can be set alongside an earlier one by Beverly Duncan.[41]

L. Schnore		*B. Duncan*
Environment	Topography	*Site*
Technology	Transport and communication	*Accessibility*
	The friction of space	
Population	Size	
	Rate of growth	*Growth*
	Ethnic and racial composition	
Organization	Economic base	*Persistence*
	Community (ecological)	
	Organization	
	(The extent to which an urban	
	area is occupied by more or less	

---

[39] W. H. Form (1954): The place of social structure in the determination of land use: some implications for a theory of urban ecology. *Soc. Forces* **32**, 317.

[40] L. F. Schnore (1965), 383 – 6.

[41] B. Duncan (1964): Variables in urban morphology; in E. W. Burgess and D. J. Bogue, editors, (1964): *Contributions to urban sociology*, 17 (Chicago).

isolated and self-contained sub-
systems)
Social class composition

Duncan's 'persistence' referred mainly to historical factors and is not
equated with Schnore's 'organization' which is particularly important since
he maintains that 'all of the broad factors listed above — environment, technology and population — affect the internal arrangement of the city by their
joint effects upon organization. In short, all of the other variables in the
'ecological complex' operate to affect spatial distribution by being mediated
through functional organization.'[42] Schnore deliberately excludes 'value
systems' (i.e. sentiment and symbolism) and 'institutional arrangements'
(i.e. public policies) from his complex.

This is a list to which, with the exclusion noted, few people would take
exception, but it does little more than abstract and enumerate the sorts of
factors which the oldest studies in land-use drew upon in explanation of
unique or exceptional situations. It seems to make little contribution to
theory. One is thus led via a long road back to the destructive critics and the
views of Gittus: 'The former theories and techniques of urban analysis have
lost much of their validity. There is need for new emphasis on the variability
of urban structure and this involves the need for an empirical rather than a
theoretical approach to the situation. . . . It is conceivable that [it] . . .
might fail, but in view of the impasse that has now been reached in this field
from the starting point of general theory, it is well worth the making.'[43]

2 Land economics and urban land-use

The earliest work of importance in this field pre-dates that of the human
ecologists by many years for Richard M. Hurd's *Principles of city land values*
appeared in its first edition in 1903.[44] Much of this enquiry, as the title of
Hurd's book implies, is directly concerned with land value, but even so it is
inextricably bound up with land-use for 'the patterns of land-uses and land
values will be mutually determining.'[45]

Hurd drew upon earlier work concerned with land value and adapted the
principles of Ricardo, propounded for agricultural land, to an urban setting. Thus he began from the principle that 'value in urban land, as in
agricultural land, is the resultant of economic or ground rent capitalized.'[46]
Further 'in cities, economic rent is based on superiority of location only, the
sole function of city land being to furnish an area on which to erect buildings.'[47] With the growth of a city more remote, and hence by definition
inferior, locations are brought into use so that rents at the most accessible
points rise. For this accessible and consequently more valuable land

[42] L. F. Schnore (1965), 383.
[43] E. Gittus (1964), 13.
[44] R. M. Hurd (1924): *Principles of city land values* (New York).
[45] W. Alonso (1964): *Location and land use*, 16 (Cambridge, Mass.).
[46] R. M. Hurd (1924), 1.
[47] R. M. Hurd (1924).

competition will take place; 'any utility may compete for any location within a city and all land goes to the highest bidder' — who therefore obtains maximum convenience or economy in time and effort by being most accessible.

Hurd summed up his argument in a succinct sentence, 'Since value depends on economic rent and rent on location, and location on convenience, and convenience on nearness, we may eliminate the intermediate steps and say that value depends on nearness.'[48] But Hurd notes that 'nearness' is a relative term and has to be evaluated in terms of the growth and physical structure of the city on the one hand and the nature of the use required on the other. He concludes by emphasizing the necessary limitations imposed by an economic investigation which does not take into account 'individual and collective taste and preference as shown in social habits and custom'.[49]

These ideas have remained as basic to the mainstream of land economics. The major restatement took place in the 1920s by Robert M. Haig[50] but in much the same terms. Haig saw rent as the charge for accessibility or the saving in transport costs and invoked a bidding process to determine the occupancy and use of land. Undoubtedly his major contribution was the introduction of the notion of the 'friction of space', that is, that hindrance to perfect or immediate accessibility, for without such 'friction' there would be no transport costs and all locations would be perfect. The purpose of transport is to overcome this imperfection or friction, but while transport partly offsets friction, site rentals and transport costs represent the charge for that friction which remains. Rent thus appears as a payment for the saving in the costs of transport and these, rent and transport costs, will vary with site since 'the theoretically perfect site for the activity is that which furnishes the desired degree of accessibility at the lowest cost of friction' so that 'the layout of the metropolis tends to be determined by a principle which may be termed minimizing the costs of friction.'[51] This involves a three-way relation of rent, transport costs and location which are interdependent.

Ratcliff, in his well known volume *Urban land economics* adopts an argument that is basically similar. 'The utilization of land is ultimately determined by the relative efficiencies of various uses in various locations. Efficiency in use is measured by rent-paying ability, the ability of a use to extract economic utility from a site. The process of adjustment in city structure to a most efficient land-use pattern is through the competition of uses for various locations. The use that can extract the greatest return from a given site will be the successful bidder.'[52] From this there emerges an 'orderly pattern of land-use spatially organized to perform most efficiently the economic functions that characterize urban life.'[53] Ratcliff follows further enquiry into the competition of users for sites by the bidding process and into

[48] R. M. Hurd (1924), 13.
[49] R. M. Hurd (1924), 18.
[50] R. M. Haig (1926): Toward an understanding of the metropolis. *Q. J. Econ.* **40**, 421.
[51] R. M. Haig (1926).
[52] R. V. Ratcliff (1949): *Urban land economies*, 369 (New York).
[53] R. V. Ratcliff (1949), 369.

the minimizing of costs of friction, by an analysis of the different demands each user will have in locational terms, for not all users are in direct competition. Nevertheless 'in summary one might say that the structure of the city is determined through the dollar evaluation of the importance of convenience.'[54]

This sort of argument can be used in the derivation of a city structure closely analogous to that proposed by Burgess. In figure 8−6 distance is used as a measure of 'convenience' in the sense used by Ratcliff. Each crude and broad category of land user can be examined by ability to pay rent against distance from a single, most accessible core.[55] Retail uses demand greatest accessibility to the whole city population in order to maximize profits, while away from the city centre this quality falls off very rapidly as does the willingness to pay high rents (figure 8−6A). Offices, such as those of legal or insurance firms or of doctors and dentists also require accessibility and a central location but the very nature of their businesses means that the very high rents of the centre can be avoided by marginal locations. The slope for rent/distance is, therefore, less steep (figure 8−6B). Multiple housing

Figure 8−6: Bid rents for different users of urban land in relation to distance from the city centre. *After B. J. L. Berry (1959)*. In each of these graphs the ability of a potential user of urban land to pay rent is plotted against distance from the city centre.

[54] R. V. Ratcliff (1949), 375.
[55] For a discussion see B. J. L. Berry, (1959): The spatial organization of business land uses; chapter 3 in Garrison *et al.*, *Studies of highway development and geographic change*, 62 (Seattle).

schemes, such as apartment blocks, will give larger returns per unit area and can, therefore, obtain a greater degree of accessibility than single family housing but will not need the central locations which the retail and commercial offices have to obtain (figure 8−6D). The advantages of accessibility are, therefore, sacrificed in the interest of lower costs, although it must be emphasized that to these costs in terms of land must be added the costs of travel for, as has been emphasized, value or the capitalized expectation of rent, transport costs and location are interdependent. Finally agricultural uses are the least intensive and although they, too, would derive advantages from location at the centre they are outbid by all the urban uses and the rent/distance slope is the least steep (figure 8−6E).

If all these relationships, that is, all the slopes, are now superimposed (figure 8−7) then it can be seen that where the slopes intersect then the user furthest away from the core will be outbidding the user nearer to the core

Figure 8−7: Superimposition of separate graphs in figure 8−6 indicates that the various lines intersect. At each inter-section from the city outskirts in towards the centre the inner use can afford to pay higher rents and takes over from the outer use. These points are indicated by the dotted lines.

and consequently that type of use will succeed. If this is converted into a two dimensional diagram then a series of rings will be generated and a cross section interpreted in terms of value will give a close approximation to that presented for Topeka by Duane Knos[56] (figure 8−8). There are a large number of assumptions which are not proven and a number of serious flaws in the argument which has been presented. For example, all users are assumed to require equal quantities of land and no allowance is made for

[56] D. Knos (1962): *Distribution of land values in Topeka* (Lawrence, Kansas).

Figure 8–8: The distribution of land values in Topeka. *After D. Knos (1962).*

possible substitution of a larger land area for a less convenient location or, in crude terms, for buying cheaper land further out. Several attempts have been made to provide a more sophisticated basis and a more complex model in place of the simple concepts so far considered.[57]

The initial outline of one of these models can be briefly considered in order to indicate its rationale rather than trace its full development which is impossible in the present limited context.

William Alonso in his work *Location and land use* introduced two further variables, first the quantity of land which each user will wish to acquire and second the amount of disposable income which will be devoted to land and travel costs on the one hand, and all goods and services, including savings on the other. The equilibrium of the individual household in the urban situation is then seen as a consequence of the relation of all the alternatives in expenditure open to the individual and the patterns of preference which can be exercised. The alternatives open define the 'locus of opportunities' which

[57] W. Alonso (1964); L. Wingo (1961): *Transportation and urban land* (Washington).

is seen as a surface generated by the interrelation of the three variables noted above, the amount of land, the amount of goods and services and distance from the centre.

To relate this back to figure 8−6, it will be observed that the ability to pay rent depends partly on the size of the land area required and partly on the desired expenditure on other things. A complex surface is generated since the relations are not simply linear. Thus if the amount of goods and services is held constant and the relationship between quantity of land and distance considered then, 'the price of land . . . decreases with increasing distance from the centre. Therefore, the quantity of land that may be bought increases with the distance, since land is becoming cheaper. On the other hand, distance enters . . . in the form of commuting costs. As distance increases, so do commuting costs and consequently the amount of land that may be purchased decreases.' The resultant curve of quantity against distance 'rises to the point at which marginal increases in commuting costs are equal to the savings realized from the decreasing price of land. Thereafter, the amount of land that may be bought with increasing distance decreases.'[58]

The locus of opportunities surface defined along the three axes − of quantity of land against distance, quantity of land against quantity of goods and services and quantity of goods and services against distance − is set against the pattern of preferences, defined as a surface from the possibility of substitution amongst the three variables so that the individual household would be equally satisfied by different combinations of land, goods and accessibility (distance). From this the equilibrium of the household is derived, the desires in terms of preferences being linked to the possibilities in terms of the locus of opportunities. This individual equilibrium solution is then reformulated in the terms of market equilibrium, but this is a complex process for land and distance are so intertwined that the individual demand curves cannot be amalgamated into a demand curve for the market.

It will be apparent that this model is working, as the sub-title of the volume states, 'towards a general theory of land rent'. The assumptions on which the model is built are clearly set out. These include a featureless plain, all land of equal quality, all land ready for use without improvement, land freely bought and sold with both buyers and sellers having perfect knowledge of the market, no legal or planning restraints, no social restraints, sellers who wish to maximize revenue and buyers their profits or satisfaction, and the city regarded as a two-dimensional unit with no vertical element. The result is a deductive argument with clear premises explicitly rejecting all but purely measurable economic factors. It is rigorous, internally consistent and far removed from the reality of the city as it comes closer to pure economic theory.

3 Activity systems and urban land-use

The discussion so far has revealed that work on the structure of towns in

[58] Alonso (1964), 23.

human ecology has reached an impasse, while economic models contribute but partially to the solution of the problem. There is a third approach which while presenting no model seems to provide a stimulating way of looking at urban land-use structure and leads to a coherent framework for interpreting it. This is the approach via activity systems which can be defined as 'behaviour patterns of individuals, institutions and firms which occur in spatial patterns'.[59] F. Stuart Chapin has attempted to sketch 'a conceptual framework to describe some of the major elements and dynamics of human behaviour as they relate to land-use.'[60]

Figure 8–9 indicates the sequence which Chapin invokes to provide a

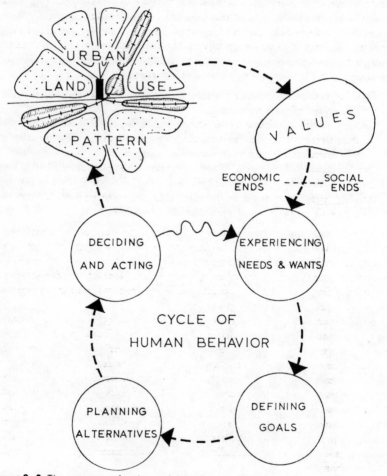

Figure 8–9: The sequence of action and the influence of values in bringing about a change in the urban land-use pattern. *After F. S. Chapin, Jr. (1965).*

[59] F. S. Chapin (1965): *Urban land-use planning*, 244 (Urbana, Ill.).
[60] F. S. Chapin (1965), 29.

framework consisting of values, behaviour patterns and outcomes. 'Certain individual- or group-held values concerning the use of a particular parcel or area set in motion a four-phase cycle of behaviour which culminates in the parcel or area being put to a particular use.'[61] These phases are part of the 'cycle of human behaviour' or of the behavioural pattern indicated above and are classified as: experiencing needs and wants; defining goals; planning alternatives; deciding and acting. Because of his particular interest, Chapin puts this in the context of planning, but it will be seen that he accepts explicitly the views of Firey in starting with culturally determined values which find no place in any other construct. From these values, both conscious and subconscious, or explicit or implicit, of individuals or groups of individuals, patterns of behaviour are generated leading to those actions in the urban setting which are the determinants of the land-use pattern. The behaviour patterns can be interpreted as constituting systems of activity and this is as equally applicable to the firm or the individual. Rannells has classified these activities into three states of elaboration:[62]

1　*Routine activities*. Standard patterns of movement of the individual, for example the journey to shop.
2　*Institutionalized activities*. These are concentrated onto particular points by institutions, as for example, onto a theatre which necessarily focuses a number of individual systems upon it.
3　*Organization of processes*. This is the most complex situation where there is a whole series of patterned cross relationships. For example the 'activity system' of a bank by the very nature of its business will be made up of a wide array of associated but different links.

The word 'link' used above indicates that the study of these systems leads directly into the examination of linkages, for few 'establishments', or indeed individuals, are isolated for they are associated with others by a series of linkages, where a linkage is defined as 'a relationship between establishments characterized by recurrent interactions which require movement of persons or of goods or the exchange of information.'[63]

Thus, for example, the emergence of a well defined legal area in a city can be seen as a consequence of a system of activities and linkages which bind legal firms together. There is a relation to the general public demanding accessibility in the sense which it has previously been used in this chapter; there is a relation to the law courts, the location of which may be due to essentially historical circumstances; there is a relation to standard sources of information such as a registry of wills and of births, marriages and deaths; there is a relation of firm to firm in negotiation which involves face to face situations; there is a relation in Britain of solicitor to barrister. For any such area these links can be traced, indeed they could to an extent be measured and quantified.

The result is a land-use element which can be seen as the product of a

---

[61]　F. S. Chapin (1965), 30.
[62]　J. Rannells (1956): *The core of the city* (New York).
[63]　J. Rannells (1956).

complex of linkages which are the creation of the activity systems of the various components. The tracing of the systems and the identification of the linkages is a prerequisite to the understanding of the components or the pattern of land use.

It is perhaps worthy of note that the sort of model proposed by the economists attempts to do just this by ignoring all the complexity and identifying one link only — that with the centre of the city. It follows that this approach is extremely broad in one context in that the values-behaviour-patterns framework permits the introduction of the widest range of operative factors for there are no limiting assumptions and no deductive arguments. Indeed the 'activity system' concept is much nearer the ecological framework presented by Schnore. At the same time it is very restricted in that instead of generalizing from the aggregate condition, it attempts to examine the real city in microdetail — for example in the actual movements of individuals — and from this to build up to an explanation of larger segments. In this way it presents a different method of looking at the city, for while maintaining contact with reality it still identifies the framework of forces which shape the aggregate, the total structure.

An attempt has been made in this chapter to survey in general terms those studies which attempt either to construct a model of the entire city or to introduce a conceptual framework in relation to which it can be understood. It is apparent that generalization on such a vastly complex topic must inevitably be unreal — hence the flight away from classical ecology either to the discipline of theoretical economics or the rationality of an approach via the detail of individual or corporate activities. It would seem that in these two directions useful contributions may be found; either in the clear delineation of assumptions and the erection of a rigorous model which can only examine the interaction of highly selected variables, thereby illuminating brightly a small part of the whole picture; or in the construction of a meaningful conceptual framework which might indicate significant bases from which to interpret the complexity of land-uses.

Notes on further reading
The most important material is that referred to in the footnotes to this chapter and these standard works should be consulted. The most useful general volumes on activity systems, urban land economics and human ecology are respectively:

Chapin, F. S. (1965): *Urban land-use planning* (see footnote 59). This deals with a larger range of topics and is accessible and straight-forward.
Ratcliff, R. V. (1949): *Urban land economics* (New York). This is still the most rewarding general volume to consult.
Theodorson, G. A., editor (1961): *Studies in human ecology* (New York).

A good number of books on urban economics have been published recently as the specialism becomes more popular in relation to the universal relevance of urban problems. Among them are:

Button, K. J. (1976): *Urban economics* (London).
Evans, A. W. (1973): *The economics of residential location* (London).
Goodall, B. (1972): *The economics of urban areas* (Oxford).
Hallett, G. (1979): *Urban land economics* (London).
Parry Lewis, J. (1979): *Urban economics: a set approach* (London).
Perloff, H. S. and Wingo, L. Jr. editor. (1968): *Issues in urban economics*. (Baltimore).
Rasmussen, D. W. (1973): *Urban economics* (New York) and, (1974): *The modern city: readings in urban economics* (New York).

The following should also be considered:

Alonso, W. (1964): *Location and land use* (see footnote 45).
Wingo, L. (1961): *Transportation and urban land* (see footnote 57).
Harvey, D. (1973): *Social justice and the city*. Chapter 5.

There are two areas of investigation which have not been introduced into this chapter but which need to be reviewed. The first of these concerns the relationship of population densities to distance from the city centre. Here the main works are:

Berry, B. J. L., Simmons, J. W. and Tennant, R. J. (1963): Urban population densities: structure and change. *Geog. Rev.* **53,** 389.
Clark, C. (1951): Urban population densities. *J. Roy. Stat. Soc.,* **A64,** 490.
Newling, B. E. (1969): The spatial variation of urban population densities. *Geog. Rev.,* **59,** 242.

A useful review can be found in:

Berry, B. J. L. and Horton, F. E. (1970): *Geographic perspectives on urban systems,* chapter 9: The urban envelope: patterns and dynamics of population density. (Englewood Cliffs, N.J.)

The second concerns the development of models of urban growth. Two general introductions are to be found in

Perloff, H. S. and Wingo, L. Jr., editors (1968): *Issues in urban economics; Part II: Intrametropolitan development;* particularly the chapter by Britton Harris: Quantitative models of urban development. (Baltimore.)
Kilbridge, M. D., O'Block, R. P. and Teplitz, P. V. (1970): *Urban analysis*. Div. of Research. Grad. School of Business Admin. Harvard (Boston). This contains an extensive bibliography.

A further general source which includes not only papers but a series of useful reviews is: *J. Am. Inst. Planners* (1965) **31** (2), Special Issue: Urban development models. While a widely quoted study is:

Lowry, I. S. (1964): *A model of a metropolis* (Santa Monica). Rand Corp. Memo RM−4035−RC.

Further reading on characteristic areas within the city is included at the end of succeeding chapters, but a very convenient collection of readings is:

Bourne, L. S. (1971): *Internal structure of the city* (New York).

9

The Central Business District

Insofar as the central business district (CBD) is regarded as the organizing centre about which the rest of the city is structured, it is appropriate that the concept be isolated for special consideration; it identifies one of the 'typical' areas of the city.

Investigators have tended to approach the CBD in three ways. First by attempting to provide the idea with a clear spatial identity through seeking means of defining its limits objectively. Inevitably such attempts at definition lead into consideration of the many specialized sub-units which make up the composite notion of a CBD. The second line of investigation has been by considering the composing elements in isolation, that is by considering locational requirements, say of department stores, quite independently of the existence or character of a CBD as such. The third approach has been by way of generalizing these individual locational requirements in terms of activity systems and linkages. These three approaches are by no means clearly distinctive and each must of necessity involve elements of the others, but in the order in which they have been placed here they can be looked upon as representing a process of growing incisiveness and insight as the emphasis swings from a conventional aggregate land-use basis towards the consideration of the multiplicity of decision making situations through which the CBD is built up.

1 Criteria for areal definition

The earliest concern with the CBD was related to the traditional geographical problem of areal definition, the notion of such a region having been derived from the ecologists' model of the city. The terms 'retail core' or CBD or other equivalents had long been in use, but the procedures employed in definitions were extremely crude and depended on visual inspection of land-use maps in the search for discontinuities between retail and other specified central uses and a non-central uses, and upon local opinion as to what constituted the shopping or 'downtown' area. Perhaps significant geographical work was not attracted to this problem because the challenge of a process of change was not always apparent. Indeed the very idea that the CBD was surrounded by a 'zone of transition' implied that it was itself immutable. This was confirmed by an apparent lack of areal extension, accompanied by the failure to materialize in this context of the invasion-succession syndrome of the classical ecologists.

For a variety of reasons—the role of vertical as opposed to horizontal development and the growth of suburban shopping centres among them—the CBD has not extended rapidly in area terms over the last forty years and process, therefore, has not been as clearly apparent as in the vast extension of residential areas. The result was an odd lack of concentrated analysis of the CBD in geographical literature and it was not until 1954 that R. E. Murphy and J. E. Vance Jr[1] by their work set in motion a series of studies concerned directly with this important part of the city.

Murphy and Vance were primarily concerned with the problem of definition, with the attempt to provide a uniform method for the physical delimitation of the CBD which could replace the fixing of boundaries by haphazard and local procedures. Accepting the view that any boundary must be zonal (and impermanent) they sought to 'draw a line which would approximate this zonal edge'. Undoubtedly the major problem in this exercise resides in the most appropriate criteria to be used. A number of these can be reviewed and since it has been argued in the previous chapter that use is, in general terms, the determiner of the value which can be put on land, and vice versa in a given situation, then it would seem that the most effective tool for definition would reside in land value or some derivative.

(*i*) *Appraised or assessed land values.* It is implicit in many studies, such as that of Topeka, for example, reproduced in the last chapter (figure 8–8), that land values, reduced to some comparable unit of area or of street frontage, would be powerful indicators of the CBD at whose margins values should fall rapidly. But there are many difficulties that arise in the attempt to employ this apparently ideal basis. In Britain, as in most parts of the world, the simple and outstanding one is that reliable data are just not available.

In the report of the proceedings of a colloquium under the Acton Trust on 'Land values' published in 1965, 'there was general agreement that lack of reliable data was a serious handicap to understanding' and again, 'because of lack of data many details . . . could not be studied at present.'[2] A contributor to the volume who was presenting an isopleth map of land values (figure 9–1) wrote 'I have chosen to enclose the residential part of the Barbican area with a land value contour of £4 per foot super, or say £175,000 per acre. The process by which I arrive at this figure is long and complicated and largely infra conscious but I am sure it is just about right! The best valuations are usually made at this level—some valuers would describe it as "according to the stomach". This is because one gets a sinking feeling when it is wrong.'[3] Clearly at this level there is no way at all to precision in definition. Murphy and Vance discuss the problem in some detail,

[1] R. E. Murphy and J. E. Vance, Jr. (1954a): Delimiting the CBD. *Econ. Geogr.* **30,** 189–222. (1954b): A comparative study of nine central business districts. *Econ. Geogr.* **30,** 301–36.

[2] P. Hall, editor (1965): *Land values,* 17 (London).

[3] P. Hall, editor (1965): chapter 2: A study of certain changes in land values in the London area in the period 1950–64 (by B. Anstey).

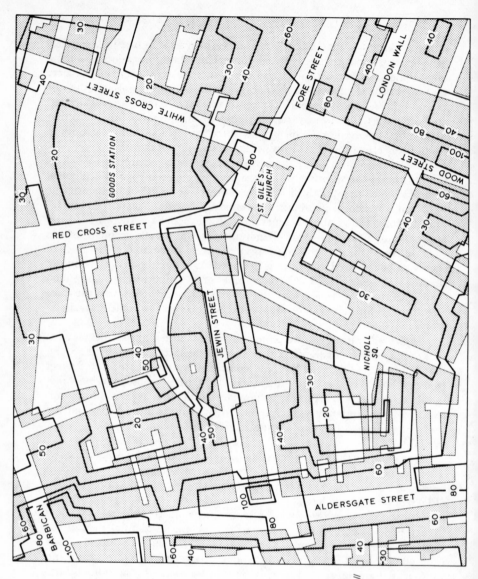

Figure 9–1: Isopleths of land values in the Old Barbican area of London. *After B. Anstey in P. Hall (1965).* This is part of a map which was drawn in 1953. The values are expressed in terms of pounds sterling per foot frontage. This is a sample map of 'isovals' – that is, lines joining points of equal value – and an interpretation will be found in the source referred to in the text.

considering both appraised values, that is the values approximating to a market value, and assessed values, which are used for taxation purposes. Their main criticisms are the differences between cities so that comparisons are impossible, the subjectivity of many of the assessments, the occasional lack of data because of confidentiality, the fact that values are unrelated to building height and, largely, that they do not directly reflect use.

Whilst accepting the operational problems, it is difficult to sustain the last two more fundamental objections. Value should reflect demand for a scarce commodity and building high is an attempt to squeeze maximum use out of a limited resource, that is central city land, and therefore, *a priori*, there should be a clear relation between value and height. There is a whole range of other influences at work in the development of the skyscraper[4] but essentially it is related to excessive demand for limited space. There is some truth in the view that the skyscraper is merely a three dimensional variant of the grid-iron street plan made to stand up vertically instead of horizontally.[5] Building high increases floor space on valuable sites: hence it is impossible to maintain that a height of building/land value relationship does not exist. Likewise if it is maintained that land value does not discriminate between uses, then this presents a fundamental challenge to the view of the land economist as outlined in the previous chapter, except in so far as, related to their needs and resources, two potential users make equal bids.

It is maintained, therefore, that, through the critical measure of value, the nature of the CBD boundary can be examined and the extent of its zonal or abrupt character evaluated. But one is forced to conclude that the problems concerning land values are associated with the impossibility of obtaining satisfactory, uniform, objective data for a large number of cities, rather than with the concept of using values themselves.

(*ii*) *Rent*. If land values are not easily obtained then clearly rent per unit area or street frontage is a good substitute since the relation is clear, as indicated in the last chapter; land value is rent capitalized. This criterion of rent was used by William-Olsson in an effective study of the shopping streets of Stockholm though no attempt was made to delimit an area by a critical value.[6] A shop rent index was derived by dividing the total rents for any premises by the frontage. But here, too, the same difficulties arise, for although rent is a fixed sum and less nebulous than appraised value, the data are generally not available and are treated as confidential. On detailed scrutiny a good proportion of William-Olsson's figures are seen to be estimates and to some extent the objectivity of the maps is superficial rather than fundamental.

---

[4] J. Gottmann and R. A. Harper, editors (1967): The skyscraper amid the sprawl. Part IV of *Metropolis on the move*, 125–50 (London).

[5] J. Gottmann and R. A. Harper, editors (1967), 133. Gottmann quotes this view from John A. Kouwenhoven.

[6] W. William-Olsson (1960): Stockholm structure and development, *International geographical congress, Norden*, 63–5.

(*iii*) *Rateable values.* In Britain this value is used as a basis for the fixing of contributions towards local finances. It is easily available for all properties and can be taken as a substitute for rent. The method of rating is fixed by the Rating and Valuation Act of 1925 modified by the Rating and Valuation Miscellaneous Provisions Act of 1955.[7] By this the gross rateable value is defined as 'the rent at which the hereditament might reasonably be expected to be let from year to year, if the tenant undertook to pay all the usual tenant's rates and taxes, and if the landlord undertook to bear the cost of repairs and other expenses, if any, necessary to maintain the hereditament in a state to maintain that rent.'[8]

Here, then is an easily available figure which is at least indirectly linked to land value, indirectly since the rateable value is assessed as the rent of a building not simply of the urban land, so that other complexities are introduced. In making this assessment two main factors are considered. The first is the physical condition, including space, nature of frontage and access; the second is site advantages, a less tangible factor which includes the potential value of the site based on experience and on current rents which are known to the assessor. In special cases the valuation officer can demand the turnover figures of a business. These rateable values have been used frequently in British work, perhaps most consistently by D. T. Herbert who in 1961 proposed a rate index[9]

$$ \text{RI} \ = \ \frac{\text{Gross rateable value}}{\text{Ground floor space}} $$

This index was to be used to identify, 'a part of the town which, without attempting to define it too closely, might be termed the core of the central business district'[10] (figure 9—2); there is deliberately no attempt to put forward a method of delimitation. The crux of the problem lies in the selection of a value, which must be an arbitrary process unless isopleths can be drawn and some form of gradient analysis introduced. Undoubtedly these figures will continue to be used in Britain and they do provide a most useful basis for investigations of city structure.

Two qualifications are needed. These are assessed figures and no more than the view of the valuation officer, and though he works from experience and extensive evidence and though by the process of objection each decision can be subject to scrutiny, nevertheless the value is still at root a personal assessment and is in danger of being given a specious objectivity by appearing in numerical form in an official source. The second qualification is to repeat that the value is an assessment of land plus building and not of the land alone.

Apart from these criteria for delimitation which are in some way related

---

[7] D. M. Lawrance and W. H. Rees (1956): *Modern methods of valuation,* fourth edition, 264—83 (London).

[8] D. M. Lawrance and W. H. Rees (1956), 266.

[9] D. T. Herbert (1961): An approach to the study of the town as central place. *Sociol. Rev.* **9,** 273—92.

[10] D. T. Herbert (1961), 280.

Figure 9–2: The distribution of rate indexes in Newcastle-under-Lyme. *After D. T. Herbert (1961).* The calculation of the rate index is given in the text.

RATE INDEX

32 and over

24 — 31

16 — 23

8 — 15

4 — 7

4 and under

to land value, there is a series of other bases which have been suggested from time to time. Among these are population densities,[11] pedestrian flows and even retail turnover.[12] All are faced with the same problem of availability of data on a sufficiently detailed scale to be usable. The result is that most investigators turn quite properly to the land uses themselves as the simplest, most direct evidence to be utilized in determining the spatial characteristics of the CBD.

2 Methods of areal definition

The inadequacy of simple inspection methods for delimiting the CBD has already been noted whilst the attempt to identify characteristic edge uses although interesting cannot be applied in detail. Murphy and Vance were, therefore, forced to elaborate a standard procedure. This they did as follows:

(*i*) *Definition of uses to be accepted as characteristic of the CBD.* Such uses were isolated in a negative way by elaborating non-central uses as: permanent residence, government and public buildings, organizational establishments (churches, colleges, etc), industrial establishments (except newspapers), wholesaling, commercial storage, vacant lots and buildings. This is a list can be accepted, though at this crude level of generalization most of the real problems of assignment of uses to or not to the CBD do not appear. But the essential point is that the decision made at the outset is crucial and subjective: the eventual area defined depends upon these bases put forward in a list of excluded uses. It is both interesting and amusing to include here a definition of a central use by John Allpass and his colleagues at the Institute of Centre-planning at Copenhagen: 'A CBD function: A function which has not yet left the central business district.'[13] This clearly underlines the circularity of the reasoning by which the central uses are isolated.

(*ii*) *Measurement of floor space devoted to the various uses.* Having identified central uses, then, from the detailed land-use map which is made for all floors to include total use, not merely the ground floor, the amount of floor space devoted to each use category is calculated. The unit for this process is the city block which is an obvious basis in the American city with its well-high universal grid pattern, but which is not so clear-cut in European cities where intricate and irregular plans make blocks much less amenable units.

[11] R. E. Murphy (1966): *The American city*, 286–90 (New York).

[12] L. H. Russwurm (1964): The central business district retail sales mix. *Ann. Assoc. Am. Geogr.* **54**, 524–36.

For examples of a variety of methods see: W. F. Heinemeijer, M. Van Hulten and Hans D. de Vries Reilingh, editors (1967): *Urban core and inner city* (Leiden). See particularly parts II and III.

[13] J. Allpass *et alia* (1967): Urban centres and changes in the centre structure; in W. F. Heinemeijer *et alia* (1967), 103.

(*iii*) *Calculation of ratios*. For each of the blocks a series of ratios or indices can be calculated. These are:

1 *Total height index* (HI)

$$\text{HI} = \frac{\text{Total floor space}}{\text{Ground floor space}}$$

This is the height of each block in floors if all the space, whatever its use, were to be spread evenly over the whole block. This is not the most valuable of measures for it merely generalizes a direct mapping of building heights. By reducing these heights to a block basis it provides a stage in the generalizing of actuality to a line boundary.

2 *Central business height index* (CBHI)

$$\text{CBHI} = \frac{\text{Total CB uses floor space}}{\text{Ground floor space}}$$

This is the height of each block in floors if all the central business uses were evenly spread over the whole block. It is a more useful measure since a CBHI of 1 indicates a complete ground floor coverage by central business uses. However, while showing the importance of central business uses, it does not indicate dominance for it fails to show the proportion of total available space in central uses.

3 *Central business intensity index* (CBII)

$$\text{CBII} = \frac{\text{Central business floor space}}{\text{total floor space}} \times \frac{100}{1}$$

This measures the proportion (percentage) of all available floor space in central business uses and is by far the most useful of the ratios, for it indicates the relative dominance of central business uses in any block and the choice of some limiting value (say 50 per cent) can be used as a universal in delimitation.

4 *Central business index* (CBI)

$$\text{CBI} = \text{CBHI of 1 plus CBII of 50 per cent}$$

To define the CBD Murphy and Vance took a composite measure as indicated above and called it the CBI. All blocks meeting the requirement were regarded as part of the CBD.

(*iv*) *Application of ratios or indices*. The application of these indices requires a set of further rules as, for example, that a non CB block surrounded by CB blocks should be included within the CBD boundary. The application of these techniques in the definition of the CBD of Worcester, Mass., is shown in figure 9−3.

(*v*) *Remaining problems*. Even after this set of rules has been applied some clear objections remain:

Figure 9–3: The definition of the central business district: Worcester. Mass. _After R. Murphy and J. E. Vance, Jr. (1954a: see footnote 1, p. 199)._ **1:** Central business height index (CBHI) of 1 or more. **2:** Central business intensity index (CBII) of 50 or more. **3:** CBHI of 1 or more and CBII of 50 or more. **4:** CBD boundary. **5:** Peak land value intersection.

1   Variations in block size are not taken into account and could have a marked influence on the location of a boundary in detail. This becomes especially relevant in comparative studies and the whole purpose of this procedure is presumably to establish a basis for comparison.
2   The central business uses are subjectively determined even if they are uniformly applied. This repeats an earlier comment.
3   No account is taken of the 'quality' of use of an area. A small corner shop and a specialized and expensive central store are classed the same and the floor space used could be the same.
4   Even if the operational difficulties are overcome the main objection to the method is still outstanding. What is the whole point and purpose of defining such a boundary?

The earliest modifications, whilst still dominated by the delimitation problem, were directed towards the fact that the CBD so defined has a 'hard core' — 'where the definitive qualities reach their greatest intensity.'[14] Hence there were attempts to separate 'core' from the 'frame' in which it was held.[15] Perhaps the most intensive of these was the study of central Cape Town by D. H. Davies.[16] Beginning with the principle that 'in the heart of the CBD more intensive use of space, higher land values, heavier pedestrian traffic and generally taller buildings indicate the presence of a "hard core" ', Davies went on to outline procedures for the identification of this area. As one would anticipate, these were based on a revision upwards at the two points where major arbitrary decisions were made by Murphy and Vance. First the necessary minima for the CBD were increased to a CBHI of 4 and a CBII of 80 per cent. Second the marginal areas which constitute the frame were further diminished in the CBD context by restricting those uses regarded as 'central'. Cinemas, hotels, head offices, newspaper establishments, government and municipal offices and retail stores offering low quality goods (subjectively defined) were regarded as non CBD hard core uses. This process is a neat illustration of the sorts of decisions made at various points in the defining procedure — why a CBII of 80 per cent? The eventual delimitation of these areas in Cape Town is indicated in figure 9—4, where the exclusions resulting from the application of these more rigorous conditions are depicted.

3 Purpose of definition

At this stage it is as well to turn aside to review the purpose behind this type of analysis for it would seem that the first approach by geographers to the study of the CBD was dominated by the search for definition. From definition there are advantages to be gained. If some universal method were to be

[14]   R. E. Murphy, J. E. Vance, Jr., and B. J. Epstein (1955): Internal structure of the CBD. *Econ. Geog.* **31**, 21—46.
[15]   E. M. Horwood and R. R. Boyce (1959): *Studies of the central business district and urban freeway development* (Seattle).
[16]   D. H. Davies (1965): *Land use in central Cape Town: a study in urban geography* (Cape Town).

Figure 9–4: The delimitation of the hard core of the central business district of Cape Town. *After D. H. Davies (1965).* **A:** A stage in the definition process. **1:** CBD boundary. **2:** CBII of 80. **3:** CBHI of 4. **4:** Hard core as identified by **2** and **3** above. **B:** Final definition. **1:** Blocks omitted by exclusion rule in which government and municipal offices and department stores offering lower quality and restricted ranges of goods were counted as non-central uses. **2:** Blocks still retained after application of exclusion rule. **3:** The final, continuous hard core boundary. In this a discrete area has been isolated and the outlying qualifying blocks have been discarded.

adopted, then the size, structure and nature of these areas could be considered in relation to rank in the urban hierarchy, and an important function/form link could be established.

Few attempts have been made to follow these lines of enquiry. One of them is the study of land-use in the urban core by Hartenstein and Staack.[17] Six German cities (figure 9−5) were studied and by using Murphy and Vance methods a 'hard core' and 'fringe' were identified. Data relating to these areas were then used for a series of analyses, from which generalizations were derived, such as: the larger the total floor area of the urban core, the larger the floor area for all uses; with growing size of the core area, the floor area for retail use does not grow at a parallel rate — probably due to the fact that larger cities have decentralized their retail functions; with growing size of the core area, the floor area in office use grows at a higher rate — probably due to the fact that larger cities fulfil a number of regional, national and international functions which smaller cities do not.[18]

Many of these conclusions are not very startling or unexpected, but they are important, for if analysis is to be based on the locational decisions of individual firms then this study shows that they are not simply concerned with making decisions in the abstract in relation to location. The different combinations of users in cities of different size must inevitably be part of the decision-making process. Undoubtedly Hartenstein and Staack have made good use of a uniform method of definition, but even so their conclusions are linked to a number of fairly obvious statements about the relative density of uses in the core and the rate of diminution of those uses away from the centre. To a large extent in other studies the fixing of a boundary has become an end in itself, devoid of purpose and hence academically barren. In some ways the search for regional boundaries in the city centre followed the earlier search for regional boundaries in geography and in doing so fell into all the same traps.

Murphy and Vance in their CBD studies were aware of this problem and seem to have realized that definition for its own sake was hardly a stimulating end product of their research. A consideration of the internal structure of the CBD[19] revealed its dynamic and changing nature, for the edges were seen to be either advancing or contracting, and zones of assimilation and of discard were identified and related to surrounding uses. This is an appropriate development, for, as assimilation and discard are considered, attention is directed towards process and away from definition. But these are still only a part of the whole complex of processes operative in the city centre and determining land-use. Inevitably one is led towards a more realistic evaluation of the central area not being made up of a CBD (with or without a hard core) but of a number of closely associated areas or sub-cores, constantly subject to pressures and with, in consequence, changing boundaries. These areas have emerged and have crystallized out in the long

[17] W. Hartenstein and G. Staack (1967): Land use in the urban core. Part I of W. F. Heinemeijer *et alia* (1967), 35−52.
[18] W. Hartenstein and G. Staack (1967), 43.
[19] R. E. Murphy, J. E. Vance, Jr. and B. J. Epstein (1955), 21−46.

STUTTGART

DUSSELDORF

NURNBERG

DUISBURG

BREMEN

ESSEN

Block Types
▨ Hard Core
▧ Core Fringe
▨ Public

Borders
—— Hard Core
– – – Core Fringe

Figure 9–5: The hard core and fringe area in six German cities. *After W. Hartenstein and G. Staack, in Heinemeijer et alia (1967).* This figure illustrates the general application of the core and fringe (or frame) concept to a series of large German cities.

historical process of the town's growth.

Once Davies had relaxed the notion of a single, simple CBD in Cape Town and had lifted out a hard core he was inevitably faced with the problem of these remaining areas and logically proceeded to identify them by means of cluster analysis.[20] This is carried out for each category of use by using floor space per lot (the basic areal unit). Each lot with a particular use is plotted and the centre of gravity is found by the standard method of drawing two axes to contain the distribution and by finding the mean of all the distances from each lot to each axis (figure 9−6). Davies weighted the distance values by amount of floor space in each use by multiplying each measurement by the floor space devoted to the use in the lot and then dividing the totals by the total floor space in that use, so that the weighted centre of gravity takes areal extent into account as well as locational pattern.

The conventional method of establishing the cluster boundary is to draw a

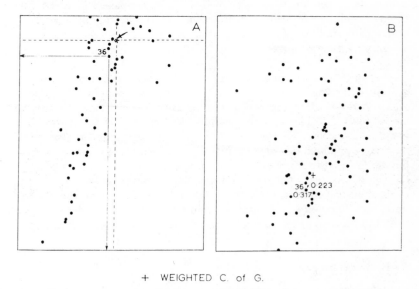

+ WEIGHTED C. of G.

°ᴋ UNWEIGHTED C. of G.

Figure 9−6: The process of cluster analysis. *After D. H. Davies (1965).* The use is household furnishing. Each dot represents a lot or areal unit and **A** shows the southern part and **B** the northern part of the total distribution, with some overlap. For each lot (e.g. lot 36 on diagram) the distance to X and Y axes is measured, and the mean distances to the X and Y axes for all lots give the centre of gravity. This is weighted by floor space to give the weighted centre of gravity (see text). The process of inclusion is represented in the graph (figure 9−7, p. 213) where the percentage of the distance of each lot from the centre of gravity of all distances is plotted against the percentage floor space in any use in each lot of all floor space in that use. The graph lines of 50% and 97% are drawn as described in the text (p. 212).

[20] D. H. Davies (1965), 39 *et. seq.* This does not refer to the statistical process of the same name.

circle of radius equal to the mean of all the distances from the individual lots to the centre of gravity, or in more sophisticated studies to draw in standard deviational ellipses. This was rejected on account of its arbitrary areal character. Instead each lot distance was expressed as a percentage of the distance of all lots from the centre of gravity, and likewise the floor space in any use was expressed as a percentage of all the floor space in the use under consideration. These were then plotted against each other. In order to bring together strong representation, increasing distance was associated with decreasing size by plotting 1/area. On this graph the lots which were to be regarded as forming the cluster were identified by a factor of inclusion (F), where $F = A/D$ where A is percentage area and D percentage distance. A series of curves for F, expressed as values of $(1/A)/D$, were used to identify inclusion by totalling the percentage of floor areas of lots to the left of the curve (figure 9–7). Eventually the very high figure of 97 per cent was chosen to identify clusters and a line was drawn which encompassed all the lots identified as making up this proportion. The superimposition of these cluster boundaries produced a complex map of city centre 'regions' (figure 9–8). These were then analyzed as part of the structural make-up of the city centre.

The conclusions which Davies draws are related to the complexity of the spatial patterning, which has to be set against the discrete CBD concept, and also the relation of this patterning to concentric zones, sectors and nuclei, a backward look to the generalizations of whole city structure which is not illuminating. Rightly he comments, 'it is suggested that currently there may well be diminishing returns in any delimitation studies per se',[21] but he lets his study end rather inconclusively, neither following up the concept of linkages which he introduces, nor the historical emergence of the areas identified, that is, the way present linkages have come about; for he states 'cause and effect are interwoven in a manner too complex to unravel without historical investigation beyond the scope of the present study.'[22]

4 Historical process and the CBD[23]

Historical investigation is best exemplified by Ward's study of the evolution of central Boston.[24] Three maps (figures 9–9A, B, C) indicate the basic pattern of development as successive specialized areas crystallized out as the city grew rapidly.

From an early nineteenth-century pattern where specialized business, was restricted to a small section of the waterfront and the market halls, there was a progressive segmentation of specialized activities into financial,

[21] D. H. Davies (1965), 87.

[22] D. H. Davies (1965) 74.

[23] H. Carter and G. Rowley (1966): The morphology of the central business district of Cardiff. *Trans. Inst. Br. Geogr.* **38**, 119–34.

[24] D. Ward (1966): The industrial revolution and the emergence of Boston's central business district. *Econ. Geog.* **42**, 152–71.

Figure 9–7: Identification of clusters in central Cape Town, household furniture sales. *After D. H. Davies (1965)*. The process is explained in the text page 218 and in figure 10–6. **A**: inclusion process, **B**: limits of Cluster.

Figure 9–8: The overlapping of major clusters in central Cape Town. *After D. H. Davies* (*1965*).

A: retail uses; **B:** office uses; **C:** Automobile, industrial wholesale and commercial storage uses; **D:** public and government uses. (PVLI: peak land value intersection.)

administrative, retail and wholesale commercial functions, occupying by the early twentieth century an area larger than the original town.

The first distinctive area to emerge was that devoted to financial and insurance services which were valued by the merchant community, and warehouse accommodation developed nearby. The development of 'mass consumption' and 'mass transit' resulted in the emergence of distinct retail and wholesale sections whilst manufacturing was displaced. At the same time financial and administrative functions were enlarged to form an extensive segment. Thus Ward depicts how from a small nucleus, and related to changes brought about in the nineteenth century, the distinctive parts of Boston's CBD emerged. At no point in his illustrative maps is the CBD as such defined nor is there any attempt at objective definition, indeed no direct evidence is produced at all to support the identification of areas or directions of growth. The prime concern is with process rather than with definition.

It is, however, possible to generalize the situation to indicate the way in which the composing elements of the central area crystallize out from the amorphous general central area of the pre-nineteenth century city (figure 9–10).

In figure 9–10 which relates mainly to Britain, diagram A represents the situation early in the eighteenth century with a regionally undifferentiated kernel surrounded by a fringe belt (eventually the Inner Fringe Belt, IFB). By 1850 (diagram B) the segregation of central city land-uses has appeared with the emergence of specialized financial and warehouse or wholesale districts (F and W on figure 9–10B). These overlap the retail core which was still in an 'incipient' form. The new industrial areas (I) had much in common with the warehouse district and there was considerable overlap. Industrial housing (Ih) of low quality was closely associated with the industrial region itself and spread on to the estates of the IFB. The core still retained upper class housing (U) but, under the pressure of changes, a sectoral extension was underway. Vance would argue that the merchants still needing rapid access, especially to the financial area, tended to remain at or near the centre often in imposing newly built squares, but the non-working elite were beginning to move further out.

By 1880 (diagram C) a clear retail core had emerged and also by that date the first chain shops were appearing within it. The sectoral extension of the well-to-do exerted a significant influence on the town centre pulling it outward in a zone of assimilation into what had been the IFB. The further development of working men's houses had led to the further deterioration of the oldest inner areas into which filtered the derelict from the indigenous society (WCS) and immigrant ethnic groups (E), in the case of Britain mainly the Irish. At the margins a middle class area had developed, deteriorating both zonally into the centre and sectorally towards the industrial areas. A Middle Fringe Belt (MFB) had come into being characterized by public utilities, including cemeteries (C), waterworks (W) and asylums (LA).

Figure 9–9: The development of the central area of Boston, Mass., from 1850 to 1920. *After D. Ward (1966).*
A: 1850 to 1875; **B:** 1875 to 1890; **C:** 1890 to 1920.

Figure 9–10: A suggested generalization of the development of the industrial town, 1880–1900. For explanation of the abbreviations, see text pp. 215–219. WCS = Working class slum; E = immigrant ethnic area.

By the end of the century the modern city, before Second World War destruction and renewal, had come into being (diagram D). The distinctive retail area continued to be dominated by chain and specialist stores and its continued migration towards the sector of upper class housing had created zones of assimilation (+) and discard (−). The remaining areas were largely as they had been twenty years earlier. The MFB had been assimilated by intermediate class housing in which the public utilities remained lodged, but an Outer Fringe Belt was coming into being.

This simple descriptive generalization of the internal structural changes in British cities during the nineteenth century indicates the way in which an approach via the evolutionary sequence can be made to the modern city centre. To it must be added post war change which in many cases has left the old core isolated by the conversion of the surrounding zone by comprehensive redevelopment programmes into an inner ring road or urban motorway with new high rise municipal housing closely related to it.

5 Cluster identification and process

From the various studies to which reference has been made there does emerge a methodology for studying the central areas of cities. It is concerned with areal definition and the unravelling of process, both at an aggregative level. It can be briefly stated as follows:

1   Define distinctive contemporary areas by means of cluster analysis or some like technique, the greater the degree of objectivity the better.
2   Interpret these areas in terms of the growing city by taking cluster analysis back into the past and by identifying movements in the centre of gravity of clusters and changes in the size and shape of clusters. This identifies not merely zones of assimilation and discard, but the larger and more complex process by which special uses become segregated and by which the locational characteristics of uses become fixed − by which the amorphous core develops into the city centre.
3   This interpretation is carried out by means of tracing the emerging spatial linkages between functions and the spatial incompatibility between functions, which respectively attract and repel and are the operative factors in the developmental process.

A study of central Manchester by R. Varley has attempted to follow through this method.[25] At the outset by using the location of establishments from directories, centres of gravity and indices of dispersion (the mean of all distances from the centre of gravity) were calculated. The sorts of results produced are illustrated in the table on page 221.

If the distribution of stock and share brokers and of travel agents is examined (figure 9−11A and B) then the difference in the degree of scatter indicated in the table below is apparent and this has clear implications in relation to linkages. The very close links of the stock brokers with the

[25] R. Varley (1968): *Land use analysis in the city centre with special reference to Manchester*. University of Wales: unpublished M. A. thesis).

Figure 9–11: A: The distribution and centre of gravity of stock and share brokers in Manchester in 1965. **B:** The distribution and centre of gravity of travel agents and wholesale jewellers in Manchester in 1965. *A, B, after R. Varley (1968)*. The distribution patterns of stock brokers and travel agents is discussed in the text (pp. 219–21). The pattern of wholesale jewellers reveals a characteristic clustering and a distinctive area; see also figure 9–12A.

Legend within figure:

MANCHESTER 1965
- • Wholesale Jewellers
- ▲ Travel Agents
- – – Boundary of area studied
- × Centres of Gravity

0 Feet 500
0 100 Metres

STOCK & SHARE BROKERS'
OFFICE IN MANCHESTER IN 1965
× Centre of Gravity
– – Boundary of area studied

0 Feet 500
0 100 Metres

River Irwell
Market Street

Type of establishment	Index of dispersion
Stock and share brokers	1·77
Barristers	2·33
Wholesale jewellers	2·70
Building societies	3·24
Insurance offices	3·28
Solicitors	3·36
Estate agents	4·03
Accountants	4·22
Manufacturers' agents	4·30
Merchants	4·69
Cotton spinners and manufacturers	5·17
Travel agents	5·95

Exchange and the associated financial area produce a tight distribution. On the other hand travel agents have a number of different links partly with the business office area, partly with transport facilities or their termini and partly with the retail area where a shop front is necessary in terms of public service. Moreover, in Manchester there is another factor, for whereas stock broking is a long established profession, having built up associations and developed concentration over a considerable time, travel agents are relative newcomers and have had little time to move together to produce a well marked area. It is possible to carry these methods back into the past and to construct similar maps, and movement over a considerable period of time can be shown (figure 9–11C). The close-knit areas devoted to stock brokers,

Figure 9–11: C: Changes in the centres of gravity of selected functions in Manchester between 1850 and 1965. *After R. Varley (1968).*

as well as to legal professions, are clearly apparent in Manchester where total movement of the centre of gravity over a hundred years has been no more than two hundred feet. Travel agencies did not exist at these earlier dates.

This preliminary analysis was followed by the employment of land-use data (floor space in square feet) for thirty basic categories made available for blocks and parcels within blocks, by the Manchester County Borough (figure 9–12A). A combination method was used by which the various uses in each block were ranked according to the percentage of floor space occupied. A direct map can be made of first (and indeed each succeeding) ranking use for each block and this can be used to identify core areas, which can be closely related to those established by cluster analysis of establishments. But a real problem remains, since rank gives no notion of degree of dominance of a use or of the association of uses in any block, a feature essential to the identification of linkages. To solve this, land-use combinations were evaluated by a least squares method[26] (figure 9–12B).

The method is as follows: for each block the percentages of each use are ranked in descending order. Theoretically if the block were to be a single-use block then there would only be one use which would account of 100 per cent of the floor space. The percentage of the first ranking land-use is compared, therefore, to 100. The difference of the actual value from the theoretical value is squared and added to the squares of the remaining percentages in the block so that a total is obtained. The next assumption is that the block is a 'two-use block' in which case each use should account for 50 per cent of the total. The first and second ranking uses are each compared with the theoretical distribution, this time 50 per cent. The differences from 50 are squared and these are added to the squares of the remaining percentages of other land-uses represented. This process continues, comparing actual with theoretical until all the uses in a block have been dealt with.

When all the totals have been obtained then the lowest one marks the point at which a block is nearest the theoretical or ideal situation, that is where all the floor space is equally divided between the types of use present. Thus if the fourth total is the lowest then the block is regarded as a four-use block and the four particular uses are regarded as in combination, and 'combination' in this context can be regarded as the equivalent of in-block linkages. Each block can be mapped according to the number and sorts of land-uses in combination and distinctive areas can be identified.

It is not possible or necessary here to follow the detail of this study, but it is worthy of note that a virtual mono-retail area does emerge (figure 9–12C) though most other areas are characterized by combinations of use. Thus Area 1 is identified by Varley is predominantly one of storage, largely wholesale in character. But there is also a strong retail element intermingled including four single-use blocks. This is probably due to a variety of small retail establishments serving the wholesalers (indeed some establishments are both wholesale and retail) particularly confectioners, tobacconists and

[26] This is derived from: J. C. Weaver (1954): Crop combinations in the middle West. *Geogrl. Rev.* **44**, 175–200; D. Thomas (1963): *Agriculture in Wales during the Napoleonic wars* (Cardiff); see particularly chapter 5, 79–95.

Figure 9–12: A: The distribution of first ranking land-uses by blocks in central Manchester in 1966.

The key to the shading is as follows: **1:** Churches and public places. **2:** Entertainment. **3:** Cultural including museums and libraries. **4:** Indoor games. **5:** Wholesaling and covered storage. **6:** Open storage including builders' yards. **7:** Commercial art studios. **8:** Radio, T.V. and film studios. **9:** Open land including parks and playing fields. **10:** Waste and derelict land. **11:** Special industry (mining, smelting or casting). **12:** Light industry — those which could be carried out in a residential area without detriment to the amenity. **13:** All general industry excluded from 11 and 12. **14:** Health. **15:** Education. **16:** Cleared building sites and buildings under construction. **17:** Miscellaneous including abattoirs, kennels and riding stables. **18:** Government offices. **19:** Financial offices. **20:** Professional offices. **21:** Commercial offices. **22:** Other offices. **23:** Public services. **24:** Hotels. **25:** Residential uses. **26:** Retail. **27:** Public houses. **28:** Car parks. **29:** Transport, including filling stations, railway land and airports. **30:** Vacant. *Note*: all the uses are not represented on the keys since only the relevant have been included. The full list is given here as an indication of the bases of analysis.

Figure 9–12: B: Land-use combinations in central Manchester in 1966. For method see text. The complexity of the original makes it impossible to reproduce the whole. This area is the north eastern corner of **A**, although a different shading scheme is used.

Figure 9–12: C: Dominant land-use regions in central Manchester in 1966. This is part of Varley's summary map. Area **1** is predominantly an area of storage and wholesaling with a strong retail element, whilst Area **6** is the traditional office area. The main retail areas are **3** where retail is virtually a mono use, **4** where it is in combination with a wide variety of uses, and **8** which is the quality retail area where office uses are in combination. The location of the areas on this map can be identified by comparison with **A** where the boundaries of the study area are indicated. This figure covers the northern part only. Rather than give conventional names, such as 'retail core', Varley has used the neutral terminology of Area **1**. Each area has a characteristic combination of uses. *A, B, C after R. Varley (1968)*.

cafes. Light industry, clothing manufacture and printing, are also represented but heavy industry is excluded owing to congestion and high land values. Area 6 emerges as the financial area already discussed which is dominated by financial offices. Varley calls this 'the traditional office area' in the light of its stability, which he has already identified.

At this point a similar study by Goddard of London's central area can be considered.[27] Only six basic uses were included but these provide a basic pattern of combinations from which land-use zones can be derived (figure 9–13). 'The historic dual-centred core ("the City" to the east and Westminster to the west) has both the strongest vertical development and the greatest segregation of uses, offices, having virtually eliminated all other functions.' These office areas are themselves composed of distinctive subgroups as Goddard has shown elsewhere using multivariate analysis techniques.[28] A third sub-core is formed by the West End distinguished by a retail-office-residence combination and characterized by the lateral extension of retailing into the residential areas to identify areas of conversion. These are very different from the conversion about the city core which is characterized as 'decaying fringe', where deteriorating residential areas unsuitable for office conversion are taken over for commercial and industrial use. Finally the 'mixed area' is the area of earliest expansion west of the

[27] J. Goddard (1967): The internal structure of London's central area. In W. F. Heinemeijer *et alia* (1967), 118–40.
[28] J. Goddard (1968): Multivariate analysis of office location patterns in the city centre; a London example, *Reg. Stud.* **2**, 69–85.

O Offices
S Shops
C Commerce
I Industry
P Public Buildings
R Residence

city which originally was one of fashionable squares—Covent Garden and Soho Square. These degenerated in the nineteenth century as the fashionable areas moved further west and Regent Street was constructed as a western limit. The result in modern London is a mixed area containing a variety of uses with property in a variety of conditions. The end product of Goddard's analysis is similar to those already considered.

It will be apparent that these areas are still arbitrarily defined, although it would not seem difficult to devise an objective method of association by linkage analysis as Goddard does for his office areas. Even so, and without much objectivity in areal identification, they seem vastly more useful than an area ringed around and labelled CBD, or even split into core and fringe. The above analyses demonstrate the multiplicity of relationships that exist between uses and lead directly to the questions as to what are the precise needs of any use of central urban land and how can these be satisfied in locational terms within the structures that comprise the city centre.

There seems little point in providing here an exhaustive catalogue of the considerations which will influence each category of urban land user, even if it were possible. But it is apparent that the decisions made at the micro level of the firm, or the individual, build up into the aggregate pattern and the more that is known about this decision-making process the more realistic will be the appraisal of the aggregate condition. Thus Nelson[29] put forward eight principles operative in the selection of a retail site.

These are as follows:

1   *Trading area potential.* A minimum volume of business is an obvious first necessity. In central place theory terminology it must be possible to tap sufficient custom to pass the minimum threshold requirement.

2   *Accessibility to trading area.* Maximum accessibility to the population of the trading area is needed. Presumably this operates on a regional and on a local city centre scale. It results in peak land value intersections or, in more everyday terms, competition for corner sites at main cross roads or squares.

3   *Growth potential.* Access to areas with growing populations and rising incomes is needed.

4   *Business interception.* A site between the main concentration of working population in the downtown area and the main shopping centre will enable customers to be intercepted along the main lines of daily movement.

[29] R. L. Nelson (1958): *The selection of retail locations*, 52 (New York).

Figure 9–13: Land-use combinations and land-use zones in central London. The upper diagram shows the uses in combination and is similar to that in figure 9–12**B**. The lower diagram shows a resolution of these combinations into land-use zones. The detail of use and the scale of work is cruder than that for Manchester but the basic principles are the same. In this lower map W. End stands for the West End (Mayfair and St James) giving an office, shop, residence combination; 'core' refers to the City of London and to Westminster. *After J. Goddard in W. J. Heinemeijer et alia (1967).*

5   *Cumulative attraction.* A number of similar units in a small specialized area can exert a much greater influence on potential customers than an isolated store. The possibility of inspecting several shops offering similar goods and provinding a wide choice, that is a number of complementary units, will generate a pull of its own.

6   *Compatibility.* The location in an area of compatible uses will generate maximum customer interchange.

7   *The minimizing of competitive hazard.* This is self-explanatory for it is common business sense to avoid a location where competition is critical.

8   *Site economics.* A site which provides maximum economies through ease of access and shape is obviously an advantage.

Not all these principles work together for cumulative attraction, and compatibility may well bring a store into an area of competitive hazard; but nevertheless they form a basic group of tenets relative to store location. At the same time and at a level of detail, these kinds of principle have to be reconciled with those relative to social power, which have been discussed earlier. Competition for sites is not resolved simply in terms of the market but in terms of the play off between competing interests and the power they can exert at a particular time and relative to an existing set of structures.[30] If comparatively little is known of the needs of users still less is known about the powers they can deploy. Thus in a sample of 373 establishments in Worcester, Mass., Ames has shown how variation in rank order occurs according to number, space occupied and size establishment.[31]

Type of establishment	Number	Rank of establishments by Space occupied	Size by employees
Retail	1	3	6
Services	2	4	5
Manufacture	2	1	1
Wholesale	4	2	2
Transport	5	5	3
Finance	6	6	7
Government	7	7	4

The implications of this table are of greatest significance in terms of the way users can obtain central sites; indeed they lead on to a consideration of the very heterogeneity of the central area and the external economies to firms which result from it.[32] At this point one is merely outlining the many problems about the central area of the city still to be studied.

The general conclusion which emerges from the previous pages, however, is that attempts to resolve the heterogeneity and complexity by cluster

---

[30] See page 187.

[31] Personal communications, from D. Ames formerly of the University of Cincinnati Department of Geography.

[32] B. Thorngren (1967): External economies of the urban core. In W. F. Heinemeijer *et alia* (1967), 413–22.

analysis or by land-use combination methods and attempts to isolate and examine decision-making situations are trying to do the same thing at different levels of generality. Clusters are created by the linkages generated by systems of activity which characterize the users of central urban land. This was apparent in the structure of a legal area outlined in the last chapter and it is a theme taken up by a number of writers concerned with urban land-use. Bourne writes that an approach can be taken which focuses on 'communication or linkage requirements between activities. By tracing the linkages or "movement systems" for and between establishments, some additional insight is provided into the locational pattern of urban land-use and variations in the degree of spatial association between individual users. . . . Although it is difficult to extract theory from these discussions, the emphasis on the dynamic interaction between location and activity rather than on accessibility alone represents an important addition to existing generalizations.'[33]

Undoubtedly the most effective analysis of this situation was that by John Rannells in his book *The core of the city* which was published as long ago as 1949.[34] At this point a further complexity must be introduced which is inherent in the analysis of Ward and which is the particular concern of Bourne. All the generalized models assume that there is a constant plane surface to be developed whereas in fact to the entrepreneur, faced with making a locational decision, the city consists of an existing stock of buildings. As change takes place, as associations of uses develop, they have to fit into and adapt, or replace, a given set of structures.

In summation, therefore, 'the physical city exists because of the patterned activities of its population as they accumulate and are accommodated at definite locations in establishments.'[35] It follows 'that individuals and establishments in action make the city, which in turn shapes their activities; that ongoing patterns of action explain the uses to which available structures are put, with the result that the physical environment is sustained by continuance of activities, while physical changes reflect shifts in the underlying activity systems into which the whole complex of urban life is separated for analysis.'[36]

Davies's work on Cape Town, which has been considered already, was largely derived from Rannell's study of central Philadelphia. But Davies was sidetracked by his concern for definitional problems on the argument that spatial notions were the basic geographical concern. Rannells was less concerned with defining any preconceived area than with identifying the interlinked systems of activity which were lodged in a general central area. He used the city block as his basic unit and the number of establishments and amount of floor space in each block as a measure of activity, divided into manufacturing, wholesaling with stocks and without stocks, business

[33] L. S. Bourne (1967): The private redevelopment of the central city. *Univ. Chicago Dept. Geogr. Res. Pap.* **112**, 19 (Chicago).
[34] J. Rannells (1956).
[35] J. Rannells (1956), 16–17.
[36] J. Rannells (1956), 17.

services, consumer services and retailing.

Rannells uses a number of conventional measures, such as centre of gravity and index of dispersion, but as part of his analysis he establishes a reference core (not a CBD) which is an arbitrarily defined area to which specialized distributions can be related.[37] This is defined by isolating those blocks, ranked in order, which contain half the total of establishments of all types (34 in all) and half the total floor space (55 in all). These two measures include 30 which are common to both measures so that the reference core consists of 59 blocks, i.e. 30 + (34 − 30) + (55 − 30). A similar reference core can be worked out for each separate use and by superimposing these maps the implied relationships (linkages) can be identified.

In a sense Rannells's work is not locational, he is using locational data to establish a patterning of relationships (hence Davies's objection). This he does by presenting his conclusions as showing the central area of the city as affected by a three way screening (figure 9−14).[38] The three screens are accessibility, which is the traditional factor emphasized relative to the central area but which needs to be related both to people and to the goods handled; availability, which is concerned both with the amount of space required and with the particular advantageous location required; and the linkages, to other businesses and the public. To a large extent Rannells was responsible for presenting the CBD in a new light, not as an area to be

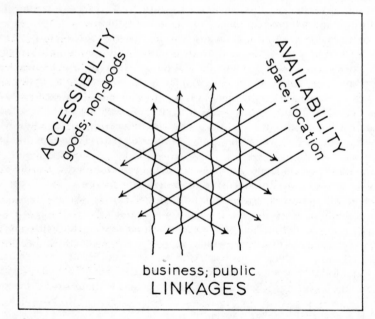

Figure 9−14: The threeway screening of city centre locations. *After J. Rannells (1956).*

[37] J. Rannells (1956), 117−21.
[38] J. Rannells (1956), 151.

defined but as the product of a complex of forces which determined locational decisions, a complex which had to be unravelled before anything useful could be said about the area.

The most recent contribution to this complex problem has been made by Whitehand, especially in relation to the availability of buildings.[39] He has been concerned in particular to identify innovation in building technology as it effects the city centre and the diffusion of change within the centre. The location of change will be determined by profitability, 'Thus the probability of structural modification and renewal tends to increase as physical structures diverge from the "optimum" (or most profitable) for the sites concerned. Physical structures may diverge from the optimum in terms of the amount of floorspace and/or in terms of the suitability of that space for a particular function'.[40] This sets up a complex problem for a variety of other factors is also involved including the role of central and local government, landowners and even bomb or fire damage. Whitehand's study of central Glasgow, however, points the way in which future investigation is likely to trend.[41]

6 The zone in transition

It is relevant here to introduce the notion of the Zone in Transition (Tz), for immediately the attempts at rigid definition of the CBD are relaxed then the surrounding area, conventionally making up the Tz, is brought into consideration. Indeed much of the discussion following the work of Murphy and Vance has been of the whole central area rather than an isolated CBD. It was inevitable that following the work of Murphy and Vance attempts should be made to define the Tz on similar grounds. Among those making this attempt are Robert E. Preston and D. W. Griffin.[42] The Tz, they point out, has been traditionally viewed as an area of mixed commercial and non-commercial land-use, tending towards deterioration and blight, and locationally separating the retail heart of the city from surrounding residential neighourhoods or heavy industrial districts. Usually present are such intensive non-retail activities as off-street parking, warehousing, light manufacturing, wholesaling with stocks, special professional organizational services, transportation terminals and multifamily residences.[43]

The basic notion of this zone is simple. Residential uses are extending outward and as more space is demaded by central users so the inner residential areas are taken over in a process of invasion and succession. The greatest change of use is concentrated in this inner zone which is, therefore,

[39] J. W. R. Whitehand (1978): Long-term changes in the form of the city centre: the case of redevelopment. *Geografiska Ann.* 60B, 79–96.

[40] J. W. R. Whitehand (1978), 81.

[41] See also: M. J. Bowden (1971): Downtown through time: delimitation, expansion, and internal growth. *Econ. Geog.* 47, 121–135.

[42] R. E. Preston and D. W. Griffin (1966): A restatement of the transition zone concept. *Ann. Assoc. Am. Geogr.* **56**, 339–50. R. E. Preston (1966): The zone in transition: a study of urban land use patterns. *Econ. Geog.* **42**, 236–60.

[43] R. E. Preston and D. W. Griffin (1966), 341.

in transition. To some extent the upward growth of the CBD, together with the suburban development of industry and of retail trade in suburban or out-of-town shopping centres, results in a diminution of demand for space in the zone and consequently in a lack of renewal of what is the oldest building stock; this in turn results in deterioration and blight.

Preston and Griffin depict the Tz as in figure 9–15. It is seen as consisting of a sector of active assimilation where new uses are in process of development, often of being taken into the CBD, characterized by high-quality uses. Second there is a sector of passive assimilation where changes are slower and, indeed, to some extent it is a zone of discard from the CBD with non-CBD uses such as warehousing taking over. Third, there are discontinuous sectors of general inactivity where little change is in progress. These notions are closely linked with the zones of assimilation and discard proposed by Murphy, Vance and Epstein.[44]

In attempting an areal definition of the Tz, Preston adopts a procedure parallel to that of Murphy and Vance and postulates a contrast between 'transitional-zone' and 'non-transitional-zone' uses. It is simpler here to note

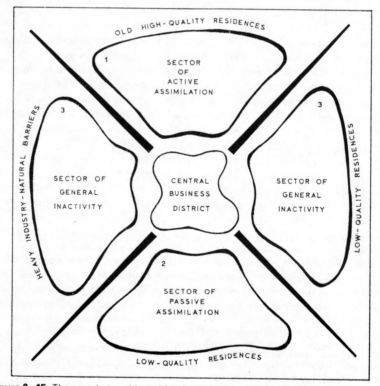

Figure 9–15: The zone in transition. *After R. E. Preston and D. W. Griffin (1966).*

[44] R. E. Murphy, J. E. Vance and N. Epstein (1955), 43.

the non-transitional zone uses as the list is much shorter: these are residences, heavy industry, vacancy, public open space and railroad yards. The Tz is isolated by taking out from the centre the CBD as identified by the Murphy and Vance method and then by establishing an outer boundary where the amount of land in transition-zone uses falls below thirty per cent, a value chosen by a trial and error process. This provides (with some need for other minor rules) a neat boundary (figure 9 — 16). The proportions of uses found in these areas as averages derived from three cities were:

Government organizations	24·5
Wholesale and storage	10·9
Light industry	7·8
Retail	7·0
Transport	4·1
Parking	4·6

Among the non-transitional-zone uses residence accounted for 19·6 per cent, heavy industry 7·0 and vacancy 7·7. These results themselves cast some doubt on the whole procedure, for a non-transitional-zone use accounts for the second highest proportion of space. But the definition is itself circular, the uses chosen defining the area and the area reflecting the uses.

Consideration of the patterns revealed by analysis of three cities led to a further development of the Tz concept. 'Within the zone the clusters (of uses) are generally arranged in sectors and are separated from one another by areas of less intensive and less specialized land-use.'[45] The outstanding clusters identified were:

1 Wholesaling, private and commercial storage, light industry and transport.
2 Public organizational and headquarters office establishments.
3 Automobile sales and services and parking.
4 Financial establishments, general offices, variety stores and transient residences.
5 Food, household, service trade and various retail establishments.

It is immediately apparent that Preston is directly echoing the sort of analysis that Rannells carried out. He is identifying clusters derived from linkages so that his first group, the members of which are strongly associated together, directly reflects the category 'goods handling' which Rannells used. Like Davies, however, the study of the Tz is dominated by definition of areas as an end in itself, so that obvious lines of development are not followed. The nature of the links which result in these associated groups, their coming together over time, their relationship to available space and locations, and their relationship to existing structures are not traced.

Bourne has developed a critique of the Tz concept which is particularly

---

[45] R. E. Preston and D. W. Griffin (1966), 344.

Figure 9–16: The boundary of the zone in transition, Worcester, Mass. Compare with figure 9–3 where the CBD was defined. *After R. E. Preston (1966).*

pertinent.[46] It is based on 'emphasizing the concept of structural adjustment, as a continuous process of change in the spatial structure of the city as a system, in contrast to the approach of defining areas which offer certain characteristics of transition. Certainly the whole city is in a process of change not solely the area adjacent to the CBD and in many ways the real problems are related to the areas which are *not* experiencing change and are not in

[46] L. S. Bourne (1968): Comments on the transitional zone concept. *Prof. Geog.* **20**, 313–16.

transition in that sense but are derelict and decayed. Ageing and decay are inevitable and the older city centre suffers first. Normally there is renewal and the real problem is why does deterioration persist and why is the sequence of decline and renewal disrupted.'[47]

7 Conclusion

To a great degree our understanding of the operative processes and consequent usage patterns in the city centre is completely inadequate. To chop out arbitrarily defined pieces and give them names is useful in so far as it advances comprehension of the complex, but it is no solution. Careful and detailed study of process is essential. This involves an effective realization of the interests of users of central land, the activities in which they are involved, the links which they require and the resources, both economic and political, which they can deploy. This must be carried out in the context of continuing change and flux over time. This presents a fascinating if formidable range of influences to be taken into analysis but will bring some understanding of the city centre that much nearer.

Perhaps some objection may be taken to the rather cavalier dismissal of spatial definition of regions which is so traditionally a geographical approach. But the time when extrapolation of complex cause from a pattern of areas was productive of progress in this field has long gone.

Notes on further reading

The early papers by R. E. Murphy and J. E. Vance, Jr. (1954a and 1954b, see footnote 1; 1955, see footnote 14) referred to in the text should be read, whilst a convenient summary is available in:

Murphy, R. E. (1966): *The American city* (see footnote 11).

Various contributions have been brought together and summarized by Murphy in:

Murphey, R. E. (1971): *The central business district* (London).

The two works by Rannells and Davies are also essential.

Davies, D. H. (1965): *Land use in central Cape Town: a study in urban geography* (see footnote 16).

Rannells, J. (1956): *The core of the city* (see footnote 34).

Davies's study has been updated in:

Davies, D. H. and Beavon, K. S. O. (1973): Changes in land-use in central Cape Town. *Dept. Geogr. and Envir. Studs. Univ. Witwatersrand, Occasional paper* **10.** (Johannesburg).

A volume devoted entirely to the city centre but with contributions of varying quality is:

---

[47] L. S. Bourne (1968), 316. See also pp. 269–70.

Heinemeijer, W. F., Van Hulten, M. and De Vreis Reilingh, H. D., editors, (1967): *Urban core and inner city.* Proceedings of the international study week, Amsterdam (Leiden).

An older symposium is:

Norborg, K., editor (1960): *Proceedings of the I. G. U. Symposium in Urban Geography, Lund 1960, part IV; the city centre* (Lund).

The following two papers on the zone in transition should be read:

Preston, R. E. and Griffin, D. W. (1966): A restatement of the transition zone concept (see footnote 42).

Preston, R. E. (1966): The zone in transition: a study of urban land use patterns (see footnote 42).

as should the critique by:

Bourne, L. S. (1968): Comments on the transitional zone concept (see footnote 46).

On linkages an early but useful paper is:

Morgan, W. T. W. (1961): A functional approach to the study of office distributions. *Tijdschrift voor Econ. en Soc. Geog.*, **52**, 207–210.

whilst a more thorough statistical investigation is:

Goddard, J. B. (1968): Multivariate analysis of office location patterns in the city centre: A London example (see footnote 28).

General studies on office location are:

Cowan, P. (1969): *The Office, a facet of urban growth* (London).

Daniels, P. W. (1975): *Office location: an urban and regional study* (London).

Goddard, J. B. (1975): *Office location in urban and regional development* (Oxford).

and another work which indicates the direction in which the study of offices is moving is:

Goddard, J. B. (1973): Office linkages and location. *Progr. in Planning* 1(2), 111–232.

A paper dealing with intra-urban shifts is:

Pritchard, G (1976): A model of professional office location. *Geog. Annaler.* 57. Ser.B, 100–108.

While a review of the significance of the shift of offices to the suburbs is undertaken in:

Leland, S. B. and Pang, W. N. (1977): Big business in the big city: corporate headquarters in the C.B.D. *Urban Affairs Quarterly*, 12(4), 533–544.

A series of research papers of the Department of Geography at the University of Chicago forms a most stimulating and valuable source of further reading. The relevant publications are:

Berry, B. J. L. (1963): *Commercial structure and commercial blight.* No. **85.**

Bourne, L. S. (1967): *Private redevelopment of the central city.* No. 112 (see footnote 36).

Simmons, J. W. (1964): *The changing pattern of retail location.* No. **92.**

Simmons, J. W. (1966): *Toronto's changing retail complex.* No. **104.**

The works on marketing geography (see chap. 6, p. 139–40) include consideration of the central business district, especially:

Davies, R. L. (1977): *Marketing geography* (London), chaps. 5 and 6.

Scott, P. (1970): *Geography and retailing* (London), chap. 6.

One of the few comparisons of the C.B.D. in eastern and western contexts is made in:

Pannell, C. W. (1976): Cities east and west: comments on theory, form and methodology. *Prof. Geogr.,* **28**(3), 233–40.

A paper which deals with retail site selection and the quality of the entrepreneur is:

Green, H. L. et alia (1978): When are store locations good? The case of the National Tea Company in Detroit. *Prof. Geogr.,* **30,** 162–7.

10

The Residential Areas of the City: Structures, Social Areas and Residential Choice

An interpretation of residential distributions at a general level was offered when the structure of the whole city was examined in chapter 8.[1] The outline of this interpretation has been most clearly sketched by Alonso in his comparison of historical and structural theories of urban form.[2]

At the heart of the generalized residential pattern lies the paradox that the richest people live on the cheapest land and vice versa or, in other words, that land values decrease with distance from the centre. The historical explanation is that derived from the analyses of E. W. Burgess[3] and in its simplest form maintains that as the city grows outward from the centre so new houses are built on the periphery. New fashions in housing appear at these points and such houses are desired, and can only be afforded, by the richer elements in the population and they, in consequence, move progressively outward. As this happens the outmoded houses they abandon filter down the income scale. This produces concentric residential zones with increasing income, and by implication increasing social status, from the centre out. These are conventionally named working or lower class, middle class and upper class zones.

Structural explanations on the other hand are based on the play off between accessibility, the costs of commuting and the costs of land. If one assumes typical cultural values and tastes which are 'a liking for ample land and a relative willingness to commute, it is clear that more distant but cheaper per square foot sites are more attractive to the wealthy than the poor.'[4] The resultant is a distribution of income groups which is similar to that of the historical type of explanation, for structural forces and historical process have been, over the last-century, working in the same direction.

This simple picture can quite obviously be modified. Thus in structural terms it is possible to introduce the diminishing returns that occur with distance from the city centre. The greater the distance the larger is the city and hence the attractions of the facilities at the centre are very high. At the same time the larger the city then the greater is the distance to be traversed to the central facilities and the more irksome the journey. It follows that the richest part of the population, the upper classes, will also be found in luxury

[1] See chapter 8, page 169.

[2] W. Alonso (1964): The historical and structural theories of urban form: their implications for urban renewal. *Ld. Econ.* **40**, 227–31.

[3] See chapter 8, pages 170–72.

[4] W. Alonso (1964), 229. Structural explanation has taken a different meaning since this was written.

houses or apartments adjacent to the centre where the nature of the buildings can shut out the environmental problems. Moreover, the very wealthy can maintain the town apartment and the country house, maximizing the advantages to be derived from both residential locations and minimizing travel difficulties by cutting them down to less frequent intervals than the daily journey, such as weekends only.

In terms of historical explanation the introduction of a sector interpretation, based on the maintenance of an upper class residential area at the centre and extending outwards, accomplished much the same sort of variation on the over-rigid concept of zones. In this way the early simplistic schemes have been modified.

At this point it is necessary to consider precisely what are being employed as the defining criteria within the overall concept of the 'residential areas'. Undoubtedly the earliest geographical concern was with structures, that is with houses as part of the physically visible scene, rather than with areas defined in the more nebulous terms of income or social status. Again the problem of use and structures arises and once more the general trend has been to divorce the two in order to clarify procedures. This divorce is seldom complete, studies of social areas often include the physical condition and amenities of housing as a variable, while studies of housing as such usually employ terms such as 'working class houses'; but this sometimes reflects lack of clarity in research design as much as a desire to reconcile use (in this case interpreted as social class) with structure. In general the study of structures has become the domain of the historical geographer and has strong links, therefore, with historical interpretations of city patterns. The study of income, class and status as spatial variables has been pursued by social geographers and is linked more closely to structural theories of city patterns.

In view of the haphazard way in which references to contrasted city areas are couched, now in terms of a type of housing (inter-war semi-detached), now in terms of income (upper income bracket housing), now in terms of class (working class areas) it becomes vital to identify quite clearly which particular notion is being employed as the key criterion of definition.

The two bases of identifying areas, by type of building or by social category, can be separated for purposes of analysis, though once more it must be emphasized that this is only a convenient simplification even if it is preferred to the confusion of terminology that has occasionally been employed even to the extent of 'very large residence' combined with such terms as the 'middle wealthy'.[5]

1 Structures: the analysis of house types

It is not difficult in general terms to integrate the consideration of structures with some of the ideas prevalent in social studies. 'Filtering down' has long been used to interpret the broad changes in major housing fashions. In Britain in the late eighteenth and early nineteenth centuries the terrace was the main element in urban building reaching its apogee in the Regency

[5] H. C. Brookfield (1952): Worthing. *Tn. Plann. Rev.* **23**, 145–62.

terraces of west London and in the great squares by which the rapid westward extension of the city was accomplished. It appeared too in the growing provincial cities, such as Bath and Cheltenham. But in those towns which were expanding most rapidly and without the architects to design them or the resources to sustain them, the terraces degenerated into little more than rows of cottages or long, monotonous lines of mean houses. The result was to put the terrace completely out of fashion, so much so that only at present has any attempt at revival of this compact and characteristically urban form been possible. As the terrace filtered down in esteem its place was taken by the attempt of the Victorian bourgeoisie to imitate their social betters by building separate houses in their own grounds, a middle class version of the great country house.

As this in turn was transferred to the 'mass consumption society' it degenerated into the suburban villa or semi-detached house, the garden front and back a poor remnant of the large estate, the dog of the livestock! It is appropriate that many of these villas were built in imitation of the country house and 'Stockbrokers' Tudor'[6] epitomizes much, even if it does add a social class qualification to the structural characteristic and reintroduces the separation which has been adopted.

The filtering down of the separate house, the deterioration of its social cachet, has in turn rehabilitated the terrace and it has become identified not only as a respectable but even a stimulating element in contemporary townscapes. Fashions are essentially cyclical but there is also clear evidence that types of town residence respond in popularity to a clear process of innovation, adoption and filtering down the social scale, abandonment and then readoption once the 'lower orders' have given them up.

There have been few studies of the above sort in a geographical context, though some have been closely related,[7] for the conventional analysis of residential areas has been by age of building. Even this approach is seldom retained as such and most studies soon resolve themselves into a consideration of the historical growth of the city and the identification of characteristic areas in the conventional 'growth plan', and only occasionally in the more complex 'age of buildings' map.

Whilst these are necessary adjuncts to general studies they are not very incisive methods for the study of the urban house. Indeed while a large number of studies have dealt with rural or regional house types few have ventured into the intricate detail of the city. It is true that most maps of city growth include structural elements. Thus one is familiar with maps having areas labelled, 'early nineteenth century terraced housing' or, 'inter-war semi-detached housing', where an approximate date is linked with the grossest of structural descriptions. R. E. Dickinson reproduces the types of housing recognized in the County of London Plan as being applicable to the whole of England.[8] The categories identified are:

[6] For by far the best and most amusing comments on these changes in style see O. Lancaster (1959): *Here of all places* (London).

[7] See pages 246–48 of this chapter.

[8] R. E. Dickinson (1951): *The west European city* 502 (London).

1   Old cottages which formed part of the pre-nineteenth century villages and pre by-law housing of the two storey terrace type.
2   Relatively large houses of three storeys plus basement built 50 to 80 years ago.
3   Buildings originally used as stable and coach accommodation attached to large houses, now used as dwellings (mews houses).
4   Isolated or detached villas in the suburbs with large gardens and spacious layout.
5   Two storey and three storey houses built 50 to 60 years ago and covering large areas. By-law housing.
6   Tall tenement blocks erected between 1875 and 1920.
7   Spacious and dignified terraces and squares of the seventeenth and eighteenth centuries.

This is not a very impressive categorization but it is sufficient to indicate the method.[9] With a scheme of this order established the investigator proceeds to map the city by observation and divide it into broad areas (figure 10–1A). In extension of this Smailes has called for 'special maps that depict the town, not only in terms of functional land-use, but also of the building forms and materials that contribute much both to the general appearance of the town and to the distinctiveness of its general parts, the urban regions'[10] (figure 10–1B). He himself has suggested a classification which for Britain would identify in structural terms the following:

1   Residential hotels and boarding houses.
2   Blocks of flats or apartments.
3   Terrace houses with front gardens.
4   Terrace houses without front gardens.
5   Detached or semi-detached villas and bungalow residences with garages or adequate garage space at the side.
6   As 5 but without garages or garage space.
7   Large detached houses in extensive grounds.[11]

In addition he commends a mode of mapping and analysis which includes date and building and roofing material so that an entry reads, 'A large three storeyed early Victorian detached house in extensive grounds, that has now been converted into apartments: it is built of stone with a slate roof.'[12] This would presumably correspond to the second of the categories of the County of London Plan.

This same problem has been considered with admirable attention to detail by R. J. Solomon in a study of Hobart, Tasmania. The theme is clearly that of A. E. Smailes: 'We must learn to recognize the architectural elements

---

[9] For a general discussion of townscapes by a geographer see E. Johns (1965): *British townscapes* (London).

[10] A. E. Smailes (1955): Some reflections on the geographical description and analysis of townscapes. *Trans. Inst. Br. Geogr.* 21, 161.

[11] A. E. Smailes (1964): Urban survey; in J. T. Coppock and H. C. Prince, editors, 1964: *The geography of greater London*, 210 (London).

[12] A. E. Smailes (1964).

Figure 10–1A: The urban regions of St Albans, 1950. *After H. S. Thurston (1953).* **1:** city centre; **2:** industrial areas (F. Fleetville Camp area); **3:** inner zone of mixed development; **4:** east suburban fringe; **5:** Kingsbury promontory; **6:** northern residential belt and southern residential areas (whether detached or semi-detached, all the houses possess a generous street frontage and deep gardens so that there are only 3–5 houses per residential acre); **7:** Gombards ('late nineteenth-century villas, many with three storeys, set in wider more pleasant streets'). **8:** inner Hatfield Road professional quarter; **9:** city station environs; **10:** northwest and southwest suburbs ('a haphazard intermingling of different types and classes of dwellings from the best detached houses to the worst types of shack bungalows'); **11:** medieval remnant; **12:** small areas of better houses within the east suburban fringe. This is a characteristic map of residential areas in conventional terms. In spite of Thurston's detailed mapping method the various areas have been given locational names (rather than names indicating their physical character) largely because of the variety of structures. (see page 241.)

(B)

Growth Phase	Functional Zone	Function-form Relation	Relief	Fabric Materials
Old town (KERNEL)	Enclave(s)	Residues	Architectural dominants	Traditional, or imported stone
	Commercial CORE with prongs outside kernel Ousting of residence	Extensive replacement or new facades	High buildings; point blocks; rugged profile; irregular street cornice	Concrete replacing traditional
I Late eighteenth and early	Decayed inner zone of mixed use	Conversion rather than replacement	Low buildings; little relief except churches; terrace housing in formal lay-outs; some replacement in flat blocks	Mixed
N nineteenth century	Workshops, warehouses, high density residence (slums) and high flats); railway space			
T				
E	Professional and administrative quarters	Converted houses		Brick or stucco and slate
G Railway age before 1914	Industry and tightly-packed housing mixed	Some conversion but mainly obsolete forms still in use	Terrace-ribbing with factory and neo-Gothic church salients; gas-holders	
U				
M Railway and automobile age since 1919	Industry and housing segregated	Forms conforming to current functions	Villa studding	Brick (much Fletton) rough cast, and tile
E	Villa housing in open, bourgeois suburbs and municipal estates	Chain-store facades in shopping centres	Intermixture of roofs and tree tops	Much foliage
N	Spacious factory lay-outs		Factory scaling: power-station chimneys and cooling towers	
T				
S Urban fringe	Village enclaves			Traditional
	Interim development; residential ribbons and outliers; urban utilities, e.g. cemeteries, sewage works; amenity space and surviving farmland, allotments and market gardens			

Figure 10–1B: British Town Structure. *After A. E. Smailes (1964).* This table attempts to present in summary form the sorts of influences which have been operative in creating British town structure and generalizes the specific case of St Albans in figure 10–1A. (see page 241.)

and constructional materials which in combination comprise an authentic fabric of particular style and period. They become the diagnostic agents in the process of analysis and classification; any significant alteration to their basic characteristics is reflected in the structural entity of the building unit, and its impact may be assessable.'[13] Solomon follows this by a study of Hobart in which the present townscape is examined in terms of extant and modified buildings which existed at the time of survey and could be identified on an 1840 map (figure 10−2). This is essentially a process of carefully identifying relict elements in the present townscape,[14] and by virtue of its nature all elements are relict in one sense.

But as soon as buildings are described in the way proposed by Smailes or indeed as suggested by Solomon then the real nature of the problem appears. It is clearly a multivariate problem with no one variable being dependent, and some form of factor analysis which would isolate components of the complexity, or of association analysis which would isolate the key criteria of variation, are required.

As yet there is very little literature in which these methods are employed but studies are beginning to be made. Kenneth E. Corey has been attempting work of this nature in Cincinnati, Ohio. 'It is proposed,' he writes, 'that the major dimensions of variability and the major dimensions of classification of an example of urban housing be isolated by means of principal component analysis and discriminant analysis respectively.'[15] Corey takes a twenty block area in an older residential neighbourhood of Cincinnati (Corryville) which contains 247 houses and based upon preliminary survey 40 variables are used. The first thirty-three of these are attributes, the last seven interval scale values where a critical point has to be chosen. These variables are reproduced below in table 10−1.

It is worth noting that this list would be easily adapted for most western countries with only minor modifications, such as the amendment of the ubiquitous American porch: certainly it is close to the lists of features which have been used in Britain.[16] The analysis revealed that 53 per cent of the variability was accounted for by the first six components, the first two accounting for 15·89 and 12·02 or 27·91 per cent of the total variation. The loading of each variable on the first factor is shown in table 10−2.

As with all component analyses the real problem is the interpretation of the components and in a complex situation such as this it is particularly problematical. Corey suggests that the first component can be identified as a dimension of 'rather youthful houses constructed of relatively inexpensive

[13] R. J. Solomon (1966): Procedures in townscape analysis. *Ann. Assoc. Am. Geogr.* 56, 255.
[14] J. W. Watson (1959): Relict geography in an urban community; in R. Miller and J. W. Watson, editors (1959): *Geographical essays in memory of A. G. Ogilvie*, 110 (Edinburgh).
[15] K. E. Corey (1966−7): Urban house types: a methodological experiment in urban settlement geography. *Dept. Geogr. Univ. Cincinnati Disc. Pap.* 3 (1966), appendix III (1967), page 45. See also, K. E. Corey (1969): *A spatial analysis of urban houses.* Univ. of Cincinnati, unpub. Ph.D. dissertation.
[16] H. S. Thurston (1953): The urban regions of St Albans. *Trans. Inst. Br. Geogr.* 19, 107−21.

Figure 10–2: Relict buildings in Hobart, Tasmania. *After R. J. Solomon (1966).* This map, which is a portion of the original, shows the buildings of the 1840s and their degree of preservation in the townscape of 1962–3.

table 10–1: Variables used in a study of housing in part of Cincinnati

1	Classification	Single	20	Roof	Flat
2		Double	21		Pitched
3		Duplex	22		Composition
4	Construction	Frame	23		Metal
5		Brick	24		Asphalt
6		Stone	25		Wood shingle
7		Stucco	26		Asphalt
8	Foundation	Concrete			Shingle
9		Cement block	27		Slate
10		Stone	28		Tile
11	Walls	Siding	29	Porch	Covered
12		Shingle	30		Uncovered
13		Wood	31		Enclosed
14		Asphalt	32		Wood
15		Asbestos	33		Masonry
16		Stucco frame	34	Year built	
17		Stucco	35	Age	
		masonry	36	Building length	
18		Common	37	Building width	
		brick	38	Building area	
19		Face brick	39	Total building value	
			40	Total assessed value	

table 10–2: Adjusted factor loadings on the variables shown in table 10-1

Variable	Factor 1 Loading
4	0·394
5	−0·415
8	0·826
9	0·484
10	−0·827
12	0·341
16	0·391
18	−0·618
20	−0·534
21	0·538
23	−0·582
24	0·479
25	0·339
26	0·331
34	0·816
35	−0·815
36	−0·676
37	0·424

Note: All loadings lying between +0·30 and −0·30 have been omitted. For description of variables see table 10-1.

materials. The houses of this dimension are wide, with pitched roofs . . . characterized by recent date of construction; concrete and cement block foundation; roof materials of asphalt, wood shingle and asphalt shingle; and general construction and walls of frame stucco and asphalt. The negative scores reinforce the inexpensive building dimension by denoting lack of the more expensive materials — stone and brick, and building length. Empirical correlation suggests a "California bungalow" type of house.'[17] The next stage in this work would be to examine each house in relation to factor scores and from these to derive a regionalization of house types. This ends at the same stage as the more empirical methods already described and interpretation must be undertaken in relation to the growth of the city and all those forces of fashion and cost which control building style. But the regional pattern has now been objectively derived in so far as selected variables permit this.

The problems of employing a method of this sort are very great. The information Corey used, limited to 247 houses, was available from a central source (the real property assessment files of the Auditor of Hamilton County, Ohio); to obtain this information for the whole housing stock of a large city presents a very formidable task of data collection. One has also to question whether this statistical process will justify itself by results, for there seems little doubt that the types of house identified and the regions described will accord fairly closely to those of the empirical investigator basing his work on experience. But this is a valid and useful area of experiment that might add a very desirable element of precision to the rather vague categories which have been employed in the past.

The same sort of problem has been approached in a different manner by C. A. Forster in a study of the development of physical characteristics in by-law housing in Hull.[18] This type of housing was built between 1854 and 1914 and from it Forster selects one special sort, the cul-de-sac court. A total of 1479 of these was identified in the whole of the city. Thirteen variables were listed from inspection (table 10−3). Ten of these were concerned with the general configuration of the houses and three with building materials. In the list it is worth noting that the absence of one variable implies the presence of another. Thus all the houses without slate roofs had pantiles. In

table 10−3: List of variables. By-law housing in Hull

Rear access to house
Stub carriage road
Double fronted house
Three floors
Front garden
Red brick
Slate roof
Ornamented brick
Tunnel entrance to cul-de-sac
Bay window
Double bay window
Garret
End house in terrace faces street

---

[17] K. E. Corey (1966−7), 47.
[18] C. A. Forster (1968): The development of by-law housing in Kingston-upon-Hull: an example of multivariate morphological analysis. *Inst. Br. Geogr. Urban Study Group. Salford conference.* 115−31.

this way the list is restricted. To these were added two variables of dimension which were not basically dichotomous. Critical values were selected by assessment to give:

cul-de-sac courts over 100 feet long, and
cul-de-sac courts over 20 feet wide.

1479 cul-de-sac courts were then surveyed to show the presence or absence of the fifteen variables. A form of association analysis (multiple chi-square analysis) is used in a process of dichotomous division of the courts. Caroe has described association analysis, 'At each stage in the analysis the collection of individuals under consideration is divided with respect to a single attribute so that in the resulting two sub-groups this attribute is possessed by all members of one and lacked by all members of the other.'[19] This process is continued until a point is reached where the maximum association between variables in the undivided classes is not significant at the $0 \cdot 01$ confidence level. The process is shown in figure $10-3$. Each of the final groups can be described by the critical dividing attributes so that Type B, the most common, can be summarized as:

Cul-de-sac terrace over 20 feet wide
Lower bay window
Less than 100 feet long
The end houses face the street
Red brick

Although the data are derived from groups of houses, the courts, and not single houses as was Corey's, the end product is the same, the identification of dominant and recurrent types. Forster carries his analysis forward on a chronological rather than a regional basis. An examination of a 25 per cent sample of plans is undertaken and the number of houses built per year is divided into the morphological groups A to V (figure $10-4$) which have been identified. The result is a clear chronology of change. 'The major morphological developments in the cul-de-sac terrace by 1893 can be summarized as the transition from local to national building materials which became almost completed by the late 1880s; the provision of rear access to houses by 1878 and the widening of the courtyard and the provision of lower bay windows and front gardens in the 1880s and 1890s.'[20] But in 1893 a new set of by-laws came into being rendering all but Groups B and D (figure $10-3$) illegal. Type F appeared in 1908 with bay windows on both upper and lower floors and these houses were solid and spacious and, in purely structural terms, remain adequate today. Again there is no doubt that a meticulous historical study without recourse to statistical analyses would have revealed the same features but Forster's study is most valuable in

[19] L. Caroe (1968): A multivariate grouping scheme: association analysis of East Anglian towns; chapter 16 in E. G. Bowen, H. Carter and J. A. Taylor, editors (1968): *Geography at Aberystwyth*, 253–69 (Cardiff).

[20] C. A. Forster (1968), 129. See also, C. A. Forster (1972): Court housing in Kingston upon Hull. *Univ. of Hull, Occ. paps* 19.

HULL: GROUPING OF TERRACES BY ASSOCIATION ANALYSIS

Figure 10–3: Grouping of cul-de-sac by-law terraces in Hull by association analysis. The progressive breakdown into the final morphological groups is indicated as well as the critical feature in each case. *After C. A. Forster (1968).*

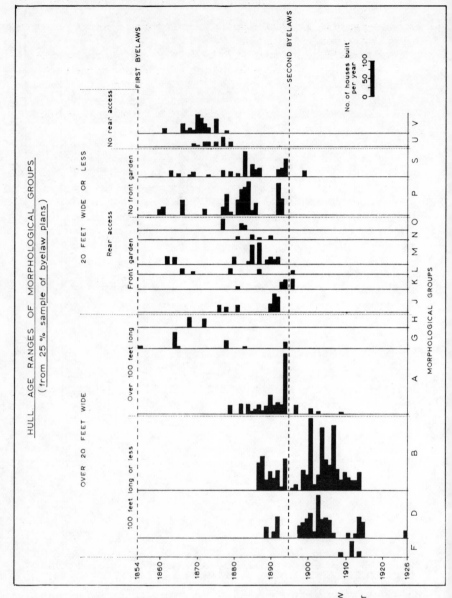

Figure 10—4: The age ranges of the morphological groups of by-law terraces. This is a diagram based on a 25 per cent sample and indicates the time range over which the various groups identified in figure 10—3 were built. *After C. A. Forster (1968).*

indicating another method of approaching the study of house types which has clear direction and precision.

The two studies which have been sketched are preliminary examples of work which is likely to increase in scale as the application of new analytical techniques to old problems proceeds. The clear sorting of innovations in building characteristics in a historical sense, together with studies of their diffusion, coupled with the objective identification of regional groups from component analysis must certainly provide much sharper tools for the job of understanding the way townscapes are created.

To some extent this section under the heading of 'structures' has diverted attention away from the concept of land-use of which residential areas are part. But it is important that one of the oldest concerns of the urban geographer, indeed one which at one time was thought to be *the* concern since it dealt with the visible landscape, should not be abandoned. 'I believe that the primary concern of cultural geography is with the nature, genesis and distribution of the observable phenomena of the landscape directly and indirectly ascribable to man, and of course including man himself. By "observable" I mean in general "visible". '[21] That is a view to which few now would subscribe without qualification, but there has been a tendency to abandon too completely the old emphasis on the visible phenomena in the rush to advance the more fashionable study of social areas.

2 Social characteristics of residential areas

The zones and sectors which were identified by the Chicago ecologists were presented in social terms and it is, therefore, with such terms that the bulk of investigation of residential areas has been concerned. The first stage was the empirical testing of hypotheses which followed from the ecological models. These hypotheses were that populations are segregated residentially by social class and, that since social distance can be translated into physical distance, then observable patterns of residential segregation in spatial terms can be discerned within the city. The classical model implied that social class increased with distance from the city centre, but this was hardly tenable even within America.

In these hypotheses the concept of 'social class' is a little vague and for most operational purposes it has been equated with 'occupation' which is the most easily accessible parameter. 'Occupation is only one of the criteria of social stratification, however. Its significance is clearly twofold because it relates to an economic relationship with the means of production but also defines a work-situation which will in turn have consequences on both the consciousness of class identity and also will help to define patterns of status estimation and attitude to the stratification system both within and outside the work situation.'[22]

The major testing of the first of the above hypotheses, using occupation as

[21] F. Kniffen (1957) in S. D. Dodge, chairman (1957): Round table on problems in cultural geography. *Ann. Assoc. Am. Geogr.* **27**, 155–76.
[22] J. A. Jackson (1968): *Social stratification*, 3 (Cambridge).

a measure of social class, was that by O. D. and B. Duncan.[23] They used two basic measures. The first is the index of dissimilarity:

$$\sum_{i=1}^{n} \frac{(x_i/\Sigma x_i) - (y_i/\Sigma y_i)}{2} \cdot 100$$

Where x_i represents one occupation and y_i represents another occupation residing in zone i. Essentially it measures the percentage of an occupational group (x) which would have to move to make its distribution identical with another occupation group (y). If this is computed between one occupation group and all others combined it gives the second measure, an index of segregation. Table 10−4 indicates the index of residential segregation for each major occupation group, for employed males, in Chicago in 1950.

table 10−4: Index of residential segregation of each major occupation group, employed males, Chicago 1950. *After O. D. and B. Duncan (1955).*

Occupation group	By census tract	By zone-sector segments
1 Professional, technical and kindred workers	30	21
2 Managers, officials and proprietors, except farm	29	20
3 Sales workers	29	20
4 Clerical and kindred workers	13	9
5 Craftsmen, foremen and kindred workers	19	14
6 Operatives and kindred workers	22	16
7 Service workers, except private households	24	20
8 Labourers, except farm and mine	35	29

From this the Duncans argue there is a U shape pattern of indices of segregation. With high values at the top and bottom of the social scale, professional workers and managers and service workers and labourers, but with low values in the intermediate occupations where status is less clearly marked—'residential segregation is greater for those occupational groups with clearly defined status than for those groups whose status is ambiguous.'[24] Table 10−5 reproduces the indices of dissimilarity in residential distribution and from this the Duncans conclude that there is an 'essential correspondence of social and spatial distance among occupation groups'. The result of their study was to demonstrate that segregation in residential terms does exist and that the most segregated occupation groups are those at the extremes of the socio-economic scale.

It also shows that this segregation, in terms of social distance, is paralleled by a spatial segregation, in terms of physical or locational difference. A further study by J. O. Wheeler using Pittsburgh data confirms these conclusions from the Chicago study corroborating 'the generalizations of other researchers that the most segregated occupations are those at the highest and lowest ends of the socio-economic scale. Futhermore, occupations

[23] O. D. and B. Duncan (1955): Residential distribution and occupational stratification. *Am. J. Sociol.* **60**, 493−503. For a recent review see: B. S. Morgan (1980): Occupational segregation in metropolitan areas in the United States, 1970, *Urban Studies,* **17**(1) 63−69.
[24] O. D. and B. Duncan (1955).

table 10—5: Indices of dissimilarity in residential distribution for major occupational groups, employed males, Chicago 1950. *After O. D. and B. Duncan (1955)*.

| | *The groups are numbered as in table 10-4* | | | | | | |
	1	2	3	4	5	6	7	8
1	–	13	15	28	35	44	41	54
2	8	–	13	28	33	41	40	52
3	11	7	–	27	35	42	38	54
4	20	18	17	–	16	21	24	38
5	26	23	25	12	–	17	35	35
6	31	29	30	16	14	–	26	25
7	31	31	30	19	25	19	–	28
8	42	41	42	32	30	21	24	–

Note: Above diagonal the indices are by census tract, below diagonal by a zone-sector arrangement. The index is explained in the text.

that are most alike in residential location are also similar in socio-economic rank; those with the greatest locational differences represent the extremes of status level.'[25] But this evidence only goes part of the way toward a spatial interpretation for even if segregation is accepted and social distance is translated, in the city as a spatial entity, into physical distance, these do not carry any implication of *relative* location within the city. Here the evidence becomes less clear. The Duncans' material is thin and can carry no real conviction, while Wheeler concludes that his 'study finds little relationship between the relative concentration of an occupational group's residence and distance from the central business district.'[26] Certainly there is general confirmation of 'the centralization of residence' being inversely related to socio-economic status.[27]

A study by Kain using data from Detroit has postulated and demonstrated 'that if households had the same location rent function, the same transportation cost function, the same space preference, and the same valuation of time, but different incomes, the length of the households' journey to work would increase as an increasing function of income.'[28] Again in his conclusions Kain writes 'workers employed in higher-income occupations and working in inner rings (distance rings from the centre) tended to make longer journeys-to-work and resided in outer rings. When employed in outer rings they made shorter journeys-to-work and lived within the same ring and adjacent rings at very high rates. Lower income workers made short journeys-to-work and resided within the workplace ring and in nearby rings regardless of the place of work.'[29] This is only in small part a confirmation of a zonal pattern of residential segregation, indeed the latter part of the quotation does not conform to the zonal model.

There is a considerable danger that the multiplication of studies such as

[25] J. O. Wheeler (1968): Residential location by occupational status. *Urb. Stud.* **5**, 24.
[26] J. O. Wheeler (1968).
[27] O. D. and B. Duncan (1955), 502.
[28] J. F. Kain (1962): The journey to work as a determinant of residential location. *Pap. Proc. Reg. Sci. Assoc.* **9**, 147.
[29] J. F. Kain (1962).

these provides no more than a series of exercises derived from and, more importantly, limited by the context of the ecological models or the abstractions of the land economists. Use of the single variable of occupation means that they fail to take into account the great variability within residential areas. This failure was to be compensated in the attempt to increase the range of variables which are to be taken as diagnostic of distinctive social areas.

The immediate stimulus to derive acceptable social areas came from the need to provide 'community areas' for a study of Los Angeles, as well as from the awareness that one variable was an inadequate means of approaching a complex problem. It followed that the first departure was via the attempt to build up a more satisfactory and, *ipse facto*, more complex means of classifying basic census units into homogeneous social areas. The early statement of Shevky and Williams[30] in their study of Los Angeles in 1949 was followed by a volume by Shevky and Bell, *Social Area Analysis*, in 1955 in which an attempt was made to put the study on a broader basis.[31] The basic principle on which the key variables were selected is contained in the sentence, 'we conceive of the city as a product of the complex whole of modern society; thus the social forms of urban life are to be understood within the context of the changing character of the larger containing society.'[32] From this three aspects were isolated epitomizing this changing character. These were:.

1   Change in the range and intensity of relations.
2   Differentiation of functions.
3   Complexity of organization.

Via the arguments which are set out in table 10–6 these were translated into three constructs which were identified as social rank (economic status), urbanization (family status) and segregation (ethnic status). These were measured for statistical purposes by the data indicated in table 10–7 to provide the three indices.

Implicit in this whole process, as indeed the authors propose, is the assumption that the selected indices relate to the observed social differentiation between urban sub-populations, and at the same time they are unidimensional, that is, that they do not include similar aspects within them and therefore repeat the same measure three times. This point will be considered later. In order to classify areas the index of urbanization was plotted against that of social rank as a base divided equally into three. Urbanization was also divided into three intervals, 'with the middle or average interval determined by the space of two standard errors about the regression line of urbanization related to social rank'[33] (figure 10–5).

[30] E. Shevky and M. Williams (1949): *The social areas of Los Angeles; analysis and typology* (Berkeley and Los Angeles).
[31] E. Shevky and W. Bell (1955): *Social area analysis; theory, illustrative application and computational procedure* (Stanford).
[32] E. Shevky and W. Bell (1955).
[33] E. Shevky and M. Williams (1949).

table 10–6: Social area analysis: steps in construct formation and index construction. *After E. Shevky and W. Bell* (1955).

Postulates concerning Industrial society (aspects of increasing scale) (1)	Statistics of trends (2)	Changes in the structure of a given social system (3)	Constructs (4)	Sample statistics (related to the constructs) (5)	Derived Measures (from col. 5) (6)	
Change in the range and intensity of relations	Changing distribution of skills: Lessening importance of manual productive operations – growing importance of clerical, supervisory, management operations	→ Changes in the arrangement of occupations based on function	→ Social Rank (economic status)	→ Years of schooling, Employment status, Class of worker, Major occupation group, Value of home, Rent by dwelling unit, Plumbing and repair, Persons per room, Heating and refrigeration	→ Occupation, Schooling, Rent	} Index I
Differentiation of function	Changing structure of productive activity: Lessening importance of primary production – growing importance of relations centred in cities – lessening importance of the household as economic unit	→ Changes in the ways of living – movement of women into urban occupations – spread of alternative family patterns	→ Urbanization (family status)	→ Age and sex, Owner or tenant, House structure, Persons in household	→ Fertility, Women at work, Single-family dwelling units	} Index II
Complexity of organization	Changing composition of population: Increasing movement – alterations in age and sex distribution – increasing diversity	→ Redistribution in space – changes in the proportion of supporting and dependent population – isolation and segregation of groups	→ Segregation (ethnic status)	→ Race and nativity, Country of birth, Citizenship	→ Racial and national groups in relative isolation	} Index III

table 10–7 Indices used in social area analysis. *After E. Shevky and W. Bell (1955)*

Index 1   Social Rank
A   Occupation ratio. Total number of craftsmen, operatives, and labourers per 1000 employed persons.
B   Education ratio. Number of persons who have completed no more than grade school per 1000 persons 25 years old and over.
C   Rent – omitted from the list.

Index 2   Urbanization
A   Fertility ratio. Number of children under 5 years per 1000 femals age 15 through 44.
B   Women in labour force. The number of females in the labour force per 1000 females 14 years and over.
C   Single-family detached dwelling units ratio. The number of single-family dwelling units per 1000 dwelling units of all types.

Index 3   Segregation
       The number of persons designated 'negro', 'other races', and 'foreign-born white', the last from south and east Europe. Shevky and Bell give a list of the countries. The sum of these is divided by the population of each tract and multiplied by 100 to give the index.

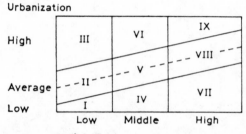

Figure 10–5: The derivation of social areas. *After E. Shevky and M. Williams (1949)*. The criteria used are indicated in the text. Urbanization is plotted against social rank which is divided into three. The regression of urbanization on social rank is plotted and divisions drawn two standard errors away. This gives nine divisions.

Segregation was added to this basic classification by high and low categories related to the mean figure.

Figure 10–6 shows a part illustration of the map of social areas of Los Angeles produced by Shevky and Williams using 1940 data. The wedge of high social rank and average or low urbanization picks out one of the best known areas of Los Angeles, swinging from the Pacific Ocean at Santa Monica along Sunset and Wilshire to Beverly Hills. To the east the suburban areas of Glendale and Pasadena also emerge quite clearly, although here a low index of urbanization reflects the suburban character of those parts.

Figure 10–6: The social areas of Los Angeles: **1:** census tracts with high social rank and average and low urbanization (i.e. categories VII and VIII on figure 10–5); **2:** census tracts with low social rank and average and high urbanization (i.e. categories II and III on figure 10–5). This is a simplified extract from the original coloured map, but the major contrasts appear particularly in the area of high quality residence extending from the coast at Santa Monica through Beverly Hills to Hollywood. *Derived from E. Shevky and M. Williams (1949)*.

The work of Shevky and his associates has been the subject of a great deal of criticism. It has been urged that it has no theoretical background and is merely an attempt to delineate areas for their own sake, a view as already noted not unfamiliar in regional geography or attempts to define the CBD. To some extent this limitation is not surprising, especially in the light of the many expressions of dissatisfaction with the existing ecological models and the need for empirical work upon which reformulation could be based. What theoretical background there was can be discerned if the way in which Shevky derived his constructs is examined in relation to the characteristics of the urbanization process as set out in chapter 2. The dominance of Wirth's ideas becomes evident and the parameters which Shevky selected were intended to examine in small scale areas the changes which were taking place in society at large as urbanization increased. There are immediate problems in this transfer of scales and to the extent that Wirth's ideas themselves are not accepted the whole conceptual basis of social area analysis in this context is undermined.

If the whole notion of the constructs is open to question so, too, is the selection of the statistical measures. For example, in most subsequent studies rental has been eliminated from the measure of social rank. 'In considering the whole range of possible parameters which might be selected as measures of aspects of urban social structure one might, therefore, have even graver doubts as to the validity of isolating those few indices which Shevky suggested.'[34]

The third line of criticism relates to the unidimensional nature of the indices which was noted earlier, that is whether the three are discrete and unrelated to each other and not, in fact, overlapping measures of the same thing. Thus it can be shown that fertility is closely associated with occupation and education and hence has a significant linkage with social rank and does not stand outside it as a measure of that most nebulous construct which Shevky called 'urbanization'.

It will be apparent that a very familiar problem is raised, precisely the same one as in urban house styles, and that is how to collapse a large number of variables, which are somehow related to social character, into a smaller range of significantly associated variables denoting underlying components of social character. Factor analysis was clearly called for and hence the growing number of studies which have been published which attempt to reduce the large number of possible variables to a smaller number of uncorrelated factors by the use of this statistical technique.

At this point some difficulty arises over the use of principal component and factor analysis in geographical research.[35] It is not possible here (it is far

---

[34] B. T. Robson (1969): *Urban analysis*, 52 (Cambridge).

[35] Chap. 5 in R. J. Johnston (1978): Multivariate statistical analysis in geography (London) is the best introduction.

[36] Two worth consulting are H. H. Harman (1968): *Modern factor analysis* (Chicago); L. Rummel (1970): *Applied factor analysis* (Evanston). In addition *The Statistician* 23 was devoted to multivariate problems in geography: a most useful paper here, with an extensive bibliography, is D. Clark, W. K. D. Davies and R. J. Johnston (1974): The application of factor analysis in human geography. *The Statistician* 23 (3/4), 259–81.

from the purpose of this book), to review statistical techniques. There are many sources where component analysis is considered;[36] it is only necessary to insist on three points:

1   Component analysis is only a taxonomic procedure not to be confused with a theoretical formulation.

2   The variables included will determine the components (factors) abstracted. If data on occupation and wealth, age and ethnic origin are put into an analysis, it will not be very surprising if socio-economic status, life cycle and ethnicity emerge as the main components of variation. The critical decision is what variables are included and this is often dictated by what data are available in usable form.

3   The labelling of the components (factors), although related to the loading of variables, is subjective and there is a strong incentive to 'find' the accepted components.

It follows from the above that in conceptual terms there is no great advance on Shevky's procedure: indeed the theoretical basis is even more tenuous. The uncorrelated character of the components ensures, however, that the 'constructs' do not overlap and hence it does provide a real test of this nature of the three measures which Shevky proposed. At the same time by use of grouping techniques the individual areas can be associated into regions by the scores on each component so that the spatial arrangement of the social areas can be studied from an objective and uncommitted basis. These two aspects can be considered separately.

1   *The components of social variation.* Murdie has produced a table of the components which have been identified from a number of analyses, mainly of American cities.[37] In nearly all these cases three are outstanding, and usually make up the first three extracted. They are economic status, family status and ethnic status. To these two more recent British studies can be added where the components identified are social class, housing conditions and subdivided housing losing value in the first[38] and housing condition, ethnic status and family status in the second.[39] There is a fairly clear element of agreement in all these studies, although the British evidence emphasizes housing conditions rather than economic and social status. The components which emerge are, therefore, closely allied to those constructs proposed by Shevky and Bell.[40] The rather vague 'urbanization' construct is, however,

---

[37] R. A. Murdie (1969): Factorial ecology of metropolitan Toronto, 1951–61. *Univ. Chicago Dept. Geogr. Res. Pap.* 116 (Chicago), table 3, pages 52–8.

[38] B. T. Robson (1969), 162–4.

[39] D. T. Herbert (1970): Principal component analysis and urban social structure: a study of Cardiff and Swansea; chapter 5 in H. Carter, W. K. D. Davies and C. R. Lewis, editors (1970): *Studies in the geography of Wales* (London).

[40] See also M. D. Van Ardsol, S. F. Camilleri and C. F. Schmid (1968): The generality of urban social area indexes. *Am. sociol. Rev.* 23, 277–84.

reinterpreted as a measure of 'family status' or family characteristics. This gives three basic components which play a part in urban social variation and since by the nature of their abstraction they cannot be overlapping, then it is possible to look at the next problem which is how are these distributed within the city and so bring the consideration back to the basic geographic concern of spatial variation.

2   *The spatial articulation of the components of social variation.* Once again it is true to contend that most studies which have been concerned with the spatial characteristics of identified components have not propounded any new theory of city structure, but have examined the results in relation to the earlier ecological models. To a large extent these studies have been placed in the context of zonal as against sectoral characteristics of distribution. The terms 'zonal' and 'sectoral' are to some extent pejorative and the real crux is whether the locational character of the component is controlled by distance or directional forces in relation to the city centre.

The two aspects of social area analysis, component content and spatial articulation, were the subject of a study by Anderson and Egeland.[41] They selected four American cities, Akron and Dayton in Ohio, Indianapolis in Indiana, and Syracuse, New York, which were roughly comparable in size and circular in shape. Variance analysis was used to test two measurements, urbanization and social prestige, by distance zones and by sectors. The principal findings of the study were 'that urbanization . . . varies primarily concentrically or by distance from the centre of the city, while prestige value (or social rank) varies primarily sectorially with very little distance variation.'[42]

This conclusion would support Hoyt's sector hypothesis as far as social rank is concerned, that is, there is no basic distance pattern whereby the prestigious residential areas of a city are found in an outer surrounding zone. The basic reasons which Hoyt put forward for this sectoral development have already been outlined.[43] They can be effectively summarized: 'High status residents have great freedom in choosing the origin for the sector, usually selecting the most attractive area topographically which is closest to their work places in the office quarter of the central business district and near to the residences of the community's leaders. Once this has been chosen, however, other status groups distribute themselves around it so that the high status area becomes the pivot of the city's residential structure.'[44] As the high status area is tied to this base by its inherited tradition it expands outward as a sector along a main artery of communication.

The sorts of factors involved in this process have been clearly depicted in a

[41] T. R. Anderson and J. A. Egeland (1961): Spatial aspects of social area analysis. *Am. sociol. Rev.* **26**, 392–8.
[42] T. R. Anderson and J. A. Egeland (1961), 398.
[43] See chapter 8, page 180.
[44] R. J. Johnston (1966): The location of high status residential areas. *Geogr. Annaler* **48B**, 25 (Stockholm).

Figure 10–7: The development of the high prestige residential areas of Melbourne, 1860–1960. *After R. J. Johnston* (*1966*). The circles represent the mean deviation of the distance at which high status persons live from the centre of gravity of the distribution. These were computed separately for the eastern and southern sectors. The basic definition of 'high status' was the home addresses of those Melbourne persons recorded in 'Who's Who in Australia'.

study of Melbourne by R. J. Johnston.[45] Using as a definition of high social status residents' inclusion in *Who's Who in Australia* he has traced the development of the prestigious residential areas over a hundred years. Figure 10–7 summarizes the evidence for the last half-century. Residential development by the high status group has been separated into two parts and is traced by calculation of the mean centre of gravity and the mean distances

[45] R. J. Johnston (1966).

of deviation which indicate the degree of dispersion about the centre.[46] The map shows a southern sector where the centre of gravity had moved five miles between 1913 and 1962 from its original emplacement in St Kilda on the coast and four miles south of the city centre. In the other eastern sector of Toorak movement had not been as marked or as direct only covering two miles from its original source. It was also a tighter and more compact sector with a smaller mean distance of deviation.

In explanation of these sectors and the differences between them, Johnston adds to the sector interpretation of Hoyt the socio-cultural variables which Firey introduced.[47] Toorak, he argues, has not expanded physically because of the larger mansions with extensive estates which on subdivision allowed intensification rather than expansion when demand for space arose since the area had long been 'the peak of residential aspirations'.[48] Individual and institutional restraints have been operative in the preservation of the area's character. This brief study indicates that the detailed mode of extension of high status residential areas does conform to Hoyt's sectoral interpretation and where a class dimension is revealed in social area analysis it conforms to the same spatial arrangement. Prestige, too, is a self-perpetuating influence and generates an element of stability in the location of high status areas which are often tied to their points of origin.

The second component which many analyses have revealed is the one Shevky and Bell termed 'urbanization' but which is usually renamed 'family status' to give it a clear connotation and detach it from wider implications. According to Anderson and Egeland[49] it does not conform to the location pattern of social status groups and most other investigators agree.[50] Perhaps the most convincing study is that of Toronto by R. A. Murdie in which not only was a component analysis carried out for 1951 and 1961 using 86 and 78 variables respectively, but change during the decade was also analyzed. Murdie concludes, 'the economic status dimension moved outwards in a general sectoral arrangement with the wedges of high and low status widening towards the periphery of the metropolitan area. . . . The family status dimension tended to move outwards from the city centre in a concentric fashion.'[51]

Family status in this context is defined by a factor characterized by large, young families, few women working outside the home, single family dwellings and high car and home ownership at one end and the converse at the other. For this situation there is a contrasting set of explanations to those

---

[46] See J. F. Hart (1954): Central tendency in areal distribution. *Econ. Geogr.* **30**, 48−59.
[47] See chapter 8, page 186.
[48] R. J. Johnston (1966), 33. For a further study see R. K. Middleton (1966): Measuring intra-urban residential quality: a method for determining residential morphology. *Prof. Geogr.* **18**, 352.
[49] J. R. Anderson and J. R. Egeland (1961).
[50] B. J. L. Berry and R. J. Tennant (1965): Metropolitan planning guidelines. *Comml. Struct.* (Chicago). P. O. Pedersen (1967): Am empirical model of urban population structure: a factor analytical study of the population structure in Copenhagen. *Proc. First Scandinavian-Polish Reg. Sci. Seminar, Warsaw.*
[51] R. A. Murdie (1969), 142−4.

for the social class factor. This lies generally in the different needs of the family at different stages in the cycle of development. Alonso remarks on this in recording the increase of apartment construction in the USA. 'We have mentioned the convection-flow life cycle of the American middle class family. The young and the old need apartments while it is those in their thirties that power the demand for single family homes.'[52] The implication is that the young adult will seek an apartment near the city centre and will only look for the more spacious single family house with its garden or yard when he is married and has a family. As the family leaves home then there is considerable attraction in a more easily managed apartment near the city centre. The individual, therefore, in the context of his life cycle moves across the city setting up the distance-to-centre/family relationship which is revealed by these analyses.

The whole crux of the matter was summarized by one brought up in a city—'houses are for kids, apartments are for adults.' Robson provides a more elegant version, 'Whether a family chooses to live in the inner or the peripheral parts of a town can therefore be determined by its assessments of the importance of land inputs as against commuting inputs and the balance of this equation of family budgeting will change depending on which stage of its life cycle the family is in as much as upon its income level.'[53] There is an increasing array of empirical evidence to support this view derived as it is from a generalized level of investigation. Rossi from a series of intensive interviews and follow up studies concluded, 'the major function of mobility [is] the process by which families adjust their housing to the housing needs that are generated by the shifts in family composition that accompany life cycle changes.'[54]

The conclusion from these studies is that the two major controls on the decision where to live in a city are socio-economic status, including both the ability to pay rates and rents, the picture the individual has of himself and the sort of social group into which he wishes to opt, and life cycle 'status' where the family's needs exercise a strong influence. Both of these operate through a nexus of institutional and cultural constraints.

The third component of social variation in cities which was isolated by Shevky and has been confirmed by many component analyses is 'ethnicity' or ethnic status. This was called by Shevky, segregation or the group phenomenon of isolation. It is concerned with the degree to which cultural and racial groups become separated in the city and hence with the urban ghetto. It was appropriate that a study of the ghetto emerged from the Chicago ecologists and Wirth's book, entitled *The ghetto*,[55] treated it as a phenomenon within the context of human ecology. The ghetto was 'not the product of design but rather the unwitting crystallization of needs and practices rooted in the customs and heritages, religious and secular, of the Jews themselves.'[56] Jews drifted into separate cultural areas not due to external

[52] W. Alonso (1964), 230.
[53] B. T. Robson (1969), 243.
[54] P. H. Rossi (1955): *Why families move*, 9 (Glencoe, Ill.).
[55] L. Wirth (1956): *The ghetto*.
[56] L. Wirth (1956), 18.

pressures but largely through the desire to associate in an area where religious observances could be followed without arousing alarm, and also for security. 'The voluntary segregation of the Jews in ghettos had much in common with the segregation of negroes and immigrants in modern cities. . . . The tolerance that strange ways of living need and find in immigrant colonies, in Latin quarters . . . is a powerful factor in the sifting of the population and its allocation in separate cultural areas. . . .'[57] This is, however, too simple an identification and certainly two types of ghetto can be recognized which play diametrically opposite roles.

1   *The temporary ghetto.* This is a segregated area through which populations become adjusted to new ways of life. In particular immigrants to a
country or a city find immediate refuge with people of their own kind
until they have adjusted to urban living in a country and, with a rise in
their socio-economic status and acquisition of native mores, they
become diffused through the population. This process can act for native
rural immigrants (the slum) or culturally alien elements (the ghetto).
This is the traditional function of the ethnic area in American cities. As
acculturation progresses, the family moves out, loses its ethnic
character and becomes part of urban America.

2   *The permanent ghetto.* This is, perhaps, contrasted in degree rather
than in nature, but it is the means by which a cultural group can actively
resist being weakened and lost in the larger community of which it is a
part. In this case it is not part of a process of assimilation but quite the
reverse, the means by which assimilation can be resisted and identity
preserved.

At the moment the black in the USA is in the dilemma of not knowing in which of these two ways to regard the ghetto, as a temporary phase which will see him become diffused throughout and integrated with American society or as a permanent feature which will enable him to develop his own way of life, opting out of the value system of white, middle-class America. If the latter course is taken the problem then becomes one not of dissolving the ghetto but rather of emphasizing it and obtaining a fair share of community investment. This could lead to an ironic reversal to the 'separate but equal' principle of the pre-anti-segration legislation and to apartheid.

To a large extent the difficulties of the blacks in the USA are derived from the fact that instead of being the temporary feature it has been for almost all other immigrant groups the ghetto became permanent whether the blacks wanted it that way or not. 'The early pattern of negro settlement within each metropolitan area followed that of immigrant groups. Migrants converged on the older sections of the central city because the lower cost housing was there, friends and relatives were likely to be there, and the older neighbour-hoods then often had good public transport.'[58] But unlike other incoming

[57]   L. Wirth (1956), 20.
[58]   O. Kerner, chairman (1968): *Report of the National Advisory Commission on Civil Dis-orders*, 243–4 (New York).

groups a subsequent pattern of dispersal has not happened. Morrill[59] has suggested four reasons for this:

1   *Prejudice and discrimination.* These need no elaboration in this context.

2   *Characteristics of the black.* By this Morrill means to include all those difficulties faced by members of a minority group when they leave the shelter of the ghetto. This is especially acute when physical differences are evident.

3   *Real estate and associated financial institutions.*[60] Apart from any ideological commitment the interest of these people is to avoid any change in the character of an area that would result in prices falling. Once they do begin to fall the greatest profit is to be derived from encouraging rapid selling.

4   *Legal and governmental barriers.* These have been nominally eliminated over the last decade.

'In summary, the concentration of negroes in central cities results from a combination of forces. Some of these forces such as migration and initial settlement patterns in older neighbourhoods, are similar to those which affected previous ethnic minorities. Others — particularly discrimination in employment and segregation in housing and schools — are a result of white attitudes based on race and colour. These forces continue to shape the future of the central city.'[61]

Morrill, in the same paper quoted above, identified the expansion of the ghetto as a process of spatial diffusion. The mechanism is related to the gradual spread of black occupancy as marginal blocks are penetrated and then rapidly change in character (figure 10−8) so that any form of racial integration is most difficult to sustain. There can be identified for most blocks or streets what is called a 'tipping point', 'once the proportion of non whites exceeds the limits of the neighbourhood's tolerance for inter-racial living (this is the tip point) the whites move out.'[62] A figure of 30 per cent black occupancy has been suggested as this figure, though it will vary in relation to a wide range of other factors.[63]

The effective result of these forces is the emergence in large cities of clearly marked ethnic areas representing this third component of social area make-up. The location of these areas is implicit in their history. As the exodus of white population from the centre of the city to the suburbs has proceeded, so the ghetto has been intensified as a portion of the inner city. If one accepts a spatial diffusion process for ghetto expansion then this will

---

[59]   R. L. Morrill (1965): The Negro ghetto: problems and alternatives. *Geogrl. Rev.* **55**, 339−61.

[60]   For a valuable study see Joe T. Darden (1973): *Afro-Americans in Pittsburgh: the residential segregation of a people* (Lexington, Mass.).

[61]   O. Kerner, chairman (1968).

[62]   M. Grodzins (1958): *The metropolitan area as a racial problem*, 6 (Pittsburgh).

[63]   H. Spiegel (1960): Tenants' intergroup attitudes in a public housing project with declining white population. *Phylon* **21**, 30. E. P. Wolf (1963): The tipping point in racially changing neighborhoods. *J. Am. Inst. Tn. Plann.* **29**, 217−22.

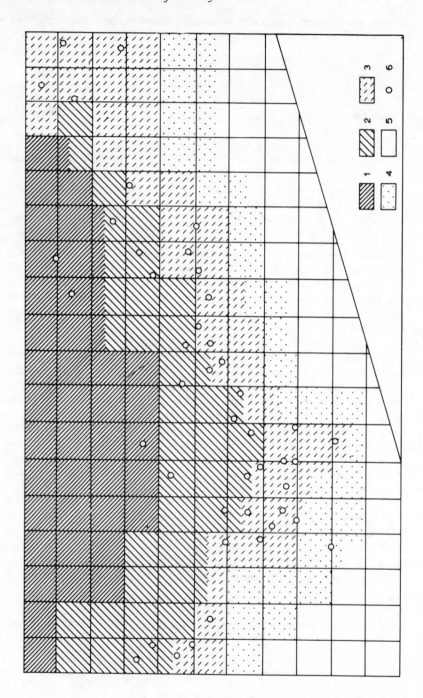

take place where white resistance is least effective. Since areas high in socio-economic status are sectoral, often retaining a link with the centre, the ghetto will tend to be squeezed into a sector-like arrangement, made up of a series of blobs around the inner city. This is the situation which Murdie proposed for the ethnic areas of Toronto from his survey of that city.

A broad comparison can be made with the areas in British cities where immigrants have clustered. In a study of Birmingham P. N. Jones has argued that these are not to be called ghettos in the strict sense of the term since they are not exclusively dominated by one cultural group but are rather mixed areas.[64] In the clusters of immigrant areas he identified in Birmingham the coloured population only forms some 14·6 per cent of the population, with a maximum of 18·5 per cent. This compares with figures for example from Cleveland. Ohio, which show that 80 per cent of the black population lived in census tracts which were 75 per cent black in composition.[65] K. and T. Taeuber[66] employed the segregation index (see page 252) and found that for 207 of the largest US cities it was 86·2 in 1960. Jones is probably right, therefore, to argue that he is not dealing with ghettos in the proper sense.

Nevertheless most studies of change between 1961 and 1971 showed that 'intensification has remained the dominant spatial process rather than a hoped-for dispersal and suburbanization. Movement to areas of post-1920 housing, whether private or municipal, is clearly not enough to make any significant impact in comparison with the concentrations of the middle ring of the city.'[67] Figure 10−9 shows 11 clusters of immigrants Jones could identify in Birmingham in 1960. This suggests an arrangement both zonal and sectoral. There is a clear zone of occupation apparent whích avoids the inner city and is closely linked to the high density middle-zone. This is a consequence partly of structural, partly of institutional factors. The inner zone is an area of late nineteenth-century slums, particularly of small houses or

[64] P. N. Jones (1967): The segregation of immigrant communities in the city of Birmingham, 1961. *Univ. Hull occl. Pap. Geogr.* **7**.
[65] O. Kerner, chairman (1968), 249.
[66] K. and T. Taeuber (1965): *Negroes in cities* (Chicago).
[67] P. N. Jones (1970): Some aspects of the changing distribution of coloured immigrants in Birmingham, 1961−66. *Trans. Inst. Brit. Geogr.* **50**, 217. See also, P. N. Jones (1976): Coloured minorities in Birmingham, England. *Ann. Assoc. Amer. Geogrs.*, **66**, 89−103.

Figure 10−8: Black purchases on the edge of a ghetto in one year. *After R. L. Morrill (1965).* The five shaded boxes refer to five identified areas within which the proportion of purchases in 1955 was as follows:

Area	No. of white purchases	% total purchases	% area negro
1	8	3·9	32
2	26	4·3	16
3	67	40·6	5
4	72	98·7	1
5	112	100·0	1
6	New street fronts with sales to negroes in 1955.		

Figure 10–9: Immigrant clusters in Birmingham. *After P. N. Jones (1967)*. The immigrant clusters were identified by including all contiguous enumeration districts which belong to the upper quartile (10·1 per cent immigrant population). Completely surrounded districts which fell below the critical value were included. The 'colour' definition is derived from foreign born residents from the West Indies, India and Pakistan. The clusters are: **1:** Saltley; **2:** Small Heath; **3:** Sparkbrook; **4:** Highgate; **5:** Balsall Heath – North Moseley; **6:** Cannon Hill; **7:** Calthorpe Park; **8:** Summerfield Park; **9:** Newtown Aston; **10:** Handsworth; **11:** Aston.
For a recent summary, using 1971 census data, see:
Jones, P. N. (1976): Colored minorities in Birmingham, England. *Ann. Assoc. Amer. Geogr.* 66(1), 89–103.

cottages built around courts. These are inherently ill suited to immigrant needs because of their very small size. Moreover large tracts are now municipally owned and scheduled as comprehensive redevelopment areas.

The immigrant clusters have, therefore, been pushed out and have taken over the high density, later by-law terraces and even larger but contemporary houses and villas. These have often leases with only a short time to run, which makes normal mortgages difficult to obtain, so that they become available for a quick cash sale and are large enough to house immigrant families. This 'invasion' is made all the easier since the houses lack modern amenities, not only internally but externally as well, as for example in the absence of garages or garage space. The result is that 'the clusters are not typically sited in the slum-ridden heart of the city, but in the tree lined, often attractive townscapes of the middle ring.'[68]

Two spatial influences have been at work to create this situation in Birmingham. The first is the physical and institutional restraints operating in the city centre which have prevented the take over of the oldest, poorest properties. The second is the resistance from the suburbs, together with the particular conditions required by the immigrants, the economic resources they have, and their need to associate with people of a like cultural background. The result is a zone which is almost complete. Indeed if other immigrant groups, such as the Irish, are added the zonal picture becomes even clearer. This conforms to the generalized notion of a black collar around the CBD which is used in the Kerner report. In detail, however, this ring is rarely complete and often extends out as invasion and succession proceed. It is better to think of it as combining zonal and sectoral qualities.

Before concluding this section on the ethnic dimension it is necessary briefly to consider a characteristic part of most cities where economic and social forces react most clearly on the physical fabric — the slum. The slum has much in common with the ghetto and the classifications which have been proposed — slums of hope and slums of despair,[69] the 'urban village' and the 'urban jungle'[70] — correspond with the 'temporary' and the 'permanent' ghetto. The basic cause of central blight has already been examined: new building takes place progressively further away from the centre and slums occur where the reciprocal process of central redevelopment does not take place.

There are several reasons for this imbalance. Buildings are long-term investments and modification is costly. They are also not easily detachable from the area in which they are sited. The result is that with age and use the value of a building declines in terms of the net return on investment. A point can be reached when redevelopment would give a greater return: that is, it would compensate the cost of removing the building, the cost of a new one and the loss of returns during the process. Rising land values imply an increasingly intensive use[71] (figure 10–10). This can be achieved by the subdivision of houses thus creating the situation where slum rents per unit area and return on capital are among the highest. If this does not happen a wide range of problems faces the potential developer, among them the difficulties of widespread ownership of small units and of acquisition. Moreover, any large area will include property in a variety of conditions — many planning authorities have been accused of the demolition of houses of good quality in a policy of comprehensive redevelopment.

The result is that capital can be better devoted to the commercial

---

[68] P. N. Jones (1967), 22.
[69] C. Stokes (1962): A theory of slums. *Land Econ.* **48**, 187–97.
[70] H. J. Gans (1962). *The urban villagers*, 4 (New York).
[71] L. S. Bourne (1967): Private redevelopment of the central city. *Univ. of Chicago, Dept. of Geography Research Papers* **112**, 40–49 (Chicago).

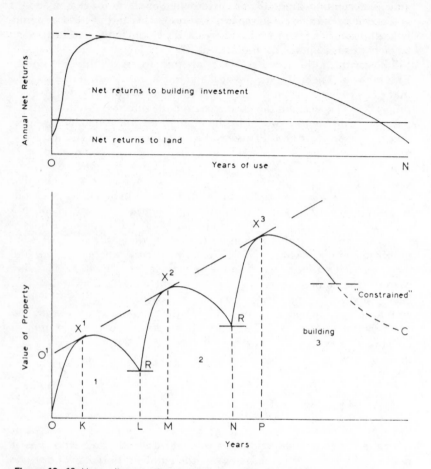

Figure 10—10: Upper diagram: the expected net returns from investment in a new building: Lower diagram: idealized replacement cycle for individual buildings. *After L. S. Bourne (1967).* The upper diagram is self explanatory. In the lower diagram O represents the time of original construction while K, M and P indicate the time of the theoretical optimum net returns on the original investment. R is the level at which replacement occurs and L and N redevelopment in the form of a new building. The line $X^1 - X^2 - X^3$ represents the theoretical increase in total property value with replacement by more intensive uses.

property of the centre or the residential suburb. It is not economically viable for private capital to provide housing for low income groups, and thus the inner areas must either deteriorate into slums, be redeveloped by private capital as luxury apartment blocks or by public capital for housing. As they deteriorate they provide the milieu where the newcomer to the city can find refuge together with the dropout. In relation to the urban society at large those on their way to integration within it and those on their way to rejection of it, find common ground in an environment of decay and dilapidation.[72] Comments of this kind have been drawn together by J. A. Rex in a study of the 'sociology' of the zone in transition,[73] a characteristic area of the city already discussed in the context of the CBD. Rex presents a model based on three elements:

1 *A general theory of housing classes in the city.* This to a large extent accepts standard notions of the decay of central property and the flight to the suburbs. 'I suggest that the basic process underlying urban social interaction is competition for scarce and desired types of housing. In this process people are distinguished from one another by their strength in the housing market or, more generally, in the system of housing allocation.'[74] Since Rex writes in a British context he has to pay more attention to the allocation of municipal housing than is found in work on the United States.

2 *A theory of ethnic group relations and rural-urban culture change.* This takes in the situations already discussed under the 'ethnicity' component and the role of the ghetto.

3 *A theory of conflict and conflict resolution as between associations in the urban zone of transition.* This has not been discussed in this book since it is marginal to the primarily spatial concern of the geographer. But most certainly the way formal and informal associations mediate in the conflicts that arise out of ethnic and other group relations is of significance. Rex argues that such associations aim at overcoming social isolation, affirming meanings, values and beliefs, administering 'pastoral' care and the attainment of group goals. The result is to modify conflict so that the tensions which must arise are offset, 'but the situation in the zone of transition is a highly unstable one and in any sudden crisis ethnic and class conflicts which are temporarily contained may crystallize and be pursued by more violent means.'[75]

Rex has effectively systematized the role of the slum and ghetto areas of the city, or the zone of transition conceived as 'that area of the city where the least privileged housing classes live, especially the landlords and tenants of lodging houses.' He is, however, concerned with a structural rather than a locational notion of the zone of transition which he conceives as only partly tied to the physical fabric of the city by the first of his three elements. At an earlier point in this volume (chapter 9, pp. 231–35), when the zone in transition was reviewed as part of the CBD margins, it was noted that, in spite of the attempts to define it in terms of commercial and industrial uses,

[72] For a general study see: D. R. Hunter (1968): *The slums, challenge and response* (New York). J. A. Casasco (1969): The social function of the slum in Latin America: some positive aspects. *Ekistics* **28**, 168–75. M. Fried and J. Levin (1968): Some social functions of the urban slum; in B. J. Frieden and R. Morris, editors (1968): *Urban planning and social policy* (New York).
[73] J. A. Rex (1968): The sociology of a zone in transition; in R. E. Pahl, editor (1968): *Readings in urban sociology*, 211–31 (London).
[74] J. A. Rex (1968), 214.
[75] J. A. Rex (1968), 231.

the second largest single use was residential. It has already been demonstrated that there is no 'zone' as such in spatial terms but rather segments of land. The structural ideas put together by Rex illuminate the processes which are in operation. These must be integrated with the study of economic processes at work at the city centre before any meaningful study of spatial patterns can progress.

3 An overview of social areas

It is possible to combine the ethnic variable with socioeconomic status—including the lowest groups living in the so-called slum—and family status and to adopt Murdie's model as an indicator of the essential elements in the residential structure of the city (figure 10−11). This can be stated in terms of the hypotheses that Murdie proposed:

1   Economic status tends to be associated with measures of income, occupation, and education and tends to be distributed sectorially.
2   Family status tends to be associated with fertility, type of household, and labour force participation by women and tends to be distributed concentrically.
3   Ethnic status tends to form 'groupings' which can be superimposed upon the cellular structure created by combinations of sectorial and concentric patterns.[76]

Figure 10−11: A model of the residential structure of the city. *After R. A. Murdie (1969).*

[76] R. A. Murdie (1969), 7.

In spite of the brief inclusion of Birmingham, England, in the earlier discussion, the conclusions have been those derived from American literature and based on American experience. Certainly the 'family status' variable would not play anything like as important a role in Britain or western Europe as in the United States. In his study of Sunderland, Robson found that an analysis of thirty variables resulted in a first component which could be interpreted as associated with social class. The second component was a measure of housing conditions.[77] Neither family status nor ethnicity emerged. It is also worthy of note that a study of Cardiff and Swansea produced a first component associated with housing conditions.[78]

The view that British cities produce somewhat different dimensions in terms of factorial ecology as compared with North American examples has been challenged by Davies and Lewis in a study of Leicester.[79] From their analysis they state that 'it has proved possible to demonstrate that the basic urban dimensions of Leicester conform much more closely to the standard North American patterns than has hitherto been suggested.' Moreover it was also found appropriate to relate these dimensions in Leicester to concentric, sectoral and clustered spatial patterns as shown in figure 10−11.[80]

Again, R. J. Johnston[81] in a study of four New Zealand cities (Auckland, Wellington, Christchurch and Dunedin) reaches a similar conclusion and proceeds to quote Timms's view that 'the demonstration that there are consistent patterns in the factorial invariance of cities in different parts of the world poses a major challenge to urban theory.'[82] This is certainly true although three relevant areas of work need to be noted:

1   Both Davies and Lewis and Johnston note that the standard dimensions can be considered as being made up of lower order components. (See section 4 below.)
2   Undoubtedly such theory will need to be related to ideas on the processes of modernization and the social changes which take place. (See section 5.)
3   Like studies of central place systems at an aggregate level, social area analysis leads to an impasse: it provides an effective description but explanation tends to move away from the aggregate to the individual level. (See section 6.)

---

[77]   B. T. Robson (1969), 159−67.

[78]   D. T. Herbert (1970), 82−88. See p. 259, footnote 39.

[79]   W. K. D. Davies and G. J. Lewis (1973): The urban dimensions of Leicester, England; in B. D. Clark and M. B. Gleave, editors (1973): Social patterns in cities. *Inst. Brit. Geogr. Spec. Pub.* 5 (London).

[80]   G. J. Lewis (1972): Leicester — urban structure and regional relationships; in N. Pye, editor (1972): *Leicester and its region* (Leicester). G. J. Lewis and W. K. D. Davies (1974): The Social patterning of a British city: the case of Leicester 1966. *Tijds. voor econ. en soc. geogr.* 65(3), 194−207.

[81]   R. J. Johnston (1973): Residential differentiation in major New Zealand urban areas: a comparative factorial ecology; in B. D. Clark and M. B. Gleave, editors (1973).

[82]   D. W. G. Timms (1971): *The urban mosaic: Towards a theory of residential segregation* (Cambridge). See also, R. J. Johnston (1972): Towards a general model of intra-urban residential patterns. *Progress in Geography* 4, 82−124.

4 Subdimensions of social areas

Davies and Lewis in their Leicester study first establish an eight factor (first order) solution from the initial set of variables. The eight factors are identified as: socioeconomic status, mobility, stage in life cycle, substandardness (of housing), mobile young adult, ethnicity, economic participation, urban fringe, females. They then proceed to factor-analyse the matrix of correlations between the eight factors and to derive from the exercise three (second or higher order) factors which they label: social status, family status, ethnicity. The levels of generalization can be identified as follows:

First order title   Loading   Second order title

Substandardness ──────── − 0·61 ──────────→

Urban fringe ──────── + 0·76 ──────────→ } Social status

Socio-economic status {── + 0·69 ────────→

── + 0·54 ── ── ── ── ──→ Family status

──────── First ranking correlations

── ── ── ── Second ranking correlations

The social status dimension is made up of three subdimensions one of which refers to the quality of housing and another to characteristics of the rural-urban fringe. The point of real interest, however, is that in Britain socio-economic status is not entirely separated from family status.

This has been most clearly demonstrated in a paper by Barrie Morgan in which the bases of family status segregation are examined in Exeter.[83] After careful analysis Morgan fails to identify the patterning of life-cycle stage as predicted by standard ecological models. He comments that the investigation was prompted by his concern that theory regarding the residential structure of British cities was too dependent on empirical work carried out in North America. His central finding is summarized as, 'that residential immobility among households who enter new housing in the family cycle is a more important influence on the residential patterns of family status groups than changing household needs generated by life-cycle changes'.[84] This suggests that limited economic resources lock people into a housing situation so that the independence of the dimensions (factors) assumed by Murdie's resolution in Toronto is not achieved. This is in line with Berry's view (see p. 56−7) that 'in every society the principal dimensions of socio-economic differentiation are those of social status and age structure, or stage in life cycle. However, only at the highest levels of development do these factors appear to operate independently. At somewhat lower levels of welfare (Britain) there remains a correlation between income and family structure . . only the rich elderly can segregate themselves . . . . . . at lower income

[83] B. Morgan (1976): The bases of family status segregation: a ~ase study in Exeter. Trans. Inst. Brit. Geogrs. New Series, 1(1), 83−107.
[84] B. Morgan (1976), 105.

levels there is a great mixture of family types in the same residential areas'.[85] This seems the case in the significant loading of the first (lower) order factor of socio-economic status on to the second (higher) order factor of family status in the table above. This suggests some inhibition in the separation of socio-economic status from that of family status[86] which can be related partly to stage of development, implying some sort of sequence, and partly to the institutional forces of the housing market. A developmental model is briefly considered in the next section and institutional influences in the next chapter.

5 A developmental model of social areas

A starting point is the work of Abu-Lughod on Cairo. Thirteen variables were employed in her analysis and the first factor abstracted was identified as representing 'style of life', for the highly associated variables reflect 'economic aspects of a life style which, in today's Cairo, is increasingly finding expression in more "modern" family patterns of female education, delayed age of marriage and lower fertility.' The second factor is interpreted as representing a 'male dominance' and the third social dis-organization. But for present purposes 'the most significant finding is the close association between certain variables of family status and variables of social rank.'[87] There are many possible explanations for such a situation, which is at odds with that in American studies: for example, in Egypt the extended family is so pervasive an element of urban life that various stages of the family cycle are played out within the same households rather than isolated in sequential residential settings.[88] Even if such a relationship between social rank and family type is accepted it would still be possible to have a variable which could be called 'family status' and disassociated from social rank, providing two conditions were met — firstly that stages in the family cycle were clearly associated with changes in residence, and secondly that a stock of sufficiently specialized housing existed to meet the changes in residence demanded at the different stages in the family cycle.

These conditions do not obtain in most western countries: indeed, the Leicester evidence above indicates that they do not do so in Britain. It could be argued that the model presented by Murdie is particular to North America. Abu-Lughod argues further that the conventional western variables are of little meaning in situations where contrasts derive from cultural variations between ethnic or tribal groups, and where there is a low level of differentiation of housing type and a residual element of extended households. Immediately these points are made, it becomes clear that an

[85] B. J. L. Berry (1972): *City classification handbook: methods and applications* (New York), 56.
[86] But see:
H. Morikawa (1976): A comparative study of factorial ecologies of Hiroshima and Fukuoka. *Geog. Review of Japan*, 49(5), 303–313, where the first two factors derived are family status, with a zonal pattern and socio-economic status with a sectoral pattern.
[87] J. L. Abu-Lughod (1969), 207.
[88] J. L. Abu-Lughod (1969), 208.

extended model is needed to take account of these variations in 'the scale of society', and which will present a developmental continuum,[89] that subsumes the contrasting locations of high quality residential areas in both pre-industrial and industrial cities and the changes in development dealt with earlier (pp. 174−6).

Such a developmental model is implicit in the polarized situations epitomized for the pre-industrial city by Sjoberg and for modern industrial cities by contemporary factorial ecologies. We urgently need to establish the process of translation from one situation to the other. Indeed several studies explicitly portray this metamorphosis.

In a study of four Latin American cities — Bogota, Quito, Lima and Santiago — Amato demonstrates the collapse of traditional patterns and the emergence of new spatial arrangements. 'With the advent of industrialization, the concomitant development of new transport facilities, and the growth of commerce . . . many cities moved away from (the) colonial model. The most dramatic occurrence, signalling the breakdown of traditional land-use patterns, was the flight of the upper classes to suburban locations.'[90] Morris and Pyle write of Rio de Janeiro that though many would see it as an industrial city, in terms of its social organization it clearly 'maintains many of the features of the pre-industrial city and of the transitional city.'[91] Here the explicit use of the word 'transitional' suggests a developmental model. Writing of Calcutta, Berry and Rees argue that 'there is increasing functional differentiation of land-use, alongside regional occupational differentiation. And consistent with the notion of a city in transition, alongside these bases of differentiation are a strong land-use and familism gradient, comparable in many ways to "modern" American formulations of urbanization.'[92]

The bravest attempt to provide a synthetic framework for these changes has been made by Timms in *The urban mosaic*. Timms maintains that in premodern society 'there is a high degree of coalescence between the criteria of social differentiation: an individual's status in one institutional realm is highly predictive of his standing in others. Status is ascribed and differences in prestige, way of life, ethnic identity and place of residence are intimately related. With modernization this coalescence breaks down. An individual's kinship connections no longer provide an almost perfect basis for predicting his social rank, his place of residence, or, even his ethnicity.'[93] Perhaps, the most interesting feature of Timms's statement is its quite remarkable parallelism with the notions of Wirth: these were introduced earlier and they were seen as the basis from which Shevky and Bell developed social area analysis. Timms implies that a change takes place from a single axis of differentiation

[89] B. J. L. Berry and P. H. Rees (1969): The factorial ecology of Calcutta. *Am. J. Sociol.* 74, 445−91.

[90] P. Amato (1970): Elitism and settlement patterns in the Latin-American city. *Jl. Am. Inst. Town Planr.* 36 (1), 96−105.

[91] F. B. Morris and G. F. Pyle (1971): The social environment of Rio de Janeiro. *Econ. Geogr.* 47 (2. supplement) 286−99.

[92] B. J. L. Berry and P. H. Rees, (1969).

[93] D. W. G. Timms (1971), 143−4.

in the pre-industrial state to the more complex dimensions of the contemporary city. This is accompanied by spatial resorting of the type already noted in Latin American cities, but much more work is needed to identify this process of spatial change.

A considerable amount of recent research has concentrated on the nineteenth century city in the western industrializing world and the notion that parallels can be drawn with the contemporary city are implicit in much of this work. Thus Carter and Wheatley[94] in a study of the iron and steel town of Merthyr Tydfil at the mid-nineteenth century have introduced the notion of internal colonialism to explain a situation where both factor analysis and clustering procedures reveal associations of social class, occupation, migration and ethnic status, very much in line with Timms's identification of a colonial situation. The clearest exposition of the social areas of a nineteenth century city is that by Lawton and Pooley relating to Liverpool.[95] The arrows on the diagram (figure 10—12) of mid-Victorian Liverpool indicate the dynamic elements of change. In particular the sectoral extension of the high status area to the south-east of the CBD is noteworthy.

The whole process can be summarized by the notion of the differentiation of land uses and the segregation of populations and an effective intermediate stage in the move towards the situation of contemporary factorial ecologies is caught. This is an oversimplification and points of detail have yet to be resolved, but the growing range of nineteenth century investigation should eventually result in an effective tracing of the transformation that century witnessed. This in turn will enable more valid comparisons to be made with contemporary changes in developing countries.

6 Residential location: The problem of disaggregation and residential choice

It is possible to introduce this problem by the examination of household activity systems, in much the same way as the activities of firms were suggested as providing a profitable approach to the CBD.

Household activities include a vast range extending from work to social and recreational activities and to shopping. There are few studies of this sort and results from investigations are not very fruitful,[96] but one study from Detroit[97] illustrates the principle and relates back to the previous discussion in this chapter. For each of five major sectors of metropolitan Detroit, the centres of white and black populations had been calculated in a previous

[94] H. Carter and S. Wheatley (1978): *Merthyr Tyafil in 1851: A Study of Spatial Structure*. S.S.R.C. Project. Working Paper 2 (Aberystwyth, Dept. Geog.).

[95] R. Lawton (1978): Population and Society 1730—1900, in R. A. Dodgshon and R. A. Butlin eds. (1978): *An historical geography of England and Wales*, 352 (London).

[96] G. C. Hemmens (1968): The structure of urban activity linkages. *Univ. of N. Carolina at Chapel Hill Centre for Urban and Regional Studies, Urb. Stud. Res. Monog.*

[97] R. V. Smith, S. F. Flory, R. L. Bashshur and G. W. Shannon (1967): *Community interaction and racial integration in the Detroit area; an ecological analysis*. Report derived from project 2557, US Office of Education (Eastern Michigan University).

Figure 10–12: The urban structure of mid-Victorian Liverpool. This schematic diagram, which is not to scale, attempts to summarize the main residential and social areas within Liverpool in 1871 and the associated processes of migration to the city and of residential mobility within it. The high-status sector south-east of the Central Business District should be noted and the contrasting working-class residential areas of the dock-side and the North End. Stages of growth may be seen in the sequence of suburban zones around the historic core, the CBD of 1871. Based on R. Lawton and C. G. Pooley, *The Social Geography of Merseyside in the Nineteenth Century*, (Liverpool, 1976), Fig. 26.

study[98] and joined to form a 'centre line' of white and negro population (figure 10–13). A similar technique was now used to define a centre line based on a stratified sample of population questioned as to 'the location of meeting places of all formal associations they belonged to, as well as the residence location of all friends, neighbours, relatives and co-workers with whom they interacted. In this manner point locations were derived for all formal and informal associational activities of each respondent.'[99] From these points a mean centre of gravity was computed for each sector and joined to form an interaction line (figure 10–13). From this it is clear that residential segregation is associated with segregated interaction. The activity systems of these two populations, in the study context, are related to different areas.

To some extent it can be suggested that residential choice—particularly in intra-urban relocation which plays a large part in determining the total pattern—is the function of the total of these activity systems. But there are two sorts of activity which could control residential choice. The one is directed towards employment and place of work and the other to social and leisure activities.

Moriarty has examined the relative stress to be put on these two controls considering them as competing hypotheses.[100] The first he calls the 'economic competition' hypothesis in which the ability to pay is the basic factor and in consequence journey-to-work and site costs are the major influences in the residential decision. 'Differences in the locational behaviour of residential decision makers are due to differences in their budget costs and income resources, and it is this difference that determines the spatial distribution of socio-economic groups in urban space.'[101] Moriarty maintains that such a proposition is nowhere supported by empirical evidence and sets out in contrast the second 'social choice' hypothesis which argues that residential decisions stem from conscious, or indeed subconscious, social choice related to the differing values, needs and desires of people.

Most empirical studies reject the 'economic competition' interpretation and find no relation between social class and distance to work. For example, Halvorson reports, 'the major conclusion to be drawn from the data summarized is a negative one . . . the journey to work or work access constitutes a rather minor factor in the residential location decision.'[102] Halvorson goes on to positive conclusions which relate residential location decision to the quality of housing and the quality of the housing environment. Similar results have been widely reported and have led to an emphasis on

[98] A. J. Mayer and T. F. Hoult (1962): *Race and residence in Detroit*. Wayne State University, Institute for Regional and Urban Studies.

[99] R. V. Smith *et alia* (1967), 13.

[100] B. M. Moriarty (1970): A test of alternative hypotheses of urban residential growth. *Proc. Assoc. of Am. Geog.* **2**, 97–101.

[101] B. M. Moriarty (1970), 98.

[102] P. Halvorson (1970): *Residential location and the journey-to-work in Charleston, West Virginia*, 178. Univ. of Cincinnati: unpublished Ph.D. thesis.

RESIDENTIAL INTERACTION PATTERNS
DETROIT AREA
1965

Miles
0 2 4 6 8
0 2 4 6 8 10 12
Km

DETROIT CITY
MEAN CENTRE
RESIDENTIAL LINE (WHITE)
INTERACTION LINE (WHITE)
RES. LINE (BLACK)
INTER LINE (BLACK)

Figure 10–13: Residential interaction patterns in the Detroit Area, 1965. The method of construction of the residential and interaction lines is indicated in the text. *After R. V. Smith, et alia. (1967).*

decision making and environmental perception as main areas of current investigation.

These areas of present investigation are best presented in a residential location decision model which sets out the reasons operative in the selection of a particular location. This has been done in diagrammatic form by Herbert and fig 10−14 is derived from his model.[103] The key concepts are to be found in the work of Wolpert[104] and of Brown and Moore.[105] The individual household can be considered to be under the influence of two sets

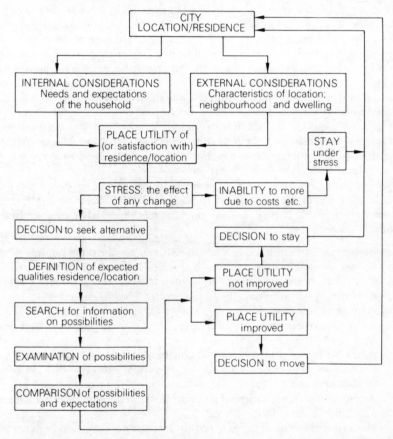

Figure 10−14: A residential location decision model. *Modified from D. T. Herbert (1972).* Note that 'place utility' is a complex notion and will be determined by a complex series of 'trade-offs', of which the most obvious is a desired house in an undesirable location against an inadequate house in a desired area.

[103] D. T. Herbert (1972): *Urban Geography. A social perspective,* 246−256 (Newton Abbot).

[104] J. Wolpert (1965): Behavioural Aspects of the decision to migrate. *Papers Reg. Sci. Assoc.* 15, 159−169.

[105] L. A. Brown and E. G. Moore (1970): The intra-urban migration process: a perspective. *Geogr. Annaler,* (Series B) 52, 1−13.

of forces. One is internal, in that it is generated by the household itself and defined in terms of its own needs and expectations; the other is external and defined by the characteristics of the locale. These two sets interact in creating 'place utility', which essentially measures an individual's level of satisfaction or dissatisfaction with a given location. 'If the place utility of the present residential site diverges sufficiently from his immediate needs, the individual will consider a new location.'[106]

The divergence between present site and possible new locations is set up by the operation of 'stressors', or by any change which alters, or threatens to alter, the status quo. These could be related either to internal factors—for example, an increase in family size by the birth of children or the coming of in-laws to live with the nuclear family—or to external forces such as the building of a nearby motorway or the buying up of proximate houses by people of different ethnic origin. They need not be as tangible as these examples: for instance, a change in the way the household regards its social status could give rise to stresses. From the impact of such stresses comes the decision to consider the possibility of an alternative location. Two related problems face the household in their consideration. The first is to define the qualities to be expected at a new location and the second to carry out a search in order to find such a location.

A number of studies have attempted to list and compare desirable qualities. Perhaps the most useful is that by Butler, Chapin *et alia*[107] who from a nationwide survey in the United States report that metropolitan households prefer:

1 Better neighbourhood quality with either a less desirable housing unit or less accessible location over a less desirable neighbourhood with either a better housing unit or better accessibility. (Overwhelmingly—approximately 70 per cent to 27 per cent.)

2 A house that is desirable inside but appears less so outside to one where an attractive exterior belies the interior. (Overwhelmingly—80·4 per cent to 14·2 per cent.)

3 Access to better than average schools in an area with higher taxes to lower taxes and less desirable schools. (Overwhelmingly—78·3 per cent to 15·2 per cent.)

4 A conflicting combination of a new or fairly new house together with a well-established neighbourhood.

5 Modern architectural style to traditional (But barely—45·5 per cent to 37·6 per cent.)

6 A housing unit all on one floor.

7 Few children in the neighbourhood.

8 Large lots to small lots.

[106] L. A. Brown and E. G. Moore (1970), 1.

[107] E. W. Butler, F. S. Chapin *et alia*. (1969): Moving behavior and residential choice. A national survey. *US Highway Research Board, National cooperative highway research report* **81** (Washington DC).

A listing of possible qualities is also presented by Brown and Moore.[108] Attempts to identify the most consistently emphasized features have isolated two — the house itself, that is the various physical features of the dwelling especially the space available, and its social and physical environment. Perhaps the most interesting attempt to approach this problem has been G. L. Petersen's.[109] Respondents were asked to detail their judgements on photographs of residential areas rated in relation to ten selected variables. The replies were factor analyzed to produce a first factor which was essentially physical quality closely associated with age of the structures, and the second an environmental quality named 'harmony with nature' as reflected in such things as amount of greenery, privacy and open space.

After the definition of expected qualities, the household is then faced with the problem of searching for information on the possibilities available. A diagram constructed by Silk is reproduced (figure 10−15) to indicate some aspects of the search procedure.[110] It is a truism that one limitation on the individual will be the extent of his knowledge: he will be restricted to a choice in a known area which can be called his awareness space, modern jargon for the *terra cognita* of the ancients. This is the area with which he is familiar through his varied activities such as journeys to work, shop or to visit friends. It is virtually the same as the alternative term 'action space', although that is best reserved for the area that which he is familiar through direct personal activity as opposed to indirect contact space which would include familiarity derived from the media and reports from relatives and friends. To this must be added the information provided by real estate agents.

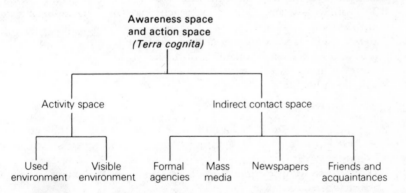

Figure 10−15: Components of spatial search in residential location decisions. *After J. A. Silk (1972).*

[108] L. A. Brown and E. G. Moore (1970), 5.

[109] G. L. Petersen (1967): A model of preference: quantitative analysis of the perception of the visual appearance of residential neighbourhoods. *J. Reg. Sci. Assoc.* **7**, 19−31.

[110] J. A. Silk (1972): Comments on 'historical' factors influencing residential choice and associated research problems. Paper read to *Inst. Brit. Geogr. Urban Study Group.* See also J. A. Silk (1971): Search behaviour: general characterization and review of literature in the behavioural sciences. *Univ. of Reading, Geographical Papers* **7**.

Having considered the desired qualities of a new location and where these are, the household will proceed to review all the possibilities and compare them with the existing location. From this a decision to stay or move will be made in relation to the measuring rod of place utility.

At this point it is worth recalling the consideration of consumer behaviour introduced in chapter 6 (pp. 128–33) for buying a house is an aspect of consumer behaviour.

A further resolution of intraurban mobility at an individual scale remains. The intense mobility associated with modern urbanism makes Webber's non-place urban realms all the more significant.[111] If people structure their lives within these realms then the problem arises of identifying this structuring and assessing its impact on spatial behaviour, and so one enters the field of 'social networks in urban situations.' The book edited by J. C. Mitchell with that title[112] is concerned with central African towns, but the basic notions set out there can be generally applied to the various realms in which the individual operates. In order to give some indication of the flavour of Mitchell's work it is worthwhile outlining very briefly his identification of the morphological and interactional characteristics of social networks.[113] The morphological characteristics are:

1   *Anchorage*. This defines the point of origin of the network but this can have no absolute meaning, it must be defined in the context of an investigation as the individual on whom the network is fixed or anchored.

2   *Reachability*. This defines the degree to which an individual can be contacted via the network or the extent to which he can contact others. The ease with which others can be reached is of obvious importance to any network.

3   *Density*. This is a different concept to reachability for it measures the interaction between all members of the network.

4   *Range*. This assesses the number of people in regular and direct contact with an individual.

The interactional criteria are:

5   *Content*. This defines the basis on which contacts within the networks are made. It could,' for example, be kinship, religion, work or friendship.

6   *Directedness*. This is a measure of reciprocity, of the extent to which contacts are one way or not.

7   *Durability*. Some networks come into being for a very specific purpose, perhaps to advocate a public policy of some sort, and then disappear. Not all networks are permanent.

8   *Intensity*. Individuals will vary in the degree to which they feel

[111] M. M. Webber (1964): The urban place and the nonplace urban realm; in M. M. Webber *et alia*, editors (1964): *Explorations into urban structure* (Philadelphia). See p. 310.
[112] J. C. Mitchell (1969): *Social networks in urban situations* (Manchester).
[113] This outline is from J. C. Mitchell (1969): The concept and use of social networks; in J. C. Mitchell, editor (1969), 1–50.

themselves committed to the network, ranging from the complete commitment that its members may feel to an organization like the Mafia to a much more casual involvement in minor causes. It is worth observing that in common everyday terms the word 'Mafia' is used to denote a network.

9 *Frequency.* The frequency of contact between the members will vary and this becomes a measurable feature of interaction.

These nine measures can be applied to any interactive situation whether it be a complex of business links or a pattern of golf club membership. It is implicit in the ideas of Wirth, and the reasons of Webber, that in an urban context these various reticules become discrete as the urbanite segregates the roles played. In all this the geographer has a tenuous interest but, although the networks display aspatial interactions between populations, implicit within them are relative locations and hence spatial manifestations. As Connell writes 'the content of these spatial links remains critical and morphological networks alone are inadequate; social networks, by definition, are only marginally spatial.'[114] The investigation of the spatial articulation of urban social networks presents a research problem for the geographer. It might well reveal the extent to which new small-scale 'communities' are emerging within the larger urban region and the relevance these have in the residential location decision.

The end result of these studies of the individual or household's residential location decision should be to build up from this microscopic level to the explanation of the location and characteristics of residential areas. This supposedly avoids the impasse of inadequate explanation to which macro-scaled studies are tied, just as consumer behaviour studies supposedly provide new directions from the unsatisfactory aggregate model of central place theory. But reference to central place will reveal that here again the problem of scale is fundamental (see above, pp. 415–16) and that the dilemma presented earlier in this chapter in the paper by Moriarty is not properly posed or resolved.[115]

The priority of influences in residential decision making will be related to the scale at which the decision is being made. Unless that scale is very carefully specified then confusion will arise. At the crudest aggregate scale of the whole city, decisions will relate to the ease of journey to work and *cost*, for to suggest that price is not a highly pertinent factor is to fly in the face of reason. At this level, and appropriately, the various aggregate models are pitched, such as those derived by Wilson[116] from the Lowry formulation. At a somewhat larger scale the constraints of workplace and of crude cost will be set aside and general neighbourhood characteristics might well become pertinent as 'residential neighbourhoods', sieved out at the first scale of the search, are compared. Finally, at the largest scale the qualities of the house

[114] J. Connell (1973): Social networks in urban society; in B. D. Clark and M. B. Gleave, editor (1973).
[115] See page 279.
[116] A. G. Wilson (1973): *Urban and regional models in geography and planning* (London).

itself become paramount. It is certainly not easy to disaggregate into a logical system the various scales of decision for this presupposes that individuals structure complex decisions rather than act on impulse or without logic. The argument here presented assumes an unreal hierarchical ordering in decision.

Perhaps the most interesting point is to relate the standard dimensions of factorial ecologies to the stressors in the location decision model. The family cycle is certainly one of the major precipitators of household moves: marriage, the production of children and the schooling of children are obvious stressors. Socio-economic status is a complex notion but it certainly subsumes the household's own view of its social standing, which it might wish its house to display, and also the money it can deploy to externalize that view in bricks and mortar or stone. Finally ethnicity can be related broadly to the notion of territoriality which might define those parts of the city acceptable to the household. To equate territoriality with action space is perhaps open to criticism but the basic notions are not far apart. Thus the interaction study of Detroit presented earlier (page 277) as one of an aggregated scale of study is not as far apart as is sometimes suggested from behavioural studies at the micro-scale.

Future progress seems to lie in the attempts to specify scale in order to analyze the way in which the pay-offs between scales are operated. But like studies in consumer behaviour the ultimate reduction of this approach is to the individual level where the psychologist should be most competent. Even the individual has to be specified, for many studies refer to 'his' decision, but it is the household which moves and which married partner predominates in the process is relevant. This creates a field of study a good deal removed from the conventional geographic basis of pattern analysis.[117]

7 Social areas and social relevance

There is a danger that academic discussion of statistical niceties, or an increasingly complex review of the locational selection processes of those who can afford to choose, can become somewhat remote from the city in reality. The direct relevance of these ecological studies, however, can be found in the growing field of the study of the indicators of deprivation. There is the initial problem of the extent to which deprivation can be considered in areal and ecological terms and as a problem in a complex or multiple situation rather than as a series of discrete situations. If this is set aside it can be argued that, if parts of or areas within the city are underprivileged or relatively deprived, then identification can be derived from the

---

[117] This chapter has made no attempt to review those studies which have attempted to simulate residential growth of cities. The more important are: R. Main, Gunnar Olsson and O. Warneryd (1966): Approaches to simulations of urban growth. *Geogr. Annlr.* **48B**, 9–22. E. J. Kaiser and S. F. Weiss (1968): Some components of a linked model for the residential development decision process. *Proc. Assoc. Am. Geogr.* **1**, 75–9. This is a convenient source which includes reference to work on a similar theme published elsewhere by the two authors. B. Malisz (1969): Implications for threshold theory for urban and regional planning. *J. Tn. Plann. Inst.* **55**, 108–10. Threshold theory is somewhat different in approach but has the same end in view.

social area studies which this chapter has reviewed. At the same time the dimensions of social malaise will be revealed, whether these are related to physical housing conditions and the incidence of disease, economic disadvantage through employment situations, or to delinquency, crime and the problems of deviant behaviour.

This short section cannot hope to consider the growing range of literature in relation to delinquency or criminal areas[118] and the social indicators of deprivation.[119] Nevertheless the identification and characterization of areas is a basic geographical concern and the techniques have been developed through work in social area analysis and factorial ecology. A good example of this is the work of Giggs who has attempted to identify socially disorganized areas in Barry,[120] and to analyze the spatial patterning of schizophrenics in Nottingham.[121]

This theme is taken up in chapter 15.

Notes on further reading

There is not a great deal of material which deals in a geographical context with the physical character of residential areas. A general volume of use is

Giedion, S. (1959): *Space, time and architecture*, third edition (Cambridge, Mass.)

Smailes's early contribution is still of value:

Smailes, A. E. (1955): Some reflections on the geographical description and analysis of townscapes. *Trans. Inst. Brit. Geogrs.*, **21,** 104.

while the volume by Johns also noted in chapter 7 is relevant:

Johns, E. (1965): *British townscapes* (see footnote 9).

The main references to residential patterns are included in the footnotes but the following recent works should be consulted (they all contain bibliographies):

Evans, A. W. (1973): *The economics of residential location* (London).

Johnston, R. J. (1971): *Urban residential patterns* (London).

Herbert, D. (1972): *Urban geography: a social perspective* (see footnote 99).

Muth, R. F. (1969): *Cities and housing. The spatial pattern of urban residential land use.* (Chicago).

[118] For one of the earliest British works see T. Morris (1957): *The criminal area: a study in social ecology* (London); but the use of the term 'delinquency area' is much earlier and derives from the work of the Chicago ecologists, see C. R. Shaw (1929): *Delinquency areas: a study of the geographic distribution of school truants, juvenile delinquents and adult offenders in Chicago* (Chicago).

[119] D. Donnison (1974): Policies for priority areas. *Journal of Social Policy* 3, 127–35. A general volume is: R. E. Pahl (1970): *Whose city?* (London).

[120] J. A. Giggs (1970): Socially disorganized areas in Barry: a multivariate analysis; chapter 6 in H. Carter and W. K. D. Davies, editors (1970): *Urban essays: studies in the geography of Wales* (London).

[121] J. A. Giggs (1973): The distribution of schizophrenics in Nottingham. *Trans. Inst. Brit. Geogrs* 59, 55–76.

288   The residential areas of the city

Robson, B. T. (1969): *Urban analysis. A study of city structure with special reference to Sunderland* (see footnote 34).

Timms, D. W. G. (1971): *The urban mosaic. Towards a theory of residen tial segregation* (see footnote 82).

Two resource papers of the Association of American Geographers provide useful summary references:

Mayer, H. M. (1969): The spatial expression of urban growth. *Resource Paper* 7.

Rose, H. M. (1969): Social processes in the city: race and urban residential choice. *Resource Paper* 6.

The working papers of the Centre for Environmental Studies, London, are also useful reading including

Martin, D. B. (1969): The housing market. *CES-WP* 28.

Wilson, A. G. (1968): Development of some elementary residential location models. *CES-WP* 22.

In relation to residential choice a work still frequently quoted is

Rossi, P. H. (1955): *Why families move* (see footnote 54).

Also worthy of consultation are

Butler, E. W., *et alia* (1969): Moving behavior and residential choice: a national survey. *Nat. Co-op. Highway Res. Progr. Report*, 81. (Washington D.C.)

Lansing, J. B. and Bath, N. (1964): *Residential location and urban mobility: a multivariate analysis* (Ann Arbor, Mich.).

Pickvance, C. G. (1973): Life cycle, housing tenure and intra-urban residential mobility: a causal model. *Sociological Review*, 21(2), 279–297.

Taafe, E. J., Garner, B. J. and Yeates, M. H. (1963): *The peripheral journey to work: a geographic consideration* (Evanston, Illinois).

Vance, J. E., Jr. (1966): Housing the worker: the employment linkage as a force in urban structure. *Econ. Geog.* 42, 294–325.

Vance, J. E. Jr. (1967): Housing the worker: determinative and contingent ties in nineteenth century Birmingham. *Econ. Geog.* 43, 95–127.

Wolpert, J. (1965): Behavioural aspects of the decision to migrate. *Papers Reg. Sci. Assoc.* 15, 159–69.

Wolpert, J. (1966): Migration as an adjustment to environmental stress. *J. Soc. Issues* 22, 92–102.

Social area analysis has now built up an extensive literature. The most useful introductions are in the books by Robson and Timms cited above and also:

Berry, B. J. L. and Kasarda, J. D. (1977): *Contemporary urban ecology* (New York).

Herbert, D. T. and Johnston, R. J. eds. (1976): *Social areas in cities.* Two vols., vol. 1, *Spatial processes and form*; vol. 2, *Spatial perspectives on problems and policies* (London).

Herbert, D. T. and Johnston, R. J. eds. (1978): *Social areas in cities. Pro cesses, patterns and problems* (London) This is a shorter, soft-covered version of the two volumes above.

Robson, B. T. (1975): *Urban social areas* (Oxford).

A complete issue of *Economic Geography* was devoted to urban ecology and this is an essential element in the literature:

Berry, B. J. L., editor (1971): Comparative factorial ecology. *Econ. Geog.* **47** (2 Supplement), 209–367.

See also for alternative solutions and higher order factors:

Davies, W. K. D. (1978): Alternative factorial solutions and urban social structure: a data analysis exploration of Calgary. Canadian Geog. **22,** 273–297.

Giggs, J. A. and Mather, P. M. (1975): Factorial ecology and factor invariance: an investigation. *Econ. Geog.* **51,** 366–2.

An introduction to the study in the context of human ecology appears in

Theodorson, G. A. (1961): *Studies in human ecology*, 226–53 (New York).

In relation to the social indicators and the relevance issue, three good introductory items, each with bibliographies, are:

Knox, P. L. (1975): *Social well-being: a spatial perspective* (Oxford).

Smith, D. M. (1973): *The geography of social well-being in the United States* (New York).

Smith, D. M. (1974): Crime rates as territorial social indicators: the case of the United States. *Dept. of Geog. Queen Mary College, Univ. of London. Occasional Papers* 1.

Further material on welfare issues is included in Chapter 15.

The social areas of cities in developing countries are considered further in Chapter 16.

For the most convenient source for material on social areas in socialist countries see:

French, R. A. and Hamilton, F. E. I. eds. (1979): *The socialist city: spatial structure and urban policy* (Chichester and New York), especially Chapter 14:

Weclawowicz, G. The structure of socio-economic space in Warsaw in 1931 and 1970: a study in factorial ecology, pp. 387–424.

Studies of cities in the western world continue to be published; a good example is:

Houriham, K. (1978): Social areas in Dublin. *Econ. and Soc. Review,* **9**(4), 301–318.

While a review of twelve U.S.A. metropoles can be found in:

Rees, P. H. (1979): *Residential patterns in American cities.* Univ. of Chicago, Dept. of Geog., Research Paper No 189.

A consideration of South African cities is available in:

Hart, T. (1978): Factorial ecology and the South African city: some problems and prospects. *South African Geographer,* **6**(2), 123–130.

11

The Residential Areas of the City: the Housing Market and Institutional Influences

A critical and unconsidered assumption has been made in regard to all the material considered in the last chapter. That assumption is that distinctive social and residential areas are the consequence of choice, or in more general terms, of demand. Because people want properties of certain types, located in particular areas, then the market responds by providing for those demands. The assumption, it is true, has been hedged around with limitations, but they have appeared as asides rather than direct statements. If socio-economic status, or the ability to pay, is a fundamental control of residential segregation, then only those who deploy the greatest resources will be able to choose freely, and very few of those without some limitations. At the lower end of the scale it has already been noted that municipal or public housing can greatly modify the patterns implied in the standard models of urban structure. But the location of this housing is in no way the free choice of the residents, nor is the acquisition of an individual house, which is the consequence of an allocation process. Again, in dealing with disaggregated residential choice, it was indicated that although many households would find themselves subject to 'stresses' no action could be taken in the form of search for a different house or location because of the problems of cost — such households remained where they were 'under stress'.

All this implies that the basic creators of urban residential patterns are not those demanding, for income limits 'free' choice, but those supplying. There obviously is a demand but it is only met insofar as the supplier can see a potential profit. The minimal returns to building cheap housing mean that a minimal quantity is built. The form of the city is, therefore, a product of the combined interests of the developer and the builder operating within a nexus of institutional stimuli and constraints. Such a simple reversal of the earlier approach is too elementary a reaction, but it does carry the implication than in order to understand the aggregate pattern of residential areas which factorial ecologies only describe, the geographer must turn aside to consider the housing market. Patterns are insufficient, processes must be pursued. Residential location decisions are not free and unconstrained, even assuming income variation, for they are made in relation to an existing stock of buildings and a complex market situation. Figure 9–14 (p. 230) presented Rannells's three way screening of city centre locations[1]; it can be adapted to meet the residential sector. 'Accessibility' is significant, in this

[1] See page 230.

case to goods and services and also to facilities such as golf courses or schools. 'Linkages' are important to friends and social peers and to work. The third element is 'Availability' in terms both of space and location, but it is the availability of a given stock, rarely of an open choice. Indeed, in the allocation of a municipal house availability becomes the dominant, perhaps the sole, control.

To some extent most of the argument in this book has assumed a degree of universality derived from the conventional freedom of western democracies where price is the arbiter and where, in consequence, a similar suite of locational forces will operate. From the working out of these forces over standardized space, generalizations can be established. However, as one moves into the housing market, then intervention by government becomes more apparent and in such a context it becomes difficult to sustain generality. Accordingly the consideration in this chapter will be largely, though not exclusively, concerned with Britain. But Britain is merely being used as an example of how the supply side imposes on distribution patterns; the purpose is still not to describe a unique situation.

The total housing stock in Britain in 1976 was 18·1 millions.[2] It can be considered from a number of points of view. 'Fitness', for example, would be one criterion. From the viewpoint of housing provision, however, the critical division is by tenure for that identifies the providers of accommodation. Figure 11−1 indicates the categories of housing tenure in England and Wales at three dates and from it two features can be noted.

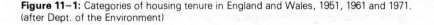

Owner−Occupied

Private rented

Public sector (local authority, new town, and housing association)

Figure 11−1: Categories of housing tenure in England and Wales, 1951, 1961 and 1971. (after Dept. of the Environment)

[2] Department of the Environment (1977): *Housing policy. A consultative document* (London), 10.

The first is that two types of tenure—owner-occupier and public sector (mainly though not exclusively municipal housing)—dominate and together account for 85 per cent of the total stock. The second feature is that this has come about mainly as the result of a large and rapid decline in the privately rented sector for over the quarter century from 1951 to 1976 the proportion of such accommodation has declined from 52 to 15 per cent.[3]

A more extreme condition can be demonstrated by going further back in time. Thus, in Leicester in 1914 only 5 per cent was owner occupied and 95 per cent was rented whereas by 1971 private renting had fallen to but 15 per cent, owner occupancy had risen to 50 per cent and council renting had reached 28 per cent.[4] There have been two causes of this decline. The first was the rapid increase of municipal housing and the second the active decline of rented private property particularly after the Rent Acts of 1965 and 1974. These are reciprocal elements in the changing pattern. Over the last decade the renting of property by private landlords, especially at the bottom end of the market, has become much less attractive, largely due to the Rents Acts which have controlled rents, laid down minimum standards and, above all, given security of tenure to the tenant. Britain has thus moved from an extreme where exploitation of tenants was widespread to one where renting is so constrained as to be hardly worthwhile and where the supply has been greatly diminished.

If, at this stage, the now small private rented sector is ignored, then the supply side can be considered under the two dominant tenures of municipal or council housing and owner-occupied housing. But there are two aspects common to both forms of provision. The first is the actual construction of new houses and the second is the obtaining by, or the allocation of the houses to, individual families. These have to be considered separately in relation to each tenurial type.

Before this consideration is undertaken, however, there are three preliminary issues which need to be cleared:

1   Housing as a political issue
2   The variety of 'markets' relating to housing
3   The notion of 'housing classes'.

1 Housing as a political issue

It is now widely urged that urbanism cannot be considered apart from political systems. This is at once true and a truism. However, issues relating to housing provision have such an overt political context that it is necessary to set these out. The range of views can be indicated under four groupings.

a   The far left. Housing should, like education and health, be a social service provided wholly by the state and in which no advantage should

---

[3] Dept. of the Environment (1977), 14.
[4] B. T. Robson (1975): *Urban social areas* (Oxford), 43. Robson is quoting from, R. M. Pritchard (1972): *Intra-urban migration in Leicester, 1860–1965* (1972): Unpub. Ph.D. thesis (Univ. of Cambridge).

accrue to accumulated wealth. Just as everyone should be educated in a
state system with no private/public schools, and that no private
medicine should be accessible outside a public health service, so, too,
there should be no private housing. All property should be state (or
municipally) owned, state built and state allocated. Allocation would
be according to need, a concept difficult to define but related to such
measures as family size and place of work. Since housing is regarded as a
state service there would be no rents or rates, these being covered by that
part of the gross national product appropriated by the state. Only by
these procedures can social justice be guaranteed; but at the price of
state control.

b   *The moderate left.* Housing is again regarded as a social service like
health care and education. But the attitude to private provision of such
services is ambivalent and reaches a greater degree of tolerance in relation to housing where owner occupation is considered permissible. This
is usually justified by the argument that owner-occupiers acquire
property for use rather than for accumulation in the Marxist sense and,
therefore, have more in common with tenants than with landowners
and exploiters of property. 'While ownership of housing may involve an
accumulative potential, it does not constitute ownership of a productive
resource, and thus does not form the basis for class formations of any
kind. Landowners, developers, and others involved in the supply of
housing have a monopoly over productive capital in the city which is not
in any way shared with those who buy their own houses. Thus in terms of
Marxist political economy, owner occupiers are not a distinctive class
since although they accumulate wealth, they do so through consumption rather than production, their property does not reproduce itself,
and their "profit" (if such it is) does not represent the extraction of surplus value'[5]. Private profits from renting accommodation are clearly of
a different nature. The state must, therefore, be the active, preferably
the sole, provider of properties for rent. The rents charged by the state
should, because housing is a service, be nominal rather than economic,
rather like the charge for medicines in a health service. There should be
no means test so that any subsidy is based on the house not on the individual or family.

c   *The far right.* Housing is a commodity like any other good and should
be bought and sold on the open market through the bidding process and
without any state intervention. The individual provides his own
housing, as health care and education, and has the choice of how much
of his disposable income is allocated to it as against other desired goods
and services. The ultimate goal is the exact opposite of the extreme left.
A rising standard of living would enable everyone, in theory, to make a
successful bid for some property and so the archetypal 'property owning
democracy' would be achieved. In the meantime a Darwinian 'law of

[5] P. R. Saunders (1977): *Housing tenure and class interests.* University of Sussex, Urban and
Regional Studies. Working paper 6.
It should be added that Saunders is not agreeing with this viewpoint but setting it out.

the jungle' operates where the wealthy and successful become the owners of the most expensive property and housing filters down the social hierarchy. The poorest people, and the worst housing, drop out at the bottom. However, the rich can obtain profit by renting to poorest sections of the population and so accommodation is provided for all. Choice is maximized, although only for those who have the money to ensure it, for it becomes zero for the destitute. Only by these procedures, it is argued, can individual freedom be assured, but at the price of inequality.

d   *The moderate right.* Housing is essential for all, like education and health care, but the amount which any individual wishes to consume is related to his own decisions. However, there must be a basic provision below which no one falls. This is best achieved in a mixed economy where the most desirable state is to be an independent owner-occupier; where this is not possible (or desired), rented accommodation is made available by both private and public landlords. Since the form of tenure and the sums spent constitute a choice in the family resource allocation, rents cannot be subsidized and a full economic rent must be charged. In order to ensure the basic provision, however, subsidies or rebates on rents and rates (taxes) are paid to individuals or families who can show that they have not the means to meet these charges. Subsidies go to means tested people, not to housing as such, and the state provides a 'safety-net' to ensure minimum standards are met for all families.

Each political group will, no doubt, feel that its views have been grossly oversimplified or misrepresented in the foregoing section. An attempt has been made, however, to assume that each group has laudable ends and to indicate the fact that different means are considered essential to achieve these ends.

2 The variety of markets in housing

The existence of housing markets presupposes a non-socialist economy, for if all housing is state owned no markets exist and the critical process is that of allocation. This will be discussed later (see p. 298). Given the mixed economy of the United Kingdom, however, the varieties of tenure and the demand for finance will generate a number of associated markets. These have been set out in simple diagram form by Susan Charles and this is reproduced in figure 11−2.

There is no point in describing the diagram which is self-explanatory but it does carry implications for the geographer seeking process explanation, for, however briefly, some discussion of these markets becomes necessary. As with the political issue, this will be introduced where relevant in the succeeding sections.

3 The notion of housing classes

Given the variety of political attitudes and the complexity of the housing

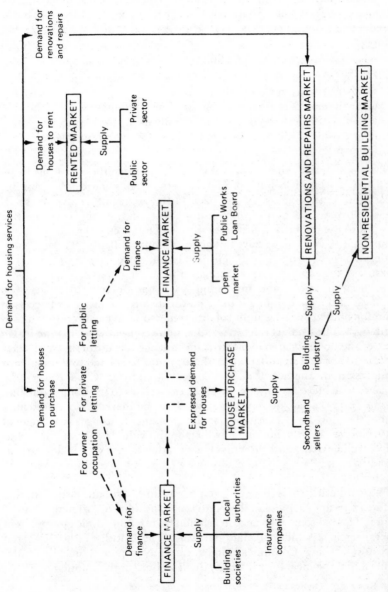

Figure 11–2: The housing markets (*after S. Charles*)

markets, it has been suggested that the only successful way to approach the problem in hand is to identify the varying degrees of 'strength' with which people can participate in the housing market. The most widely quoted attempt to suggest such groups has been that of Rex and Moore who proposed a set of 'housing classes'[6]. These are, arranged in order of strength to compete:

1   The outright owners of large houses in desirable areas.
2   Mortgage payers who 'own' whole houses in desirable areas.
3   Council tenants in Council built houses.
4   Council tenants in slum housing awaiting demolition.
5   Tenants of private house-owners, usually in the inner ring.
6   House-owners who must take lodgers to meet loan repayments.
7   Lodgers in rooms.

The point of immediate geographical interest is that these housing classes are explicitly given locational characteristics. Thus the words 'desirable areas' and 'inner ring' carry one back to the aggregate analysis of social areas, whereas the notion of housing classes carries the consideration forward to the underlying processes with which this chapter is concerned.

Rex and Moore's views have not gone without challenge. Three types of criticism have been developed[7]. The first is that current tenurial status is no measure of the capacity to gain access to the housing market and it is therefore both superficial and misleading as a basis of classification. 'The emphasis of the analysis ought to be on the means and criteria of access to desirable housing and the ability of different people to negotiate the rules of eligibility'[8]. The second criticism is rather more conceptual than practical in nature, and not unrelated to the first. It challenges the use of the word 'class' and maintains that in no sense can these groups be related to the standard connotation of the word in sociological literature. 'Class power — the capacity to achieve favourable life chances — relates to the ability to realize income from the sale of goods or services on the market. Housing tenure cannot therefore form a basis for classification since housing is an element of consumption, and the housing to which an individual achieves access thus *reflects* rather than *constitutes* his class situation'[9]. This view is close to that already set out relating to the view of private housing taken by the moderate left (page 293).

The third criticism is that the grouping assumes, without justification, a uniform system of values in relation to the desirability of different forms of tenure. This has some relevance in relation to different ethnic groups but in general seems a somewhat marginal issue. The British Market Research Bureau's Housing Consumer Survey certainly reported unequivocally, 'ownership is the ideal for a majority in *all* sections of the community'[10].

[6] J. Rex and R. Moore (1967): *Race, community and conflict* (London), 274–5.
[7] This critique is based on that by P. R. Saunders (1977), 1–5.
[8] R. Haddon (1970): A minority in a Welfare State society. *New Atlantis*, 2, 129.
[9] P. R. Saunders (1977), 4.
[10] National Economical Development Office (1977): *BMRB housing consumer survey. A survey of attitudes towards current and alternative housing policies* (London), 5.

All these are relevant comments. In relation to the first two, Pahl's suggestion that means of access should be stressed rather than current tenurial status has much to commend it[11]. His classification is:

1   Large property owners and capitalist speculators.
2   Smaller landlords.
3   a   Owners of capital sufficient to own their own houses and owning.
    b   Owners of capital sufficient to own their own houses and renting.
4   Those who must rent.

But although this avoids many of the above criticisms of Rex and Moore's scheme it is essentially impractical, for how are those who 'must rent' to be identified and distinguished from those who 'prefer to rent'?[12].

Before the foregoing diversion to consider political attitudes to housing, the varied markets relating to housing and the notion of housing classes, a point had been reached where a division was accepted into the two major tenancy groups of owner-occupiers and council tenants. With the above considerations as background the basic theme of the housing market can be taken up again under the headings of the tenancy divisions.

4 Municipal council housing

(*i*) *The building of houses*. The British government's consultative document on housing policy set out the 1977 situation. 'Public sector authorities provide houses for roughly a third of all households in England and Wales. Their stock has grown from 2·2 million houses in 1951 to 5·5 million 1976. In this period, 3·2 million new houses have been completed by local authorities, 0·2 million by new towns and 0·5 million by housing associations'[13]. This form of provision has a long history extending back to the legislation of the nineteenth century and the Housing of the Working Classes Acts. 'Local authorities had been given powers to build working class houses by Lord Shaftsbury's Act of 1851, but the amount of new building for which they were responsible was quite insignificant . . . Municipal building remained unimportant because it was regarded as undesirable and unnecessary'[14]. It was not until 1949 that the words 'working classes' were dropped and subsequent measures became simply 'Housing Acts'. There seems little purpose here in discussing the not irrelevant but complex problem of the capacity of the building industry, but rather it is more useful to concentrate on the critical provision of finance, which is at the heart of the municipal housing issue.

Each local government authority operates a statutory Housing Revenue Account (HRA) relating to the accommodation it rents. In 1975/6 the

---

11 R. E. Pahl (1975): *Whose City? And further essays on urban society* (London), 245.
12 A. Murie, P. Niner and C. Watson (1976): *Housing policy and the housing system* (London), 78–79.
13 Dept. of the Environment (1977), 75.
14 W. Ashworth (1954): *The genesis of modern British town planning* (London), 91–2.

proportion of the HRA costs met by rents was 45 per cent[15], so that in order to operate the system the remainder, which involves both operating costs and the financing of new building, has to be obtained from elsewhere. There are three sources. The first is the local rates (taxes) which make an essential but limited contribution. In 1975−6 the Rate Fund accounted for but 244 million pounds of a total investment in the public sector of 2798 million. The second source is capital borrowed on the open market at current rates, and the third is government subsidy.

In 1975−6 general subsidy accounted for 966 million and rent rebates added a further 292 million. It is the nature of this subsidy which has become a political issue. In 1967 the then Labour Government, in an attempt to meet electoral promises in relation of the number of houses to be built, introduced a system by which local authorities were able to borrow on the open market at going rates of interest but government subsidy maintained that interest rate for the authority at a standard 4 per cent. The conditions allowed central government control of standards but established an open financial commitment which inevitably caused problems. The response of the succeeding Conservative Government in 1972 was the Housing Finance Act which attempted to shut off the open commitment and introduced the controversial notion of 'fair rents'. Although there were provisions made for phasing, the basic intention was to introduce economic rents which covered the costs of building and expenditure on maintenance, and ensured a balanced HRA. In order to cushion the less well off, a rent rebate scheme was introduced by which those who could show need were given rebates on the economic or fair rents paid. In 1975 the Labour Government, which came into power in 1974, repealed the 1972 Act and substituted the Housing Rents and Subsidies Act, although it is only intended as an interim measure. By this the notion of a fair or economic rent was abolished and subsidies restored (for example 66 per cent of the annual loan charges on approved capital works) though the rent rebate principle was retained.

The legislation is far more complex than this simplified summary, but essentially it revolves around the political issues set out earlier. Public sector housing can either be looked upon as an economic venture where the HRA is balanced, but with rebates to help the less well off, or as a social service where the bulk of the HRA will come from subsidy derived from taxation, local and national. The main point to the urban geographer is that from these situations come the finances available to build houses and hence the extent and, indeed, the nature of municipal estates.

(*ii*) *The allocation of houses.* The allocation of public housing is in itself a matter of considerable interest since it is indicative of the system which might operate in a non-market, non-capitalist situation. There are two stages in the process. The first is the sieving out of the eligible and the ordering of families into degrees of priority. Eligibility might not seem to

---

[15] These data and those in the following account are taken from the DoE publication *Housing Policy.*

apply where there is only a state source of housing but even under such circumstances it could have a regional or locational reference. That is, in a totalitarian situation migration of population is contained and controlled by assigning eligibility for housing in a regional context. Within contemporary Britain there is no uniform system of establishing eligibility and priority and each local housing authority operates its own system.

Two bases can be identified. The first, which is more concerned with eligibility and is the most controversial, is length of residence or of working in the area. Because eligibility through a residential qualification has resulted in immigrant homelessness it has become an issue of public concern. The result has been a declaration against it by Government, at least in terms of eligibility if not explicitly in terms of priority.[16] To some extent this is a response to situations easily exploited by the media; the disadvantages and the injustices of abandoning qualification by residence are hidden and less exploitable. The second basis is need, and a wide variety of criteria is used in its establishment. Included are measures such as size of family; separation of family; accommodation available, especially in number of bedrooms related to the sex of children; disability; ill health; the sharing of facilities such as a kitchen or a bathroom. Each authority can score those families on its housing list by such criteria and allocate accordingly.

Ultimately all schemes give rise to ill-feeling for none can be totally objective, even if need could be defined. Moreover, incompatible criteria have to be played off against each other, such as length of residence against need. At best, a whole complex of influences are brought to bear, personal, social and political, at the worst, powers over people are placed in the hands of gatekeepers, that is those who within the bureaucratic system control access to housing. The powers of such gatekeepers are every bit as alarming, perhaps more alarming because they are absolute, as the exploitive ability of capitalist landlords. The role of the manager or gatekeeper in urban society although central to this whole theme, cannot be considered at length in this brief chapter. Pahl's essay, *'Urban managerialism, reconsidered'*, is an excellent elaboration.[17]

In summary, there are three problems related to eligibility and priority. The first is the difficult assessment of the significance of residence in a geographically mobile society. The second relates to problems engendered by the requirement to show need, for it offers no encouragement to improve existing conditions; improvement of conditions lowers need and reduces priority. The third is the power given to gatekeepers. However idealized a society, there are unlikely to be all the houses required, of the appropriate type, in the right location and as long as there is a shortage these problems will remain.

The second stage in the allocation process is that of matching individual families with particular houses. This might seem to be an actuarial problem in relating houses built to family sizes, and a managerial problem in detail.

[16] Dept. of the Environment (1977), 79—80. Note also the Housing (Homeless Persons Act) Act of 1977.
[17] R. Pahl (1975), 265—287.

A characteristic difficulty, arises, however, in relation to life cycle changes. A large house allocated at the peak period of family formation and child rearing becomes inappropriate at a later stage after child launching when an elderly couple or a single person is left. But the direction of families in parallel with the free market pattern of life cycle movements is socially unacceptable. People cannot, in a reasonably free and caring society, be moved around like so many pieces on a chequer board.

A much more contentious procedure arises, however, where the managers attempt to concentrate problem families on one estate. This practice is both condemned and denied, but Gray in a study of Hull has been able to show that it is operated.[18] He established that all new tenants were in 1972 interviewed by a 'housing investigator' who not only recorded standard details but also assessed households in general terms as 'good' or 'bad' tenants. An accompanying table (Table 11.1) shows the results.

table 11–1: Status of Tenant and Type of Property, Hull, 1972.
(After Gray)

		Local Authority Grading of Tenants		
		Poor/Fair	Fair/Good	Very Good/Excellent
Percentage of household	1919-44	62·5	13·9	10·7
Occupying dwelling	1945-65	29·2	38·0	28·6
By age of	Post 1965 used	8·3	23·4	17·9
Dwelling	New	0·0	24·8	42·9

Gray's summary of these results is significant. 'In terms of the class structure of residential areas, the effects of local authority policies both in Hull and elsewhere is to accentuate the social and spatial contrasts between classes: the worst-off groups in the city are increasingly segregated in the poorest council estates and the contracting private-rented sector, whilst the most privileged (and generally higher class) council tenants tend to be concentrated in the new high-status estates elsewhere in the city'.[19] Here, then, is a detailed illustration of the process by which socially contrasted city areas are created, not by demand in the market but by the manipulation of supply and allocation by managerial decisions. Whether this is a 'proper' procedure is another matter and a subjective one. It can be argued that it gives an element of providing compatible neighbours which those in the owner-occupied sector can and do value highly in their purchasing strategy.

5 Owner-occupied housing

(*i*) *The building of houses.* A complex of interests is involved in the provision of houses for sale and it is useful to follow the order set out by Robson who considers in turn the land owner, the developer and the planner.[20] To

[18] F. Gray (1976): Selection and allocation in council housing. *Trans. Inst. Brit. Geogrs.* New Series 1(1), 34–46.
[19] F. Gray (1976), 44.
[20] B. T. Robson (1975), 53–58.

his three interest groups it is worth adding the builder. It is not, however, easy to keep these apart since they both overlap and clash in the business of building houses.

The land owner at one time held a predominant control over residential development and it is one of the standard exercises in historical urban geography to show how land ownership patterns, and the willingness or otherwise of owners to release land, were determinants in the nature of town extension[21] Such absolute control has, however, been whittled away during this century. Even some nineteenth century legislation modified the extreme laissez-faire situation and from the first Town Planning Act of 1909 constraints have been successfully built up. The 1947 Town and Country Planning Act marked a significant step, for the initiation of compulsory development plans and development control, together with powers of compulsory purchase, meant that influence on the internal structure and external extension of towns was placed more firmly in the hands of planning authorities.

Land-use was by this time effectively nationalized and state-controlled via local government representation. What remained was the critical issue of betterment. Once agricultural land is scheduled for residential development, or when such scheduling seems likely, its value vastly appreciates and the question arises as to whom this increased value should go. Again this is a political matter. The left maintains that it is the community which creates this increase which therefore should revert to the community; that is, that all land should change hands at current-use value. Beyond this is the view that all land should be nationalized in any case, or should come into public ownership at development. It would be thus expropriated at current-use values. The far right argues that it is a basic guarantee of freedom that the individual should hold property and should be free to sell it where and when he wishes for as much as the free market will offer. If an entrepreneur takes the risk and is enterprising enough to buy land and hold it in anticipation of development he should reap the reward of his risk taking and initiative.

In 1974 Britain moved substantially (though far from completely) to the left with the Community Land Act. In briefest summary, this gave local authorities the right to purchase land needed for 'relevant' development in the next ten years from 1976 at is undeveloped cost. In order to achieve this each authority has to set up Land Acquisition Management Schemes (LAMS). To cover the interim period of change, during which land could be sold privately, a Development Land Tax on profits at 66·6 per cent was levied on such transactions. Eventually all development land was to be acquired by the local authorities. Behind all this also lies the critical issue of the supply of land for residential building. Prior to the Act it certainly paid the large development companies to build up large land banks where both inflation and betterment on release for building provided rich profits.

After the general election of 1979 a Conservative government came to power and the leftward trend of the mid and late 1970's is being reversed.

---

[21] T. Slater (1976): Estate ownership and nineteenth century suburban development, in A. McWhitt ed. *Archaeology and history of Cirencestero* (Oxford), B. A. R. Reports 30, 145–157.

The Community Land Act has been repealed. To ensure an adequate supply of land, a public sector land register is being compiled in order to identify land which could be released for development. Thus the see-saw effect of party politics continues to exert a critical influence on the land market.

Already in considering the supply of building land both developer and planner have been introduced. The word 'developer' now has pejorative overtones. A developer's interest is profit and to achieve this the main aim is to upgrade use, that is to change land from a low revenue to a high revenue use.[22] This can be done by raising rents, intensifying use by such means as adding floors to an existing building, or by upgrading use, that is, for example, by replacing housing with offices.

It can be argued, therefore, that the developer has had three major influences on British cities. The first is that he has concentrated on the construction of large residential estates on greenfield sites at the city margins, thus strongly reinforcing if not creating suburbanization. This involves a simple and profitable process of upgrading land in agricultural use. The second is that having no interest in building low cost housing, especially on high value city centre land, he has been active in increasing returns by the construction of office blocks on decaying residential areas. An excellent example of this is given by Ambrose and Colenutt in their book *'The property machine'*.[23] A chapter is devoted to 'The Property Development System in Brighton' which considers in detail the redevelopment of the twenty-five acre Brighton Station site. The alternatives were either a new station, a hotel, conference facilities, a hypermarket, a vast car park, a telecommunications centre, a recreation centre, general offices and a small amount of housing, or restoration of the Victorian station and council housing. There is no room here to trace the details of this conflict but the situation neatly points the opposition between maximizing returns in either economic or social contexts—and there are justifications for both views.

The third influence is via that of the builder. The builder, like the developer and land-owner is in the market to make a profit and like anyone in such a situation responds to demand, not need. Moreover, 'the price of houses for sale is not determined by what they cost to build but by what buyers can afford. And what buyers can afford depends on levels of wages, credit and subsidies. But if wages rise, house prices rise. If government subsidy increases, house prices rise. If credit gets cheaper and easier to get, house prices rise. As soon as decent housing comes theoretically within reach of the poorest workers, house prices rise and takes (sic) it out of reach again'.[24] The undefined adjective 'decent' in the quotation makes the statement that much weaker but it does set out the injustices the market creates.

The planner, too, as has been indicated, operates as a major influence on residential character. In a situation where land-uses are designated by

[22] C.D.P. Information and Intelligence Unit (1976): *Profits against houses. An alternative guide to housing finance* (London), 9.
[23] P. Ambrose and B. Colenutt (1975): *The property machine* (London), 104–133.
[24] C.D.P. (1976), 11.

planning authorities, decisions can have critical effects on the value of land, either blighting it or raising it to a level which, without compulsory powers of purchase at current-use value, the local authority cannot meet. The planner, as bureaucrat, has to hold the ring between individual and community interest and so is usually the most easily accessible for condemnation. But the planner can only operate within the framework of national legislation and some indication of the nature of this has already been given.

(*ii*) *The obtaining of houses.* In terms of owner-occupation the fundamental control of who gets which house is the ability to pay and since few people have sufficient capital to buy outright then the control is access to loan finance, usually through a building society. It is estimated that between 80 per cent and 95 per cent of all advances for house purchases have come from the building societies[25], with small contributions from local authorities, insurance companies and banks. Building societies in Britain are non-profit making and also, unlike other financial institutions, they borrow short and lend long. Because of this, and the fact they depend on investment money, the societies maintain that they have an absolute duty to ensure security for their loans. This they do by using two restrictions on advances, the one related to the individual concerned, the other to the property. The personal restriction is a measure of credit worthiness. Most mortgages are limited to some 80–90 per cent of the purchase or valuation price, whichever is the smaller. The criteria employed are usually that monthly payments should not exceed weekly income or that the amount advanced should be not more than two to three times the annual income. Mortgages are usually for terms of 25 years and any building society therefore looks for stable career prospects and secure earnings.[26] A salary from a professional career which increases with age and experience is far more attractive than the wage of a manual worker in heavy industry which might peak with physical capability and then decline. The government publication "Housing Policy", concludes that 'there are probably a lot of people who want to become home owners, but whose needs do not quite fit into the conventional pattern of mortgage facilities and lending criteria applied across the building society counters'.[27]

The second restriction on mortgage relates to the property. Since this is the security on which the loan is made it has to be judged as a sound investment. Certain rules of thumb seem to be applied though there are no firm, fixed guide lines. The property should be characteristic of the district in which it is located; public transport should be reasonably available; the district should not be showing evidence of deterioration. In general, the more 'standard' the type of property the easier it is to obtain a mortgage. Thus in Britain the best regarded property is the three bedroom semi-detached house.[28]

[25] Dept. of the Environment (1977), 50.
[26] A. Murie *et al.* (1976), 163.
[27] Dept. of the Environment (1977), 51.
[28] A. Murie *et al.* (1976), 164–170.

Building societies dislike new, idiosyncratic styles of housing but it is their attitude to older property which gives rise to most criticism. Property which is old, in poor condition and in deteriorating areas does not offer good security and the building societies, therefore, refuse to advance loans.[29] Taken to its furthest extent this involves the controversial process of redlining, that is of identifying whole areas, usually of the deteriorated inner city, where mortgages are refused. Lambert in a study of Birmingham concluded that 'the building societies either deliberately steered clear of certain of the older areas . . . or exercized extreme caution, although they usually emphasized that there was no written policy which precluded all houses in those areas. However two or three managers did say that they had marked off areas on a map (in one case we were shown this) and rarely looked at any property falling within these boundaries'.[30] Where such red-lining had occurred it was often said to be done at the instigation of surveyors who it was argued knew the city well and all the trends and markets involved. After a review of the evidence Peter Williams writes, 'Although our conclusions must be tempered by the lack of any comprehensive analysis, there can be no doubt that red lining exists and that building societies, at least, believe themselves to be justified in this practice'.[31]

The real problem remains to produce mapped evidence. The authors of *'Profits against houses'* do include a map of Newcastle (figure 11 – 3) but it is not discussed in the text and no indication of the evidence upon which it was based is given.[32] Presumably, it is only an impression derived from experience rather than either a map actually used by one society or drawn from a meticulous examination of all mortgages offered in Newcastle over a set period. The immediate conclusion is that the building societies, through the mortgage system, exert a considerable influence upon city structure.

At this point it is useful to introduce parallel evidence from the United States. Owing to increasing concern with regard to declining residential areas the Home Mortgage Disclosure Act was passed in 1975. By this all depository institutions were required to disclose the number and value of all mortgage loans issued in all SMSA's. Such data are amenable to spatial analysis and they have been used by Dennis Dingemans in a study of redlining and mortgage lending in Sacramento. He contends that although his investigation 'does not enable him to determine the exact role of mortgage lenders as causal agents of neighbourhood change . . . it does contribute a basic understanding of the geography of mortgage lending in a relatively untroubled metropolitan area'.[33]

Dingemans's conclusions are that mortgages and home improvements are

[29] C. Lambert (1976): *Building Societies, surveyors and the older areas of Birmingham.* Centre of Urban and Regional Studies, Univ. of Birmingham. Working Paper No. 38, 30–35.
[30] C. Lambert (1976), 33–34.
[31] P. Williams (1978): Building societies and the inner city. *Trans. Inst. Brit. Geogrs.* New Series 3(1), 32.
[32] But see M. Boddy (1976): The structure of mortgage finance: building societies and the British social formation. *Trans. Inst. Brit. Geogrs.* New Series 1(1), 68.
[33] D. Dingemans (1979): Redlining and Mortgage lending in Sacramento. *Ann. Assoc. Amer. Geogrs.*, 69(2), 225–239.

Areas where the Building Societies refuse to lend

Housing Action Areas & General Improvement Areas

Council Estates

Mostly Non-Residential

Old city of Newcastle

Figure 11–3: The Redlined areas of Newcastle after Community Development Project's 'Profits against houses'. For a more detailed map see M. Boddy (1976) footnote 32, p. 304.

strongly associated with several of the traditional measures of the socio-economic status of neighbourhoods. He adds, 'many of the pioneering students of intra-urban mortgage lending patterns have found these patterns elsewhere and have been quick to reach the conclusion that lenders were redlining—discriminating against mortgage loan applications from certain areas regardless of their personal qualifications for the loan sought'. Properly, however, he contends that specific investigation of the processes and behaviours underlying these patterns is essential rather than the making of direct assumptions from aggregate data.

There is a further group which can operate to influence social areas within cities. These are the estate agents. The traditional role of the realtor in the U.S.A., for example, was either to preserve or tip, that is to change rapidly, the racial character of areas. This rather crude impact upon social space has to a great degree been modified by legislation against racial discrimination both in the U.S.A. and Britain. Even so the influence of the estate agent can still be significant for he is not a passive and neutral gatekeeper but brings both unconscious and conscious influences to bear. Palmer writing of the influence of realtors in the U.S.A. in the late 1960's identified three control techniques.[34] The first was the automatic matching of a customer to an area where no specific area is specified by the client. The second is by warnings of unhappiness, indications that a household will not fit in easily to an established ethos, whilst the third is the simple distortion of facts, for example describing a house as sold if the client seems inappropriate.

The general argument is that the agent feels a 'commitment' to residential areas and that a successful business is run by avoiding mismatches and mistakes. Even if such blatant management does not occur, it can be shown that estate agents cover only limited portions of the housing market and will recommend in relation to perceived social categories.[35] Peter Williams's summary of the influence is, 'thus through their role as advisers to landlords, building societies and property companies, as well as having personal control of all the different organizations, estate agents are in an important position with regard to the generation and manipulation of change as well as being crucial intermediaries in the process whereby households obtain accommodation'.[36] There is the danger, however, of assigning predetermined and, indeed, malevolent intentions to estate agents. They themselves are only operating within a social context, carrying out what the community around them wishes, otherwise they would soon go out of business. They have no brief to be agents of social change in directions perceived as 'good' or 'bad'. The notion of 'manipulation' and still further of 'generation' of change needs some qualification. It can be argued that the change derives from large scale social processes and the realtor is literally merely the 'agent'.

6 Three examples

This review of the impact of the supply side on the structuring of the city has, like many such studies of process, had some difficulty in firmly linking the matters considered to patterns on the ground. In order to demonstrate the link three specific topics can be considered.

(*i*) *The high rise block in public housing.* One of the distinctive features of nearly all large British cities during the 1960's and the early 1970's was the building of high-rise tower blocks to accommodate council tenants. The result has been a very distinctive contribution to the townscape as well as to the pattern of social areas. The construction of these blocks shows a very distinctive peaking towards the end of the 1960's and then a marked tailing

[34] R. Palmer (1955): *Realtors as social gatekeepers, a study in social control.* Unpub. Ph.D. thesis. Yale University.

[35] R. Palm (1976): Real estate agents and geographical information. *Geog. Review*, 66(3), 266–280 and (1976): The role of real estate agents as information mediators in two American cities. *Geografiska Annaler.* Ser. B. 58, 28–41.

[36] P, Williams (1976): *The role of financial institutions and estate agents in the private housing market: a general introduction.* Centre for Urban and Regional Studies, Univ. of Birmingham Working Paper No. 39, 61.

off in the 1970's. This is clearly illustrated in table 11−2.

Two points can be derived from the table. The first is the growth in the contribution of high-rise blocks to total accommodation provided, to reach a level of just under a quarter between 1964 and 1967. The second is that the percentage of total costs in each year is greater, that is high-rise development was a more expensive form of provision. This had been clearly demonstrated by 1959, the year before the data in table 11−2 began. P. A. Stone had indicated that the net construction costs per three bed-roomed dwelling with a standard floor space, were just under twice as much in a twelve storey block as in the traditional two floored house.[37] These special costs were met by additional subsidy from central government to the Local Authority. But the question must be put as to why this form of development occurred, for there was certainly no demand for it from the populations involved. For an explanation one has to turn to consider the influence of two of the controllers of supply.

table 11−2: Local Authority High Rise Construction: Tenders Approved 1960 to 1975

Year	Percentage of dwelling in 5 or more storeys of all Dwellings	
	By Numbers	By Cost
1960	11·91	17·27
1961	10·92	16·15
1962	13·35	19·43
1963	19·99	26·93
1964	29·08	28·30
1965	19·49	24·99
1966	21·81	27·25
1967	21·38	26·67
1968	15·78	19·84
1969	9·93	12·66
1970	6·80	8·65
1971	5·16	6·61
1972	2·80	3·76
1973	2·63	3·79
1974	1·58	2·37
1975	0·042	0·48

Source: C.D.P., *Profits against houses* p. 29.

The Local Authorities and their professional representatives, the planners, faced a major difficulty in the post-war period. On the one hand there was the need for a massive slum clearance and redevelopment programme, especially in relation to very high density working class housing dating back to the nineteenth century. On the other hand the urban sprawl which had characterized the inter war period had been the source of much criticism. Ian Nairn's book *'Outrage'* of 1955 was a characteristic blast, 'The city is to-day not so much a growing as a spreading thing, fanning out over the land surface in the shape of suburban sprawl . . . This thing of terror, which will get you sweating at night when you begin to realize its true proportions, we

[37] P. A. Stone (1959): The economics of housing and urban development. *Journal of the Royal Statistical Society*. Series A (General), 122 (4), 426−427.

have called . . . Subtopia. It consists of the universal suburbanization not merely of the country, or of the town, but of town-and-country—the whole land surface'.[38] Moreover, some of the most distinguished urban theorists urged the same point. The city, argued Le Corbusier, should be compact, lively and concentrated.[39] The way forward, therefore, seemed evident. High rise, high density development would solve critical problems. In a foreword to a Ministry planning bulletin of 1962 called 'Residential Areas: Higher Densities', the then Minister of Housing and Local Government wrote, 'over the next 20 years we are going to need at least six million more houses. This is formidable problem with two inescapable consequences; we need to allocate more land for housing and we need higher densities especially in pressure areas. We need not one or the other, but both—more land and higher densities'.[40] There seemed no reason why such a policy should not succeed. Some of the most expensive and exclusive of luxury accommodation was in high-rise apartments. In many European cities life in high density apartments was a commonplace, even a tradition, and caused no apparent problems.

The second influence involved was that of the big construction companies and their architects. The authors of 'Profits against houses' accuse them of having a clear interest. 'In the 1950's many big civil engineering firms wanted to move into council housing; they wanted to develop new technology and use mass production methods—to make a profit. High rise flats fitted the bill'.[41] The argument continues that a massive persuading programme, together with the corruption of local officials which has since come to light, enabled them to achieve their ends, including large public subsidies for this expensive form of provision which went directly to the builders. Having obtained their profits, and acquired an expertise, these firms moved out and on to the lucrative field of high-rise office block construction.

Much of the criticism of high-rise building is ex post facto in character. There is no doubt that at the time the tower block was seen as a solution to a range of problems and a means of keeping the city compact and lively. That it went disastrously wrong is now widely agreed, although the reasons are perhaps not quite as obvious and are worthy of a brief review.

The first reason put forward is that such accommodation is completely alien to the British tradition (apart from the tenements of Glasgow), and, therefore, greatly disliked by those allocated to it. That this is so is unchallengable. Surveys both by government and by other groups have revealed a consistent dislike of high-rise flatted dwellings. A review of an Opinion Research Centre report in 1967 began, 'One in six of the homes currently being built by local authorities in Britain are flats in tall blocks of ten stories (sic) and upwards, yet only one person in a hundred wants to live in a block

[38] I. Nairn (1955): *Outrage* (London), 365.
[39] Le Corbusier (1947): *Concerning town planning* (London).
[40] Ministry of Housing and Local Government (1962): *Residential Areas. Higher densities.* Planning Bulletin 2 (London), 3.
[41] C.D.P. (1976), 29.

that high'.[42] Mere dislike is, perhaps, too weak a reason to account for the disastrous physical decline of many of these blocks, but it significantly shows that the general pattern was determined by the supplier and not by demand which was overwhelmingly for detached or semi-detached houses (79 per cent in the Survey quoted and 71 per cent of a government survey of families living at high density).[43]

The explanation for the rapid deterioration of these high-rise blocks must, in part at least be an environmental one. But as Michelson has pointed out, it is necessary to make a distinction between the properties inherent in high-rise building and properties that appear connected to them insofar as the buildings are constructed in a particular way. 'A good number of the social implications of high-rise apartments are, in fact, implications of these buildings *as they are conventionally constructed*. It takes no great stretch of the imagination to contemplate buildings with total sound proofing, with cavernous living space, with service and recreational facilities near every suite, and so on. We may not expect such buildings under current economic conditions or under current methods of finance, but the limitations of the status quo are not necessarily limitations to high-rise buildings per se'.[44]

The two major problems which derive from high-rise living are related to density and access. High density generates noise in particular, but a whole range of other less easily identifiable conditions which are often said to be associated: physical ill-health, 'heightened aggression, family breakdown, inadequate child care and personal disorder'.[45] But this is the complex field of environmental psychology and little has been convincingly demonstrated. There are in Michelson's words, many frightening insinuations, but few firm conclusions.[46] More immediate is the second problem of access. There is the direct problem of playing space for children within the parents' direct view, but indirectly there is the problem of access via lifts, which are either inadequate or break down and remain out of order, and concrete walkways. The ill-lit corridors and balconies and the graffiti covered lifts become the ideal locations for petty crime, which soon escalates into major crimes of violence. Once this happens the whole situation degenerates into an uncontrollable sequence of vandalism and destruction until the block, with windows broken, doorways boarded up and every fitment broken and wall defaced, becomes uninhabitable for all but the criminal.

The classic case of a well intentioned project designed by a specifically commissioned architect which moved from inauguration in 1954 to demolition in 1974 is, in fact, not British but the Pruitt-Igoe complex in St. Louis, Missouri. Pruitt-Igoe consisted of 33 blocks each 11 storeys tall intended to

42 The Sunday Times (1967): Why so few can have the house they want. May 21, 2. A review of an Opinion Research Centre investigation for local authorities into national attitudes to housing problems.
43 Ministry of Housing and Local Government (1970): *Families living at high density*. Design Bulletin 21, 33.
44 W. Michelson (1977): *Environmental choice, human behaviour, and residential satisfaction* (New York), 43.
45 W. Michelson (1977), 47.
46 W. Michelson (1977), 49.

house 12,000 residents. It was conceived as a revolutionary project to free the blacks of St. Louis from 'the vicious circle of poor housing, unemployment, crime, disease and eternal poverty which had haunted them so long'. It was intended to be the best possible low-rent housing.[47] It was a utopian endeavour which utterly collapsed. The history of the debacle is too long to narrate here[48] but has been ascribed to the complete lack of provision of shops, nurseries, play areas, day care centres and general services. As one commentator recorded, 'The fact that so many people were crammed into so small a space, and that so many of the people came with problems far in excess of their ability to cope, added mercilessly to the dilemma'.[49]

This discussion can be taken a little further into the field of environmental psychology which has already been opened up. Oscar Newman in his book *'Defensible space'*[50] was much concerned with the sorts of minor crimes and senseless violence and vandalism which characterizes housing projects like Pruitt-Igoe. Newman starts from the isolation that characterizes high-rise living where access to neighbours 'across the garden fence' is not possible. This, he argues, leads to a withdrawal from community life and hence there is no consensus community control of anti-social behaviour. All space is public space and designed and made to look so. Nobody owns it, so nobody defends it. From this comes Newman's notion of defensible space, whereby such anonymous areas are fenced and attached and made subject to surveillance. In short a 'territory' is established which can be clearly identified and defended. 'Another feature of many low-rent housing projects . . . that exacerbates crime statistics is that they tend to be designed so that they stand out from the surrounding context by virtue of their starkness and lack of architectural embellishment'. It is almost as if they were being set up as a target for attack. The interiors, too, tend typically to be 'institutional' in character, with tiled walls, uncarpeted floors and 'vandal proof' fitments. The message is defiance, a physical challenge to those who do not wish to be contained to show that they are superior to their symbolic prison walls. Newman argues that 'such environments make the residents devalue themselves, lose their self-esteem and self respect and so create a vicious circle of damage and repair and greater damage'.[51] One, thus, returns to Pruitt-Igoe where a situation was reached where, because of the danger of attack, workmen were unable to make any repairs and by 1968 copper sheeting was being torn off roofs. The result was flooding and in the winter of 1971 hundreds of flats were inches deep in ice.

This brief foray into the field of environmental psychology has been made to demonstrate the direction in which process studies lead. From aggregate social areas as the consequence of demand, consideration shifted to the need

---

[47] An excellent account appeared in *The Guardian*, May 15, 1974, 16. S. Winchester (1974): They've come a long way in St. Louis. The information that follows comes from this source. See also L. Rainwater (1970): Beyond ghetto walls: black family life in a federal slum (Chicago).

[48] S. Winchester (1974), see above footnote 47.

[49] S. Winchester (1974), 16.

[50] O. Newman (1972): *Defensible space* (New York).

[51] C. Mercer (1975): *Living in cities. Psychology and the urban environment* (London), 93.

to consider supply. The details of supply of municipal housing led, in turn, to a review of the characteristics of one type of provision and some of the social and physical responses which followed. A position has now been reached where at least the groundwork has been established for a study of the process by which such an aggregate social areas as 'The Piggeries' in Liverpool can be undertaken. But, as in behavioural studies of individual choice, a substantial departure has been made from conventional geographical analyses of spatial patterns into studies of the impact of the built environment on social and community character.

Here, too, the assessment of the failure of high-rise accommodation will be related to political viewpoints. Those to the left, starting from the romantic egalitarian assumption that all people are alike and inherently good, will ascribe these disasters to the economic system and the social and physical environment it necessarily generates. Those to the right, starting from the realistic assumption that all people are not alike and are inherently selfish and competitive and that there is only varied redemption from something approaching original sin, will relate the degeneration of such buildings to the fact that they become the social sinks into which the indolent and the criminal descend. In the words of nineteenth century morality, 'those who wish to be clean, clean they will be' or in the more modest phrase quoted about Pruitt-Igoe, 'so many of the people came with problems far in excess of their ability to cope'. Neither extreme is justified. It is probably unfortunate that those families most unable to cope and seeking public help are those given accommodation where there are severe environmental stresses. But as Michelson comments, it is not high-rise living of itself which creates those stresses but rather the way it is established when costs have to be kept to the minimum. It is not very logical to rail against the luxury of penthouse suites on the one hand, and against high-rise blocks for council tenants on the other, without looking a little more carefully at the total context.

(*ii*) *The suburban estate.* It could be maintained that few wish to live on a suburban housing estate and that given an unconstrained choice most families would probably opt for a large house in its own extensive grounds but with immediate accessibility to all desired services. The decision to buy a house on an estate is, therefore, a compromise accepted as being a feasible solution. From this rather elementary point of view it is evident that the creator of the settlement form, indeed the house design itself, is not the demanding customer but the supplying developer. In a more complex way this can be seen as the product of the market system.

These arguments have been most cogently advanced by David Harvey with empirical exemplification from Baltimore.[52] 'Residential differentiation in urban areas has long been explained in terms of social ecological processes, consumer preferences, utility maximizing behaviours on the part of individuals and the like. The Baltimore evidence suggests that financial

[52] D. Harvey (1974): Class-monopoly rent, finance capital and the urban revolution. *Regional Studies*, 8, 239–255.

and governmental institutions play an active role in shaping residential differentiation and that the active agent in the process is an investor seeking to realize a class-monopoly rent'.[53] Harvey defines such a rent as a form of absolute rent which arises 'because there exists a class of owners of "resource units" — the land and the relatively permanent improvements incorporated in it — who are willing to release the units under their command only if they receive a positive return above some arbitrary level'.[54] It follows that the class-monopoly rents obtained will depend upon the outcome of a conflict of interest between the owners and the consumers. The characteristic middle class seeker of housing has, to use Harvey's terms for the process, been subject to a 'blow-out' from the inner city which has been subject to an influx of low income populations and a rapid decline in the services of all sorts.

Here then is a well defined market which the land owner can exploit. The population concerned can be convinced of the advantages, and especially of the relative prestige, of living in a particular area and hence led to house purchase and the creation of a positive return to the owner. The whole operation is conducted within the institutional framework of national and local government but the home buyer is led, he does not do the 'demanding'. The residential structure of the city is, therefore, shaped by the derivation of profit returns for the owners of the monopoly rents and the financial institutions which support them. 'This is not to say that considerations of race and ethnicity, social status and prestige, life style aspirations, community and neighbourhood solidarity and the like, are irrelevant to understanding residential differentiation. Ironically, all of these features *increase* the potential for realizing class-monopoly rent because they help to maintain the island-like structure, to create the absolute space of the parochially minded community'.[55] Indeed as Harvey goes on to maintain, it is possible to argue that consumer preferences are produced systematically from this process rather than generated spontaneously from the community. They are certainly as liable to manipulation as are preferences for consumer goods, and effective manipulation within the sub-market can increase returns.

The argument advanced above is one slanted from a particular angle and the simple notion of house seeking populations led by the nose to a situation which they are manipulated to believe they want, is far from completely credible. But the view of residential segregation by socio-economic status presented by Harvey is sufficiently impressive to emphasize that the middle class suburban estate can equally be regarded as the creation of the realizers of class-monopoly rents, as the spontaneous generation of an environment out of the wishes of the families who live on it.

(*iii*) *Tenure and mobility.* Most surveys of household movers in Britain have demonstrated convincingly that the majority of moves occur within the two major types of tenure, owner occupiers and council tenancies, with private renting fuelling them both. Figure 11−4 illustrates this quite clearly.

[53] D. Harvey (1974), 249.
[54] D. Harvey (1974), 241.
[55] D. Harvey (1974), 249−250. See also Chap. 15, p. 374.

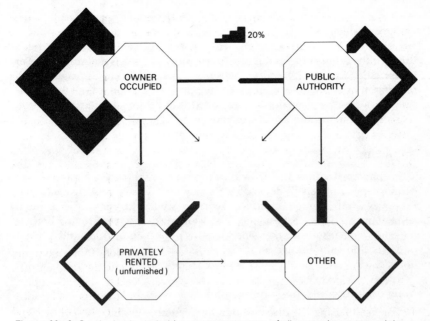

Figure 11–4: Continuing household movers: percentage of all moves by tenure, origin and destination. England and Wales (excluding Greater London) 1970–71. *After Murie, Niner and Watson (1976).*

In the owner-occupier sector 33 per cent of all the movers were within the sector as against 6 who moved out, while in the public authority sector 15 per cent were within as against 8 per cent who moved out.[56] If there are such restrictions related to tenure then it would seem likely that they would conflict with that essential mobility on which is dependent the flexibility which creates social areas. Since the tenure types are themselves class related it is unlikely that there would be any clear impact on socio-economic status areas, except in so far as they would be reinforced. But the second component of variation has been identified as a life cycle one and that is most certainly dependent on easy change of residence in relation to age and family status. This has been investigated by Morgan in Exeter.[57] He defines his central finding thus; 'that residential immobility among households who enter new housing early in the family cycle is a more important influence on the residential patterns of family status groups than changing housing needs generated by life-cycle changes' and maintains that his conclusion is likely to apply to other British cities. In order to emerge clearly, a family status component must be linked to differential attractiveness of different parts of the city to different family types. But that apparently does not apply in Exeter, and by extension, in Britain.

[56] A. Murie *et al.* (1976), 42.
[57] B. S. Morgan (1976): The bases of family status segregation: a case study in Exeter. *Trans. Inst. Brit. Geogrs.* New Series 1(1), 83–107. See also p. 274.

In brief the tenurial problem breaks across the simple operation of the life cycle component and explains why it is far from convincingly apparent in British studies. 'It is demonstrated', writes Morgan, 'that progression through the family cycle is not associated with changes in housing tenure or accessibility to the city centre, but that households are associated with housing built at the time of, or soon after, their formation; that is to say, the distribution of family status groups is better understood in terms of inertia than changing housing needs associated with life cycle changes'.[58]

7 Conclusion

This chapter attempted to show that the residential patterning of the city cannot be completely understood either by inferring large scale ecological processes from aggregate patterns or from seeking to identify individual behaviour in relation to residential decision making. Over arching both of these is the housing market operated by public authorities and private interests, and only within the context of that market can the complex mosaic of residential areas be properly comprehended.

Notes on further reading

For British housing the direct source for present issues is:

Department of the Environment (1977): *Housing policy. A consultative document* Cmd. 6851 (London).

With the best source for data being the:

Technical Volume which was published in three parts. Part 1 deals with the historical background, current situation and forecasts; Part 2 with fairness between tenures and with owner occupation; Part 3 with Local Authority housing and the private rented sector as well as with the physical condition of the housing stock and a review of housing policies in other countries.

A useful bibliography is:

Stewart, John M. (1978): *Housing bibliography*. University of Lancaster, Occasional Papers in Social Administration 2.

The Centre of Urban and Regional Studies at Birmingham has made a special study of housing and a number of working papers have been published and are referred to in the chapter. The most useful general works are:

Murie, A., Niner, P. and Watson, C. (1976): *Housing Policy and the housing system*. Urban and Regional Studies No. 7 (London).

Lambert, J. Paris, C. and Blackaby, B. (1978): *Housing policy and the state* (London).

A general review is also available in:

Berry, F. (1974): *Housing: the great British failure* (London).

---

[58] B. S. Morgan (1976), 83. For a rather different view see: J. R. Short (1977): Patterns of Residential mobility in the private housing market: a case study of Bristol. *Bristol Housing Studies No. 2*. Dept. of Geography, Univ. of Bristol.

The best brief consideration in a specifically geographical context is:

Bassett, K and Short, J. (1980): *Housing and Residential Structure* (London).

Whilst relevant chapters appear in:

Herbert, D. T. and Johnston, R. J. eds. (1976): *Social areas in cities* (London), especially Chap. 4, L. S. Bourne. Housing supply and housing market behaviour in residential development.

Most texts in urban economies have a section on housing and reference may be made to those listed at the end of Chapter 8, p. 197. An elementary introduction with a helpful bibliography is:

Charles S. (1977): *Housing economics* (London).

Two journals, one geographic the other concerned with planning have devoted issues to housing. These are:

Institute of British Geographers (1976): *Houses and people in the city.* New Series 1(1). (1978): *Housing and employment in the inner city.* New Series 3 (1).

Royal Town Planning Institute (1973): *Housing,* 59(2); (1976): *The Community Land Act,* 62(1); (1977): *Housing renewal—is the strategy working,* 63(2).

The role of gatekeepers is best considered in:

Pahl, R. (1975): *Whose city?* (London), especially Parts 2 and 3.

For redlining see the references given in footnotes 32 and 33.

Housing is both an emotive and political issue and much of the writing is polemic rather than academic in purpose. Two examples which are stimulating reading but must be treated as falling into the former category are:

Ambrose, P. and Colenutt, B. (1975): *The property machine* (London).

Community Development Project (C.D.P.) Information and Intelligence Unit (1976): *Profits against houses. An alternative guide to housing finance.* (London).

For the reaction of the British Conservative Government elected in 1979 to the issues discussed on pp 297–301 see: *Local Government Planning and Land (No2) Bill* (1980).

12

The Rural-Urban Fringe

The space into which the town extends as the process of dispersion operates has created the concept of a rural-urban fringe, an area with distinctive characteristics which is only partly assimilated into the growing urban complex, which is still partly rural and where many of the residents live *in* the country but are not socially and economically *of* it. The foregoing introductory sentence reveals two somewhat different terms of reference. The first refers directly to the physical characteristics of area, the second to the social characteristics of the occupants and it is as well that these are kept carefully apart. Three aspects can therefore be considered:

1 The notion of the fringe as a distinctive physical area or region of the city, primarily designated by characteristic land-use associations.
2 The notion of the fringe as that area where urbanization impinges on rurality and, therefore, where the processes envisaged by Wirth[1] can best be observed and, indeed, should be in operation. The rural-urban continuum should most effectively be studied within the confines of this geographical area.
3 The impact of urban expansion on agricultural land.

1 The rural-urban fringe as a region of the city

A large amount of literature appeared roughly during the period from the mid-1940s to the beginning of the 1960s, which was concerned with the physical delimitation and the defining features of the rural-urban fringe.[2] In land-use terms Wissink[3] has called it an area of 'great differentiation', while Golledge[4] used the term, 'a geographical no-man's land'. Both these expressions are derived from the wide variety of uses found in an area which has been only partly brought into the urban complex. The city does not grow outwards in well defined, advancing rings of rapidly completed development. It extends haphazardly, making rapid advances at one point and hardly moving at all at another. It is this process which occasions the

---

[1] See chapter 2.
[2] For a consideration of definitions see. R. A. Kurtz and J. B. Eicher (1958): Fringe and suburb: a confusion of concepts. *Soc. Forces* 37, 32–7.
[3] G. A. Wissink (1962): *American cities in perspective; with special reference to the development of their fringe areas*, 201 (Assen).
[4] R. G. Golledge (1960): Sydney's metropolitan fringes: a study in urban-rural relations. *Aust. Geogr.* 7, 243–55.

incoherent land-use pattern which is taken as representative of the fringe. This is not something associated particularly and uniquely with present metropolitan growth. The fringe belts which Conzen and Whitehand have recognized as significant determinants of the morphology of urban settlements[5] represent the continuing influence of former fringes long after they have been encompassed by the advancing urban front. Schnore and Knights[6] have demonstrated how early a feature metropolitan expansion was in the United States.

At the city margins, therefore, in the context of the fringe, a wide mix of land-uses is characteristic ranging from the old, untouched rural villages to modern residential estates; from a variety of commercial developments, including out-of-town shopping centres to the city services and industries which are conveniently located at the margins. Wehrwein[7] described the fringe in the USA as an 'institutional desert' because of the uncontrolled location there of unpleasant and noxious establishments such as slaughterhouses, junkyards and wholesale oil storage, and of utilities such as sewage plants and cemeteries. Once again it is worth emphasizing that the latter, too, are not a feature of the twentieth century. Figure 12−1 presents a good example of the way in which public services had grown outside the intensely built up area of Paris by the end of the nineteenth century.[8] The range of defensive works, mental hospitals, cemeteries and waterworks, while characteristic of the period, illustrates the process convincingly.

In a contemporary context the various land-uses, older villages, newer residential extensions, commerce, industry, city services and the underlying farming, are not neatly sorted out into homogeneous areas but are intermingled in random fashion and it is this which gives its distinctive quality to the land-use pattern of the rural-urban fringe.[9] It is also possible to translate this somewhat static narrative of land-uses into a more dynamic statement of process. Golledge in a study of Sydney presented seven propositions:[10]

1   There is a constantly changing pattern of land occupance.
2   Farms are small.
3   Crop production is intensive.
4   The population is mobile and of low or moderate density.
5   Residential expansion is rapid.
6   The provision of services and public utilities is incomplete.
7   Speculative building is common.

These conditions reflect the nature of the fringe as already outlined and represent the push into rural surrounds of young, mobile middle class populations and the attempts by speculative builders to provide for them at

---

[5] See chapter 7, p. 165.
[6] L. S. Schnore and P. R. Knights (1969): Residence and social structure: Boston in the ante-bellum period; in S. Thernstrom and R. Sennett, editors (1969): *Nineteenth century cities*, 247−57 (New Haven and London).
[7] G. S. Wehrwein (1942): The rural-urban fringe. *Econ. Geogr.* **18**, 217−28.
[8] J. Bastié (1964): *La croissance de la banlieu parisienne*, 186 (Paris).
[9] G. A. Wissink (1962).
[10] R. G. Golledge (1960).

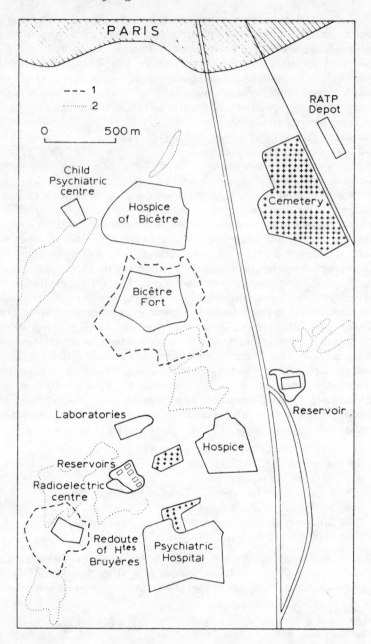

Figure 12–1: Fringe uses to the south of Paris at the beginning of the present century. *After J. Bastié (1964).* **1:** Military installations and the limits of the zone *non aedificandi* about the forts; **2:** quarries. This map indicates a characteristic assemblage of uses generated by the central city at the period and taking up space on the fringes.

a rate which, in some cases, outreaches the input of services and utilities. The only additional features Golledge includes are farm size and crop production, presumably related to urban demand.

More recently other aspects of the fringe have become conspicuous. In the U. K. two of the most notable land-use modifications are the growth of a considerable number of nurseries and garden centres, selling plants and equipment to the newcomers, and the development of horse riding schools and stables catering especially for the young female members of the incoming middle and upper class families. A further use is as recreational land, for instance where the fathers of the horse riding daughters can play golf ! Similar developments can be identified both in the U.S.A. and Australia but perhaps the major feature in the U.S.A. has been the out-of-town shopping centre which planning legislation has limited in the U.K. Dawson has indicated how the increasing size of such shopping centres has made them leaders in the expansion into fringe areas, 'While developers of large centres seek 40 hectares of flat land at motorway intersections in high-income neighbourhoods in the suburbs, it would be false to assume that all centres have been located in this way. For the very large centres a single segment of suburbia is not large enough and land requirements cannot be met by a location in present suburbia or on its fringe. Centres of 150,000 m^2 and more may seek locations between major suburban tracts and in open agricultural land. Midway between Los Angeles and San Diego for example, work began in 1977 on a multi-purpose centre which is to have 750,000 m^2 of retail and business space on a 190 ha site in the triangle formed by three freeways. Green-field and inter-urban sites are almost inevitable for developments of such size.'[11]

R. E. Pahl[12] has also attempted to summarize the characteristics of the fringe and his four main headings take in many of the characteristics proposed by Golledge:

(*i*) *Segregation*. The ability to pay for the new housing of the fringe results in a pattern of segregation appearing. Giggs in a study of Nottingham[13] showed that not only are there basic differences between the north and west which was built up and industrialized in the nineteenth century and is suburb rather than fringe, and the south and east, which is still underdeveloped and can be considered part of the fringe, but that within the south and east clear differences can be identified. A cluster analysis of 78 parishes using 15 variables was carried out, the variables representing population growth, age structure, housing characteristics, socio-economic status, employment, work-place and mode of travel, mobility and dependency. Significant differences between the parishes were revealed and four sets were identified. Giggs recognizes these as: Set 1, modern mining

[11] J. A. Dawson (1979): *The marketing environment*, 308 (London).
[12] R. E. Pahl (1965): Urbs in rure. The metropolitan fringe in Hertfordshire. *London School of Economics and Political Science, Geogr. Pap.* **2**.
[13] J. Giggs (1970): Fringe expansion and suburbanization around Nottingham; a metropolitan area approach. *E. Midland Geogr.* **5**, 9.

settlements; Set 2, large residential suburbs; Set 3, small residential suburbs; Set 4, small villages, i.e. unmodified villages.

He concludes, 'the major residential tracts of the suburbs—old villages, private housing, council estates and miners' estates—are all clearly segregated, with the private estates generally located closer to the old village cores. Large planned tracts are given to commercial, educational and institutional uses.'[14] A characteristic variety of settlement form is accompanied by segregation of population by 'class'. To such an extent is this developed that many parts of the fringe become status symbols in a residential context, they are *the* places in which to live.

(*ii*) *Selective immigration*. The rural-urban fringe will attract in particular 'mobile, middle class commuters who tend to live and work in distinct and separate social and economic worlds from the established populations'.[15] Those who come to live in the fringe constitute a small section of the whole urban community and they tend to retain their orientation towards the city. Many studies have demonstrated a pattern of linkages that is unrelated to the fringe itself. Rodehaver[16] as early as 1946 in a study of Madison, Wisconsin, identified the strong pull on the urban migrants to the central city for work, shopping, church-going and social activities. Martin[17] in Eugene, Oregon, found similarly that people of the fringe considered themselves urbanites, while Kurtz and Smith[18] in a study of Lansing, Michigan, concluded that the urban migrants to the fringe returned to the city, even to the areas of previous residence for social activities.

(*iii*) *Commuting*. This follows from the previous point and needs little comment except to note that it is not confined to the more wealthy but the availability and cost of transport necessarily confine the less well-off.

(*iv*) *The collapse of geographical and social hierarchies*. This is one of the most interesting of Pahl's conclusions and advances the concept of a distinctive fringe. With the populations partly directed towards other parts of the city for certain services, then the service content of fringe settlements becomes modified. They do not need to carry an array of goods and services commensurate with the population they serve, but can become specialized in particular directions. It is possible that conventional central place ideas would not apply in direct fashion and that something akin to the dispersed city[19] is appearing in the fringe. Instead of rounded bundles of functions at

---

[14] J. Giggs (1970), 17.
[15] R. E. Pahl (1965), 72.
[16] M. Rodehaver (N.D.): *The rural-urban fringe; an interstitial area*, 66−9 (Univ. Wisconsin: Unpublished Ph.D. thesis).
[17] W. T. Martin (1952): A consideration of differences in the extent and location of the formal associational activities of rural-urban fringe residents. *Am. sociol. Rev.* **17**, 687−94.
[18] R. A. Kurtz and J. Smith (1961): Social life in the rural-urban fringe. *Rur. Sociol.* **26**, 24−38.
[19] I. Burton (1963): A restatement of the dispersed city hypothesis. *Ann. Assoc. Am. Geogr.* **53**, 285−9.

particular hierarchical levels collected at appropriate nodes, the various functions are being dispersed in several nodes in specialized or segregated bundles, the whole process being precipitated by the mobility of the population. This is the basis of the out-of-town shopping centres noted above. Likewise the segregation of incoming groups, with their links back to the city, undermines the traditional social hierarchies of the rural areas.

Pahl summarizes the above points by maintaining that 'a new population is invading local communities, bringing in national values and class consciousness at the same time that a new type of community, associated with dispersed living is emerging.'[20] Here, however, the argument has moved far away from the concept of a fringe as a physical area to one associated with particular social processes. One view considers the rural-urban fringe as identified by static features, a mix of land uses brought about by the incomplete extension of the city as well as the demands which it makes on its marginal areas. The other view sees the fringe as showing distinction in the nature of the communities which occupy it, brought about by the migration of mobile, middle class families orientated to the city and dominated by urban life styles.

2 The rural-urban fringe and the rural-urban continuum

In the context of the geographical study of city structure and the fringe as part of it, this aspect is not as immediately relevant. But it reflects both on the conclusion in the last paragraph and on the earlier discussion in chapter 2 of the urbanization process. If a transformation takes place on a rural-urban continuum as proposed by the followers of Wirth then internationally it can be demonstrated by national comparisons if that scale is meaningful, but intra-nationally the changes should be most apparent where the urban frontier extends into rural areas. But the simple urban-rural dichotomy cannot be maintained against the existence of the 'urban village' and the 'metropolitan village'.

The concept of the 'urban village' has already been introduced and many studies have shown the existence in city centres of distinct enclaves where the kinship linkages are intense and where there is a high density of social contact giving a cohesiveness conventionally ascribed to rural settlements.[21] The notion of 'anomie' does not easily fit into relationships in older working class areas. Not only does London's East End provide examples of this but also the mining settlements of South Wales where the intense nexus of family and social relationships, based on face to face contacts provided a social context anything but 'anomic'. Indeed the *preservation* of the Welsh language in this *urban* situation contradicts ideas of its solely rural survival.

As a complete opposite Pahl argues the case for the 'metropolitan village' where the characteristics are largely derived from the four features of

---

[20] R. E. Pahl (1965), 79.
[21] H. J. Gans (1962): *The urban villagers* (New York).

fringe populations examined earlier. This is, in other words, the commuter village, where the mobile middle class builds a highly dispersed pattern of activities based not on a place, but on the region. To a large extent their choice of residence is associated with class and life-cycle stage, but Pahl adds two other features which influence the way of life. These are the necessary associations with other life styles in small and heterogeneous settlements and the relationships developed in the general social organization of the village, an involvement and an interaction. 'The sociologically most significant feature of this settlement type is the interaction of status groups which have been determined nationally—by the educational system, the industrial system and so on—in a small scale situation.'[22]

If this line of thought is carried on it has a marked reflection on the idea of a rural-urban continuum, or the process of urbanization. 'Whether we call the processes acting on the local community "urbanization", "differentiation", "modernization", "mass society", or whatever, it is clear that it is not so much communities that are acted upon as groups and individuals at particular places in the social structure. Any attempt to tie particular patterns of social relationships to specific geographical milieux is a singularly fruitless exercise.'[23] This last view is especially worthy of discussion for not only does it reject the notion of 'rural' and 'urban' contexts for categorizing behaviour but thereby reflects on any idea that the fringe is characterized by the sorts of transformation that are associated with the rural-urban continuum. But to some extent the argument is illusory. It must be accepted that the sociologist is concerned primarily with aspatial structural processes that differentiate society, and one can accept Pahl's view that the relationships that are derived cannot simply be assigned a spatial context.

The contrast between what is 'local' and what is 'national' may well be a better way of looking at the contrasts between what are usually termed 'rural' and 'urban' although the impact of the modern mass media, particularly television, make these substituted terms hardly more appropriate.[24] It is the direction of orientation that matters and one feels that terms like 'inward orientation' and 'outward orientation' are preferable to the rather meaningless 'local' and 'national' dichotomy[25].

Indeed the most useful concept to introduce is that of Melvin Webber's 'nonplace urban realm'—'an urban realm is neither urban settlement nor territory, but heterogeneous groups of people communicating with each other through space.'[26] Everyone participates in different realms and shifts from one to another. 'This is, of course, especially true of the highly specialized man who may turn from a transatlantic phone call to arbitrate an intra-office personnel problem, then read his mail from customers in

[22] R. E. Pahl (1968): The rural-urban continuum; in R. E. Pahl, editor (1968): *Readings in urban sociology*, 268 (London).

[23] R. E. Pahl (1968), 293.

[24] R. E. Pahl (1968), 276.

[25] J. H. Johnson (1967): *Urban geography; an introductory analysis*, 142—3 (London).

[26] M. M. Webber (1964): Urban place and nonplace urban realm; in M. M. Webber *et alia* (1964): *Explorations into urban structure*, 116 (Philadelphia).

various places, then join other motorists in the peak-hour rush, before reassuming his roles as parent, newspaper reader, and member of a friendship circle.'[27] Webber goes on to assert that no urban settlement is a unitary place but a part of an array of shifting and interpenetrating realm spaces.

In this interpretation the conflict in the rural-urban fringe is between the limited realm participation of the rural or local population and the large range of realms in which the immigrant participates. Nevertheless, 'the intensely 'local', or an 'inward orientation', or limited realm participation can be found lodged in the city centre in the urban village, or in the mining village, 'the "national" outlook or outward orientation' and, above all, wide ranging realm participation can be found in the semi-rurality of the city fringe. Even so this does not destroy the concept of the fringe areas as those where this conflict of orientation is particularly acute, even if one is in danger of ascribing derived social patterns to geographical milieux!

3 The impact on agricultural land

Agriculture in the fringe becomes inevitably influenced by urban penetration, although the most controversial issue in smaller, highly industrialized countries is related to the loss of productive farmland. The changes in land-use and farm size have already been noted. The purchase of land for development leads to both smaller units and fragmentation of holdings. Where 'betterment' is not exacted for the benefit of the community, speculation by the purchase of fringe land in anticipation of development can create a deterioration in agricultural standards. Also where the 'urban fence' is ill defined or not well defended, vandalism from the encroaching housing estates can create problems, for such anti-social activities are not restricted to the inner city.[28] Again the advance of the actual urban frontier spreads the wave of 'rural retreaters' and the rather large scale 'hobby farmers' who seize opportunities to live in a rural environment and work on the land.

The most significant impact, however, in small intensively developed countries is the encroachment on farmland and its assimilation into the urban territory. There is an extensive literature to which R. H. Best[29] and A. G. Champion[30] have made substantial contributions. It is best summarized in recent figures published by Best which indicate that the present rate of gain in land provision for the urban area of England and Wales is at an annual rate of 1·6 hectares per 1000 people. If this rate is projected forward, by the year 2300 all land, other than protected land, will have been

[27] M. M. Webber (1964), 118.

[28] M. Elson (1979): Urban fringe management problems. *The Planner*, 65(2), 521—54.

[29] R. H. Best (1968): Extent of urban growth and agricultural displacement in post war Britain. *Urban Studies* 5(1). R. H. Best (1976): The extent and growth of urban land. *The Planner*, 62(1), 8—11.

[30] A. G. Champion (1975): *An estimate of the changing extent and distribution of urban land in England and Wales 1950—1970.* Centre for Urban and Regional Studies. Report 10 (Birmingham). R. H. Best and A. G. Champion (1970): Regional conversions of agricultural land to urban use in England and Wales, 1945—1967. *Trans. Inst. Brit, Geogrs.* 49, 15—32.

used up and by 2800 all land will be covered by urban uses.[31] These figures are in themselves sufficient indication of the problem and it must be emphasized that much recent extension is not a function of population growth but of the relaxation of urban densities. Zero population growth is not a simple solution to the in-take of rural land.

The demand on rural land, together with the desire to preserve the discrete character of towns, have been the main motivations in the development of green belt policies, the preservation by legislation of open, rural terrain about cities. In Britain such attempts go back to the reign of the first Elizabeth and have seldom been greatly successful against the pressures of urban extension. Where a green belt is maintained it often simply pushes development still further into the countryside as it is 'stepped over'.

4 Conclusion

Writing as long ago as 1967, Harold Mayer identified problems of competition for land and preservation of open space as the two most important areas of research interest in the rural-urban fringe.[32] Ten years later a conference on Research on the Urban Fringe organized by the British Countryside Commission[33] revolved around five topics:

1   Agriculture and the urban fringe.
2   Land management and development pressures.
3   Recreation in the urban fringe.
4   Land-use relationships and conflicts.
5   Interaction between policies in the urban fringe.

All these are more detailed presentations of the basic two problems identified by Mayer. Agriculture through the fragmentation of holdings and an unwillingness to undertake long term investment takes on a distinctive character. Speculative buying of land in anticipation of development creates a complex land market, difficult to monitor. Recreational demands increase, not only from the affluent but from the urban poor and deprived. All these interact, creating conflicts in which some sort of mediating institutions are sought. The manner in which a city expands as its fringes, the process by which land is taken into the city, the whole mechanisms of the various decision processes, all these are critical in the interpretation of the urban fringe which, indeed, has a claim to be the real transition zone of the city.

---

[31] R. H. Best (1976), 11.
[32] H. Mayer (1967): A survey of urban geography; in P. M. Hauser and L. F. Schnore, editors (1967): *The study of urbanization*, 99 (New York).
[33] J. C. Phillips and A. J. Veal (1979): *Research on the urban fringe* (Centre of Urban and Regional Studies. Conference and Seminar Papers no. 6, Birmingham, England).

Notes on further reading

A general bibliography is to be found in:

Phillips, J. C. and Veal, A. J. (1979): *Research on the urban fringe*. (Conference and Seminar Papers No 6. Centre for Urban and Regional Studies. Univ. of Birmingham, England)

Two most useful books are:

Johnson, J. H. editor (1974): *Suburban growth: geographical processes at the edge of the western city* (London)

Masotti, L. H. and Hadden, J. K. editors (1973): The urbanization of the suburbs. *Urban Affairs Annual Reviews* **7**.

The first of these is primarily concerned with the United Kingdom but with some references to European areas, the second with the United States. They both have useful bibliographies.

For the rural-urban fringe as part of the city, early works providing definition and comment are

Kurtz, R. A. and Eicher, J. B. (1958): Fringe and suburb: a confusion of concept (see footnote 2).

Myers, R. B. and Beegle, J. A. (1947): Delineation and analysis of the rural-urban fringe. *Appl. Anthropl.* **6,** 14–22.

Pahl, R. E. (1965): Urbs in rure. The metropolitan fringe in Hertfordshire (see footnote 12).

Wehrwein, G. S. (1942): Rural-urban fringe. *Econ. Geog.* **18,** 217–28.

Wissink, G. A. (1962): *American cities in perspective; with special reference to the development of their fringe areas* (see footnote 3).

More recent studies are:

Archer, R. W. (1973): Land speculation and scattered development: failures in the urban fringe land market, *Urban Studies* 10(3), 367–72.

Brodsky, H. (1973): Land development and the expanding city, *Annals of the Association of American Geographers*, 63(2), 159–66.

Clawson, M. (1971): *Suburban Land Conversion in the United States: an economic and governmental process* (Baltimore).

Gavish, D. (1976): Changes in rural land-use on the urban fringe in D. H. K. Amiran and Y. Ben-Avieh eds. *Geography in Israel* (Jerusalem), Israel National Committee, International Geographical Union.

Hart, J. F. (1976): Urban encroachment on rural areas, *Geographical Review* 66(1), 1–17.

Hushak. L J. (1975): The urban demand for urban-rural fringe land. *Land Economics* 51(2), 112–123.

Raup, R. M. (1975): Urban threats to rural lands: backgrounds and beginnings, *J. of the American Institute of Planners*, 41(6), 371–78.

Srivastava, B. and Ramachandran, R. (1974): The rural-urban fringe, *The Indian Geographical Journal*, 54(1), 1–9.

Strachan, A. J. (1972): The social and economic interactions of urban and rural land-uses on the western periphery of Edinburgh, *Geographica Polonica*, 24, 113–26.

The papers by Whitehand referred to in chapter 7 are also relevant.

The literature on 'suburbs' as distinct from the fringe is extensive:

Carver, H. (1962): *Cities in the suburbs*. (Toronto).

Dobriner, W. M., editor (1958): *The suburban community* (New York).

Dobriner, W. M. (1963): *Class in suburbia*. (Englewood Cliffs, N.J.)

Douglas, H. P. (1925): *The suburban trend* (New York).

Gans, H. J. (1962): Urbanism and suburbanism as ways of life, in A. M. Rose, editor (1962): *Human behaviour and social processes* (Boston).

Gans, H. J. (1967): *The Levittowners* (New York). The references include Gans's extensive work on suburban themes.

Harris, C. D. (1943): Suburbs. *Am. J. Sociol.* **49,** 1–13.

Schnore, L. (1965): *The urban scene.* (New York). This includes reference to Schnore's wide range of publications on this topic.

Spectorsky, A. C. (1955). *The exurbanites* (New York).

Material on the rural-urban continuum was introduced in chapter 2 but the following which are related to the notion of the dispersed city should be consulted.

Burton, I. (1963): A restatement of the dispersed city hypothesis (see footnote 19).

Stafford, H. A. Jr. (1962): The dispersed city. *Prof. Geogr.* **14,** 8–10.

Webber, M. M. (1964): Urban place and nonplace urban realm (see footnote 26)

A book dealing with a specific problem is

Thomas, D. (1970): *London's Green Belt* (London).

while problems of planning are usefully considered in a book which has excellent short studies of major cities:

Hall, P. (1966): *The world cities* (London).

For a popular work on the whole topic of city fringes see:

Masotti, L. H. and Hadden, J. K. (1974): *Suburbia in transition* (New York).

13

The Location of Industry in the City

It is perhaps surprising that there are fewer studies which seek to generalize the pattern of industrial land-use in the city, than for most other types of use. This is probably due to the concern of research in locational analysis with the larger problems of a regional scale rather than with the intra-urban scale, and also to the intractable nature of the problem itself since such a wide universe of activities is included even under the restricted definition of 'manufacturing industry'. To this the conventional division into heavy and light makes no useful contribution.

It has already been noted that E. W. Burgess identified a zone which was described as being dominated by working class homes and heavy industry.[1] This was largely the product of historical forces and relevant to the earlier part of this century. The rapid growth of industry during the nineteenth century meant that it took up a location, when associated with pre-existing towns, outside and on the margins of the old nuclei. This resulted, in some cases, in the neat concentric zone envisaged by Burgess, as for example in Cologne prior to the Second World War.[2] The construction of defensive walls on an even site had constricted the city into a series of zones while the area *non aedificandi* outside the 1880 defences was preserved as a green belt. Outside this the large industrial developments of the latter part of the century took place, since they were barred from the river frontage for military reasons. Along with them were built the industrial suburbs to produce a classical zonal pattern (figure 13-1). The main industrial areas themselves were associated with the main radial railway lines, whilst the working class residential areas filled in the areas between.

In contrast to the arrangement exemplified by Cologne, most of the towns which were created by industry, and had no previous existence, grew around the formative elements, the factory and the mine. In consequence multiple nuclei schemes tended to emerge, as suggested by Harris and Ullman.[3] The point location of exploited resources produced a number of nuclei in relation to which the residential areas were disposed. These often coalesced (the origin of the concept of conurbation) to form urbanized areas dominated by the separate nuclei and often in the process creating another, the central business district. A good example of this is Merthyr Tudful[4] in South Wales

[1] See chapter 8, page 172.
[2] R. E. Dickinson (1951): *The west European city*, 81–90 (London).
[3] See chapter 8, page 182.
[4] H. Carter (1968): Urban systems and town morphology; chapter in E. G. Bowen, H. Carter and J. A. Taylor, editors (1968): *Geography at Aberystwyth*, 229–33 (Cardiff).

Figure 13–1: The industrial areas of Cologne in 1939. *Adapted from R. E. Dickinson* (*1951*). The black areas indicate railways and goods and marshalling yards. Areas to the east of the Rhine have been excluded.

where four early ironworks established between 1750 and 1790 created four distinct nuclei, while the central area emerged as the fifth (figure 13–2).

But these schemes are at the most general level of interpretation and it is in progress from the stage that comparatively little has been accomplished. Four attempts, by Isard, Loewenstein, Hamilton and Pred can be considered in turn and in conclusion some attempt can be made to establish what ground there is in common.

In his volume *Location and space economy* Walter Isard[5] presented a diagram which purported to represent urban-land use patterns. The city is viewed as using localized raw materials and ubiquitous raw materials or none at all. Industries using ubiquitous materials are extremely important within the city, but are linked either with the central area or with all industrial areas since their locational requirements are less stringently defined.

[5] W. Isard (1956): *Location and space economy*, 278–9 (New York).

Figure 13–2: Merthyr Tudful in 1850. The separate industrial nuclei can easily be distinguished. To the northwest lay the Cyfarthfa Works, to the east the Penydarren Works and the Dowlais Works. The fourth southern nucleus is not shown on this map. The old village was located on the extreme southern edge of the map and new developments in a church and market hall (M) indicate the growth of the industrial town. This is an admirable example of a 'multiple nuclei' situation.

These apart, all other industries, implicitly using localized raw materials, are seen to be concentrated in one of several industrial areas which are accordingly characterized by certain industrial associations. These areas are located, it would seem from the diagram, after the arrangement proposed by Burgess. They surround the central area and are in turn, surrounded by the less densely developed suburbs. They do not form a continuous zone, however, but constitute a series of sectors within such a zone. Isard based his assessment on intuition, logical and analytical principles relating to the interaction of general forces governing land-use, and facts.[6] His 'model' adds little to previous ideas other than the refusal to use a heavy/light division of industry and an attempt to use raw material sources as a basic divide between centrally and non-centrally located industry.

A survey based on a wider array of empirical evidence was that by Loewenstein[7] where manufacturing uses were considered alongside a number of other characteristic uses. A selection of cities was examined in which a particular use, as demonstrated by employment, was dominant: 'Only that employment in which a particular city excelled was reproduced from the basic land-use maps'[8] onto a standard format consisting of five distance rings (figure 13 – 3). From this evidence, synthesized into one map representing manufacturing land uses in total, it was concluded that 'manufacturing activities typically tend to be dispersed away from the core'[9] and to have a linear appearance due to extension along transport lines. This dispersal away from the core Loewenstein explains in a conventional way as the consequence of the high costs and congestion in the theoretically optimum location in the city centre. There are also a number of other factors:

1 Labour- or market-oriented firms are likely to be found in the city centre. This is because market-oriented firms, such as those engaged in newspaper publication, can save in terms of transport costs since distribution from the centre is much easier, whilst labour-oriented firms can draw effectively from a central location on the widest ranges of skills.

2 Manufacturing plants which are engaged in what Loewenstein calls organized, integrated industries, cluster along 'radial and belt railroads and highways'. This is particularly true of assembly industries such as the automobile industry.

3 Large, basic processing industries, such as petroleum refineries or steel mills require large areas and create a great deal of noise and pollution. They therefore, repel residential development and will be removed from it. This is only partly true; certainly high quality residential areas are unlikely to develop adjacent to heavy industry but historically this is by no means true of working class residential areas.

4 Large new plants are often located in a suburban context where land is most easily and cheaply available.

[6] W. Isard (1956), 280.
[7] L. K. Loewenstein (1963): The location of urban land uses. *Ld. Econ.* **39**, 406–420.
[8] L. K. Loewenstein (1963), 409.
[9] L. K. Loewenstein (1963), 413.

DETROIT EASTON ELKHART

FLINT SAGINAW SOUTH BEND

SPRINGFIELD MASS. THOMASVILLE YOUNGSTOWN

Figure 13–3: The distribution of manufacturing in selected American cities. *After L. K. Loewenstein (1963).* The areas in black denote manufacturing land-use. Five distance rings are superimposed in each case by taking the major CBD intersection as centre and drawing an outer ring at the mean limit of the metropolitan area. The radius of this outer ring is divided into four to give the circles shown.

This is not a very impressive breakdown of industrial distribution but it does illustrate the point which neither Burgess nor Isard make clearly. Industry is not confined to any one zone or any series of areas, it is located throughout the city because different types require different locational attributes so that any attempt at generalization, unless linked to a convincing typology, becomes extremely hazardous.

This can be illustrated from Loewenstein's own work. He calculates for each use an index of concentration.[10] This measures the percentage

---

[10] L. K. Loewenstein (1963), 418. The derivation of the index is discussed in detail here.

distribution of land-use of each of the activities, such as retail or manu-facturing, in each of the five rings as a percentage of the total land area within the ring. In the computation of the index the percentage of the total land was accumulated and multiplied by the amount of land in a particular use. The formula is defined as:

$$\text{Index} = 1 - \Sigma(X_i - X_{i-1})(Y_i + Y_{i-1})$$

where Y_i is the accumulated proportion of total area through the ith ring (the fifth if the total city is under survey) and X_i is the accumulated propor-tion of the area for the give kind of employment activity, i.e. for a given type of use. Table 13-1 illustrates the computation of the index of concentration for public administration. The index varies between -1.0000 for a com-pleted dispersal, through zero for even distribution throughout the rings to $+1.0000$ for complete concentration. An analysis of the results reveals that manufacturing had the lowest index of 0.2800 compared with 0.6896 for finance, insurance and real estate, 0.7344 for retail and 0.4816 for personal service and the 0.8400 for public administration as shown in table 13-1. Manufacturing showed the least tendency to concentration and the highest tendency to an even distribution throughout the city of all the uses con-sidered. One example (Elkart, Ind.) even shows a minus index of -0.0352, the only occurrence, which demonstrates a tendency towards complete dispersal.

The various characteristics of intra-urban industrial location derived by Loewenstein are reflected in Hamilton's attempt,[11] in considering models of industrial location, to reduce the map of London's industry to a generalized scheme (figure 13-4). On this four characteristic locations are identified:

table 13-1: Computation of Loewenstein's (1963) index of concentration for public administration

| Ring | Total area | | | Public administration | | | |
	Proportion of total area in ring (1)	Cumulation of (1) (Y_i) (2)	2 Point total of (2) ($Y_i + Y_{i-1}$) (3)	Proportion of total public administration in ring (4)	Cumulation of (4) (X_i) (5)	2 Point difference of (5) ($X_i - X_{i-1}$) (6)	Product of (3) × (6) (7)
1	0.04	0.04	0.04	0.64	0.64	0.64	0.0256
2	0.12	0.16	0.20	0.24	0.88	0.24	0.0480
3	0.20	0.36	0.52	0.07	0.95	0.07	0.0364
4	0.28	0.64	1.00	0.05	1.00	0.05	0.0500
5	0.36	1.00	1.64	0.00	1.00	0.00	0.0000
Total	1.00	—	—	1.00	—	—	0.1600

Index of concentration = $1 - $ Total column (7) = $1.0000 - 0.1600 = 0.8400$

[11] F. E. I. Hamilton (1967): Models of industrial location; chapter 10 in R. J. Chorley and P. Haggett, editors (1967): *Models in geography*, 361-417 (London).

Figure 13–4: A model of the spatial industrial structure of a metropolis. *After F. E. Ian Hamilton (1967)*. This is based on a map of industrial areas in London. The four categories shown are: **A**: central locations; **B**: port locations; **C**: radial or ring transport artery locations; **D**: suburban locations.

A *Central locations.* These are taken up by industries which require access to skilled labour, for example instrument making, to the CBD, for example the clothing industry, and to the whole urban market for distribution, for example, newspaper publishing. It is in this context that the 'swarming' of closely associated activities occurs which gives rise to sharply defined industrial quarters.

B *Port locations.*

C *Radial or ring transport artery locations.* Both these (B and C) are taken up by larger enterprises seeking cheaper land in larger quantities and good locations for assembly and distribution. In addition larger amounts of unskilled or semiskilled labour can be obtained without calling on city-wide sources.

D *Suburban locations.* Such positions are sought by industries requiring very large amounts of land for assembly or production lines and for storage or if the industry has repellent features, such as fumes or noise, which compel it to seek isolation from residential areas.

The interpretation of this pattern is presented in the context of the conventional explanatory factors. 'If the metropolis is large, then substantial cost differentials èxist between alternative locations within the city, especially with regard to land, labour and transport. The model of the metropolitan spatial structure of industry, therefore, comprises differing localizations of associated industries in different optimum conditions.'[12] This sounds perilously close to a sophisticated version of the schoolboy's answer that a cultivated plant under consideration occurs in the 'best soils'

[12] F. E. I. Hamilton (1967), 408.

and 'most suitable' climate! There is clearly a very close parallel between the generalizations of Loewenstein and Hamilton.

Finally Pred has presented an array of what he terms seven flexible types of manufacturing each of which he argues should be characterized by a distributional pattern with a unique set of attributes, including in some cases randomness.[13] Pred adopts the rationale derived from Chinitz's study of industrial plants in the New York Metropolitan Area. Chinitz proposed three broad types:

1   Those serving markets predominantly local.
2   Those serving national markets. Subdivided by size and value of product.
3   Those plants localized by external economies and not included under 1 and 2.

Pred writes 'since each type and subtype has different transportation requirements, or different abilities to absorb transport outlays, singular, but not exclusive, locational tendencies emerges.'[14] This is comparable to Hamilton's statement above, but made in relation to a useful subdivision of industries which to some extent reflects Isard's earlier basis but with an emphasis on markets rather than on raw materials. Pred's seven types are as follows:[15]

1   *Ubiquitous industries concentrated near the CBD.* These are industries whose market is coextensive with the metropolis. They often have linked wholesaling functions and can maximize distribution from the centre. Pred quotes bread, cake and pie plants as an example.
2   *Centrally located 'communication-economy' industries.* In these cases locations are determined by external economies derived from immediate accessibility to the purchaser prior to the process of manufacturing. An obvious example is job printing where the most frequent demand arises in the city centre and where face-to-face contacts are necessary. Pred characterizes the New York garment centre as archetypal.
3   *Local market industries with local and raw material sources.* Within this group are industries for the local market and using ubiquitous raw materials, such as ice manufacturing plants, and also those using raw materials which are the by-products of other industries or semi-finished goods. These often appear to have random locations since the constraints operating on site selection are not great, even nearness to railheads is not vital where intra-urban access is required. The building of freeways has resulted in some dispersion of these industries: presumably this should also influence those in group 1.
4   *Non-local market industries with high-value products.* Where the market is greater than the metropolis and where the finished product

[13]   A. R. Pred (1964): The intra-metropolitan location of American manufacturing. *Ann. Assoc. Am. Geogr.* **54**, 165–80.
[14]   A. R. Pred (1964), 173.
[15]   A. R. Pred (1964), 174–80.

has a high value-to-weight ratio then transport cost become relatively unimportant and a random location pattern can result. Fortuitous factors can govern site selection. A typical example is the manufacture of calculating machines. Other things being equal these industries will tend to locate near the CBD, especially the smaller firms.

5   *Non-centrally located 'communications-economy' industries.* Pred defines these as 'those industries which imperatively cluster in non-central locations to realize "communication economies".'[16] He suggests that these are highly technical industries which need to cluster to keep abreast of innovation but are nationally oriented and hence not related to the CBD in any specific way. This results in strip development along major expressways and space-age electronic industries are exemplars.

6   *Non-local market industries on waterfronts.* This is a well-known group of port industries and requires no comment, other than to make the reservation that all industries on waterfronts do not necessarily belong to the group.

7   *Industries oriented toward the national market.* These have extensive markets with locations strongly influenced by the bulk of the products and transport rates. The main point that Pred makes is that these locations often show distinct biases in the sector of the city in which they are located which is characterized as one looking toward the regional or national market.

At the beginning of his study Pred set out to answer two questions: 'What kinds of industry remain in or near the core of the metropolis? What patterns, if any, are to be distinguished among the decentralized industries?'[17] He answers the first question with some success but makes little headway with the second[18] and indeed admits, 'a considerable amount of evidence remains to be culled before any real understanding of intrametropolitan locational preference of industries oriented towards non-local markets is attained'.[19] The examples which he uses are mainly derived from San Francisco and to some extent the characteristic types and locations are representative of that metropolis rather than general in concept. But it is evident that there is a great deal in common between the suggestions of Loewenstein, Hamilton and Pred and the three formulations can be put together as follows:

1   *Centrally located industries:*
    a   Labour-oriented.
    b   Market-oriented — This includes the two categories of ubiquitous industries and local market industries proposed by Pred.
    c   CBD-oriented — This includes Pred's 'communication — economy' industries.

[16] A. R. Pred (1964), 177.
[17] A. R. Pred (1964), 170.
[18] For an early study of the decentralization of industry see: E. K. Kitagawa and D. J. Bogue (1955): *Suburbanization of manufacturing activity within standard metropolitan areas.* Scripps Foundation for Research in Population Problems, Miami University. See also p. 337.
[19] A. R. Pred (1964), 180.

2   *Non-local market high value industries:* These tend to have random
    locations.
3   *Large basic processing industries:* these take in Pred's last group which
    are nationally oriented. Although suburban locations are ideal since the
    problems caused by noise and pollution can be minimized, many of
    these, especially chemical and metallurgical industries, have heavy
    investments in plant in the older inner areas of cities and remain there
    near to the location propounded by Burgess. Certainly all three schemes
    tend to underemphasize this group and Pred's notion that it is located
    on the side of the city facing its markets is an interesting one and worthy
    of empirical investigation but it says little about basic location in rela-
    tion to the rest of the city.
4   *Water front or port industries.*
5   *Integrated industries along communication lines:* These would include
    Pred's 'Non-centrally located "communications-economy" industries'.
6   *Suburban industries:* the product of the process of decentralization.

This list is far from convincing and to some extent sacrifices the
consistency in classification which Pred introduced. It does, however,
emphasize that industry can be found in every zone and sector of the city
from CBD to outer suburb.

The major process at present in operation is the rapid growth of suburban
industry at the expense of city centre locations. This is not a question of the
transfer of operations from central to fringe locations, but rather that the
greater proportion of industrial closures—or deaths as they are usually
called—take place at the centre and the greater proportion of new investment—industrial births—takes place at the periphery. This point is taken
up again in Chapter 15 and reference forward to that chapter will provide a
wider based discussion of the impact of changing industrial distribution on
the inner city.

To a large extent the problems that this chapter has noticed arise from the
ubiquity of industry. The other ubiquitous use is residence and certainly the
problem of industrial location calls for a similar treatment. The isolation of
significant attributes—such as social class provides for residence—on the
basis of a scheme such as that proposed by Pred is required together with the
effective measurement of these by location within the city. Perhaps industrial areas, the equivalent of social areas, could then be identified, defined
and fitted into the layout of land-use in the city.

Perhaps one further approach needs to be mentioned as possibly productive. As in the retail complex further illumination of the whole process by
which the industrial land-use pattern is built up will be provided by detailed
studies of the locational behaviour of individual firms. Certainly the work
initiated by McNee[20] for economic locations is a national or regional context
would be profitable in an intra-urban context. A study of Logan reveals the

---

[20] R. B. McNee (1964): The economic geography of an international petroleum firm.
Chapter 17 in R. S. Thoman and D. J. Patton, editors (1964): *Focus on geographic activity*,
98–107 (New York).

strength of the conventional factors.[21] 'Firm behaviour is related particularly strongly to transfer and other costs on the demand side of the firm's operations. In the case of Sydney this has produced a spatial pattern of manufacturing firms closely oriented to the central area and conforming generally to the pattern of industrial land values.'

These and a whole range of other factors, including the problem of linkages,[22] must be unravelled through such studies and then replaced in the context of the whole city's industrial land-uses.

Notes on further reading

The four contributions on which this chapter is based should be consulted.

Hamilton, F. E. Ian, (1967): Models of industrial location (see foonote 11).

Isard, W.(1956): *Location and space economy* (see footnote 5).

Loewenstein, L. K. (1963): The location of urban land uses (see footnote 7).

Pred, A. R. (1964): The intra-metropolitan location of American manufacturing (see footnote 13).

The main area of recent investigation has been the movement of industry away from the inner city. A source with an excellent bibliography is:

Thrift, N. (1979): Unemployment in the inner city: urban problem or structural imperative? A review of the British experience, being Chap. 5 in Herbert, D. T. and Johnston, R. J. eds. (1979): *Geography and the urban environment* (London) vol. 2, 125–226.

Other studies are:

Flagg, J. J. (1973): Spatial changes in manufacturing employment in Greater Leicester, 1947–70. *East Midlands Geographer*, 5, 400–415.

Gripajos, P. (1977): Industrial decline in London: an examination, of its cause. *Urban Studies*, 14, 181–190.

Lloyd, P. E. (1977): Manufacturing industry in the inner city: a case study of Greater Manchester *North West Industrial Research Unit. Working Paper 1.*

Smith, B. M. D. (1977): Economic problems in the core of the old Birmingham industrial area, in F. Joyce ed. *Metropolitan development and change—the West Midlands: a policy review* (Farnborough, Hants)

Whitelegg G. J. (1976): Births and deaths of firms in the inner city. *Urban Studies*, 13, 333–338.

In addition earlier useful articles with bibliographies are:

Keeble, D. E. (1969): Local industrial linkage and manufacturing growth in outer London (see footnote 22).

Kitagawa, E. M. and Bogue, D. J. (1955): *Suburbanization of manufacturing activity within standard metropolitan areas* (see footnote 18).

[21] M. I. Logan (1966): Locational behavior of manufacturing firms in urban areas. *Ann. Assoc. Am. Geogr.* **56**, 451.

[22] D. E. Keeble (1969): Local industrial linkage and manufacturing growth in outer London. *Tn. Plann. Rev.* **40**, 163.

Leigh, R. (1969): Analysis of the factors affecting the location of industries within cities. *Canadian Geogr.* **13,** 28–33.

Logan, M. I. (1966): Locational behavior of manufacturing firms in urban areas (see footnote 21).

Further studies which should be consulted are:

Groves, P. A. (1971): Towards a typology of intrametropolitan manufacturing location. *Univ. of Hull. Occ. Papers in Geog.* **16.**

Struyk, R. J. (1972): Spatial concentrations of manufacturing employment in metropolitan areas: some empirical evidence. *Econ. Geog.* 48(2).

For further material on particular areas:

Dwyer, D. J. and Lai Chuen-Yan (1967): The small Industrial Unit in Hong Kong: Patterns and Policies. *Univ. Hull. Dept. Geogr. Occas. Pap.* **6.**

Gottmann, J. (1961): *Megalopolis* (Cambridge, Mass.).

Hall, P. G. (1962): *The industries of London since 1861* (London).

Hoover, E. M. and Vernon, R. (1959): *Anatomy of a metropolis* (Cambridge, Mass.).

Martin, J. E. (1966): *Greater London: an industrial geography* (London).

Moyes, A. (1971): *Post-war changes in the distribution of employment and manufacturing in north Staffordshire.* (University of Keele: unpublished M.A. thesis)

Wise, M. J. (1949): On the evolution of the jewellery and gun quarters in Birmingham. *Trans. Inst. Brit. Geogr.* **15,** 57–72. A dated but classic study.

For a paper which questions the impact of suburban shift see:

Mason, C. M. (1980): Intra-urban plant location: a case study of Greater Manchester. *Regional Studies,* 14(4), 267–284.

14

Images of the City: The Citizen's View

1 Approaches to perception studies

Over most of this book it has been implicitly accepted that the city can be treated as a natural object, a phenomenon in space which is perfectly perceived and perfectly comprehended by all those who form part of it or establish relations with it. This view has been modified at two points. The first was in the consideration of consumer behaviour in relation to the central place system where it became apparent that, although on an aggregate scale such a system was discernable and could be interpreted as the product of the activities of shoppers and entrepreneurs over time, on a disaggregated scale consumer behaviour was by no means in accord with the principles derived from the aggregate analyses. In the resolution of this apparent conflict a more sensitive behavioural approach was found to be essential. Likewise in looking at residential patterns it was evident that, although distinctive social areas could be identified, any family's decision-making process on where to live was extremely complex and derived from the way in which they assessed their needs in relation to their knowledge of the city.

Thus we may say that, for the citizen, the objective city does not exist. Every inhabitant has most certainly a partial, and most probably an idiosyncratic, view of the urban environment in which he or she lives. In chapter 7 where town plan was examined it was proposed that the totality of plan reflected culture, in this sense an aggregate concept divorced from the individuals who make it up. But the view from the drawing board, or the view from the aeroplane, is not the view of the citizen on the ground and in the street, for there the prospect is limited—as it is from any perspective, including the planner's—and the scene partial.

A strongly growing element of urban geography has therefore focused on the establishing and analysis of images of the city and, in the geographer's particular line of interest, the development of mental (cognitive) maps which translate the images into a spatial framework. These mental maps, or images, of the urban environment can then be examined in relation to the characteristics of the people concerned. There still remains, of course, the problem that these characteristics are ultimately associated with psychological or personality types. With Golledge it is possible to view consumers as Marshallians who behave as economic man, as Pavlovians who develop repetitive patterns of behaviour via a learning process, as Freudians who are fantasizers and react capriciously to stimuli such as advertisements, and as Veblenians who follow the example set by their peers.[1] But in spite of the difficulties indicated by personality characteristics it is still possible to consider images of the city in relation to the standard variables which have been consistently used in social geography—socio-economic status, sex and age for example.

Downs has proposed three types of approach characteristic of work on geographic space perception[2] as follows:

1   *The structural approach* which is concerned with the way in which the array of information about a place is perceived. It is evident that all the sense perceptions, all the impinging data, about an environment cannot be remembered. There is, therefore, a process of selection and ordering, a structuring which has to take place. On this basis it is postulated that mental maps of a city are constructed in which useless detail is discarded and the data necessary for the purposes of the individual such as finding the way from A to B, are retained.

2   *The evaluation approach* goes somewhat further in that it is not only concerned with the way the environment is structured but also how it is evaluated in relation to decisions to be made and subsequent action to be taken.

3   *The preference approach* is directed towards the way in which preferences are developed among a set of objects distributed in space.

Evaluation and the identification of preferences are somewhat similar and they have been in part considered in relation to consumer behaviour in chapter 6 and location decisions as to residence in chapter 10. This chapter will, therefore, concentrate initially on the structural approach and concern itself mainly with the physical and visible character of the townscape.

2 A typology of urban perception

Before considering more precisely how images of the townscape can be put into some structured array it is useful to consider a typology of urban perception which identifies the ways in which such images are derived. Appleyard has proposed a threefold classification.[3]

(*i*) *Operational perception.* People become aware of many elements in the city because they use them as reference points in their everyday life in getting about in the city or simply getting to work. Bus stops or traffic intersections, key buildings or distinctive physical features are noted, remembered, and probably in turn exaggerated in importance, in the process of creating a working mental structure of the city. This is undoubtedly the most universal of the types of perception, derived as it is from repetitive activity. At the

---

[1] R. G. Golledge (1970): Some equilibrium models of consumer behaviour. *Econ. Geog.* **46**, 417–25.

[2] R. M. Downs (1970): Geographic space perception: past approaches and future prospects. *Progress in Geography* **2**, 65–108.

[3] D. Appleyard 1973): Notes on urban perception and knowledge; in R. M. Downs and D. Stea, editors (1973): *Image and Environment* (Chicago and London), 109–114.

same time in this process some parts of the city will remain virtually unseen, certainly unremembered, and perceptually invisible as the individual journies from distinctive feature to distinctive feature. For example, only parts of buildings may be remembered. A shop may often be recalled only in terms of its ground floor identity and the window it displays to the public while the architectural character of the whole building may remain completely unknown.

(*ii*) *Responsive perception.* Awareness of city images will be closely related to distinctive or unusual features which generate an immediate response: 'bright, isolated, singular and distinctive elements intrude on the operational search patterns of the traveller or catch the eye of a gazing passenger.' The role of the advertising industry is to elicit this sort of response by the use of distinctive designs or colours, by employing sexual imagery or establishing a conditioned reflex to easily remembered, catch phrases.

(*iii*) *Inferential perception.* This awareness relies on past experience and is realized by inference from parallel situations. An unknown city is likely to conform in much of its general character to that of a large number of known cities. From experience it is possible to find one's way about in a strange city by using accumulated knowledge of the structuring of urban areas in general.

Given the *types* of perception the major academic problem was the devising of some analytical system which reasonably represented the way in which city images, the perceptions themselves, are structured. This was solved, at least partially, by Kevin Lynch in his book published in 1960 and appropriately entitled, *The image of the city.* Lynch proposed five elements through which the physical structure of the city was visualized:

1   *Paths* are the channels along which people move within the city and, as a result, they tend to predominate in urban imagery since movement usually promotes observation. The characteristic problem of anyone in a city is how to get from A to B and hence the path becomes the dominant remembered feature.

2   *Edges* are linear elements which represent distinctive physical breaks within the city. They can be natural features, such as breaks of slope, sea or lake shorelines, or river fronts. They can also be man-made features, such as the distinctive breaks brought about by railways or urban motorways.

3   *Districts:* sections of most cities are immediately identifiable to the inhabitants and usually have local names. The most universally known are associated with distinctive activities, cultures, or groups such as Soho in London, Montmartre in Paris or Harlem in New York.

4   *Nodes:* certain points in the city, most often road junctions, stand out as nodes or foci. The citizen can enter into or pass through these nodes and they represented easily identified stages in movement within the city. Often they are clearly demarcated physical elements, as in the city

square. Piccadilly Circus, Times Square, Red Square, the Etoile are all nodes.

5   *Landmarks* differ from nodes in that they are features which can be observed but not normally entered or passed through. The name itself indicates the role these have played to the nagivator at sea in its earliest meaning and to the stranger in the city at the present. Distinctive buildings or features stand out as being easily identifiable and easily retained as images to be used in structuring the mental map of the city. The landmark can be used to epitomize the whole city. When a tired film or T.V. producer wants to indicate that his action is taking place in Paris then the opening sequence of shots is of the Eiffel Tower, if it is in London then Big Ben appears and if it is in New York it is either The Statue of Liberty or the Manhattan skyline.

It is evident that few individuals consciously use these five elements as such, and that they constitute together an arbitrary system for analyzing the image of the city held by people or groups of people. The elements will also have different meanings for different people, or even for the same people at different times: an urban motorway is a path to a motorist but an edge to a pedestrian. Lynch compares two maps, one showing an outline map of Boston and the other 'the visual form of Boston as seen in the field'.[4] but although derived from field reconnaissance this must be described as an urban analyst's view of Boston for in this sort of study there are no absolutes, only images. Lynch's major contribution was to provide the simple but basic tools by which the way people structured their image of the city could be realized and the perceptions of different groups compared.

Lynch proceeded by means of office and street interviews to build up a number of Boston images, but perhaps the critical concept is the notion of 'different groups' and the contrasted way in which they perceive city space. The problem of the nature of such groups immediately follows and it would seem sensible to relate them to the dimensions which in factorial ecological terms differentiates the urban population. A large number of completely individual and particularistic views can be derived, but will add little to the purpose of this investigation. The psychologist might be interested in how the city appears to the sufferer from claustrophobia or agoraphobia but such abnormalities are rarely the geographer's immediate concern. The dimensions of ecological studies imply that the image of the city will vary according to socio-economic status, life cycle stage and ethnic origins.

3 City image and socio-economic status

Francescato and Mebane have reported in a preliminary way their attempt to consider images of Rome and Milan. Their respondents were broken down into groups by status, age, sex and whether or not they were natives or the respective cities.[5] Figure 14−1 reproduces the images of Rome of the

[4] K. Lynch (1960): *The image of the city* (Cambridge, Mass.), 18−19.
[5] D. Francescato and W. Mebane (1973): How citizens view two great cities: Milan and Rome; in R. M. Downs and D. Stea, editors (1970) 131−147.

The legend shows:

	PATH	EDGE	NODE	DIST	LAND
41 – 100	━━	▪▪▪	●	░	★
21 – 40	━━	━ ━ ━	◍	▨	☐
7 – 20	━━	─ ─ ─	○	▦	▽

1	Via Borghese	39%	16	Centro	16%	
2	Pza Venezia	39%	17	Monte Mario	13%	
3	Tevere	36%	18	Campidoglio	13%	
4	Colosseo	33%	19	Vatican	13%	
5	Trastevere	29%	20	C. Vitt. E.	13%	
6	EUR	26%	21	Pza di Spagna	13%	
7	Stazione Termini	26%	22	Via Aurelia	10%	
8	Altare Patria	23%	23	Raccordo Anul	10%	
9	Pza Del Popolo	23%	24	Via Veneto	10%	
10	S. Pietro	23%	25	Pza Esedera	10%	
11	Via del Corso	23%	26	Pza Mazzini	10%	
12	Fori	19%	27	Via Mazzini	10%	
13	Pza Navona	19%	28	Univ. Statale	7%	
14	Font. di Trevi	16%	29	Trin. dei Monti	7%	
15	Lungotevere	16%	30	Gianicolo	7%	

31	Appia	7%
32	Tuscolana	7%
33	Nomentana	7%
34	Salaria	7%
35	Flamina	7%
36	Via Laurent.	7%
37	Via Nazion.	7%
38	Via Cavour	7%
39	Via Delle Milizie	7%
40	Via Giulio Cesare	7%
41	Ostia	7%

Figure 14–1: Images of Rome. *After Francescato and Mebane* (*1973*). **A:** Middle-class image of Rome.

middle-class (14–1A) and lower class (14–1B) subjects using Lynch's analytical techniques. Social class was determined by using occupation and education as indices: 33 respondents were ascribed to the middle class and 27 to the lower class. The contrasts are immediate and obvious.

The middle-class group identified a much larger number of elements over a much wider spatial extent. The reasons seem straight forward; greater wealth provides greater mobility, a wider range of cosmopolitan interests and a greater propensity to use all the widespread resources of the city. Poorer people are less mobile, are more likely to have a shorter journey to work, will not use the range of city resources and so will be less exposed to city

Figure 14–1B: Lower-class image of Rome.

space. The authors suggest an alternative explanation. They suggest that the tendency for the lower class to produce maps covering only very small areas but indicating a good deal of local detail, reflects the home orientation which is characteristic of poor Roman families. This is undoubtedly a relevant feature, but such localism is itself an aspect of poverty, although certainly a stress on home life and the neighbourhood exacerbates the limitations following directly from lack of wealth.

4 City image and ethnicity

One of the most frequency quoted examples of an imagery of the urban environment is the pilot study by the Advance Planning Section of the Los Angeles City Planning Commission.[6] In this 25 respondents were asked to draw maps of Los Angeles, from which a general representation for each of the groups was produced. Three of these composite city image maps are reproduced here (figure 14−2). Figure 14−2A is the city image of the sample from Avalon, a delightfully wry name for a predominantly black area in the south of the metropolitan area and a little to the north of the better known Watts. Figure 14−2B is that of the sample from Boyle Heights,

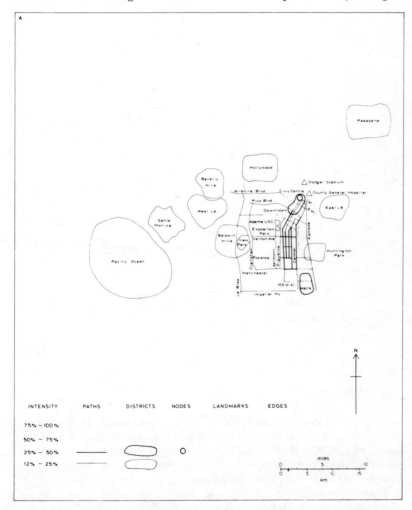

Figure 14−2: Composite city images of Los Angeles. *After Los Angeles Department of City Planning (1971).* **A:** Avalon.

[6] Department of City Planning (1971): *The visual environment of Los Angeles* (Department of City Planning, LA).

Figure 14–2B: Boyle Heights.

an almost exclusively Spanish-speaking tract adjacent to the central industrial and commercial areas. The third image of Los Angeles is shown in figure 14–2C and represents the sample from Westwood, a white upper-class neighbourhood, located on the southern fringes of the northern hills between Beverley Hills and Santa Monica.

These three maps require but little exegesis. The white upper-class image is extensive in reach and detailed in content; that of the Avalon residents is limited in reach and has less city-wide detail: only a low proportion of respondents are even aware of the universally known residential areas such as Hollywood. It is also noteworthy that the white image is dominated by the east-west grain along the lines of the well known boulevards, such as

Figure 14–2C: Westwood.

Wilshire and Santa Monica, which skirt the Hollywood Hills and Santa Monica Mountain. The black Avalon image, in contrast, is dominated by the north-south grid of the plain and related to access to the CBD. Finally the Boyle Heights composite image is most severely restricted and is limited to what is little more than the immediate neighbourhood.

Although these three images are related to ethnic and segregated groups it is not possible to sustain this argument without qualification. Socio-economic status, or access to mobility via wealth, must be invoked also. Nevertheless these results lead on to notions of ethnically based terri-toriality, and most certainly participation in the whole city-wide range of activity is related to assimilation into the larger urban community. The ghetto has been considered in its spatial context in an earlier chapter but now it can be clearly seen as a constricting feature.

Gerald Suttles in his book, *The social order of the slum*, subtitled 'Ethnicity and territory in the inner city', develops the way in which restriction grows, 'For persons in the Addams area [his name for that part of Chicago with which the book is concerned] only the adjacent neighbourhoods are well defined. Beyond this, their notions of established boundaries become vague and uncertain. . . . Each little section [of the city] is taken to be a self-sufficient world where residents carry out almost all their legitimate pursuits. A person who leaves his own area, then, is suspect so long as he has no visible and justifiable reason for straying from his home grounds.'[7] He continues (p. 228), 'Individuals in the Addams area achieve a positive association with co-residents of the same age, sex and ethnicity primarily because conflict with other persons forces them together into small face-to-face groupings . . .: so positive a role for conflict cannot be appreciated unless it is placed in a developmental sequence. At the outset parents . . do not prescribe a definite set of persons . . . [but] voice a variety of proscriptions: "Don't go out of the neighbourhood" . . . "Don't you get off the block" . . . Injunctions of this sort do not initially produce positive associations but only territorial aggregates.' In this detailed study Suttles outlines the processes by which territorial restrictions emerge and it is these which are eventually revealed in the severely restricted images of the total city which many ethnic minorities display.

The notion of the restriction of the individual's use of city space introduces the ideas contained in Hägerstrand's 'time-geography' model of society.[8] Most human activities are space consuming but 'while the space packing of urbanization allows time-savings for both individual and society it also creates interregional and intraregional social and economic inequalities . . .'[9] There are two components in the model. The first is a life-perspective environment which takes in all those places a person might encounter throughout his life and the second is a daily-life environment which is theoretically limited to the effective distance that can be covered, with return, in a single day, rather like the bounds set on a medieval market. Every individual can be thought of as contained by constraints within a time-space envelope. Some of these constraints are directly biological, like the need for sleep which restricts the reach of daily travel, but others are socioeconomic and determined by deployable resources. In this sense city-image is restricted by the nature of this inhibiting envelope.

It is worth adding one other point which is apparent from the maps in figure 14−2, although it is not related to ethnicity. Lynch discussed the

---

[7] G. D. Suttles (1968): *The social order of the slum. Ethnicity and territory in the inner city* (Chicago), 15. A paper of considerable interest is, D. Ley and R. Cybriwsky (1974): Urban graffiti as territorial markers. *Ann. Assoc. Amer. Geogr.* **64**, 491−505.

[8] T. Hägerstrand (1970): What about people in regional science? *Papers Reg. Sci. Assoc.* **24**, 7−21.

[9] A. R. Pred (1973): Urbanization, domestic planning problems and Swedish geographic research. *Progress in Geography* **5**, 37. This paper contains a full review of Hägerstrand's ideas.

imageability of the city,[10] that is, the extent to which it threw up clear and distinctive images. Examination of the Los Angeles maps will indicate that they are dominated by paths and districts and that there is a lack of nodes and landmarks. This tends to confirm the popular impression of the city as dominated by the automobile, as a mass of suburbs (districts) linked by freeways (paths).

5 City image and the life cycle

Two aspects of this relation arise:

1   *The development of spatial cognition:* this sort of study is concerned with the way in which spatial cognition develops in the child from birth. This book is most certainly not the proper place to include a review of work on this topic. It is a highly specialized field and a lengthy review of the literature is available.[11] It is included here, as a heading, since it is a part of the life cycle relation to the image of places.

2   *City image and age groups:* different age groups, different life cycle stages, will be concerned with different aspects of the city. One of the best known studies in Britain was carried out by Brian Goodey *et alia* in Birmingham.[12] A rather unusual means of collecting data was used: readers of the *Birmingham Post* were asked to send in spontaneously drawn maps of the central area of the city. Goodey reported that 'we found evidence for youth, housewives' and old people's maps of Birmingham and for the two latter the maze of recently opened city underpasses emerged as very severe blockages to mobility and urban navigation.'[13]

It would be wrong to give the impression that the three dimensions which have been discussed are the only determinants of city images, or indeed that only the visible elements that can be translated into Lynch's terminology are involved. In chapter 9 the central business district was considered as an objective area of the city and appropriate methods of delimitation sought. Even so it was noted that the earliest attempts were based upon local opinion; thus through image studies the wheel turns full circle and geographers are once more concerned with local views, for if consumers behave in a way not in keeping with the dictates of economic man then it is likely that views of the CBD will also vary.

This has been the subject of an investigation by Klein who attempted to

---

[10]   K. Lynch (1960), 9–13.

[11]   R. A. Hart and G. T. Moore (1973): The development of spatial cognition: a review; in R. M. Downs and D. Stea, editors (1973) 246–88.

[12]   B. Goodey *et alia* (1971): City-scene: an exploration into the image of central Birmingham as seen by an area residents. *University of Birmingham, Centre for Urban and Regional Studies, Research Memorandum* 10.

[13]   B. Goodey (1973): Regional and urban images in decision making and planning; in J. Rees and P. Newby, editors (1973): Behavioural perspectives in geography *Middlesex Polytechnic, Monographs in Geography* 1, 70.

establish varying definitions of the town centre by contrasted groups.[14] A random sample of subjects, 1118 in all, was selected from a number of clearly defined residential areas. These respondents were then given a set of twenty-four photographs of the city centre and were asked to divide them into three categories, 'town centre', 'not town centre', 'unknown'. Analysis of the results was then undertaken in relation to a number of variables characterizing respondents including socio-economic status, age, sex, length of residence and location of residence. This was done by calculating, for each of the photographs, the percentage of the total sample which judged it to be of the 'town centre' and then calculating the deviation from the average for each of the subgroups determined by the variables. Two of the subgroup analyses can be considered briefly.

Figure 14—3A represents a west-east profile across the city identified by five of the photographs. The responses of three groups are examined in relation to these five points, those who lived to the west of the town centre, those who lived to the east and those who lived in the inner city. These groups are represented by graphs which indicate the deviation from the average in percentages. This figure demonstrates that those who live in the west exaggerate the town centre by extending it in a westerly direction, while those who live in the east do the same in an easterly direction. Those who live in the inner city over-estimate the central point and under-estimate the extensions both to east and west and, although there are no statistical tests to match place of residence against the other variables, it seems that this locational bias is independent of them.

Klein suggests that this result may be due to the fact that people tend to use that part of the central area nearer to them, or at least to be more familiar with it. But he also adds that it may be wishful thinking and a determination to believe that the city centre is nearer than it actually is, thus, introducing another problem in this field, the notion of subjective distance. These results bring to mind the work of Brennan[15] in Wolverhampton, who found that housewives did not use the nearest shop for a good but the nearest in the direction of the CBD, that is they turned citywards not because of an intervening opportunity but possibly because movement into the city was dominant and this created the illusion that it was easier.[16]

The second example from Klein's study is shown in figure 14—3B where seven points along a north-south profile are related to length of residence in the city. Those who have been in the city the shortest time, like the younger age group, have a much more restricted view of the town centre. Especially remarkable is the disagreement over point 'j', the Festplatz. This is a point on a southern extension of the centre dominated by cultural features and a traditionally distinctive feature of the city. Those who have lived in the city most of their lives insist that it is part of the town centre whereas the newcomers have no such sentiment. Clearly there is great complexity in the

---

[14] H.-J. Klein (1967): The delimitation of the town-centre in the image of its citizens; in W. F. Heinemijer *et alia*, editors (1967): *Urban core and inner city* (Leiden), 286—306.
[15] T. Brennan (1948): *Midland city* (London).
[16] T. R. Lee (1962): 'Brennan's Law' of shopping behaviour: *Psychological Report* 11 662.

Figure 14–3: The town centre of Karlsruhe as identified by citizens. *After Klein (1967).*
A: West-east profile in relation to place of residence; **B:** North-south profile in relation to
length of residence. In these two cross sections the points labelled a to l represent the
points from which photographs were used in the study. a to e are five places ranged from
the west to the east, with f to l seven places ranged from north to south. Note also that
the city centre of Karlsruhe has tended to shift to the west in recent years. This is
reflected clearly in the responses of the inner inhabitants in graph **A** and by the newer
residents in graph **B**.

image the citizen builds up, for not only it is related to standard social variables, but to location, length of residence and to all those personal quirks which belong to the individual. Beyond the objective city is the city which people use, controlled by the images they hold for 'behaviour depends on the image.'

6 Practical and academic relevance

At this stage it is likely that the question will be put as to what use there is in these sorts of studies, for are they not just another passing geographical fad? It is possible, however, that these represent a most important area for at least a departure is made from the academic's city to that of the people who live and work in it. Four uses of city image studies can be suggested.

1   Attention is drawn to the imageability of the city. It is easy from the geographer's viewpoint to forget that the city is a built form that should give visual pleasure, 'voluptas' as the Renaissance theorists called the quality. Aesthetic pleasure must be related to the quality of the images the city creates and hence city image studies call attention to qualities too easily ignored in social science and passed over to the architect's care.[17]

2   On a large scale the efficiency of a city depends on its imageability for the ease with which people can get about, with which motorists can find their way is closely related to its legibility, that is, the ease with which distinctive images produce a sequence that can be followed. On a small scale these qualities become related to any single building, for social processes depend upon environmental organization. 'The concepts of sociopetal space and behaviour watching may be applied to explicit social areas as well as to lobbies or hallways. Every natural traffic pathway is a potential supplier of encounters which can become interactions. Therefore, the social space located at the far end of a hall, or even halfway down the hall, from the entrance has part of its therapeutic function diluted.'[18] Again it is quite evident that, though the geographer will have an interest in these studies since they are concerned with the organization of space, the prime mover in them will tend to be the architect or the psychologist.

3   The third way in which these studies are of value relates to the fact that they reveal the images of the city of the everyday user and therefore also indicate the existence of major problems. Reference has already been made to Goodey's Birmingham study, where the problem of housewives having to navigate baby carriages through an underpass system was revealed. This type of work thus seems to be a way of introducing public participation into planning processes.

---

[17] For an interesting analysis related closely to Lynch's work see: G. Clay (1973): *Close-up: how to read the American city* (Washington D.C.).

[18] M. P. Lawton (1974): The human being and the institutional building; in J. Lang *et alia*, editors (1974): *Designing for human behaviour; architecture and the behavioral sciences* (Stroudsburg, Penn.), 67.

4   The last area of relevance is one of critical importance to the cities of the twentieth century. Deprivation, and its identification by means of socio-economic indicators, is a fasionable academic study. To a great degree the emphasis here is structural and related to systems of social stratification. But it should also be locational and geographical and nowhere is this more clearly revealed than in the maps drawn by the poor and the ethnic minorities. It is true that social and economic disadvantage and locational disadvantage are part of each other, though not exclusively so. It is an ironic possibility that in Britain the drive to create a comprehensive education system may, in its early stages, have only substituted locational disadvantage for structural disadvantage, and as a result may have made the education opportunities of the intelligent working-class child much worse than they were before. If this is so it is due to the limited impact of geographical education itself and the inability, indeed unwillingness, of people to think in spatial terms. In America the 'busing' of children across cities in order to avoid schools of exclusive ethnic character is an attempt to solve a comparable problem. In this way, too, image studies link up with those of social areas which have been considered earlier.

These four uses of studies of the image of the city are practical applications in the field of planning. There remains the significance of such studies within academic geography. Here the major problem is one of circularity for image and behaviour interact and to varying degrees condition each other. Even so the key issue is not the construction of images as an exercise in itself, but the interpretation of behaviour through the images held by sets of people acting in reference to sets of opportunities. To a large extent these opportunity sets will relate to particular decisions, where to shop, where to live, where to work, and these can be considered in the appropriate contexts of consumer behaviour and residential location behaviour.

In the explanation of patterns and movements in the phenomenal — world, the observed objective city, the geographer must look to those characteristics of citizen's behaviour which play their part in structuring it. It is appropriate that a behavioural approach should play an increasingly large but by no means exclusive part in urban geography.

Notes on further reading

A series of bibliographies on environmental perception have been published by the Centre for Urban and Regional Studies at Birmingham University. Among them are:

Goodey, B. and Spencer, D. (1973); The last environmental perception check-list. *University of Birmingham, Centre for Urban and Regional Studies, Research Memorandum 2.*

Goodey, B. (1974): Images of place. *CURS. Occasional Papers No 20.*

The most useful and valuable single volume is:

Downs, R. M. and Stea, D (1973): *Image and environment: cognitive mapping and spatial behaviour* (see footnotes 3, 6, and 11) (New York).

Reference can also be made to an earlier review of the field by Downs.

Downs, R. M. (1970): Geographic space perception: past approaches and future prospects. *Progress in Geography* 2 (see footnote 2).

A more general treatment is to be found in:

Gould, P. and White, R. (1974): *Mental maps* (London).

Two classics, although very different in character, are:

Lynch, K. (1960): The image of the city (see footnote 4).
Boulding, K. (1961): The image (Ann Arbor, Mich.).

A stimulating sociological approach is to be found in:

Michelson, W. (1970): *Man and his urban environment: a sociological approach* (Reading, Mass.).

A book dealing with environmental psychology from the architects point of view is:

J. Lang *et alia*, editors. (1974): *Designing for human behavior: architecture and the social sciences* (see foonote 18).

Apart from the bibliography published by Goodey, the paper by Downs (1970) and the books edited by Downs and Stea (1973), by Michelson (1970), and by Lang *et alia* (1974) contain lengthy bibliographies.

15

Social and Economic Patterns, Spatial Inequality and Social Welfare

Previous chapters have shown that locations, both in relation to the hierarchy of towns and within the city, carry with them specific advantages or disadvantages. More and more, in seeking after explicit relevance, and in order to demonstrate an awareness of social responsibility, urban geographers have concentrated on the study of those inequalities which are derived from relative location. It can be maintained that inequalities are immediate once space is in any way differentiated, for equal access to desired points cannot be assured by any political system: the issue is an allocative one. Certainly, desirable locations (though the phrase begs the question) can be monopolized in an unconstrained system by those best able to compete through the deployment of the greatest financial resources, and in a constrained system by those who have access to the maximum power resources. The corollary of such a situation is that those who have few resources, no power base from which to operate, or who offend against the interests of monopolists, corporate or state, are relegated to the least desirable locations. Inequalities, in this way, are not offset or minimized but are, to a greater or lesser degree, exaggerated.

The contrasted images of the city which have already been described in chapter 14 are a product of this spatial differential in urban living. This concern with inequalities, or the geography of welfare, can be seen as producing three types of study. Two of them are closely related and are concerned with intra-urban situations, whilst the third is related to the inter-urban situation and the hierarchical or size contrasts between towns. These can be set out as follows:

1   Intra-urban pathology: empirical studies.
2   Intra-urban inequalities: multiple deprivation and the inner city.
3   Inter-urban inequalities: access to urban facilities and services.

1 Intra-urban pathology

Studies which fall within this group are essentially within the positivist, empirical tradition of urban geography and urban ecology. *The city'*, that seminal work of the Chicago School of Human Ecology, which was edited by Park and Burgess and published in 1925, contained the following paragraph. 'A recent study by Neils Anderson of what he calls "Hobohemia", an area in Chicago just outside the "Loop", that is to say, the down-town business area, which is almost wholly inhabited by homeless men, is a study of . . . . a human junk heap. In fact, the slum areas that invariably grow up just on the edge of the business area of great cities, areas of deteriorated houses, of poverty, vice, and crime, are areas of social junk.'[1] In the acerbic terms of the 1920's, such is the identification of a pathological condition.

Two primary aims can be identified in the context of intra-urban pathology. These are;

1   The identification of those parts of the city which are characterized by elements of social disorganization, as indicated in the quotation from R. E. Park above. Crime, in all its manifestations, and disease are the two most obvious symptoms, but others, such as the break-up of families or the failure to meet civic obligations in the inability to pay rates or taxes, can be included.
2   The identification of the socio-economic, demographic and ethnic correlates of social disorganization.

It must be stressed that the correlates are not interpreted as either the cause of consequence of the condition, but rather that they add depth to the characterization of distinctive city areas.

One of the best examples of investigations under the heading of intra-urban pathology is that of J. Giggs into the distribution of schizophrenia in Nottingham.[2] Schizophrenia is an extreme form of the set of mental disorders which are termed 'psychoses' which involve the disintegration of the personality to the extent where an individual becomes incapable of dealing effectively either with himself or his environment. Giggs mapped the distribution of this illness in Nottingham and the general pattern is shown in figure 15−1 in terms of Standard Attack Ratios (S.A.R.s). These ratios adjust the crude figures of incidence per enumeration district to take in variations in population density and population at risk by age bands. The S.A.R. is expressed in terms of the average attack rate for the city so that a ratio of 300 means that the S.A.R. for that district is three times that for the city as a whole. Setting aside minor differences between male and female distributions, the simple conclusion from figure 15−1 is that schizophrenia demonstrates a well defined locational pattern and is closely associated with the city centre. Having established the primary distribution of the condition, Giggs proceeds to undertake a factor analysis in which forty one variables for each of the 140 enumeration districts of Nottingham are employed. Of these variables twelve are related to the schizophrenic population itself, ten are demographic in nature, four are socio-economic, four relate to housing tenure and eight to housing and household conditions. The remaining one is a measure of distance from the city centre. An oblique (promax) rotated solution is developed and six factors abstracted. These are shown in table 15−1.

The distribution of these factors by standard factor scores on the enumeration districts is shown in figure 15−2, where only those districts

[1]   R. E. Park and E. W. Burgess (1925): *The city* (Chicago), 109.
[2]   J. A. Giggs (1973): The distribution of schizophrenics in Nottingham. *Trans. Inst. Brit. Geogrs.*, 59, 55−76.

Figure 15–1: Distribution of schizophrenia in Nottingham (*after J. A. Giggs*).

with a positive standard deviation of greater than 0·5 have been isolated. The relation of the first schizophrenia factor to the distribution of S.A.R.'s in figure 15 – 1 is as apparent, as would be expected. The distribution of the remaining factors can be convincingly related to the interpretation of city social space already presented in chapter 10. Simple subjective pattern matching suggests the association of the illness with rooming house areas of single people locationally at or marginal to the city centre. But since an oblique rotation was employed and orthogonally not retained, these six factors were themselves subject to further analysis (see chapter 10, p. 274) in order to derive higher order factors. This produced a stable result across all the factoring methods which were tried. The primary factor method, without rotation, gave a first factor explaining some 86·8 per cent of the variance. This second order factor, as it is called, can be interpreted in relation to the loadings of the six first order factors as shown in table 15 – 2 where a complex of factors is revealed associated with schizophrenia. The negative correlates confirm the suggestion that 'such conditions as having a stable marriage, being gainfully employed, being educated, and being intelligent may all summate to a condition called security and freedom from

table 15–1: Schizophrenia in Nottingham: Factors and Loading Variables. (After J.A. Giggs)

Factor	Positive Loading Variables	Negative Loading Variables
I Schizophrenia	All twelve schizophrenia variables	
II Life cycle	Young; mobile married	Elderly; small households
III Urbanism-Familism	Rooming house	Large households: large dwellings; married
IV Rented housing-housing amenities	Local authority housing; young; suburban	Privately rented; unfurnished dwellings; sharing amenities
V Socio-economic character	High social class (1 and 2)	Low social class (5)
VI Marital status	Single	Married

table 15–2: Schizophrenia in Nottingham: Second Order Factor 1. (After J.A. Giggs)

Strong Positive	Negative
III Urbanism	Familism
IV Rented Housing Pre 1914, Unfurnished	Rented Housing Post 1920, Local Authority
I Schizophrenia	No Schizophrenia

Moderate Positive	Moderate Negative
II Persons over 45	Persons 15 to 44
IV Single persons	Married persons

anxiety. Having all the "advantages" may be . . . critical . . . in determining how easily and successfully one copes with the tasks of living.'[3] The real problem of causation remains, however, for such an argument might well be circular. One still does not know whether people are schizophrenic because they cannot cope, or cannot cope because they are schizophrenic.

The geographical relevance of Giggs' study is that 'it has . . . been demonstrated that there are close correlations between the incidence of schizophrenia and a large set of social and urban environmental factors.'[4] The distribution of this set, moreover, takes on a very distinctive patterning for it is coincident with what is called the inner city. 'Importantly, these unfavourable social and economic traits collectively assume their greatest intensity in the inner, slum areas of the city.'[5] It is but a short step back from this conclusion to that earlier quoted from R. E. Park written in 1925, that here are the cities' junk heaps. Park's statement now seems unsympathetic, even brutal, in the way it is expressed, but it continues to pose the same problem of causation. Do these sorts of people gravitate towards the inner

[3] F. B. McNeil (1970): *The psychoses* (London), 27.
[4] J. A. Giggs (1973), 71.
[5] J. A. Giggs (1973), 71.

Figure 15–2: First order promax factors I to VI derived from factor analysis of 41 variables for Nottingham (*after J. A. Giggs*). Shaded areas are enumeration districts exceeding 0.5 standard deviation. For identification of factors see table 15.1.

city because, having a particular condition, they are unable to withstand the pressures and difficulties generated by living in an intensely competitive urban environment, or has that urban environment by its very nature created such stressful conditions that psychoses are generated? At the aggregate and descriptive geographical level the question is, of course, immaterial, for what is clear is that a section of the city can be isolated where such pathologies are located; in distributional terms they have identifiable characteristics and correlates.

In chapter 1 of this book attention was drawn to the fact that process investigation characteristically move to the behavioural level, but comparatively little has been done in this particular field of mental illness. An exception is a study by Dear of the movements and distribution of psychiatric patients discharged from Hamilton (Ontario) Psychiatric Hospital.[6] Follow-up presents obvious problems of tracking down and locating the discharged persons and, as Dear notes, it has ethical implications as well as detection problems. His study showed two clear concentrations of the sample he succeeded in tracing who has been discharged with no institutional arrangements, one in the down town area and one in the census tracts nearest the hospital. 'The former concentration may reflect the distribution of the population in need of care; it may also suggest the ghettoization of expatients. The latter concentration supports the general distance-decay hypothesis that patients in need of care will reside close to the source of care.' Here then, is some evidence as to process, although information as to pre-hospitalization location is not given. Even so, discharged patients are often mobile and without family support, so that they filter through urban space to an inner city location. 'One recurrent phenomenon of increasing prominence is the tendency for psychiatric patients discharged from mental hospitals to congregate in transient areas of the inner city core. In many ways, the discharged patients resemble other minority groups who have gravitated towards areas of cheap rental accommodation in order to 'establish' themselves. The mentally disabled, however, usually lack the skills to spiral upward along with the other self-improving groups.'[7] In this way the inner city takes in the mentally ill as it does any disadvantaged or outcast section of the community in the same sort of process that has already been discussed in chapter 10.

A similar conclusion can be derived from studies of urban crime. Again, to argue simplistically that the causes of crime can be derived from the analysis of distributional evidence is naive, but the socio-economic correlates can be sought and the characteristic areas isolated, and that is at least one step in complex research situation. The identification of particular parts of the city as showing high crime rates is long established, while the examination of regional patterns of crime goes back to the early nineteenth century. The Chicago social ecologists necessarily became involved in the consideration of criminality as an aspect of ecological processes and, as part of that tradition, C. R. Shaw published in 1929 his book, *Delinquent areas; a study of the geographic distribution of school truants, juvenile delinquents and adult offenders in Chicago*. In Britain, Terence Morris took up the same theme after the Second World War and his book, *The criminal area: a study in social ecology*, came out in 1957. Both these books had specific territorial connotations in their titles, one coining the phrase 'the delinquent *area*' and the other using the term, 'the criminal *area*'.

But it has not been until comparatively recently that urban geographers have undertaken to marry data relating to crime with the standard analyses of social areas. There are reasons for this which can be briefly reviewed. The first and most obvious relates to data. Most ecological studies rely on census

[6] M. Dear (1977): Psychiatric patients and the inner city. *Ann. Assoc. American Geogrs.*, 67(4), 588–594.

[7] M. Dear (1977), 588.

data but the figures for crimes committed are not always easy to obtain and are most certainly partial, for not all crimes are reported; and if the criminal rather than the crime is the basis for analysis, then one has to cope with the fact that only a varying proportion of those who have committed crimes are caught. In addition, there is the problem of whether to analyse crime by the location where it is committed or by the place of residence of the offender, for in studies explicitly spatial this is a decision of fundamental importance. Finally definition presents difficulties, especially at a time when the view is held, if not widely, that laws with which the individual does not agree, or which appear to be unreasonable to any dissenting group, can be broken without incurring what can be loosely called moral censure.

The associated, but legitimate, point is also argued that most studies of crime are selective and concentrate on lower class criminality rather than that of the upper social groups. Thus tax evasion, fraud and corruption are not as frequently studied in this ecological mode, as robbery and rape. D. M. Smith in considering crime rates as territorial social indicators presents a map of Washington D.C. on which the White House is marked as the location in which the Watergate break-in, or at least its cover-up, was planned.[8] He also marks the Pentagon and categorizes it under 'war crimes', an inclusion which might assist in driving home the point that the definition of crime is a controversial issue, but has a polemical rather than an ecological purpose as would be the marking of the Kremlin as the basis of the invasion of Afghanistan. In the context of this chapter, consideration will be limited to what Smith calls the 'street crimes' of violence against the individual person and against property.

Smith himself, has carried out an investigation into crime in Tampa, Florida, and figure 15 − 3 is derived from his work.[9] It shows the distribution of the ten census tracts which returned the highest rate for all criminal violations by place of occurrence in the city during 1971. At a superficial level the expected distribution patterns are revealed. The central area of the city is surrounded by a ring of tracts characterized by high crime rates. The only major break is to the north where an area under the Model Cities Programme shows some amelioration, although this might be due in part to an under reporting of crime there as a conscious element of developing better community relations. Again, the actual areas defined may reflect police activity rather than crime itself. These ten tracts lie exclusively outside the area with above average income. Smith attempts to correlate crime rates with a variety of measures of deprivation or socio-economic disadvantages but only demonstrates what he calls a 'limited correspondence' rather than a clear association. Even so, the aggregate pattern is a very familiar one.

In Britain the major geographical contribution has been made by D. T. Herbert,[10] particularly in the study of delinquency,[11] that is crime

[8] D. M. Smith (1974): *Crime rates as territorial social indicators: the case of the United States.* Occasional papers N11. Dept. of Geography, Queen Mary College, University of London, 10.

[9] D. M. Smith (1974), 33−43.

[10] D. T. Herbert (1976): Social deviance in the city: a spatial perspective, in D. T. Herbert and R. J. Johnston eds. (1976): *Social areas in the city* Vol. 2, Spatial perspectives on problems

N

0   2   4 Kms
0   2 Miles

Airport

Model Cities
Area

C.B.D.

U.S.
Air force Base

Areas with above average
per capita income

Worst ten traces for
criminal violation arrests

Figure 15–3: Aspects of crime and socio-economic status in Tampa, Fl *(after D. M. Smith)*.

committed by adolescents with the usual age limit at 20. Figure 15–4 reproduces material from his work on Cardiff with two distributions superimposed. The first is the distribution of the first factor derived from an

and policies, Chap. 3, 89–122. (1977): Crime, delinquency and the urban environment. *Progress in Human Geography* 1(2), 208–239.

[11] D. T. Herbert (1976): The study of delinquency areas: a social geographical approach. *Trans. Inst. Brit. Geogrs.*, New Series 1(4), 472–492.

analysis using 40 variables and categorized as a social class factor, since the high positive loading variables included the percentage in social class 1 and 2, having two or more cars, travelling to work by car and having exclusive use of all the household amenities recorded by the census. The second distribution mapped in the figure shows above average delinquency rates by residence per 1000 of the population at risk. A clear relationship can be seen. Once again there is the characteristic surround of the CBD by low social class areas with high delinquency rates.

It has been shown in chapter 10 that socio-economic status is essentially sectoral in its intra-urban distribution and on this map the sectoral extensions of the lower quality areas and of delinquency are well matched. Again, however, the apparent simplicity of a pattern matching exercise should not be over-stressed; even on figure 15−4 there are apparent anomalies. There

High socio-economic status factor
Areas with positive scores

Above average delinquency rates
by residence, per 1000 & at risk

Figure 15−4: Delinquency rates and social status in Cardiff (*after D. T. Herbert*).

is certainly a difference between what are conventionally called 'rough' and 'respectable' working class areas, while municipal housing tends to emphasize the sectoral extension of the delinquency distribution. It can be argued that, in like manner to those suffering from mental illness, those that are recidivist will gradually lapse into the inner city sink; those that are not will eventually take their places within standard working class areas, while those who make crime pay will graduate to the affluent suburbs. But to maintain that there is a simple association of crime with the inner city is mistaken, although it is certainly correct to argue that the inner city is associated with crime. A whole range of influences other than those of the inner city can be identified.

In chapter 11 the brief examination of vandalism considered a relationship with an impersonal physical and an anomic social environment which produced delinquency far removed from city centres and characteristic of peripheral municipal housing estates. It is also apparent that throughout the city there are deviant sub-cultures each operating what can be called a neighbourhood effect. In the public bars of the outer suburbs tax fraud becomes a laudable achievement, whilst in the ghettos of the centre mugging is translated into a permissible sport. Urban crime is, therefore, an extremely complex feature which cannot simply be reduced to a relationship to a single part of the city. Much analysis especially by process studies, remains to be done.

2 Intra-urban inequalities: multiple deprivation and the inner city

In 1925 E. W. Burgess characterized the area about the C.B.D. as the zone in transition.[12] It was called 'the zone of deterioration' or 'the zone in decay' (Chapter 8, pages 231 – 35). Some fifty years later it has been discovered by politicians and, oddly enough, by some geographers. It is true that these inner area problems have been greatly exacerbated by recent socioeconomic trends, but in all essentials they remain what they were. Perhaps this merely corroborates the radical view that such a situation is the inexorable product of the capitalist system.

The whole process of inner city decline can be regarded as a downward spiral in relation to all aspects of welfare into which it is difficult to break, but since faring well depends on secure employment the job market is an appropriate point. In that employment context the process has been one of universal decline. The areas about the C.B.D. were characterized by a high density of labour intensive, small scale enterprises, but this has greatly changed. 'Rationalization' has meant the closure or failure of small, uneconomic units, especially those with obsolete equipment. In their place large scale factories on assembly line principles have become dominant. Such operations require large extents of cheap land which is now only to be found on the outer fringes of cities. Moreover, with the problems of congestion in the city centre and the dominance of motor transport, access to motorways and urban expressways has replaced the former need to be near railway goods-yards. Skilled workers earning the highest wages have themselves looked for improved conditions away from the city centre. The result has been a massive transfer of employment away from the city to the suburbs and the creation of a job shortage in the inner city, a location from which the

---

[12] R. E. Park and E. W. Burgess (1925), 50.

skilled have been abstracted and the unskilled left behind.

A further cause of these changes is to be found in planning policies. The planning ethos of most western industrialized countries has favoured the dispersal of industry to lagging regions and, in many cases, there have been well structured government schemes to persuade industrialists establishing new enterprises or reorganizing existing ones, to look for locations away from the largest cities. Overspill schemes abounded. Moreover, on the more local scale and as a corollary, many of the central areas of cities have been subject to redevelopment, often on a comprehensive scale. Such a process often swept away a large numbers of the surviving workshops and industries which occupied poor quality premises in areas of mixed land-use. Where the business did not disappear altogether, relocation in the suburban ring followed. The planning process, therefore, has exacerbated the inner city problem which it is now trying to solve by reversing the policies which were once vigorously pursued.

This process of industrial change is clearly demonstrated in Great Britain by a study of Greater Manchester by P. E. Lloyd and C. M. Mason.[13] Figure 15−5, which is reproduced from their work, displays net total employment change between 1966 and 1972.

The dominant loss of employment from inner Manchester, as well as the inner areas of the surrounding towns, is quite unequivocally revealed. 'During a prolonged period of unfavourable national business conditions and of discrimination against small industries, manufacturing − faced with the twin pressure of the office boom and the drive for comprehensive redevelopment − has most frequently died and less often moved out.'[14] Bull has shown the same process in Clydeside, that is the peripheral location of new plants rather than intra-urban transfers, which underlies the change.[15] But whatever its nature, the result is a lack of jobs in the inner city.[16] Again in Britain, 'regional policy since the last war has brought 100,000 new manufacturing jobs to Merseyside to offset the loss of jobs in port and railway. However, all of these have been located on the periphery . . . . Between 1961 and 1971 the City of Liverpool lost 28,000 jobs in the port, railways, construction and utilities; 21,000 jobs in retail and wholesale distribution; and 30,000 jobs in manufacturing industry.'[17] The loss has accelerated since 1971.

In the U.S.A., in more general terms, in 1960 the populations of the Standard Metropolitan Statistical Areas (SMSA's) were equally divided between central city and suburban surround, but by 1970 54 per cent were suburban and by 1974, 57 per cent. During the four years 1970 to 1974 net out-migra-

[13] P. E. Lloyd and C. M. Mason (1978): Housing and employment in the inner city: a case study of Greater Manchester. *Trans. Inst. Brit. Geogrs.*, New Series 3(1), 66−90.

[14] P. E. Lloyd and C. M. Mason (1978), 88.

[15] P. J. Bull (1978): The spatial components of intra-urban manufacturing change: suburbanization in Clydeshire, 1958−1968. *Trans. Inst. Brit. Geogrs.*, New Series 3(1), 91−100.

[16] For a further study of a British city see: J. J. Fagg (1977): *The distribution of manufacturing industry in Greater Leicester.* Unpub. Ph.D. thesis. Univ. of Leicester.

[17] Dept. of the Environment (1977): *Inner area studies. Liverpool, Birmingham and Lambeth. Summaries of consultants' final reports,* 5 (London).

Figure 15–5: Net total employment change in Greater Manchester 1966–1972 (*after P. E. Lloyd and C. M. Mason*).

tion from city to suburb was some 10 per cent of the 1970 population. For New York city between 1964 and 1969 there was an annual *increase* of 47,000 jobs, but between 1969 and 1974 there was an annual *loss* of 68,000. 'The city in the last five years has been losing more than 43,000 manufacturing jobs annually, the garment industry alone losing 12,000.'[18] Elsewhere the story is the same. In 1970, St. Louis lost 43 companies to the suburbs. In two recent years, Boston lost 75 . . . . Likewise in Detroit, S. S. Kresge, the retail chain, plans to move its corporate offices, as does the Michigan Automobile Club, Delta and Pan American Airlines, R. L. Polk (publishers), not to mention Circus World, the toy manufacturers. Things

---

[18] G. Sternlieb and J. W. Hughes (1975): Is the New York region the prototype? in, *Post-Industrial America: metropolitan decline and inter-regional job shift*, 118 (New Brunswick, N.J.). The information on the U.S.A. in the above paragraph was derived from this source.

are so glum that former mayor Jerome Cavanaugh sometimes refers to 'Detroit's sister cities—Nagasaki and Pompeii'.[19] All this material, factual and prophetic, emphasizes the same pattern of decline, partly causing and in part caused by the deteriorating physical conditions of housing.

These were the earliest built parts of the city so that without constant renewal housing becomes obsolete and has none of the modern amenities. This is an added 'push' force to those who can afford to move. The 'shabby environment, the lack of amenities, the high density remaining in some parts and the poor condition of the older housing . . . contrast sharply with better conditions elsewhere. They combine to make these areas unattractive, both to many of the people who live there and to new investment in business, industry and housing,'[20] The British Department of the Environment commissioned studies of the inner areas of Birmingham, Liverpool and Lambeth (London) and the consequent reports provide a mass of detailed information on housing conditions. The Birmingham report, '*Housing policy for the inner city*', demonstrates the range of problems which include not only physical decay of fabric and the lack of standard amenities, but also paradoxically both over-crowding and under-occupation. The former is self explanatory, but to the elderly widow, characteristic of the sorts of population left in the inner areas, the problem of coping with a house which is too large, including the physical demands of cleaning and the financial demands of effective heating, can become a major one.[21] The general problems of housing have been dealt with in Chapters 10 and 11 and the characteristic inner area of decline has been indicated.

In addition to employment and housing it will be apparent from earlier chapters that these inner locations are the reception areas for immigrant populations, especially those of a culture contrasting with that of the indigeneous population. These are, as Chapter 10 demonstrated, the ghetto areas of the great cities. They are, therefore, characterized by all those tensions which are generated by the process of mutual adaptation. That process of adaptation is most difficult for the elderly, but should be easiest for the young. But the schools, like the housing, are old and outdated in structure and design.[22] The problems of teaching in these areas, where language difficulties are of a high order, result in a high turn over in employment, for only the most dedicated will accept the constant challenge. Finally, the earlier part of this chapter has shown how the inner areas become the 'sinks' to which the criminal, and those who drop out from society, gravitate.[23]

[19] B. J. L. Berry and J. D. Kasarda (1977): *Contemporary urban ecology*, 255–56 (New York).

[20] *Policy for the Inner Cities* (1977): Cmd. 6845, 3, (H.M.S.O., London).

[21] Llewelyn-Davies, Weeks, Forestier-Walker and Bor (1976): *Inner area study Birmingham. Housing policies for the inner city*, Chapter 3. (London, Dept. of the Environment).

[22] D. T. Herbert (1976): Urban education: problems and policies, in D. T. Herbert and R. J. Johnston, editors (1976), 123–158.

[23] For an interesting behavioural study see G. Rowley (1978): "Plus ça change . . . . :" a Canadian Skid Row. *Canadian Geographer* 22(3), 211–224.

The critical point is that all the above elements of deprivation or of disadvantage are not simply associated but intimately interrelated. The ill-educated and jobless immigrant, and particularly the first generation of children, form a group most likely to become involved in petty crime. The minimal physical conditions of housing not only push out the upwardly mobile, but draw in the poorest section of the population and the most rootless who cannot qualify for municipal or subsidized housing. The lack of a buoyant tax or rate base, as well as of strong and articulate community leaders, inhibits improvement. Gwyn Williams at the conclusion of his census atlas of Great Manchester records, 'numerous analyses have shown that the inner city areas of Manchester and Salford stand out as areas suffering from multiple deprivation within the fields of housing, employment and general environmental standards. The limited control they have over their own lives, and their lack of access to the power structure of society has meant that the inner city residents are unable to fully compete against other social groups with regard to the distribution of social and economic resources.'[24] The phrase 'multiple deprivation' has now become a standard designation of this situation although, again, the significant concept is not that of simple multiplication but of the functional interrelation of all the aspects of disadvantage.

The measurement of deprivation has become one of the major concerns both of urban social geographers and of administrators. There are two problems involved. The first is the choice of indicators or variables, and the second the derivation of a method by which the indicators can be combined into a single measure. The choice of variables to be used as indicators depends largely on the purpose of the survey and the availability of data. Inevitably census data make up the greater proportion of the variables used since they are easily accessible; but they necessarily cover only a section of the total situation. In the mid 1960's the U.S. Department of Commerce Bureau of Statistics undertook the identification of 'poverty areas' in the Standard Metropolitan Statistical Areas with populations of over a quarter of a million.[25] Only five measures were used:

1   Per cent of families with cash incomes under $3000.
2   Per cent of children under 18 years old not living with both parents.
3   Per cent of males 25 years old and over with less than 8 years school completed.
4   Per cent of unskilled males aged 14 and over in the employed civilian labour force.
5   Per cent of all housing units lacking some or all plumbing facilities or delapidated.

In contrast D. M. Smith in a study of Tampa[26] abstracted 47 variables to

---

[24] G. Williams (1975): *Metropolitan Manchester: a social atlas*, 39. Manchester Univ., Dept. of Town and Country Planning.

[25] U.S.A. Dept. of Commerce, Bureau of the Census (1967): *Poverty areas in the 100 largest Metropolitan Areas*. Supplementary report P.C. (S1) − 54 (Washington, D.C.).

[26] D. M. Smith (1973): *The geography of social well-being in the United States*, Chap. 9, 120−134 (New York).

assess social well-being (and its converse) grouped into six criteria, each broken down into sub-criteria and each sub-criteria into variables (not given below).

1 *Economic Status*
  a   Income
  b   Employment
  c   Welfare
2 *Environment*
  a   Housing
  b   Streets and sewers
  c   Air pollution
  d   Open space
3 *Health*
  a   General mortality
  b   Chronic diseases
4 *Education*
  a   Duration
5 *Social disorganization*
  a   Personal pathologies
  b   Family breakdown
  c   Overcrowding
  d   Public order and safety
  e   Delinquency
6 *Participation and equality*
  a   Democratic participation
  b   Equality

The British Office of Population Census and Surveys has published a volume which lists social and community indicators from the census, and a total of some 260 are set out.[27] The main issues are that a reasonable degree of economy is practised and excessive replication avoided, and that as many non-census measures are introduced as possible in order to give the necessary width of coverage. For example, Smith's 'Environment' criteria (2 above) included in its 'Streets and sewers' sub-group (b) a variable which was the percentage total length of streets needing reconstruction and another which was the percentage of area having sanitary sewer deficiencies. These are difficult to measure with any accuracy but do provide a wider range than the usual census derived data permit. An example of the measurement of deprivation from an administrative context is the attempt in Britain to establish Educational Priority Areas in which additional salary allowances were to be given to teachers. The Inner London Education Authority (ILEA) adopted the following criteria relatd to individual schools:[28]

1 *Occupation.* Proportion of occupied males in unskilled jobs.
2 *Supplements in cash from State.* Percentage of children receiving

---

[27] C. Hakin (1978): *Social and community indicators from the census.* Office of Population Censuses and Surveys, Occ. Paper 5 (London).
[28] This information is derived from: D. T. Herbert (1976), 146–151.

school meals.

3   *Overcrowding*. Percentage living at density of more than 1·5 per room.
4   *Lack of basic amenities*. Percentage of houses lacking one of the four basic amenities of the census.
5   *Poor attendance*. Average absence in a sample week.
6   *Proportion of handicapped pupils*. Percentage of children of low ability defined as the lowest twenty five per cent on a standardized test at the age of 11.
7   *Immigrant children*. Proportion of immigrant children.
8   *Teacher turnover*. Proportion of teachers who had taught in a school for less than three academic years.
9   *Pupil turnover*. Percentage of children who had spent an incomplete year in the school.

It is interesting to note that given the different aims there is considerable overlap with the American poverty area survey, except that the ILEA measure has no family composition or status input and, of course, has specific education criteria. The only remaining comment is that all the variables indicated as being used are explicitly objective and no attempt is made to measure subjective reaction to a situation.[29] It does appear at times odd that a condemnation of materialistic viewpoints and a demand for a quality of life based on community and personal relationships are accompanied by measures wholly material in their formulation.

The construction of a single index revolves around the usual difficulty in relation to such composite measures of deriving some standardizing procedure for each set of variables, and a weighting procedure for their inclusion into one summary figure. The most frequently adopted method is a Standard Score Additive Model employing what are called Z-scores. 'The Z-score is a linear transformation of the original data such that its(sic) mean becomes zero and its (sic) standard deviation becomes unity'[30]

$$ Zi = \frac{X_i - \bar{X}}{S} $$

where X_i is the value of observation i, $\bar{X}$ is the mean and S is the standard deviation. The Z-scores are then simply totalled, for it is extremely difficult to derive a satisfactory and acceptable basis for a weighting procedure.

Consideration of these measures has removed discussion from the substantive problem of those parts of the city which are deprived, to the measurement of deprivation. Smith's conclusions from the Tampa study were that 'while the worst parts of Tampa on each of these factors tend to coincide with the inner city slums, the patterns have their own distinctive features'[31] for, 'like many other cities, Tampa has its black middle-class community, its socially disorganized and highly unstable population around the prosperity symbols of the CBD, and its non-affluent white neighbour-

[29] T. J. Kuz (1978): Quality of life, an objective and subjective variable analysis. *Regional Studies* 12(4), 409–418.
[30] D. M. Smith (1973), 85–6.
[31] D. M. Smith (1977): *Human geography: a welfare approach*, 284 (London).

hoods of generally law abiding and conforming citizens'[32]. This is an appropriate warning that problem areas are not exclusively associated with one category of population or one area, but even so the predominant problem area is the inner city. Sufficient comment has been provided in this book to indicate why this should be so in locational terms.

The implications of the contrast between affluent suburbs and decaying slums has been best illustrated by Bunge's scenario for Detroit[33] (Figure 15−6 A and B). Bunge sets up an equation[34]

$$R = A(P - C) - 30\,ATD$$

where R is the rental profit in dollars per month per square mile

and A the number of dwellings per square mile,
P the rental in dollars per month,
C replacement and maintenance costs in dollars per month,
T transportation costs in dollars per mile per day, ⎫ multiplied by 30
⎬ to give
and D distance from the city centre in miles. ⎭ monthly total

Reference to Chapter 8 will show that this is the simplest of measures of land rents related to distance (compare with figure 8−7, page 191). Bunge proceeds to make the substitutions indicated on figure 15−6 A and hence arrives at the conclusion that at one mile from the city centre there are profits of $220,000 per square mile per month or $2,640,000 per annum being generated, i.e.

$$R = 5000\,(80 - 30) - 30 \times 5000 \times 0{\cdot}20 \times 1$$
$$= \$220,000.$$

Bunge's second diagram indicates the flow of these rents, together with other money transfers of a variety of natures. The implications are now apparent; those in affluent suburbs are deriving their standard of living from the exploitation of the inner city.

This exercise is, of course over simplified. It is designed to illuminate an issue rather than as an empirical investigation and hard figures are supplied for only part of the analysis. One has to accept Bunge's data, for they are presented without reference to sources of confirmation and are nothing more than subjective assessments. This is even more dangerous in figure 15−6B where flows are indicated of varying dimensions but without any values being assigned. The diagram resembles one of those elementary illustrations in economic geography where arrows of unrevealed significance identify a country's imports and exports! Moreover, none of the reciprocal inflow of money from taxes to the centre are included. Perhaps these are smaller in the U.S.A. than in Britain where the various welfare services would engender a substantial return flow which would have to be evaluated. Deliberately to omit these inflows from the calculation raises suspicions as to

[32] D. M. Smith (1973), 131.
[33] W. Bunge (1971): *Fitzgerald: geography of a revolution.* (Cambridge, Mass).
[34] W. Bunge (1971), 132−33.

The rental profit taken out of the slums at a distance of one mile from the city centre is at least $ 2,640,000 per year per square mile.

Maximum rental profit equation :
R = A (P–C) – 30 ATD
Where :
R = Rental profit – Dollars/Month/Sq mile
D = Distance from centre of city – miles
A = No of dwellings per square mile
P = Rental – Dollars per month
C = Replacement & Maintenance cost – Dollars per month
T = Transportation cost – Dollars/mile/Day

	A	P	C	T
Slums	5000	80	30	.20
Middle class	1000	200	100	.20
Affluent suburbs	100	500	300	.20

D – Distance from centre of Detroit – (Miles)

Figure 15–6: A: The urban geography of Detroit's rental profits.

the whole probity of the exercise. But Bunge's presentation makes the point which it was intended to do: there is more than simple inequality, there is also exploitation, a fact which adds a further dimension to this considera-tion of welfare geography.

Radical geographers, however, would argue that merely displaying a situation is wholly inadequate. Involvement and action are essential in order to induce change towards a situation without inequalities and free from exploitation.

3 Inter-urban inequalities

Positivist statements of the implacability of geometry are becoming unfa-shionable but even so, an axiom can be propounded that space predicates inequality and necessitates deprivation. Every point on the earth's surface cannot be provided with equal access to goods and services, nor can a total population be located on a single point. It has been maintained in chapter 4 that one of the consequences of the time-cost expended to traverse dis-tance is an urban hierarchy, or at least a size-ranking of some form: in chapter 8 it has been pointed out that the friction of distance structures intra-urban land uses. In any urban system there will be differential access

Figure 15–6: B: Direction of money transfers in Metropolitan Detroit (*after W. Bunge*).

to the highest order services, and that, for the sector of the population with least access, constitutes deprivation. No economy has yet developed, or will in any likelihood in the foreseeable future develop, in a spatially uniform way: both regional and hierarchial contrasts are part of the process of growth.[35]

At the regional scale such contrasts mean that at any one time a population will regard itself as deprived if it is situated in a lagging region. But that scale is the material of regional rather than urban studies, and although the division is arbitrary and scarcely tenable it would be odd to discuss rural multiple deprivation in a volume on urban geography, whilst growth centre policies, although specifically urban, are directed at the regional scale. This

[35] R. J. Fuchs and G. J. Demko (1979): Geographic inequality under socialism. *Ann. Assoc. Amer. Geogrs.* 69(2), 304–318.

section needs to stress a closely related but somewhat different point, the disadvantages of those who live in settlements at the lower levels of the urban hierarchy and at the periphery of the largest city hinterland. These disadvantages derive from the severely limited accessibility of populations in such settlements, a limitation which becomes a matter of critical deprivation for the unemployed, low paid, the elderly and the infirm, or any group whose mobility is in any way relatively constrained (See chapter 6, p. 139)

4 Radical or marxist urban geography

Writing on geographic inequality under socialism Fuchs and Demko conclude that 'the discussion of issues such as spatial inequalities is hardly constructive when it is done in order to condemn a specific ideological system. Since East and West share the problems of spatial inequalities, and express a commitment to their elimination or reduction, this should be recognized as a common problem to be removed from the area of political debate'.[36] This is an interesting but fundamentally mistaken reading of the critique by radical geography. Most exponents of the Marxist approach have little in common with those who emphasize welfare concerns; spatial inequalities, they assert, derive from the fundamental economic order and anything but revolution in that, a thing centrally political, is merely the rearrangement of a superstructure to make an outward appearance more attractive and defendable, while the underlying driving mechanism of the capitalist system is left untouched. It follows that it is impossible to introduce a chapter, or part of a chapter, in a book such as this dealing with radical urban geography as if it were simply concerned with stressing somewhat different issues, for the whole volume is conceived and structured in an antithetical form.

In spite of this last problem, however, it is still worthwhile to turn aside at this point, to consider how such an alternative urban geography would be structured, for it is here, over the issue of spatial inequalities, that the two approaches, conventional (capitalist) and radical (Marxist) come nearest as they pass each other on different courses.

Unfortunately there is no immediate exposition of a 'complete' Marxist urban geography to which to turn. Most radical writing has been concerned with urging the need for such a venture rather than undertaking it. David Harvey has, however, attempted a sketch of the urban process under capitalism in order to provide at least a framework for analysis.[37] He confesses that 'to broach the whole question of the urban process under capitalism in a short article appears a foolish endeavour'; to summarize his sketch must appear doubly foolish. Yet the brief diversion (or this transfer to the central thema, according to view) is worthwhile even at the risk of travesty, to present some indication of the nature of the approach.

The starting point is the main motivation of the capitalist system, the

[36] R. J. Fuchs and G. J. Demko (1979), 318.
[37] D. Harvey (1978): The urban process under capitalism: a framework for analysis. *Internat. Journ. of Urban and Regional Research*, 2(1), 101–131.

making of profit. Two basic themes follow, accumulation and the class struggle. Profit, or the derivation of surplus value, accrues to the capitalists who dominate, organize and exploit the work process. Labour can only sell its work power in the market and hence conflict arises as the capitalists ensure the securing of surplus value produced by labour, at the expense of labour. Accumulation and class conflict are in this way part of the same process. To maintain domination and speed accumulation the capitalist class behaves with increasing violence to the labouring class; to battle for its own interests the working class unites. 'Through competition, however, the inherent laws of capitalist production are asserted as external coercive laws having power over every capitalist. A world of individuality and freedom on the surface conceals a world of conformity and coercion underneath'.[38] Freedom to choose in the capitalist world is, therefore, a myth; it is part of the superstructural arrangements to conceal infrastructural impositions.

At this stage the direct question as to how all this relates to the urban geographer immediately arises. But it is still necessary to follow Harvey through his analysis of the 'laws of accumulation'. He sketches what he terms three circuits. In the primary circuit he demonstrates the tendency for the system to move towards over accumulation, for its prime raison d'etre is to expropriate surplus value, even as an end in itself. This surplus, however, can be used by being switched to the secondary circuit by progressive investment in fixed capital either to aid the production process or to support those external features which support production and which are called the built environment: housing is an example. Finally there is a further, tertiary circuit which absorbs surplus through investment in science and technology further to enhance production or in social expenditure to maintain the efficiency of labour. A health service is not concerned primarily with the total well-being of the individual but with ensuring that the labour input can be maintained. These three circuits are shown in figure 15-7.

It is against such a structure that spatial processes must be viewed. Two examples can be sketched. The first is derived from the fact that the underlying contradictions within the capitalist process of accumulation generate crises. The potential of capitalism for balanced growth is never achieved. Thus overproduction, increasing the quantity available in the market, precipitates a decrease in value and, as the potential for further productive investment is exhausted a crisis follows. Harvey identifies:

1 *Partial crises.* These occur within an economic sector or geographical region and are met by local adjustment.
2 *Switching crises.* These follow on the redirection of investment within
   a sectors of the economy
   b geographical regions
   although the two are so inter-related as to be difficult to separate.
   c *Global crises.* These affect the whole capitalist world as in the growing crisis of the late 1970's and the early 1980's.

---

[38] D. Harvey (1978), 102.

Figure 15–7: The structure of relations between the primary, secondary and tertiary circuits of capital (*after D. Harvey*).

To demonstrate the direct relevance of this analysis it can be argued that the inner city problem, which has already been considered in this chapter from a conventional cartographically based viewpoint, is a switching crisis. Investment has shifted from non-profitable to more profitable sectors/ regions to maximize accumulation. The crisis in this case becomes deeper because of the spatial immobility of investment in the built environment. But capital simply abandons the 'region' and leaves it to deteriorate with the result that costs are eventually shifted to the working class by the necessity for state intervention via comprehensive redevelopment or one of the many forms of rehabilitation. Alternatively residual profits can be made by the attraction of the poorest into these deteriorating parts of the city. Slum and ghetto are the inevitable products of the system. In the end, the community (the working class) absorbs the burden of the contradictions of capitalism either in a direct financial way or through a devalued environment.

Here, then, are the 'real' reasons, the causes of inner city decay. Mapping measures of social deprivation, devising 'enterprise regions', these are simply containing, at community expense, the costs of the contradictions of capitalism, in a cosmetic exercise.

The second example is not unrelated to the first and here it is useful to revert to a point already discussed, the explosive development of residential suburbia in the U.S.A. after 1945 (see Chap. 11, p. 311). At that time, Harvey argues, potential over-accumulation faced the country. This dilemma was 'in part resolved by the creation of a whole new life style through the rapid proliferation of the suburbanization process. Furthermore, the social unrest of the 1930's in that country pushed the bourgeoisie to adopt a policy of individual home ownership for the more affluent workers as a means to ensure social stability. This solution has the added advantage of opening up the housing sector as a means for rapid accumulation through commodity production. So successful was this solution that the housing sector became a Keynesian 'contra-cyclical' regulator for the accumulation process as a whole. . .' .[39]

It will now be apparent that these two examples of inner city decay and suburbanization are not only related to each other but have a common genesis from the operations of the capitalist system. It will also be clear why Marxist geographers argue that the initial point of departure for urban geography should be neither measurement of a real, objective world, nor the uncovering of the patterns of the perceived world, but the 'first cause' of the politico-economic system.

One final point must be made. All this is a critique of the city in the existing and real capitalist world; it goes no way whatsoever to specifying an alternative. So one returns to the authors whose views were set aside at the beginning of this section. 'It should be apparent to all but those wilfully ignorant or already ideologically committed that the imposition of a Marxist political-socialist system is in itself no panacea leading to removal of spatial

[39] D. Harvey (1978), 126-7.

inequalities; decision-makers under state socialism appear to hold values of growth, productivity, efficiency, and rewards similar to those of capitalists, leading to similar problems of spatial inequity'.[40]

5 Conclusion

The briefest of conclusions is appropriate. That there is inequality in the city which has in part a spatial aspect, is undeniable. Whether it be regarded as the product of the technical problems of organizing space common to all politico-economic systems, or whether it is the product solely of the systems themselves, must be left to the reader.

Notes on further reading

The basic work on inequality in the city is:

Harvey, D. (1973): *Social justice and the city* (London).

A clear, general presentation of major issues is to be found in:

Smith, D. M. (1977): *Human geography: a welfare approach* (London).

A volume dealing more specifically with the urban situation is:

Herbert, D. T. and Smith, D. M. (1979): *Social problems and the city. Geographical perspectives* (Oxford).

In addition to the paper by J. A. Giggs discussed in this chapter (see footnote 2). There is also a contribution by the same author to the volume noted above which is an excellent summary and has an extensive bibliography.

Giggs, J. A. (1979): Human health problems in urban areas, being Chap. 6 in Herbert, D. M. and Smith, D. T. eds. (1979), 84–116.

There have been numerous studies of urban crime from a spatial viewpoint. Two reviews by D. T. Herbert are:

Herbert, D. T. (1977): Crime, delinquency and the urban environment. *Progress in Human Geography*, 1(2), 208–239.
Herbert, D. T. (1979): Urban crime: a geographical perspective, being Chap. 7 in Herbert, D. T. and Smith, D. M. (1979), 117–138.

Other contributions are:

Brantingham, P. J. and Brantingham, P. L. (1975): Residential burglary and urban form. *Urban Studies*, 12, 273–284.
Harries, K. D. (1974): *The geography of crime and justice* (New York).
Schmid, C. F. (1960): Urban crime areas. *American Soc. Review*, 27–52 and 655–678.
Scott, P. (1972): The spatial analysis of crime and delinquency. *Australian Geog. Studies*, 10, 1–18.
Smith, D. M. (1974): Crime rates as territorial social indicators: the case of the United States (see footnote 8).

[40] R. J. Fuchs and G. J. Demko (1979), 318.

Some indicator of radical attitudes to spatial studies of crime can be gleamed from:

Peet, R. (1975): The geography of crime: a political critique. *Professional Geographer*, 27, 277–80.

Peet, R. (1976): Some further comments of the Geography of crime. *Professional Geographer*, 28, 96–100.

Harries, K. D. (1976): Observations on radical v. liberal theories of crime causation. *Professional Geographer*, 28, 100–113.

The measurement of multiple deprivation and the problems of the inner city have both now generated very extensive literatures. As far as the former is concerned a good introduction is:

Smith, D. M. (1979): The identification of problems in cities: applications of social indicators. Chap. 2 in Herbert, D. T. and Smith, D. M. eds. (1979), 13–32.

whilst a more general classic is:

Runciman, W. G. (1966): *Relative deprivation and social justice* (London).

For the inner city two references which can be taken as starting points are the British Government commissioned work quoted in footnotes 17, 20 and 21 and

Berry, B. J. L. (1980): Inner city future: an American dilemma revisited *Trans. Inst. Brit. Geogrs.*, New Series 5(1), 1–28.

Champion, A. G. and Warnes, A. M. (1978): Housing and employment in the inner city. *Trans. Inst. Brit. Geogrs.*, New Series, 3(1). This volume of the Transactions was devoted to inner city problems.

An admirable summary is to be found in:

Thrift, N. (1979): Unemployment in the inner city: urban problem or structural imperative? A review of the British experience, being Chap. 5 in D. T. Herbert and R. J. Johnston eds. *Geography and the urban Environment*. Vol. 2 (London).

No mention is made in the text, either in the section on ethnicity (Chap. 10) or on crime and violence in this Chapter of the major British example of Belfast. F. W. Boal has written extensively and with insight into this problem. Some of his studies are:

Boal, F. W., Murray, R. and Poole, M. A. (1976): Belfast: the urban encapsulation of a national conflict, in Clarke, S. E. and Obler, J. L. eds. (1976): *Urban ethnic conflict: A comparative perspective*. Univ. of North Carolina, Inst. for Research in Social Science, Comparative Urban Studies Monograph Series No. 3

Boal, F. W. (1969): Territoriality on the Shankhill-Falls divide, Belfast. *Irish Geographer*, 6, 33–4.

Boal, F. W. and Poole, M. A. (1973): Religious residential segregation in Belfast in mid-1969: a multi-level analysis in Clark, B. D. and Gleave, M. B. eds. (1973): Social patterns in cities. *Inst. Brit. Geogrs*. Special publication No. 5.

16

The City in the Developing World

The bulk of the material introduced in this book is concerned primarily with the cities of the developed west. Three assumptions (they could even be regarded as presumptions) have therefore been inherent from the start. These are: an industrialized or developed economy, a capitalist system and a western cultural environment. An ideal procedure would be to relax each of these assumed conditions in turn and to consider the consequences of such modification on cities, both in locational characteristics and internal structure. But such a procedure is difficult to carry out in any meaningful way for the second assumption, that of the capitalist system. In terms of distribution or locational pattern, that is in central place relations, socialist countries have not produced any specifically socialist modifications, whilst in relation to internal structure the lack of adequate small area data, equivalent to the census tract in the U.S.A. or the enumeration district in the U.K., makes the empirical interpretation of internal patterns broad in scale and descriptive in nature.

In spite of the increasing radical criticisms of the western city as it is, there is surprisingly little on the city as it should be, so that even on the age-old urban utopia theme there is little to consider in radical literature. In relation to undeveloped economies and other cultures, however, a great mass of material has been published in the last decade and this demands review, even if analysis in any depth is beyond the reach of a single chapter.

In relation to the material already presented in this book on urbanization and inter-urban relations, three aspects of the developing world stand out:

1 The colonial origin of towns.
2 Over urbanization and primacy.
3 Systems of periodic markets.

1 The colonial origin of towns

The colonial origin of towns is certainly not a unique feature of the developing world for many European towns and all those in the United States and Australia were colonial in origin. The great colonizing movements in medieval Europe were largely accomplished through a process of town building; the bastide towns were by their nature colonial towns and carried many colonial characteristics. The great contrast with the cities established in the developing world is, however, the major cultural differences between the predominantly European founders and the indigeneous populations. In the U.S.A. and Australia this problem was offset by the complete dispossession and virtual elimination of the native population in the process of settlement. Elsewhere the native populations remained in a condition of exploitation. The critical feature, therefore, of the cities founded in the tropical areas was the aim of exploitation. The cities tended, in consequence, to have a limited range of functions, mainly related to the export of primary raw materials and the administrative and military bases sufficient to make this viable. Where the Church went as well to convert the inhabitants to Christianity it largely relied on the administrative system.

Essentially, though certainly not completely, these cities were parasitic, rather than generative of an economic development which trickled down to the surrounding areas. For example, 'the development of the urban system in colonial Latin America gave primacy to the political and fiscal needs of the empire. The urban hierarchy of city and village, often imposed upon pre-existing native jurisdictions and urban institutions, preserved and enforced status distinctions between categories of population. The categories of Indian, slave, mestizo (of Spanish and Indian parents), mulatto (of Spanish and black parents) and Spaniard had different sets of rights and obligations in terms of tribute, forced labour, taxes, military service, trading and debt contraction. Glade[1] contrasts this form of colonization with Turner's characterization of the North American frontier as a source of economic and political autonomy and innovation . . . . 'In this situation, towns in Spanish America . . . did not serve to generate economic progress in a "backward" countryside'.[2] Again Gugler and Flanagan writing of West Africa stress that urbanization in that area owes much to the colonial past, 'This is true not only of the atmosphere and location of towns but also with regard to the nature of the role these towns have played and are continuing to play in the economic development of the independent states'.[3] Two significant consequences follow from this inheritance:

1   The large cities often have highly skewed employment structures. Development as export and administrative centres has resulted in the basic range of industrial employment remaining undeveloped. This is particularly critical at a period of high urban in-migration.

2   Because of a location initially orientated towards external linkages many capital cities are eccentrically located in the new national territories. 'As a consequence of their location on the geographic periphery of the new states, the young capitals of West Africa have acquired a political character that is more regional than national. Because of major ethnic and economic differences between the capital region and the rest of the nation, the geographically marginal capital comes to stand as a symbol of faction rather than national unity'.[4]

[1] W. Glade (1969): *The Latin American economies: a study of their institutional evolution*, 60–62 (New York).

[2] B. Roberts (1978): *Cities of peasants*, 38 (London).

[3] J. Gugler and W. G. Flanagan (1978): *Urbanization and social change in West Africa*, 26 (Cambridge).

[4] J. Gugler and W. G. Flanagan (1978), 31–2.

2 Over-urbanization and primacy

The nature of urban growth in the developing world has already been dealt with in chapter 2 when the process of urbanization was considered. Also at that point an explanation of the massive nature and rapidity of that urbanization was suggested. Certainly over simple explanations must not be accepted. At the root is the process of demographic transition characterized by a fall in the death rate and consequent rapid population growth. Milton Santos[5] shows that whereas in Sweden it took one hundred years for the death rate to fall from 21 to 14 per thousand, in Costa Rica it fell from 23 to 7·9 per thousand in 42 years (1920−1962), in Sri Lanka from 20 to 9 in 15 years (1946−1961) and in Jamaica from 28 to 13 per thousand in 29 years (1921−1950). This population 'explosion' has taken place against two critical changes. The first is in the nature of agriculture itself, which has become increasingly mechanized and commercialized and hence much less labour intensive. The second is the undermining of the traditional bazaar peasant economy by the import of manufactured goods from the developed world. In this context notions of 'dependency'[6] can be put forward or notions of the evolution of a world system using the core-periphery concept. Thus Wallerstein[7] for the early phase of European development distinguished 'between the core industrial regions, such as England, semi-peripheral regions specializing in commerce, such as Spain and peripheral regions, such as Latin America and Eastern Europe, which were organized to provide primary products for the core countries'.[8]

The expanding, modern world system has pushed the developing countries into the role of peripheral providers of raw materials, and the divergence which has characterized core and periphery on the national scale has been echoed at the world scale. A situation comes about, therefore, where not only is population growing but the bonds which held that population to the countryside are loosed and a dominant urban migration precipitated. Moreover, the attractions of the urban areas are themselves evident and much more clearly realized through kin links, as well as the growth of the media. A whole genre of studies has carried out multiple regression analyses of migration flows in under developed areas and the variables emerging as significant, apart from those of distance and size, relate to the attractive pull of the cities in terms of wages, education, health and welfare.[9]

This transfer of population into the urban areas is, as indicated above, partly related to the attraction of size and consequently there has been a trend for the largest city to grow most rapidly. This has been exacerbated by the investment policies of many countries which have diverted a disproportionate amount of funds to what is usually the national capital where political, administrative and cultural authority is centred. Gugler and Flanagan,

[5] M. Santos (1971): *Les villes du tiers monde*, 26 (Paris).
[6] H. Brookfield (1975): *Interdependent development* (London).
[7] I. Walkerstein (1974): *The modern world system* (New York).
[8] B. Roberts (1978), 15.
[9] I. Masser and W. T. S. Gould (1975): Inter-regional migration in tropical Africa (London). *Institute of Brit. Geogrs.*, Special Publication No. 8.

in a section appropriately headed 'the hubris of capital cities', present a revealing account of such a trend in West Africa. 'Anyone who ventures beyond (the national capitals) to the vast expanses of West Africa is stunned by the disparity between the concentration of resources in the capital cities and the neglect that is the fate of much of their hinterlands'.[10]

They go on to exemplify the process of concentration from the work of M. A. Cohen[11] on the Ivory Coast. There 499 out of the country's 617 industrial enterprises are located in Abidjan and 60 per cent of the jobs in the modern sector of the economy. 'In 1968, the eight storey, 500 bed Centre Hospitalier Universitaire, one of the largest and most modern hospitals in Africa, was built in the luxurious Cocody quarter, home of the high government officials, but the fund given by France was originally intended for twelve regional hospitals'.[12] This sort of bias has resulted in a population of some 5000 in 1920 and of about 36,000 in 1940, becoming 242,000 by the mid 1960's and 555,000 in 1970, with an astonishing average annual growth of 10 per cent from the 1950's to the 1970's.[13] In reviewing Asia's probable urban future Dwyer has properly used the word 'frightening'.[14] The United Nations' Department of Economic and Social Analysis estimates that even using an urban definition of 20,000 there will be 993 million urban dwellers in Asia by the year 2000 compared with 265 million in 1960 when even then the cities were described as in a state of crisis.[15]

As a result of the growth rates, which have been discussed, and the concentration of population into the capital cities, two consequences follow. The first is that of over-urbanization, a very nebulous concept but one which emphasizes the increasing urban proportion in countries whose economic bases are too feeble to sustain it. It is partly responsible for widespread unemployment. The mass of urban migrants move into a range of unproductive jobs, especially in the retail and service occupations so that the diagnostic feature of such situations is a high proportion of employment in the tertiary sector. Santos[16] has compared the state of the employment sectors in three Latin American countries with that of three industrialized countries at appropriate dates in their development. It is not that there are great differences at the present between the tertiary sectors of developed and developing countries, but that as table 16−1 reveals the countries of the so-called Third World have not undergone the prior and controlling process of industrialization. 'In developed countries technological progress, bringing about urbanization, has transformed the occupational structure, whereas in under developed countries it has been demographic evolution which has

[10] J. Gugler and W. G. Flanagan (1978), 40−41.
[11] M. A. Cohen (1974): *Urban policy and political conflict in Africa: A study of the Ivory Coast* (Chicago).
[12] J. Gugler and W. G. Flanagan (1978), 42.
[13] J. Gugler and W. G. Flanagan (1978), 41. The source for the data is P. K. Mitchell, Director of the Demographic Documentation Project, Centre of West African Studies, University of Birmingham.
[14] D. Dwyer (1975): *People and Housing in Third World Cities*, 15 (London).
[15] D. Dwyer (1975), 15.
[16] M. Santos (1971), 330−331.

table 16−1: A Comparison of employment structure in developed and under-developed countries.

Country	Date	Percentage Primary	Secondary	Tertiary
Argentina	1960	22	21	57
Chile	1960	25	17	58
Venezuela	1960	32	12	56
France	1954	28	37	35
U.S.A.	1900	38	27	35
Germany	1929	30	41	29

After M. Santos (1971)

most greatly influenced the employment structure'.[17] This is the traditional view of urbanization without industrialization.

The second consequence of urban growth rates, and especially the concentration of growth into capital cities, has been the characteristic of 'primacy'. 'The Law of the Primate City' has already been discussed (chap. 4, pp. 74−5) and the relation of primacy to under development considered. Linsky's conclusion that the concept is related to a particular process of historical change and that there is a need to relate primacy to social, economic and geopolitical conditions, must be recalled at this stage, for it would seem that the sorts of transformations discussed in this section and the dominance obtained at the core by virtue of its political and cultural authority, as well as by virtue of its economic and social supremacy, is the crucial factor in the emergence of the primate city.

3 Systems of periodic markets

A corollary of the vast population increases in the large cities, is the lack of development in the areas removed from metropolitan influence. In such conditions the lack of demand for urban services results in a time-space substitution on the same lines as that which characterized medieval Europe. In a continuation of the search for a central place geometry most investigations have attempted to indicate how markets were organized so that they could be visited in sequence by itinerant traders. The classic and most quoted study was that by G. W. Skinner relating to markets in rural China,[19] although as early as 1961 Hodder had described rural periodic day markets in part of Yorubaland. There he (Hodder) pointed out that such markets were generally evenly spaced out and independent of the village or hamlet distribution. 'Some markets . . . have been simply established in clearings in the bush at the junction of paths: others lie athwart a motorable road, sometimes near to, or in, a village. In some cases the market has in fact created a

---

[17] M. Santos (1971), 329 (present author's translation).
[18] A. S. Linsky (1965): Some generalizations concerning primate cities. *Ann. Assoc. Am. Geogr.* 55, 506.
[19] G. W. Skinner (1964): Marketing and social structure in rural China. *Journ. of Asian Studies* 24(1), 5−31.

village . . .'[20] Hodder describes the complex system as follows. Rural periodic day markets in Yorubaland operate on a ring system, each ring being composed of a complete and integrated sequence of markets taking place over four-day or multiples of four-day periods. Markets may thus occur on Monday, Friday, Tuesday, Saturday—four-day markets; or on Monday, Tuesday of the following week, Wednesday of the succeeding week—eight-day markets. This is a common phenomenon in West Africa, and appears to be related to time factors operating prior to the adoption of the seven-day week towards the latter part of the nineteenth century as European control extended inland from the coast.

According to P. Talbot, 'the original week appears always to have been composed of four days . . . The subdivisions into weeks in all likelihood originated from the necessity of differentiating between the days on which the various markets were held'. As figure 16—1 indicates, of the eight rural periodic day markets distinguished in the Akinyele ring, seven take place at eight-day intervals. These seven markets operate on successive days in such a way that each market takes place on a day on which it is the only one of the seven markets operating within the ring. After all markets have had their turn, there is one marketless day after which the process is repeated in the same order, 1—7. The eighth market, Ijaiye, occurs every four days and operates simultaneously with Akinyele on the first day with Olorisaoko on

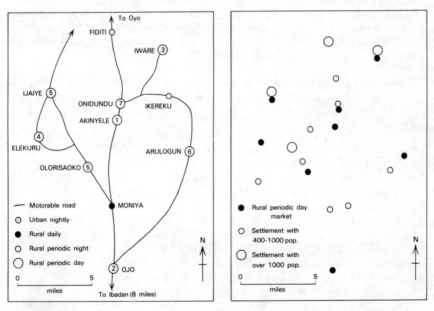

Figure 16—1: Types of local markets north of Ibadan and the population of settlements and the location of rural periodic day markets in the same area. (*After B. W. Hodder*).

[20] B. W. Hodder (1961): Rural periodic day markets in part of Yorubaland. *Trans. Inst. Brit. Geogr.* 29, 151.

the fifth day of each eight-day period. The Akinyele ring also operates in such a way that successive markets are not normally adjacent markets. The first market is at the centre at Akinyele, the second at the extreme southern edge at Ojo, and the third at the extreme northern edge at Iware; there are subsequent further movements back and forth until the seventh day, when the market near the centre at Onidundu takes place before the eighth or rest day.

In this way the timing of marketing activities is evened out over the whole ring so that no hamlet or other settlement is far from a market for more than three days. This integrated pattern and timing of markets in the Akinyele ring is thus most logical and convenient and is in some form or another characteristic of most parts of the Yoruba country. It is a wholly indigenous phenomenon, expressing an intelligent mutual self-interest among neighbouring village chiefs, or *bale*.[21]

Attempts at interpretation via traditional central place theory have been criticized by Bromley, Symanski and Good.[22] They argue for a more complex situation where the periodic market is in part the product of an economic system where making (producing) and selling have not been divorced, so that time is needed for 'manufacture' and part-time retailers demand periodic markets. Again the organization of time is a controlling factor as in the Yoruba rings already discussed. The length of week, the days set aside by religion or for rest and the significance of astrology, all these determined the market timing. Finally they argue that inertia often retains a system long after it has become economically unnecessary. The consequence of these influences is that an analysis in purely central place terms is unlikely to be greatly productive.

Three aspects of the developing world have been considered in relation to the urbanization process. That process makes its visible appearance as the city on the ground and hence there are three further aspects which demand a brief review:

4   The plans of cities.
5   The social areas of cities.
6   Spontaneous or squatter settlements.

4 City plan

It has already been established that city plan is largely the product of the cultural and social characteristics of the group which lays it out. Accordingly it is impossible to follow all the variants of plan produced in the developing world, or rather more appropriately, outside the European cultural sphere. It is worth pursuing the colonial theme introduced into this chapter, however, by considering the impact of English colonialism on the cities of India where unlike America or Australia, movement was taking place into

[21] B. W. Hodder (1961), 152.
[22] R. J. Bromley, R. Symanski and C. M. Good (1975): The rationale of periodic markets. *Ann. Assoc. Amer. Geogr.* 65(4), 530–537.

culturally alien areas with high densities of population and long standing urban cultures. The two cultures of coloniser and colonized continued side by side, certainly interacting, but engendering a distinctive urban form made up of the two elements. In writing on 'comparable urban ecology' London and Flanagan[23] have proposed a typology of cities as set out in table 16−2.

table 16−2: A typology of cities with differing ecological structures (After London and Flanagan)

1   Preindustrial cities influenced by colonialism.
2   Preindustrial cities uninfluenced by colonialism having indigenous invention of indus-trial technology.
3   Preindustrial cities uninfluenced by colonialism *not* having indigenous invention of industrial technology.
4   Cities reflecting the 'pure' impact of industrial technology.

Although the 'types' are based on ecological structure they can be as appropriately used for the examination of physical structure. In such a context no better example exists of the first type than that brought about by British colonial rule in India. That the interaction was not only one way can be seen in the many terms which found their way back to the colonizing country. In the physical or built structure of the town what in the U.S.A. is called a 'ranch style' house still remains in Britain the term derived from colonial Asia, a bungalow. This whole problem of the colonial city in India has been the subject of an excellent and thorough study by A. D. King in his book entitled *Colonial urban development*[24] and accordingly only a brief outline is presented here based largely on that source.

A most effective introduction to the colonial city is a consideration of the linguistic terms which were used to describe the various parts of the city. King sets these out in a table which is reproduced, in part, below (table 16−3).

'These words represent "physical-spatial-social" elements in the urban system which are expressed in the metropolitan rather than in the indigenous language (i.e. English rather than Hindi). Such terms however are either not found in the system of urban nomenclature in the metro-politan society (e.g. civil lines, civil station, cantonment, chummery . . .) or, if they do exist, are used with different meanings to those prevailing in the ex-colonial society (e.g. compound, bungalow, bazaar)'.[25] Perhaps the most common word which King does not mention, since it has no spatial connotation, though most definitely a social one, is the word 'pucca' which described a bungalow of masonry construction, brick or stone with tiled

---

[23] B. London and W. G. Flanagan (1976): Comparative urban ecology: a summary of the field, in J. Walton and L. H. Masotti eds. (1976): *The city in comparative prospect* (New York. London).
[24] A. D. King (1976): *Colonial urban development. Culture, social power and environment.* (London, Henley and Boston). There is a succinct account in J. E. Brush (1962): The morphology of Indian Cities, in R. Turner ed. (1962): *India's urban future* (Berkely and Los Angeles), 57−70.
[25] A. D. King (1976), 71.

table 16–3: Key terminology in the language of colonial urbanization (After A.D. King)

	Scale or Level	
Urban	Urban Sector	Urban Unit
Civil station	Bazaar	Barracks
Civil lines	Colony	Bungalow
Cantonment	Esplanade	Chummery
Lines	Mall	Club
Circuit House		Compound
Dak (bungalow)		Lodge
		Quarters
Residency		Rest House

roof, and which brought a widely used adjective into English. The location of the berth on the ships taking the representatives of the colonial power to India also provided a keyword. Port Out, Starboard Home gave not only a location away from the heat of the sun but in the mnemonic POSH, a lasting social categorization also. A review of these terms can be used to describe the major spatial elements of the colonial city, grouped as they were about the three elements critical in the morphology of Indian urbanism. The first was the garrison, the basic physical representation of military control. The second element was the civil administration developed by the colonizing power 'to run' the country, whilst the third was the native city which predated the colonial grafting-on of the newer parts.

Figure 16–2 shows how many of these elements characterized the city of Allahabad during the nineteenth and early twentieth centuries. The settlement was located at a confluence of the Ganges and the Jumna rivers and was a sacred site, the ancient city of Prayag. It was also supposedly at the confluence of the legendary Saraswati, the lost river of the Punjab.[26] The Mogul emperor Akbar had built a fort at the angle where the two rivers met and this was taken over by the British to form the Fort Cantonment. It constituted, however, a very limited area, far too small in extent for the effective deployment of the military arm of the Raj. The site of Allahabad was itself constricted, for it lay between the Ganges and the Jumna. The latter was bordered by steep bluffs while the Ganges was characterized by moving sandbanks liable to inundation. A more extensive old cantonment was developed within the confluence core, but eventually a still more extensive site was developed to the west, called the New Cantonment. The demand for space, derived both from basic military needs and from the large compounds in which the bungalows were set, is well illustrated by this progressive development. Figure 16–2 clearly shows the distinctive elements. The New Cantonment was lavishly laid out in spatial terms. The core was dominated by the Brigade H.Q. which was surrounded by the European Infantry Lines, the Cavalry Lines and the Artillery Lines. Tucked away from these and well segregated to the north east were the Native

[26] O. H. K. Spate and E. Ahmad (1950): Five cities of the Gangetic plain. *Geog. Review*, 40, 260–278.

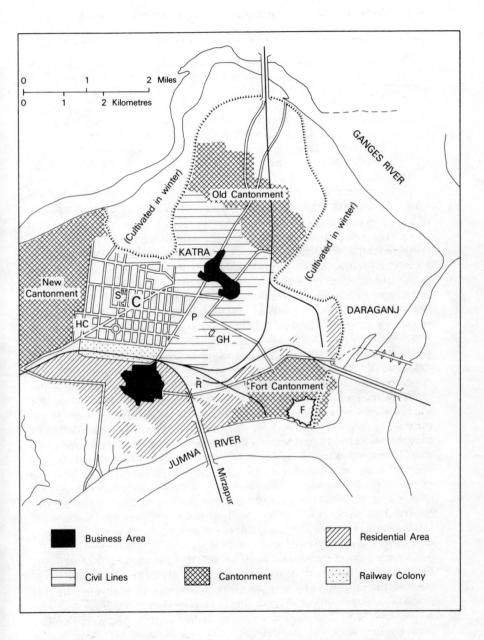

Figure 16–2: The structure of Allahabad as portrayed in a map of that city in 1931 from the Imperial Gazeteer of India. C = Cannington (part of Civil Lines), HC = High Court, GH = Government House, S = Secretariat, P = Alfred Park, R = City Railway Station. (Reprinted [Adapted] from the Geographical Review vol. 41, 1950, with the permission of the American Geographical Society.)

Infantry Lines. Adjacent to them was the Bazaar[27]. The burial ground was located well away from the living areas, from which it was separated by Macpherson Park.

The Civil Lines were situated to the east of the New Cantonment and were established on an extensive grid plan cut through by the main route which was related to the axis of the old Mogul city. Within the area were all the standard representatives of English culture in India: the Government Offices, the Law Courts, the Hotel, Hospital and the Allahabad Club. It was neatly segregated: to the north was the river Ganges while the New Cantonment was to the west: to the south were the railway lines and to the east Alfred Park provided a break. The native city was to the south, nearer the Jumna river and on the other side of the tracks. It was a densely populated and unplanned maze of narrow streets in complete contrast to the Civil Lines. Not only the railway, but the Junction Station and the accommodation for the railway staff set out in severely rectangular fashion, separated Indian city from European quarter[28].

Brush points not only to the ubiquity and the formal lay-out of the railway settlement, but also to its internal social distinctions. 'The most distinctive features of the railway towns are the perfectly uniform grid of streets and the monotonous rows of brick dwelling, graded and rented strictly according to the wage scale and occupational status of the employees. For the lowest-paid semi-skilled workers, who were from the start invariably Indians, a single room with attached kitchen and enclosed courtyard was considered sufficient. These dwelling units are built in contiguous rows of ten and twelve, or multiples thereof, allowing little or no open space between street and entrance. The quarters designed for the intermediate grades of personnel, often including Eurasians as well as Indians, have more rooms, some in a second storey, and are set back farther from the street. The two-storey bungalows built for the employees with the highest technical skills or managerial capacity and receiving the highest salaries, who at first were mainly British, stand amid spacious landscaped grounds with small row houses for the servants in the rear'.[29] 'In Allahabad the railway area was effectively deployed to block access to the north, there being no crossing for wheeled traffic for more than a mile. The railway thus completely shuts off the crowded and irregular Indian city from the broadly planned rectangular Cantonment and Civil Lines, a district of large bungalows and public offices in spacious compounds and gardens'.[30]

There is no need to labour the point. Society in nineteenth century India had a distinctive character and organization of its own. That organization with all the crudities and niceties of its ethnic and social distinctions was quite faithfully reflected in the forms of the towns it developed.

[27] Government of India (1899); *Cantonments Code* (Calcutta), 64.
[28] O. H. K. Spate and E. Ahmad (1950): Five cities of the Gangetic Plain, *Geog. Review*, 40, 260–278.
[29] J. E. Brush (1962), 62–63.
[30] G. H. K. Spate and E. Ahmad (1950), 267.

5 The social areas of cities

In the earlier section of this book dealing with the social areas of cities as part of residential patterning (Chap. 10), some attention was directed to cities of the developing world in the context of establishing a dynamic model which could epitomize the mode of evolution of the urban mosaic. In this chapter it is appropriate that some further consideration be given towards the topic of social areas in Third World cities in its own right.

There are problems, however. The first is that it would be inappropriate to imply that there is any such thing as uniformity within the greatly differing cultural traditions and politico-economic structures which make up that somewhat nebulous notion of a Third World, or even of developing countries. It is true that the evolutionary model noted above implies at least common characteristics of economic change. 'The accumulated evidence indicates that economic and technological factors are the dependent varia bles which tend to produce ecological similarities, while culturally unique factors are the independent variables which tend to foster ecological differences'.[31] Even in relation to the penetration and impact of western, industrial technology, however, too easy an assumption of a single path of change should be questioned until a good deal more is known from a wider range of examples. Nevertheless, a basic factor in all studies of the social areas of Third World cities is the degree of modernization and the consequent existence of both 'traditional' and 'modern' areas.

The second problem is that data availability and economic development are highly correlated and as a result it is difficult to obtain adequate small area data to provide the input to detailed analyses of smaller towns in the least developed areas. Indeed, in such cases the very data used in western studies could be completely inappropriate. It follows that factorial ecologies have been produced for those cities where 'development' is most advanced.

The most frequently quoted studies are those of Calcutta reported by Berry and Kasarda,[32] and of Cairo, Egypt, by Janet Abu-Lughod,[33] both of which were referred to in chapter 10. The latter piece of work, although now somewhat dated, presents a valuable insight into the social and physical structuring of the capital of a developing country. Abu-Lughod used the same set of thirteen variables (table 16−4) for 216 census tracts for 1947 and 1960. A principal components analysis with varimax orthogonal rotation was employed and the loadings of the variables on three abstracted factors for 1960 are given in table 16−4 and the average scores for the first factor for thirteen communities grouped by type are given in table 16−5. The thirteen communities themselves are mapped in figure 16−3.

[31] B. London and W. G. Flanagan (1976): Comparative urban ecology: a summary of the field, in J. Walton and L. H. Masotti eds. (1976): *The city in comparative perspective*, 59 (New York).

[32] Berry, B. J. L. and Kasarda, J. D. (1977): *Contemporary urban ecology* (New York), 134−157.

[33] Abu-Lughod, J. (1969): Testing the theory of social area analysis: the case of Cairo, Egypt. *Amer. Soc. Review*, 34(2), 198−211.

Abu-Lughod, J. (1971): *Cairo. 1001 years of the city invincible*. (Princeton, N.J.).

table 16—4: Factor Loadings, Cairo Census Tracts, 1960

	Factor 1	Factor 2	Factor 3
Persons per Room	−81	+01	+32
Persons per km²	−03	−10	+72
Sex Ratio	−01	+97	−03
Fertility Ratio	−89	−01	−00
Never Married Females	+95	+04	−03
Divorced Females	+52	+03	+41
Never Married Males	+76	+49	+11
Handicapped	−40	+13	+32
Male Literacy	+81	−07	−20
Female Literacy	+92	+10	−19
Female Employed	+85	+06	+15
Males Unemployed	−31	−03	+18
Muslins Per Cent	−56	−06	+55

Note Sex Ratio is males per 100 females in age group 15—49. Fertility Ratio is children under 5 per 100 women 15—49. The 'never married' rates largely reflect age of marriage. Values ± 20 are significant. Decimal points have been omitted. (After J. Abu-Lughod, 1969).

table 16—5: The Communities of Cairo 1960 (For Location of Communities see Figure 16-3)

Community. Groupings by Type	*Average Scores on Factor 1, 1960*
Rural Fringes	
North III	−1·56
West VI	−1·39
Cemetery IX	−1·54
South XIII	−1·84
Interior Slums	
Būlāq I	−0·35
Medieval X	−0·37
Misr a Qadimah XII	−0·54
Urban Working Class. Low	
Zaytūn IV	−0·08
Urban Middle Class	
Transition XI	+0·63
Shubra II	+0·95
Silver CoastVIII	+1·18
Upper Middle or Better	
Heliopolis V	+1·48
Gold Coast VII	+1·97

(After J. Abu-Lughod, 1971)

The interpretation of Factor 1 has already been discussed (p. 275) where it was identified as a 'Life Style' factor, contrasting those sections which were most modern, which can be read as European or cosmopolitan, with those which were predominantly traditional in their way of life. The high positive loading variables stress male and female literacy, female employment and, via the never-married surrogate, later age of marriage. All these reflect the emancipation of women from traditional roles and a modern-traditional polarization. The second factor is seen as identifying male dominance, for the sex ratio and never married males are the highest loading variables. This is brought about by the selective in-migration of unattached males. The third factor identifies social disorganization. There are clear contrasts with the factors that characterize the western city, with the nature of regional and intra-city migration appearing as critical controls.

It is too lengthy a task to follow the detailed spatial analysis which Abu-Lughod presents by identifying thirteen communities within the city (table 16−4 and figure 16−3), but the main features can be sketched. At the physical heart of Cairo is Community X which is virtually co-extensive with the medieval city. Through it runs the *Qasabah* along which all the market activities were located. It still retains that character, but away from it is 'a world never glimpsed by the tourist. It is a dark and dense residential *cum* industrial *cum* commercial quarter, mud splattered and garbage strewn, penetrated by winding, narrow dirt paths, terminating here at the gate to a thirteenth century *khan*, terminating there at a cul-de-sac . . . '.[34]

In complete contrast is Community VII, called The Gold Coast by the

Figure 16−3: Cairo, Egypt: Factorial Ecology. The thirteen sub-cities defined by Factor 1, Lift Style, according to J. Abu Lughod. The northern and southern fringes of the city have been omitted.

[34] Abu-Lughod (1971), 190.

author, perhaps as a tribute to the role of Chicago in urban ecology for it must be emphasized that it is not a name used in Cairo. It is the westernized, modern central business area of the city, once the domain of foreign colonials but now the terrain of the capital's elite. Between these two extremes lies Community XI which, forming a bridge between X and VII, a connection between the modernizing forces of the Golden Coast and the deterioration of the old city, is appropriately called 'Transition'. On the west bank of the river, that is the opposite flank of the Gold Coast, Abu-Lughod names Community VIII the Silver Coast since it is a somewhat down-market version of Community VII.

The old city, Community X, forms one of the city's slums, but the location of these poorest areas is neither characteristically 'inner city' nor peripheral, but rather related to the oldest sections. Community I, Bulaq and Community XII, Misr-al-Qadimah, were both port suburbs which have been engulfed by city growth, although extension along the river has given them a fringe character also. But the fringes are made up of distinctive communities, especially to the north where low and middle class residential areas penetrate sector-wise into the rural surrounds producing 'five sector cities'. The eastern fringe, however, made up of Community IX is dominated by 'the cemetery cities', and here is a section that can be compared to the squatter peripheral settlements classically associated with cities of the developing world.

From even this brief summary 'three types (of population) that co-exist within Cairo may be identified . . . (1) the rural; (2) the traditional urban; and (3) the modern or industrial urban'.[35] It is the differential intermingling of these that gives character to the constituent communities. In this context 'traditional' is defined as referring 'primarily to the persistence of economic activities, forms of social relationships, and systems of values which were once typical within the Cairo of a hundred years ago'.[36] To a degree it can be linked to the notion of the lower of the two circuits of the urban economy in undeveloped countries proposed by Milton Santos in his book 'Shared Space'.[37] The two circuits not only characterize the economy but must appear in the spatial structure of the city also, though never divorced into discrete areas for as Santos avers, the space is shared.

A conclusion, generally in parallel with the above, emerged from a study of a city in a contrasted part of Africa. This was an analysis of the spatial organization of residential areas in Accra, Ghana by R. R. Brand.[38] Thirteen variables which could be derived from the 1960 census were assembled for 268 enumeration areas. Four components were abstracted from a principal components analysis (table 16−6) explaining 28·5, 17·0, 12·2 and 9·8 per cent of the variance respectively.

Component I is characterized by Brand as 'bourgeois migrant commu-

---

[35]   Abu-Lughod (1971), 218.

[36]   Abu-Lughod (1971), 219.

[37]   Santos, M. (1979): *The Shared Space* (London). Translated by C. Gerry.

[38]   Brand, R. R. (1972): The spatial organization of residential areas in Accra, Ghana, with particular reference to aspects of modernization. *Econ. Geog.* 48, 284−298.

table 16–6: Component Structure for Accra (after R.R. Brand)

Variables	Factors			
	I	II	III	IV
Local born	− 77	− 27	− 17	30
Foreign Africans	39	76	− 21	− 10
Non-Africans	70	− 37	08	− 13
Child/Women ratio	− 77	10	04	17
Sex Ratio	69	29	− 18	− 05
Educated adults	06	− 82	06	− 16
Unschooled children	10	85	11	− 01
Working-age males	23	12	− 53	− 15
Employed males	11	11	10	− 84
Unemployment	− 10	23	05	78
Unemployed females	71	05	37	25
Density	− 35	− 06	− 62	28
Distance	14	10	86	− 07

Note Distance is straight-line distance from G.P.O. in C.B.D. Decimal points have been omitted and the signs in Component IV inverted.

nities' given the high loadings of non-Africans. 'These sub-areas exhibited very low proportions of local-born persons, relatively few children per women, and medium to low gross population densities. They also had a large proportion of economically non-active females (and) large representations of non-African expatriates'.[39] The distribution pattern is clearly sectoral, with a wedge extending north-east from the city centre. There was one outlying area in Tesano (A on figure 16–4), 'a European enclave analogous to the wealthy commuter suburbs ringing many western cities'.[40]

Component II shows high positive loading variables of foreign Africans and unschooled children, with a high negative loading on educated adults. This is interpreted as 'urban villagers—the sub-culture of traditionalism among migrants'. Three areas can be identified on figure 16–4. The first two, Nima and New Town (B on figure 16–4) and Sabon Zongo (C) are areas of squatter dwellings and subdivided houses in a peripheral location, whilst Ussher Town and part of Jameston (D on the map) are the city centre parallels. It is significant that Brand notes one subarea, Tudu, as a popular destination node for long-distance migrants, especially Hansa and Yoruba traders, and Sabon Zongo as developed by Muslims. Component III is a distance component contrasting the low density fringe with the centre, and IV an unemployment component.

Two immediate reflections arise from Brand's study. The first is the clear parallelism with Abu-Lughod's analysis of Cairo; the first and dominant contrast is between aspects of modernization and traditionalism. The second is the way in which ethnic associations, or tribal links, remain strongly reproduced in the urban situation. Urban ethnicity[41] is itself the

[39] Brand, R. R. (1972), 291.
[40] Brand (1972), 291.
[41] Cohen, A. ed. (1974): *Urban ethnicity* (London).

Component 1 ▨   **Component 2** ▦

Figure 16–4: Accra, Ghana: Factorial ecology. Areas with high scores on the first two components are shaded.

Component 1 Bourgeois migrant communities (more than two standard deviations above the mean).
Component 2 Urban villagers: the culture of traditionalism among migrants (more than one standard deviation above the mean).

(After R. R. Brand).

product of migration chains and a feature of the largest towns and cities. The characters of homogeneous settlements, smaller in size, and in areas little affected by Western notions, are very different. It is possible, therefore, to query many of the analyses of modernizing cities and using variables closely ranged as possible to those of western factorial ecologies; it is little wonder that results first contrast those parts which are amenable to such analyses with those that are less so.

At this point it is possible to revert to another contribution by Abu-Lughod where, in relation to North Africa, she identifies 'six fairly distinctive and co-existent urban arrangements which make up the ecological structure'.[42] These are:

1   *The Medina core.* This is the medieval or traditional nucleus.
2   *The modern appendage.* This was either designed for and built by Europeans, or constructed in European style.
3   *Rapidly proliferating uncontrolled settlements.*
4   *Peripheral suburbs.* These are built for an indigenous middle and upper class and expand in sector-like fashion between the uncontrolled settlements.
5   *Rural fringe.* This is made up of wedges of undeveloped rural land, in sharp contrast to the urban sectors.
6   *Transitional working class zones.* These are usually the intermediaries between 1 and 2.

At the beginning of this section the significance of economic and technological factors was noted and their influence in setting up convergent patterns suggested. Most Third World authors react fairly sharply against the notion that their cities are becoming more like those of the west, and still more consistently against any view that their cities are following the paths of western cities at earlier periods. National and cultural pride are potent factors in such reactions; not for the first time in this book it has to be noted that the perception of the world is a relative thing. It would not be difficult to find parallels for the six 'urban arrangements' of Abu-Lughod in eighteenth and nineteenth century Britain. But most certainly modern communications, both via the mass media and in the more direct physical sense of moving populations, are so much the greater, and hence the exacerbation of many of the urban problems in developing areas. One of the greatest of these, certainly the one with the most extensive literature, is that of the uncontrolled peripheral settlement.

6 Spontaneous or squatter settlements

The huge extent of urbanward migration has already been identified. Within the cities themselves it produces immense social problems the most immediate of which is inadequate housing. Partly as a result of the size of the problem, partly as a result of the limitation of national and municipal resources and partly as a result of social systems which inhibit the equitable division of resources, little shelter is provided through formal and planned channels. The result is that the immigrant population collects in extensive peripheral areas of settlement. 'Peripheral settlements account for at least one quarter, and often one-third or even one half, of the total urban populations in most primate cities. Thirty-five per cent of the people in Manila, thirty-three per cent in Calcutta, twenty-five per cent in Kuala Lumpur, twenty-five per cent in Jakarta, forty-five per cent in Istanbul, twenty-seven

---

[42] Abu-Lughod, J. (1976): Developments in North African urbanism: the process of decolonization, being Chap. 8 in Berry, B. L. J. ed. (1976): *Urbanization and Counter-urbanization* (Beverly Hills). Urban Affairs Annual Reviews vol. 11, 202.

per cent in Rio de Janeiro, and forty-six per cent of the population in Mexico City live in slums and uncontrolled settlements'.[43]

The names for this phenomenon are widely varied, both in the academic and planning literature and in the vernacular languages. Uncontrolled settlements, as in the quotation above, spontaneous settlements, auto- namous settlements; all these have been used from time to time. Drakakis- Smith has argued for the use of the term squatter settlements or squatter housing defining it as, 'any housing which contravenes existing legislation on the occupation of land or the construction of dwellings. This juridical definition is preferred to currently fashionable neologisms, such as "spon- taneous" or "uncontrolled" urban settlements, because the illegal nature of such housing strongly affects all aspects of life in the squatter community, from the physical environment, through types of economic activity to rela- tions with the urban authorities'.[44] In this he is undoubtedly correct since the distinction between these settlements and slums is that the residents of the latter, however delapidated the physical conditions, own the legal title or formally rent the property. In the favellas, barrios, bidonvilles and bustees, perhaps the most widely used names for squatter settlements, there is no legal title to the land occupied.

It has been suggested that urban poverty is simply rural poverty displaced and such a view seems appropriate in relation to the spontaneous settlements for the move to the city, as has been indicated, is powered by rural change and rural poverty. Once arrived at the city the migrant is faced with a group of related problems. He has no skills to offer in a market which increasingly seeks skilled workers so that the best he can hope for is either sporadic labouring employment or to establish himself in petty trading of the most limited kind. Under these circumstances he can make no bid for housing and the only way out is to construct shelter from available materials, galvanized sheeting, tin cans, odd pieces of wood, cardboard boxes, attempting gradually to improve the structure. It is in this fashion, and unprovided with water, sewerage or electricity that the spontaneous settle- ments have developed. Dwyer begins his book on *People and housing in Third World cities* with a section entitled, 'A major urban form'[45] and by so doing properly calls attention to the fact that these settlements do constitute one of the major urban features of the contemporary world.

Four further features of these settlements can be briefly considered; loca- tion, character, evolution and future development.

(*i*) *Location.* Dwyer has constructed a diagram reproduced as figure 16–5 which shows typical movements of low income population in the cities of developing countries.[46] Migration takes place both characteristically to the

[43] R. Ulack (1978): The role of urban squatter settlements. *Ann. Assoc. Amer. Geogr.* 68(4), 535.

[44] D. W. Drakakis-Smith (1978): Shelter: overview, in P. J. Rimmer, D. W. Drakakis- Smith and T. G. McGee eds. (1978): *Food, shelter and transport in Southeast Asia and the Pacific* (Canberra, Australian National University, Dept. of Human Geog. Pub. H.G. 12).

[45] D. Dwyer (1975): *People and housing in the Third World* (London).

[46] D. Dwyer (1975), 34.

People and housing in Third World cities

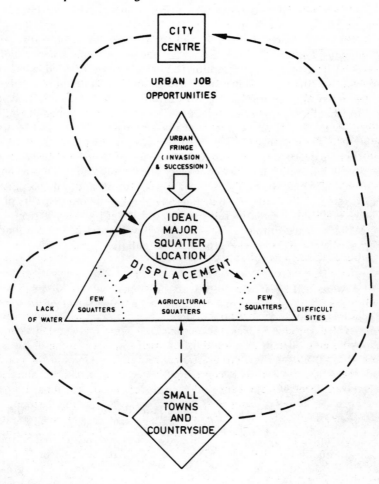

Figure 16−5: Typical movements of low income population in cities in developing countries. (*After D. J. Dwyer*).

inner city areas of reception (chapter 10 p. 269), as well as to the periphery. But, as the central city expands, those least able to meet rising rents are pushed to the periphery, and they are successfully and continually displaced into worsening environments in terms of water access and site conditions, such as steep slopes. But what jobs are available are city centred so that nearness to opportunity becomes a resisting factor that keeps the settlement as far in as possible, but inevitably a situation arises where the poorest have to pay high journey to work costs. Also, peripheral land, low in quality because of steepness of slope is likely to be that which can be 'squatted on' most easily. The spontaneous settlements, therefore, take up the least desired locations, virtually when land values have fallen to zero for the terrain can be used neither for agriculture or good quality housing.

(*ii*) *Character*. Much has been written on the degrading conditions of these settlements. Perhaps the most effective public statement has been that of the Sao Paulo Justice and Peace Commission in their report entitled, *Sao Paulo: growth and poverty*.[47] That volume points out that Sao Paulo is the fastest growing city in the world having grown from a small town a hundred years ago to 12 million at present, and if growth rates are maintained, 25 million by the year 2000. The result has been a failure to provide essential facilities, 'Only 40 per cent of the 8000 kilometres which make up the road network for local traffic in the Metropolitan Region are paved. Approximately 489,000 inhabitants live in houses without electricity. Only about 30 per cent of households in the Metropolitan Region have drains and only 53 per cent piped water'.[48] In terms of particular areas within the municipality of Sao Paulo conditions are considerably worse. In 1968 at Itaquera 89 per cent of households lacked drains, 97 per cent piped water and 72 per cent had no refuse collection. With the growth of population the situation is deteriorating not improving.

(*iii*) *Evolution*. L. J. Eyre in a study of the shanty towns of Montego Bay in Jamaica[49] proposed stages of development for these forms of settlement. These he identified as:

1   The initial occupation stage.
2   The transitional stage.
3   The stage of attaining secure tenure.
4   The stage of absorption.

This suggests a gradual change from an initial state of insecurity and lack of organization, to a gradual achievement of a feeling of permanence. This is accompanied by the improvement of dwellings and the gradual establishment of small businesses so that eventually the settlement becomes part of the city. 'Other things being equal, the older settlements have the greatest potential to become viable city communities. More recently established settlements, if their residents are not evicted and if they are upwardly mobile in a socio-economic sense, also have the potential to become part of the urban system because the city is expanding its opportunities and amenities to these peripheral areas'.[50] Ulack in a Study of Cagayan de Oro in the Philippines confirmed three hypotheses regarding the change with time; that

[47] Sao Paulo Justice and Peace Commission (1978): *Sao Paulo. Growth and poverty* (London). English translation published in association with the Catholic Institute for International Relations.
[48] Sao Paulo Justice and Peace Commission (1978), 31.
[49] L. J. Eyre (1972): The shanty towns of Montego Bay, Jamaica. *Geog. Rev.* 62, 394–413.
[50] R. Ulack (1978), 539.

the age of settlement is the most critical variable in determining the role of squatter settlements; that the oldest settlements have the best locations, closest to employment and urban amenities; that the oldest settlements have the highest socio-economic status as measured by education, income levels, jobs and housing conditions. Because of this he argues 'squatters in the older settlements have the potential to contribute more to the city. The existence of small businesses, membership in associations, better housing, and employment in more skilled jobs are all indications that the older settlements are more highly integrated into the city'.[51]

(*iv*) *Future development*. J. F. C. Turner, one of the earliest and most influential writers on squatter settlements argued that, 'It is clear that . . . . the peripheral squatter settlements do, in fact, perform the principal functions demanded by their inhabitants. So, in spite of the many, and often severe drawbacks, they often act as forward moving vehicles of social and economic change'.[52] This is the role of these settlements, similar to that of the slums of hope (see chapter 10 p. 269), that is positive and can be built upon. The direct task of rehousing the populations of the squatter settlements by the municipalities themselves is one on such a scale that it cannot be the only, even the major policy. The pattern of change has to be encouraged. The first issue is that of property titles, for the inhabitants need the security of ownership in order to have the incentive for improvement. Most of the households are too poor to want standard credit arrangements for housing improvement, preferring to add to their dwelling as opportunity permits. Figure 16−6 shows the attitudes to public and private services in the Lima barricidas after a survey by Andrews and Phillips.[53]

The intensity of dissatisfaction registers the importance of property titles and, not unexpectedly given the environmental conditions, the demand for accessible medical services. The extent of dissatisfaction indicates the demand for standard urban services. It is the provision of these services to the squatter sites that has become the dominant policy in many areas. Given the basic facilities, the initiative of the populations itself is sufficient to engender the gradual process of upgrading. Certainly solutions on western housing development concepts will be completely inadequate in face of the scale of growth in developing countries. Notions of 'slum clearance' have no meaning whatsoever under the conditions which have been discussed. The management of the spontaneous settlements and their progressive improvement is one of the critical problems in practical urban research.

7 Conclusion

This short chapter has sought to set out some of the characteristics and

[51] R. Ulack (1978), 548−9.
[52] J. F. C. Turner (1969): Uncontrolled urban settlement: problems and policies, in G. Breese ed. (1969): *The city in newly developing countries: readings on urbanism and urbanization* (Englewood Cliffs, N.J.).
[53] F. M. Andrews and G. W. Phillips (1970): The squatters of Lima: who they are and what they want. *Journal of Developing Areas* 4, 211−224.

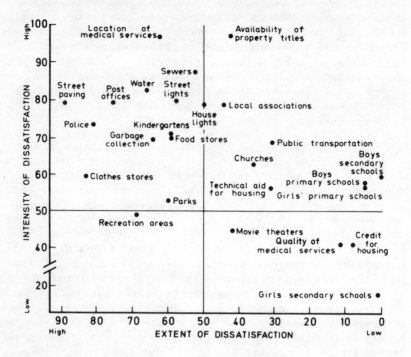

problems of the city in developing and under developed countries. Those characteristics are so distinctive and the problems are so great that they have engendered an extensive and growing literature. One limited chapter can do little more than act, in a book written mainly around the western city, as a token, an acknowledgement that the stresses and disadvantages that occur within western cities are dwarfed by the growing crisis of urbanization in the Third World.

Notes on further reading

Books which deal with the city in the developing world in general terms are:

Breese, G. ed. (1969): *The city in newly developing countries* (Englewood Cliffs, N.J.).

Dwyer, D. J. ed. (1974): *The city in the Third World* (London).

Friedmann, J. and Wulff R. (1975): *The urban transition. Comparative studies of newly industrializing societies* (London).

McGee, T. G. (1971): *The urbanization process in the Third World* (London).

Roberts, B. (1978): *Cities of peasants. The political economy of urbanization in the Third World* (London).

Santos, M. (1971): *Les villes du Tiers Monde* (Paris).

The colonial basis to cities is best presented in:

King, A. D. (1976): *Colonial urban development. Culture, social power and environment* (London).

A volume with reviews of trends is

Berry, B. J. L. ed. (1974): *Urbanization and counter urbanization* (Beverly Hills). Urban Affairs Annual Reviews. Vol 11.

Studies dealing with specific areas are:

Costello, U. F. (1977): *Urbanization in the Middle East* (Cambridge).

Field, A. J. ed. (1970): *City and Country in the Third World: issues in the modernization of Latin America* (London).

Gugler, J. and W. G. Flanagan (1978): *Urbanization and social change in West Africa* (Cambridge).

Harris, W. D. (1971): *The growth of Latin American cities* (Columbus, Ohio).

Jakobson, L. and Prakesh, V. eds. (1970): *The urbanization process in South-East Asia* (Beverly Hills, Cal.).

Mabogunje, A. L. (1967): *Urbanization in Nigeria* (London).

McGee, T. G. (1967): *The Southeast Asian city* (London).

Rimmer, P. J., Drakakis-Smith, D. W. and McGee, T. G. eds. (1978): *Food, shelter and transport in Southeast Asia and the Pacific* (Canberra) A.N.U. Research School of Pacific Studies.

There is a large number of studies of single cities but two greatly contrasted publications are:

Abu-Lughod, J. (1971): *Cairo: 1001 years of the city victorious* (Princeton).

Hinderink, J. and Sterkenburg, J. (1975): *Anatomy of an African town. A socio-economic study of Cape Coast, Ghana* (Utrecht).

Most of the material on central place studies or marketing geography contain sections on periodic markets, for example:

Dawson, J. A. (1979): *The marketing environment* (London).

but a more specialized source is:

Gormsen, E. ed. (1976): Market distribution systems. *Mainzer Geographische Studies*, 10.

A useful paper with a good bibliographical content is:

Symanski, R. and Webber, M. J. (1974): Complex periodic market cycles. *Ann. Assoc. Geogrs.* 64(2), 203−213.

while the problems of the consumer are considered in:

Hay, A. M. and Smith, R. H. T. (1980): Consumer welfare in periodic markets. *Trans. Inst. Brit. Geogrs.* New Series, 5(1), 29−44.

On squatter settlements there is an excellent bibliographic study.

404 *The city in the developing world*

Buick, B. (1975): *Squatter settlements in developing countries: A bibliography* (Research School of Pacific Studies, A.N.U., Canberra).

A specific study which has a note on further reading and a bibliography is:

Lloyd, P. (1979): *Slums of hope? Shanty towns of the third world* (Manchester).

The books listed above as dealing with the city in general all have sections dealing with squatter settlements. Two papers of value are:

Eyre, L. A. (1972): The shanty towns of Montego Bay, Jamaica. *Geog. Review*, 62, 394−413.

Ulack, R. (1978): The role of urban squatter settlements. *Ann. Assoc. Amer. Geogrs.*, 68(4); 535−550.

A volume which covers the general field of cross-cultural comparisons is:

Walton, J. and Masotti, L. H. eds. (1976): *The city in comparative per spective. Cross national research and new directories in theory* (New York).

While a paper which urges the need for a broader consideration of urbanism with considerable more attention to the developing world is:

Dwyer, D. J. (1979): Urban geography and the urban future. *Geography*, 64(2), 86−95.

17

Urbanization and Urban Geography

The nature and consequences of urbanization are of prime significance both to the developed and the less developed parts of the world. Indeed the whole future of mankind is closely bound up with the changing significance and role of the city. The urban geographer, whether he defines the scope of his work by the subject-matter he treats or by the particular perspectives he adopts, can only consider a small part of the totality which is expressed in the idea of urbanization. Even so, as the geographer reviews his work he will inevitably be strongly influenced by the attitude he adopts to the city. At the same time his study is not academically static, nor does the urban pheno-menon itself remain unchanging.

In consequence there are three topics which this conclusion needs to dis-cuss. The first of these is attitudes to the city, the second is the changing nature of the city and the third is the impact of these on urban geography as a systematic branch of the subject, a topic with which the book began and which can now be reviewed in the light of the content presented.

1 Attitudes to the city

This book has mainly, though not exclusively, been written from the context of the western industrialized world. Although attempts have been made to present a wider perspective at certain points, given the background and experience of the author it would have been over-ambitious to have ven-tured to present anything else. In western culture the attitude to urbanism has always been ambivalent; an ambivalence which it has slowly grown more popular to identify and trace so that only a brief outline is given here.[1]

On the one side the city has been seen, to use standard moral terms, as the epitome of all that is evil or, in the terminology of Wirth, anomic and alien-ating, disrupting the elemental cohesion of the social group and disinte-grating the personality of the individual. The sources of this attitude lie deep in the cultural inheritance. Prime among them are the Christian religion and its Judaic antecedents. Christianity originated among a people of the desert fringes whose folk memory and preserved tradition in the Old Testa-ment, were those of the nomadic herdsman. The city was presented as

---

[1] See for example, *The city in the history of ideas*; Part III of O. Handlin and J. Burchard, editors (1963): *The historian and the city* (Cambridge, Mass.), and G. R. Stange (1973): The frightened poets; chapter 20 in H. J. Dyos and M. Wolff editors (1973): *The Victorian city: images and reality* (London), 475–94.

destructive of the purity of religious belief and practice, bringing with it alien notions and false gods. The cities of the plain were a synonym for luxury, looseness and idolatry: Sodom and Gomorrha perished to demonstrate the fate of the urban idea. Through Christianity these attitudes became embedded in the consciousness of western man.

We may also note that Europe, as it emerged as a meaningful region after the collapse of the Roman Empire, was made up of a complex mosaic of small culture regions most of which have retained their identity, and some of which still have their distinctive languages. Brittany and Wales, Catalonia and Galicia, Flanders and Bavaria are examples.

These culture regions, often governed in the form of principalities or duchies, were subject to the process of more or less arbitrary unification, through battle or marriage bed, into the united kingdoms of the later middle ages and of modern Europe. In this nation-building operation the central and capital city played a leading role; indeed, the political unit was often forged about the city so that, for example, the name of the small area about Paris, the Ile de France, became extended to cover a whole country. By these means both symbolically and physically the city came to represent the cosmopolitan ideal, the destroyer of the folk cultures in the interests of national unity. 'In the city remote forces and influences intermingle with the local: their conflicts are no less significant than their harmonies. And here, through the concentration of the means of intercourse in the market and the meeting place, alternative modes of living present themselves: the deeply rutted ways of the village cease to be coercive and the ancestral goals cease to be all-sufficient: strange men and women, strange interests, and stranger gods loosen the traditional ties of blood and neighbourhood.'[2]

The industrial city of the late eighteenth and nineteenth centuries provided a further impetus to anti-urban attitudes, not only by contributing to the erosion of the older folk cultures but by the creation of the most appalling physical conditions and concomitant social degradation. Wirth, following the views of Tönnies and Durkheim, was able to adapt into nascent urban sociology the inherited prejudices of the past.

In the present century the history of urbanism has provided enhanced stimuli for these anti-urban views. The obsolescence of the inner city has contributed to the creation of slum and ghetto and provided an environment of urban poverty. The escape from city centre problems by the process of suburbanization, together with increasing car ownership, have brought immense pressures to bear on urban transport systems. Such are the pressures that urban motorways, to solve circulation difficulties, destroy houses and add to housing problems. The disposal of waste of all kinds, from plastic containers to sewage and the exhaust fumes from motor vehicles, has created major crises of pollution. The attempt to escape from the noise and dirt of the city generates saturating demand for what open space is accessible; yesterday's wildernesses are tomorrow's urban parks. Finally the vulnerability of the city has been revealed. It is exposed to any breakdown in

---

[2] L. Mumford (1938): *The culture of cities* (London), 4.

its complex sustaining systems. It is vulnerable to the pressure of active sectional interests, above all it is vulnerable to the urban guerrilla and to the direct political violence of a few determined and fanatical individuals.

From the sources considered so far comes an attitude which decries the city, at least in its contemporary western form. This attitude has the core of traditional romanticism buried deep within it. It reverses the Christian dogma for those on whom religion exerts no overt influence. Man may be viewed as not being inherently wicked by virtue of original sin and in need of redemption, but rather as a noble being corrupted by the vicious regime of the competitive capitalist world. That corruption is most marked in the symbol of that world, the city, the least 'natural' feature of the earth's surface which 'represents the maximum possibility of humanizing the natural environment and naturalizing the human heritage.'[3]

This romantic reaction perpetually rises to the surface in urban writing. It is nicely illustrated in Bunge's study of Fitzgerald (Detroit)[4] in which although the author attempts to deny such a basis, it nevertheless appears, almost creating a latter day version of the *Lyrical Ballads*, complete with updated versions of Ruth and Michael. Even the idea that, if natural man is corrupted in the urban world, then the nearest to innocence and virtue must be the child is strongly pressed, for Bunge writes, 'this is a book in defence of children. This book is designed to make us grow up, that is, to make us more childish.'[5] Or as Wordsworth phrased it:

> Not in entire forgetfulness,
> Not in utter nakedness,
> But trailing clouds of glory do we come,
> From God, who is our home,
> Heaven lies about us in our infancy.
> Shades of the prison-house begin to close,
> Upon the growing Boy. . . .[6]

Wordsworth's views are more tangibly anti-urban than Bunge's—

> He in the dissolute city gave himself
> To evil courses: ignominy and shame
> Fell on him. . . .[7]

—but even so this romantic view, through the notion of the geography of a revolution, is exerting active influences on urban geographers.

On the other side of this ambivalence towards the city is the view which

---

[3] L. Mumford (1938), 6.
[4] W. Bunge (1971): *Fitzgerald: geography of a revolution* (Cambridge, Mass.).
[5] W. Bunge (1971), 242.
[6] For the purist, the author is aware that the *Ode on the intimations of immortality from recollections of early childhood* was not published in the *Lyrical Ballads*.
[7] W. Wordsworth (1798): *Michael* from *Lyrical Ballads*.

maintains that the city is the greatest of all man's creations, displaying in physical form all the achievements of mankind — naturalizing the human heritage. In the city, as has been demonstrated already in this chapter, different cultures and traditions meet and mix and it is from this mixing and cross fertilization that innovation is born. New ideas and new techniques are diffused from the city and down the urban hierarchy; technical achievement and philosophical innovation are not usually related to the conservative, unchanging tradition of the countryside but to the creative flux of the city. Even if Christianity originated in a peasant community, it had to become Greek in philosophy before it could become universal and to be spread by Roman technology.

It is worthy of note that in attempting to produce a unifying theory of the town Claval has stressed that the common ground between inter-urban and intra-urban aspects of geography lies in the maximization of social interaction.[8] This is not far removed from Meier's communication theory of urban growth.[9] Whenever the crux of urbanism is sought it tends to emerge as simply a way of optimizing intercourse between people and stresses the role of the town as the meeting and mixing point.

The emancipation from the restrictions of custom is the core of the freedom which the city dweller gains. Only away from the close control of tradition can freedom to experiment, or to be different, be realized: only in the anonymous crowds of the city is true liberation possible. That very anonymity which was seen by Wirth as destructive of the individual, creates those conditions of freedom in which radical change is possible.[10] Radical change is, however, not acceptable to totalitarian regimes either of the political left or right, so the city has spawned a means of inhibiting the very freedom it generates. This is the secret or thought police, who replace in an urban situation the restraints operated by convention in rural and small scale communities.

Finally detachment from the confines of the rural community transforms an immobile situation into one where mobility is an accepted part of life. Along with physical mobility comes social mobility through opportunity, for it permits each individual to stretch his talents to their full extent whatever the ends might be.

Truth or advantage does not always lie in one of two polar extremes and discussions of urbanism have long been dominated by the notions of an ideal mid-way situation. Most explicit of all the attempts to derive such a median view is that by Ebenezer Howard in the Garden City where the two extremes are set out as magnets of attraction.[11] Perhaps earlier views of the 'citta ideale' saw the way through the creation of an apt physical environment which would of itself generate an ideal society, while a Marxist interpretation would presumably argue for a socialist economy and the elimination of competition as a means of producing the ideal city. At this point the

[8] P. Claval (1973): Une theorie unitaire de le ville. *Canadian Geogr.* 17(3), 276–9.
[9] R. L. Meier (1962): *A communications theory of urban growth* (Cambridge, Mass.).
[10] H. Cox (1965): *The secular city* (New York).
[11] E. Howard (1902): *Garden cities of tomorrow* (London).

problem becomes more clearly defined because presumably under a Marxist state, as in all ideal worlds, there would be no further development; and yet the city is the centre of change. The city is the place where people meet, where great hopes are generated and where many must be disappointed, where success is balanced by disaster, affluence with degradation, for only where people become units of production, all alike, will the static city emerge in an environment of atrophy and decay.

It is probable that most people's attitudes to the city will take in both polar extremes, now moving towards one and now the other, as illustrated, for example, by Samuel Johnson: on the one hand in *London* (1738) he writes:

> For who would leave, unbribed, Hibernia's land
> Or change the rocks of Scotland for the Strand? . . .
> Here malice, rapine, accident conspire,
> And now a rabble rages, now a fire;
> Their ambush here relentless ruffians lay,
> And here the fell attorney prowls for prey;
> Here falling houses thunder on your head,
> And here a female atheist talks you dead . . .
> LONDON! the needy villain's general home,
> The common shore of Paris and of Rome;
> With eager thirst, by folly or by fate,
> Sucks in the dregs of each currupted state.

but on the other (Boswell's *Life of Johnson*, 1971):

> "Sir, if you wish to have a just notion of the magnitude of this city, you must not be satisfied with seeing its great streets and squares, but must survey the innumerable little lanes and courts. It is not in the showy evolutions of buildings, but in the multiplicity of human habitations which are crowded together, that the wonderful immensity of London consists." . . . BOSWELL: "The only disadvantage is the great distance at which people live from one another." JOHNSON: "Yes, Sir; but that is occasioned by the largeness of it, which is the cause of all other advantages." BOSWELL: "Sometimes I have been in the humour of wishing to retire to a desert." JOHNSON: "Sir, you have desert enough in Scotland."

This argument has veered away from urban geography as such, but as geographers look for relevance, and beyond relevance for radical action, it will become clear that all the attitudes discussed impinge in their own way upon the academic study of the city. But before tracing these reactions it is necessary to turn aside to consider also how changes in the nature of the city itself are also affecting the study of urban geography.

2 The changing nature of the city

Chapter 2 of this book considered the problem of defining what is urban and it was suggested that one difficulty was that both the reality and the concept of what is urban are subject to change. The publication in 1961 by Jean Gottmann of his book *Megalopolis*, subtitled 'The urbanized northeastern seaboard of the United States', was a clear indication that new urban structures had been formed which needed new definitions.[12] Gottmann defined Megalopolis as 'an almost continuous system of deeply interwoven urban and suburban areas, with a total population of about 37 million people in 1960. . . . The cradle of a new order in the organization of inhabited space.' The nature of this new order is not as easy to identify.

Peter Hall in his massive and masterly study of megalopis England points out that 'for all his brilliant evocation of a megalopolis Gottmann never succeeds in defining it as a unique entity, and so never proves that it exists.'[13] Hall, after a careful and broadly based examination of evidence, accepts the reality of a megalopolis England but writes that it is 'a functional rather than a physical reality. Just like the comparable northeastern urban complex of the United States— Gottmann's megalopolis— it is a giant urban area only in the sense that here is a large tract of the earth's surface where the great majority of people depend on urban jobs and urban services; and where the impact of these jobs and services, in terms of measurements like commuter zones, service areas and the exchange of goods and information, expands to involve each part of the area in a complex series of interactions with other parts. It is not, and does not conceivably seem likely to be, a giant urban area in the sense that the physical growth of its parts will gradually coalesce into continuous sprawl from London to Birmingham and Manchester. That is a nightmare that has no foundation whatsoever in reality.'[14] This would equally be true of the Great Lakes megalopolis, the Japanese megalopolis extending from Tokyo to Osaka and the northwest European megalopolis extending generally about the Rhine from Randstad-Holland to Stuttgart.

Although simple physical sprawl is rejected as the basis of identity, nevertheless the complex interdependence of parts recognized not only queries the definition of what is urban but more significantly, challenges the idea that any meaningful distinction between what is urban and rural can be made. If this be the case then the sorts of study presented in this volume, all of which to a large degree assume free-standing, discrete urban entities, lose much of their central importance, or at least take on a somewhat dated appearance.

There is some overlap between the subject-matter of this book and Hall's study of urban England, but his main concern is with regional structure and much of his consideration is devoted to the broader problems of regional and economic planning. The point of emphasis moves accordingly to methods for building dynamic models in urban and regional analysis and to the sorts of study initiated by Forrester in the United States[15] and Chadwick[16]

[12] J. Gottmann (1961): *Megalopolis: the urbanized north-eastern seaboard of the United States* (Cambridge, Mass.).

[13] P. Hall, editor (1973): *The containment of urban England* (London), Vol. 1, 47.

[14] P. Hall, editor (1973), 320

[15] J. W. Forrester (1969): *Urban dynamics* (Cambridge, Mass.).

[16] G. Chadwick (1971): *A systems view of planning: towards a theory of the urban and regional planning process* (Oxford).

and Wilson[17] in Britain. It is possible to maintain, as this book does, that these are different problems demanding their own treatment, but the blurring of the urban-rural difference presents real difficulty to urban geography as a systematic study.

In spite of these difficulties it would be wrong to imply that conventional urban geography, as presented here, is now in some way outmoded. Although it is not as easy as it once was to build a study around the notion of the free-standing city clearly divorced from its rural surrounds, the basic ideas outlined in this book still remain central to the urban analyst. The question of scale will be considered later in this chapter but even here it can be maintained that the critical issue has been simply an extension of scale. The studies of regional structure, already referred to in this section, attempt to resolve the mechanics of the massive agglomeration, including its apparently rural interstices.

On the other hand in the studies of central places and of residential location presented in chapters 6 and 10, it was seen to be necessary to move into the micro-scale, behavioural approach. In spite of these extensions the basic patterns of intra- and inter-urban distributions remain the same, and the changes in the nature of the urban phenomenon from discrete city to megalopolis, even to regional city, and the development of behavioural research, only reveal a hierarchically scaled situation where the basic and essential middle ground is taken by this book.

It is probable that a real challenge to the conventions of urban geography will come from a different though related source. Most of the analyses presented in this book assume a laissez faire situation, one of relatively untrammelled competition in a capitalist system. But such conditions appertain in reality to hardly any country in the world, for some form of control is exercised by central or local government. The United Kingdom may be taken as an example where the planning process now shapes the form of towns,[18] determines the pattern of land-uses and also, by the creation of new towns,[19] the city system itself. On the larger scale, towns are nominated as

---

[17] A. Wilson (1974): *Urban and regional models in geography and planning* (London).

[18] For a general consideration of U.K. urban planning see: W. Ashworth (1954): *The genesis of modern British town planning* (London). J. B. Cullingworth (1973): *Problems of an urban society* (London); Vol. 1, *The social framework of planning*, Vol. 2, *The social content of planning*; Vol. 3, *Planning for change*. P. Hall (1973): *The containment of urban England* (London and Beverly Hills), Vol. 2, *The planning system: objectives, operations, impacts*.

[19] There is an immense literature on new towns. Some useful books mainly relating to Britain are: F. Osborn and A. Whittick (1963): *The new towns: the answer to Megalopolis* (London). (2nd edition, 1969.) L. Rodwin (1956): *The British new towns policy* (Cambridge, Mass.). R. Thomas (1969): *London's new towns* and *Aycliffe to Cumbernauld: a study of seven new towns in their regions*. P.E.P. Broadsheets **510** and **516** (London). M. Aldridge (1979): The British new towns (London).

More international studies are: P. Merlin (1971): *New towns: regional planning and development*. Trans. M. Sparks (London). J. A. Clapp (1971): *New towns and urban policy* (New York).

Books mainly concerned with the USA are: G. Breckenfeld (1971): *Columbia and the new cities* (New York). C. Stein (1966): *Toward new towns for America* (Cambridge, Mass.). R. J. Burby *et al.* (1976): *New communities, U.S.A.* (New York).

growth points[20] and every effort made to foster their development. On a small scale the planning permission required for the building of out-of-town shopping centres or hypermarkets determines the nature of the retail system.

The study of urban geography in this way necessarily becomes closely involved with the consideration of the planning mechanism and the way it operates. This is nothing novel: when town plan was considered in chapter 7 it was stressed that the physical form reflected the nature of the society in which it was generated. Planning controls are contemporary reflections of social goals. It is significant that Peter Hall's book is called *The containment of urban England*, for that containment is the result of planning restrictions and Hall has to devote a great deal of his book to the study of the regulating enactments.[21] A major difficulty for the urban geographer is this progressive involvement in the detail of planning legislation and the nature of its operation. Even so such planning may presumably be based on an initial examination of the patterns initiated by free operation under market conditions and to that extent urban geography provides the basis from which planning moves forward.

The first two sections of this chapter have indicated that numerous problems surround the idea of an independent, systematic urban geography and it is to a consideration of some of these that this conclusion must now turn.

3 Problems of urban geography

These problems which the systematic study now faces can best be considered under three headings. They are derived not only from attitudes to the city and the changing nature of the city already discussed, but also from new views as to the internal organization of geographical studies.

a The problem of identity

It has been suggested that the emergence of regional megalopoles puts in doubt the discrete urban geography which emerged in the 1950s and 1960s and which was depicted in chapter 1 of this book in diagram form. It has also been indicated that the regional model building associated with these new phenomena must impinge on the material dealt with in urban geography, although again this book has made little concession in that direction. But even further, from within the mainstream of human geography itself comes a challenge to what is a short-lived but nevertheless received tradition of dividing human geography into semi-discrete areas of study labelled economic geography, political geography, urban geography, and so on.

This problem was introduced briefly in the introduction where reference

---

[20]   Two useful books on growth-point policies are: A. Kuklinski, editor (1972): Growth poles and growth centres in regional planning, *U.N. Research Inst. for Soc. Devel. Regional planning* Vol. 5 (Paris and The Hague). A. Kuklinski and R. Petrella, editors (1972): Growth poles and regional policies, *European Coordination centre for research and documentation in social sciences, Vol.* 3 (Paris and The Hague).

[21]   P. Hall (1973): Vol. 2.

was made to the paper by Peter Gould in which the case is put most cogently.[22] Gould points to the struggle in the post-war period to get such avant garde courses as urban geography established in university departments. 'Few would object today but the irony is that just when everyone has comfortably settled down into new categories, these categories themselves have outlived their usefulness, becoming limitations upon geographic instruction and pedagogic imagination.'[23] This view has much to justify it. Gould proposes a twin orientation to geographical studies, spatial theory on the one hand and problem-solving on the other. But although his rather conversational-toned essay presents the idea, it is left unspecified in any detail.

Probably still the most convincing contribution on theoretical lines is Peter Haggett's classic, *Locational analysis in human geography*[24]. The chapter headings indicate the approach—interaction; networks; nodes; hierarchies, surfaces, diffusion. The factual context or the real-world situation is irrelevant. Indeed, the basic principle is that these analytical approaches are universal to all spatial situations: that rent gradients should be studied separately in agrarian and urban geography is seen as nonsensical and the particularity of the present systematic approach only succeeds in presenting obstacles to theory formulation. All this implies that urban geography will soon disappear. Haggett in a later volume, *Geography: a modern synthesis*,[25] presents two contrasted internal structures of geography, one called 'orthodox', with standard systematic and regional sections, the other called 'integrated'. The latter is reproduced in table 17–1.

Two difficulties stand out, apart from the somewhat imprecise content of such categories as 'natural resource geography'. The first is that it is not as easy to specify the various 'others' which appear in this scheme as in an orthodox one, but more relevant is that a close examination suggests that 'spatial analysis—applied—urban problems' may be little more than the recreation of urban geography in another guise. The critical problem is that spatial theory *is* theoretic, and presumably deductive in approach. Gould justifiably attacks a subject which consists of gobbets of fact to be learned by rote; but that is not a fair interpretation of a demand for a clear empirical content. It is possible to envisage a future where the spatial theorist will derive his generalizations and manipulate his accessible data in some remote underground cell, never having visited a city or experienced its reality, not even through the descriptions of an old fashioned regional geographer! Haggett's understandable desire to guard against this, and Gould's inclusion

[22] P. Gould (1973): The open geography curriculum; in R. J. Chorley, editor (1973): *Directions in geography* (London), 253–84.
[23] P. Gould (1973), 269.
[24] P. Haggett (1965): *Locational analysis in human geography* (London). 2nd edition, 1977 with A.D. Cliff and A. Frey; revised into two volumes: *Locational models* and *Locational methods* (London).
[25] P. Haggett (1972): *Geography: a modern synthesis* (New York), 451–4. (third edition, 1979.)

table 17–1: The integrated structure of geography. *After Haggett (1979).*

Spatial Analysis
- Theoretical — Spatial interaction theory / Diffusion theory / Others
- Applied — Watershed problems / Urban problems / Others

Ecological Analysis
- Theoretical — Environmental structures / Ecosystems / Others
- Applied — Natural resource geography / Hazard appraisal / Others

Regional Complex Analysis
- Theoretical — Regional growth theory / Interregional theory / Others
- Applied — Regional forecasting / Regional planning / Others

of problem-solving or an empirical content, can be seen as recreating urban geography as the student attempts to contain the complexity of reality by restricting the range of his empirical investigations.

This is of necessity an inconclusive discussion. It is proper that the nature and content of the systematic studies in human geography should be challenged, and urban geography particularly is in a state of change. Three overlapping areas of investigation have already been indicated in the first two sections of this conclusion: the consideration of broader urban and regional systems, the operation of the planning process and the growth of behavioural studies. These impinge on urban geography and demand modification of its content. Its separate identity is also challenged in a subject where spatial theory not surface form is seen as the heart. It is possible to question whether the theoretical bases have been sufficiently well-established, and the theoretical material sufficiently well assimilated, to provide a meaningful synthesized programme for geography. At least there must surely be room both for those who seek an elusive theory and those who believe that theory is best indicated and will be more effectively derived from a consideration of distributed phenomena like the town. Perhaps in the end this is essentially a pedagogic topic rather than one concerned with a research philosophy.

Certainly urban geography as presented in this book can do much to preserve an effective balance between abstract theory and the uniqueness of the real townscape. It also goes beyond the diktat of spatial theory in that it has to contain not only studies of the real townscape, or morphology and building types, but also to couch these in an evolutionary sequence. The city system and the fabric of the town have been built up over a long period of time and to exclude such a perspective makes nonsense of any effective view of the contemporary city.

b The problem of scale

A recent study of residential mobility concluded, 'this paper offers evidence of support of a limited directional bias in residential mobility and offers support for King's suggestion that emphasizing process or behavioural formulations in which process and structure are handled simultaneously will accomplish more than further attempting to analyse spatial structures alone.'[26] This implies that geographers must not only analyse spatial patterns (distributions in the old fashioned term), but also the bases of human behaviour which produced those patterns.

The academic issue is evident and crucial. The interpretation of any spatial pattern leads to inferences about human behaviour, in the way that the behaviour of consumers was assumed in the central place model and inferred in empirical studies designed to illustrate the operation of the model. But these assumptions and inferences are at all times open to doubt and can only be verified by specific investigation of the behaviour in question, that is, by study carried out not at the aggregate scale of the distribution pattern, but at the level of the individual. This issue has been introduced in chapters 6 and 10 (see pp. 128–32; 285–6) and no further elaboration is presented here.

In many ways this problem in geography replicates an earlier one. The environmental determinism of Ratzel and his successors was not acceptable because, in its crude form, it was manifestly inappropriate for it made no allowance for the culturally based variety of human response. In consequence a possibilist approach was derived which argued the necessity of considering the filter of human culture through which alone the man-land relationship could be properly understood. It was subsequently maintained that, with the coming of spatial analysis, the old determinist – possibilist dichotomy was irrelevant and as dead as the dodo; a new geography had emerged. But this new geography, determinist in outlook through the assumption of economic man with neither individuality nor culture, has come up against the same problem, the need to consider the motivations and decisions of human beings who are not necessarily economic maximizers. The possibilists were, in their day, charged with moving into the fields of cultural and social anthropology and including material which met the stern charge of being 'not geography'. Fortunately that sort of thinking has largely, though far from completely, disappeared.

The human geographer is thus expected to investigate process as well as pattern, but this brings him into close contact with other social scientists, particularly the psychologist, as in the quest for process he is forced to

[26] W. A. V. Clark (1972): Some vector representations of intra-urban residential mobility; in W. P. Adams and F. M. Helleiner, editors (1972): *International Geography 1972*, Papers submitted to the 22nd International Geographical Congress, Canada, 178.

consider the foundations of human behaviour. As this search for explanation advances it results in the phenomenon of reduction. Harvey writes, 'the development of general theory in the social sciences may well depend on such reduction. The postulates of economics may be reducible to a particular subset of postulates in psychology. . . . Some writers . . . have further suggested that the basic postulates of psychology might be reduced to the basic postulates of physics. Anthropologists . . . have also suggested that the route to a "value-free" and truly scientific anthropology lies through studying the neurophysiological determinants of human behaviour. The degree to which such reduction can take place, however, is a controversial issue, and even if it is conceded that total reduction is ultimately possible, this is so far from being practicable at the present time it seems irrelevant to the current problems of empirical enquiry.'[27]

Even so this problem of reduction leaves the field of geographic enquiry very ill-defined. It is certainly possible to maintain (looking back at the discussion in chapter 1) that to define an area of enquiry that is exclusively geographical is a meaningless exercise, for all investigation in the social sciences becomes multidisciplinary and none more so than the investigation of urbanism. Any subject ends where the competence of the investigator runs out. In this way the question of identity is revived once again.

The difficulties of definition and content are not real problems, except for the academic student trying to contain his field of study. The residual issue still remains. This is the one of integrating approaches at different scale levels. Reverting to the problem of teaching geography, it is possible to envisage a structure where macro-geographical theory and micro-geographical theory would form elements as in economics. In a research context it is easier to ask questions than to provide solutions, but one critical point is that in all investigations the scale of approach must be specified and care taken to avoid the confusions that arise when conclusions are not scale-related. Indeed research tackling scale problems directly needs to be initiated.

c The problem of relevance and radical geography
Two quotations can introduce this problem. The first is appropriately from Chairman Mao, 'If you want knowledge you must take part in the practice of changing reality. If you want to know the taste of a pear you must change the pear by eating it yourself.' For a western culture context it is a great pity that Mao did not refer to an apple rather than a pear, for the follow through of the implications might have made this section unnecessary. The second extract is from David Harvey's book *Social justice and the city*: 'An urbanism founded upon exploitation is a legacy of history. A genuinely humanizing urbanism has yet to be brought into being. It remains for revolutionary theory to chart the path from an urbanism based on exploitation to an urbanism appropriate for the human species. And it remains for revolutionary practice to accomplish such a transformation.'[28] A number of partly

[27] D. Harvey (1969): *Explanation in geography* (London and New York), 95.
[28] D. Harvey (1973): *Social justice and the city* (London and Baltimore), 314.

separate points arise from these quotations:

(*i*) *Learning for learning's sake.* The view that this revered piece of academic dogma is an unacceptable notion and no more than a myth which has been inherited from the conventions surrounding the education of a nineteenth-century English gentleman, is in part true. In a very limited sense the demand that geographic work should now be socially applicable has little point for there are very few urban geographers who have not at some time been involved in the use of their skills in the real world.[29] The call for applied work is an outdated one. Indeed, the wheel has turned a full circle for such involvement is now regarded by radical geographers as a prostitution of skills in the perpetuating of the capitalist regime!

(*ii*) *Objectivity and propaganda.* The more penetrating charge against 'learning for its own sake' is that it claims a specious objectivity; that for example, some ideal and discrete 'urban geography' exists whereas no social science is value free either in concept or content. The material I have presented here is derived implicitly from a set of beliefs about society, or at least an undeclared system of social values and assumptions. More explicitly this book is structured from the viewpoint of someone educated in liberal western democracy and in the context of a capitalist system modified by social responsibility. It has been bound both by its culture context and the inherited and acquired views of the author. It has sought to advance understanding within a framework rather than to criticize and overturn that framework.

On the other hand, once the idea that nothing but a value-dependent social science is possible is accepted, then academic learning, as it has been conventionally known, disappears and nothing is left but propaganda. Even what is demonstrated by the so-called scientific method has been selected, framed and devised relative to socio-culturally controlled notions. This line of argument closely parallels the views, or perhaps opinions is a better word, of Dr Goebbels and Professor Haushofer who in a clear-minded way realized that academic learning and propaganda were one and the same. We are all Winston Smiths. Most authors who subscribe to this argument seem to exempt their own work which is taken to represent some ultimate condition of ideal stability where no one, to revert to Mao's metaphor, would even dream of biting the apple. Eden has become a city. There is no point in carrying this argument further here, except to reiterate that this book has been written from a declared viewpoint.

(*iii*) *Radical alternatives.* Throughout this book reference has occasionally been made to radical and Marxist alternatives to the presentation of what can be called traditional urban geography and in Chapter 15 a brief attempt

---

[29] For example, as far as the present author is concerned, see J. A. Edwards and W. Thomas, editors (1974): *Llantrisant New Town: the case against*: a summary of the evidence presented to the public enquiry on behalf of the Heads of the Valleys Standing Conference (Cardiff), chapter 1, 10–30.

was made to outline Harvey's scheme. The most widely disseminated source of such alternatives, however, is the urban sociology of Manuel Castells.[30] Stripped of its dense verbiage the crux of Castell's argument is akin to that of Harvey, that urbanism cannot be empirically examined and interpreted as a thing in itself for it is a manifestation, and only one, of the condition of advanced capitalist societies. 'An urban sociology founded on urbanism is an ideology of modernity ethnocentrically identified with the crystallization of the social forms of liberal capitalism.'[31] His criticism of the Chicago ecologists stresses this view, 'The question is no longer to know how the social life of a neighbourhood is organized *vis-à-vis* the dominant culture, but how are to be determined the housing and infrastructure policies of the city from the relations of force between social groups structurally determined by their interests. New concepts and theories become necessary to consider problems of conflict and the decision-making processes which appear to determine the whole of urban organization.'[32]

The consideration of the housing market in chapter 11 is presumably, if only superficially, a move in Castell's direction. He is even more dismissive of geographical empiricism, which, he argues uses 'increasingly sophisticated statistical techniques but which (is) devoid of meaning in relation to theoretical categories and social issues.'[33] Indeed, the derivation of a theoretical perspective must be based on a rejection of the determinism of space, 'space in itself has no meaning because it is socially constructed',[34] a phrase which could well be found in the writings of Vidal or Febvre fifty years ago! 'Urban social science must therefore move away from a spatial empiricism, precisely in order to carry out empirical research into the spatial expression of social relations.'[35]

Put in this way there is little new in Castell's attitude. The demand for enquiry into process rather than argument from pattern is one of the longest standing in geography.

The accepted wisdom at the present is that post-war urban geography has reflected the successive movement in the subject from a basis in logical positivism, to one in phenomenology, to one in Marxism. This smacks of notions of evolutionary progress. In many ways what has occurred is a pendulum swing between attitudes which can be subsumed under the all-embracing terms 'classical' and 'romantic'. The first assumes logic, order and control from a well-defined basis, a determinism whether it be of the environment, the geometry of space or the economic system. The second accepts mutability and variability, a disorder to be comprehended through culture and personality, through the spirit rather than the system. As the pendulum swings, so approaches change resulting in an eclecticism which is likely to

[30] M. Castells (1977): *The urban question: A Marxist Approach* (London) Trans. A. Sheridan.

[31] M. Castells (1967): Theory and ideology in urban sociology, in C. G. Pickvance ed. *Urban Sociology: Critical Essays*, (London) Trans. C. G. Pickvance.

[32] M. Castells (1978): *City, class and power*, 7 (London).

[33] M. Castells (1978), 8.

[34] M. Castells (1978), 181.

[35] M. Castells (1978), 181.

characterize the work of many geographers, even as it will offend those who regard it as untenable.

4 Conclusion

This book, in the light of the literature quoted above, appears as a manual, a sort of nuts and bolts study of the city from the point of view of a British geographer or to use Harvey's description of such works, a 'partial analysis framed within the safety of a disciplinary womb'. The impatience and occasionally the naïvete of young geographers who, inspired with a desire to eliminate the ills of the city, wish to establish overriding theory or radically change the socio-economic system on which the contemporary city is based, may at times dispose them to have little patience with this constrained level of enquiry.

It might well be that the implicit philosophy of this book is a sort of nineteenth-century social Darwinism: it accepts the basic drive of competition for scarce resources and of conflict over advantageous locations, however muted, modified and regulated they may be by the operation of constraints derived from community intrusion in formal political terms either at the local or national level. Competition, the survival of the ablest competitor and the demise of the weakest, is always the key whether it be for central place status among towns, for retail sites by entrepreneurs or for residential locations by families.

No doubt when the millenium arrives and such competition is done away with, some geographer will need to write a very different book; critical discussion of the existing order will then be inconceivable for sophistry decrees that of perfection there can be no criticism which, like other aspects of Dystopia, will have withered away. In passing it is interesting to recall that in More's Utopia all cities were identical and mirror images of each other for there was complete separation and no competition. Even so, given something a little less than perfection and with the goals set by the community rather than by competing individuals and irresponsible interests, priorities will still have to be identified and there will still be competitors for the physically limited resource of urban land and the advantaged locations; even in the best of possible worlds everything cannot be located on the same spot and so inequality is written into the system in a more relevant form of environmental determinism.

This last notion of the impossibility of identical location suggests that in futurology terms the most radical revolution of the sort of urban geography this book sets out will not be brought about by political philosophies but rather by transport technologies, for only by these can the intractible problem of distance be solved. When the friction of distance is universally reduced to zero there will be no advantaged locations and inequality will have been eliminated. But then there will be no towns and no urban geography.

However, the implications to be derived from this book are apparent. The research frontier in urban geography has moved from the analysis of spatial patterns, through the disaggregated consideration of behaviour, to the study of decision making in the context of those institutions and groups which exert a dominant influence on urban function and form, and the way in which those influential groups are themselves a product of the politico-social system in which they operate.

Notes on further reading

On attitudes to the city a most useful source is:

Handlin, O. and Burchard, J., editors. (1963): *The historian and the city*, Part III: *The city in the history of ideas* (see footnote 1).

A further source is:

Hadden, J. K. *et alia*, editors (1967): *Metropolis in crisis* (Itaska, Ill.), Part III: *Ideological perspectives: The anti-urban bias*.

The problems of the modern city are dealt with in nearly every book on urbanism but a readable short book is:

Helmer, J. and Eddington, N. A., editors (1973): *Urban man: the psychology of urban survival* (New York).

On the changing nature of the city the references in the footnotes should be consulted, particularly the books by Gottmann (1961) and Hall (1973) (see footnotes 12 and 13). A general volume which is an excellent critical commentary is:

Berry, B. J. L. (1973): *The human consequences of urbanization* (London).

In relation to urban geography the paper by Gould (footnote 22) should be read while the whole volume in which it appears contains much that is relevant:

Chorley, R. J. editor (1973): *Directions in geography* (London).

Two books deal with radical solutions to the problems of the city on two different scales. For the general scale:

Harvey, D. (1973): *Social justice and the city* (London) is essential and contains further references. For the local scale:

Bunge, W. (1971): *Fitzgerald: geography of a revolution* (Cambridge, Mass.) is an excellent example of the involvement of a geographer in social change.

The most influential contemporary writer on radical urban sociology is M. Castells and reference should be made to:

Castells, M. (1977): *The urban question: a Marxist approach* (London) Trans. A. Sheridan. (1967). Theory and ideology in urban sociology, in C. G. Pickvance ed. (1976): *Urban Sociology: Critical Essays*, (London) Trans. C. G. Pickvance. (1978): *City, class and power* (London) Trans. E. Lebas.

Index of Subjects

Index of Personal Names

Index of Place Names